Essential XUL Programming

Vaughn Bullard

Kevin T. Smith

Michael C. Daconta

Wiley Computer Publishing

John Wiley & Sons, Inc.

NEW YORK • CHICHESTER • WEINHEIM • BRISBANE • SINGAPORE • TORONTO

Publisher: Robert Ipsen
Editor: Robert M. Elliott
Assistant Editor: Emilie Herman
Managing Editor: John Atkins
Associate New Media Editor: Brian Snapp
Text Design & Composition: D&G Limited, LLC

Published by John Wiley & Sons, Inc.

Published simultaneously in Canada.

Library of Congress Cataloging-in-Publication Data:

ISBN: 0-471-41580-4

Printed in the United States of America.

10 9 8 7 6 5 4 3 2 1

Contents

	Introduction	**vii**
	Acknowledgments	**xi**
	About the Authors	**xiii**
Chapter 1	**What Is XUL?**	**1**
	The Origins of XUL	3
	Leveraged Technologies in XUL	4
	Types of XUL User Interface Widgets	9
	XUL Features	11
	Implementing XUL	15
	Summary	18
	Notes	18
Chapter 2	**An XML Primer**	**19**
	XML Syntax	21
	Creating a Document Type Definition	27
	Constructing a XUL DTD	33
	Creating a Schema	36

	The Document Object Model	44
	Summary	48
Chapter 3	**Using Cascading Style Sheets**	**49**
	A Simple CSS Example	50
	CSS Fundamentals	53
	Using CSS with XUL	76
	Summary	77
	Notes	78
Chapter 4	**Building a Simple XUL Interface**	**81**
	Building a XUL Application	82
	Complete Code for xulexample.xul	98
	Complete Code for eventhandlers.js	105
	Summary	106
Chapter 5	**Creating Netscape Themes**	**107**
	Gathering Your Tools	108
	Downloading a Template	108
	Developing Your Netscape Theme	112
	Summary	130
Chapter 6	**RDF and XUL Templates**	**133**
	The RDF Model and Syntax	134
	Building and Using XUL Templates	143
	Summary	163
	Notes	164
Chapter 7	**XUL Overlays and XBL**	**167**
	Using XUL Overlays	168
	Using XML Binding Language (XBL)	174
	Summary	207
	Notes	207
Chapter 8	**The jXUL Open Source Project**	**209**
	Why jXUL?	209
	The jXUL Architecture	210
	jXUL Components	212
	jXUL Packages	227
	Getting Involved in the jXUL Project	228

	Challenges for the jXUL Project	228
	Summary	229
Chapter 9	**Case Study: Creating a Customizable Browser Portal**	**231**
	Defining the Problem	232
	Approaching the Solution	232
	Under the Hood: An In-Depth Look at Netscape's "My Sidebar"	232
	Customizing My Sidebar for the Case Study	248
	Summary	252
Chapter 10	**Case Study: Building an E-Commerce User Interface with XUL**	**257**
	Defining the Problem	257
	Analyzing the Requirements	258
	Designing the User Interface	259
	Building the User Interface	263
	Creating and Populating the User Interface	269
	Navigating the Finished Product	284
	Main XUL Interface File	285
	JavaScript Event Handling File	290
	Overlay Files	293
	Summary	296
Appendix A	**XUL Programmer's Reference**	**297**
Appendix B	**Netscape Theme Reference**	**343**
	References	**409**
	Index	**411**

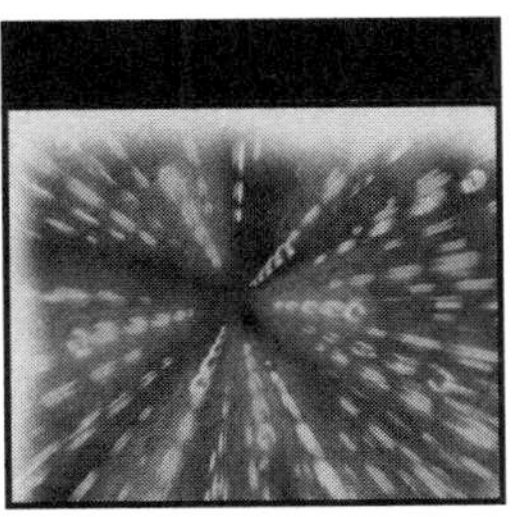

Introduction

Developing user interfaces that are easy to change and portable between platforms has been difficult. In a world of competing technologies and platforms, what are you, as a software developer to choose? If you are a seasoned software developer, chances are you have used many Graphical User Interface (GUI) toolkits: the Unix curses library, X11/Motif, Microsoft Foundation Classes, and perhaps Java AWT/Swing. In order to change your GUIs, you have had to edit your code, compile, and test your user interfaces again. In many cases, you've had to use a lot of *"ifdefs"* to separate functionality between operating system platforms. Perhaps you have used a GUI toolkit that has tied you into a proprietary vendor. As a software developer, have you ever focused too much of your time on user interfaces, when the business logic of your application seems far more important? As software developers, we have constantly struggled with user interface issues.

In the last 10 years, we have witnessed the impact of the open source movement on the Internet. As the Web has evolved, we have seen how easy it is to develop user interfaces in HTML and XML. Wouldn't it be great if developing user interfaces for applications were as easy as developing Web sites? This was the idea behind XUL—the eXtensible Interface Language.

XUL, an XML vocabulary, was designed by software developers at Mozilla.org to describe the look and feel of application-based user interfaces. In fact, the latest Netscape and Mozilla browsers are, in part, written in XUL. The Web browser's rendering engine parses XUL and creates the look and feel of all of the browser components.

Because only the rendering engine is ported between platforms, the user interface described by XUL is platform-independent. Because XUL is an XML language, it is an open standard, and it can be created, edited, and modified by any text editor, making user interface development as easy as developing a Web page.

XUL as a Solution

XUL is a standard developed for cross-platform user interfaces, and it is on the cutting edge of technology. Working together with technologies such as Resource Description Framework (RDF), XBL (XML Binding Language), JavaScript, XML, and Cascading Style Sheets (CSS), the XUL programming environment provides extreme flexibility. This book provides an introduction to XUL and some of these technologies and gives you an in-depth tutorial of how to quickly get started developing XUL-based applications.

XUL is the beginning of something very exciting. As XML standards begin to evolve and mature, XUL is a language that offers much promise. One of the side projects that the authors of this book have been working on, jXUL (www.jxul.org), is a Java-based XUL library that can be used to separate application logic and business logic in software development projects.

The work that Mozilla.org has been doing has been very exciting, and it is the beginning of something big. We feel that XUL can work together with complementary technologies, such as RDF, XBL, and scripting languages, to create powerful software applications. It is our goal to provide not only a tutorial and reference, but to provoke ideas of how this technology could be used to improve the state of software development.

How This Book Is Organized

The book is composed of four sections: “Getting Started,” “XUL In Depth,” “XUL Applications,” and “References and Appendices.” The first part of the book is intended for an audience new to XUL- and XML-based technologies. The second part focuses on XUL and its interrelated technologies in much detail. The next section provides you with case studies and advanced projects dealing with real-world XUL applications. The final part is a standalone reference containing appendices for programmers.

Getting Started. This introductory section focuses on the “basics” needed to understand the XUL language. Chapter 1, “What Is XUL?” introduces you to XUL and its related technologies. XUL's relationship with other technologies is very important, and because it is essential to know the fundamentals of XML and CSS, the second and third chapters focus on those topics. Chapter 2, “An XML Primer,” is an introductory chapter to XML and provides you with the knowledge necessary to understand the XML-based vocabulary of this book. Chapter 3, “Using Cascading Style Sheets,” is a primer on CSS and shows you how to use these style sheets to provide style and behavior to XML, XUL, and related markup languages.

XUL in Depth. The next part of this book focuses on technologies core to XUL. Chapter 4, "Building a Simple XUL Interface," focuses on the user interface elements of XUL and details a step-by-step process for creating XUL applications. Chapter 5, "Creating Netscape Themes," focuses on how browser themes are created by "skinning the browser" and using XUL and CSS to describe the look and feel of the browser. Chapter 6, "RDF and XUL Templates," shows how XUL rule-based templates can use RDF Datasources to dynamically generate user interface content. Chapter 7, "XUL Overlays and XBL," discusses XUL overlays and the XBL syntax and shows how these technologies are used for object re-use, encapsulation, composite widget creation, and extensibility.

XUL Applications. The third part of this book revolves around advanced projects in XUL and provides case studies of how XUL can be applied in the real world. Chapter 8, "The jXUL Open Source Project," discusses the open source project for developing a framework for a Java-based XUL rendering engine. Chapter 9, "Case Study: Creating a Customizable Browser Portal," is a case study that uses XUL and the design of the Netscape/Mozilla browser to provide a real-world solution for Enterprise Information Portals on the Internet. Chapter 10, "Case Study: Building an E-Commerce User Interface with XUL," is a case study that shows how XUL can be used to create interfaces for an electronic commerce Web site.

References and Appendices. The final part of this book provides reference information that you will need when developing your XUL applications. Appendix A, "XUL Programmer's Reference," details all XUL elements and attributes, DOM methods, JavaScript functions, and event handlers. In addition, Appendix A provides a few visual examples of XUL interfaces. Appendix B, "Netscape Theme Reference," explicitly details a cross-reference of Netscape themes components and cascading style sheets.

Who Should Read This Book

We wrote this book for Web developers, programmers, and forward-thinking technologists. If you picked up this book, you're probably familiar with the Internet and Web-related technologies. This book assumes a basic knowledge of Web technologies and markup languages. Some of the chapters at the beginning of this book are introductory in nature, but later chapters cover advanced topics, examples, and lessons for hard-core programmers.

This book is meant to focus on creating XUL-based user interfaces and providing a detailed reference manual and a how-to-guide. All of the technologies discussed in this book are open-source, and some of them (XML, RDF, CSS, XBL, and JavaScript) could have (and do have) entire books dedicated to their use. This book provides detailed examples and tutorials on how to use these technologies as they relate to XUL and shows you where to look for more information.

The first chapter, "What Is XUL?" is an important chapter that everyone should read to get an overview of the technology and what this book is about. After reading Chapter 1, developers very familiar with XML and related technologies may want to jump right into the next section of the book, beginning in Chapter 4. Others who are not as familiar with XML and CSS may want to read this book from cover to cover.

You may want to visit the final section of this book again and again as a programmer's reference. We will post updates, corrections to the manuscript, and extra resources on our Web site, http://www.xulbook.com/.

What's on the Web Site

Our Web site at www.xulbook.com/ will provide the following:

- Source code and examples from this book
- Corrections and updates
- Links to other great XUL resources on the Web
- XUL news

We will continue to provide support to developers with this Web site, and we hope that you visit it often.

Tools You Will Need

One of the great things about XUL programming is that you don't need expensive tools to create XUL interfaces. All you need is a text editor and a Mozilla-based browser. A few applications that would help increase your proficiency are basic XML editors. One of these editors is XML Spy, which allows you to natively create XML-based documents such as XUL, Resource Description Framework (RDF), and XHTML. However, any editor is fine! We advise you to check www.mozilla.org/ for future releases of the browser, which will provide you with a great resource with which to start.

Summary

As software engineering matures as a discipline, the mechanics of all aspects of development, including user interfaces, will become easier. If you are a software developer who is interested in a technology that can make user interface design and development easier, this book is for you. We hope that this book will provide you with the knowledge you need to get started on XUL programming and that it will help you in your professional endeavors.

All suggestions and comments from the software development community and our readers are welcome. We can be reached by email at: authors@xulbook.com.

Acknowledgments

First of all, we would like to thank Dan Gracia of Orvis.com for supplying us with images for our case study. We also would like to thank Rob Ginda and Dave Hyatt of Netscape, for answering our questions in a timely fashion.

I would like to thank my wife, Catherine, and my children, Bailey Catherine and Samuel Emerson, for giving me up for what seemed like an eternity. I sometimes work harder than I should, but it is for you. I dedicate my efforts for this book to my beautiful family, whom I adore.

I would also like to thank my family for understanding the huge undertaking that a book involves. My family includes LTC (Ret.) Ron Bullard; Cynthia Bullard; Brian, Keisha, Cullen, and Christian Bullard; JB King; Floyd and Kay Alvarez; Michelle Alvarez; Geoff, Jennifer, and Emily Alvarez; Floyd Scott, Francine, and Joseph Alvarez.

To my great friend and college roommate, Bryan Phillips, who just graduated with his law degree—I knew you would make it! Everything worthwhile in our lives requires hard work and patience. I know you will pass the bar! I would like to thank Henry Roy Sling, my cousin, whose constant support provided a foundation when I needed it most. To my friends Lonnie Hayes, Mary Hayes, Soraya Hayes, and L J Hayes, thanks for your support when we needed it most. I promise to tone down my two-ton chocolate raspberry ice cream metropolitans. To Tom and Evelyn Heard, thank you for the opportunities you have given me. To John and Cambria Sorenson, thank you for being great friends.

I would also like to thank two important people who have passed on. Mary Eloise Waller, my grandmother, was a wonderful human being. She always encouraged me and supported me. She also taught me how to cook, a skill that my wife, Catherine, sometimes wonders about. To Blake Ramsey, you are a dear friend, and I will miss you.

To Emilie Herman from John Wiley & Sons, who created what I feel is a finely crafted manuscript. I guess writers like us have a tendency to be temperamental beings. To my coauthor, Kevin T. Smith, who has afforded me new opportunities, thank you. My other coauthor, Michael C. Daconta, who over the past six years has provided me the continued opportunity for professional growth.

Most of all, I would like to thank the readers for supporting XUL. It's hard to create an environment in which we can all learn. In the words of a Charles Dickens' character, "But the umblest persons may be the instruments of good." I hope that you find our words useful to you and your quest for knowledge.

—Vaughn Bullard

First of all, I would like to give thanks to my wonderful wife, Gwen, who was so supportive while I spent endless hours writing chapters in this book during late nights and long weekends.

I would like to express my thanks for the many people who helped me with this project. Dave Bishop, David Hyatt, Eric A. Meyer, David R. Musser, and Clay Richardson reviewed/edited several of the chapters that I wrote in this book, and their feedback was critical. Helen G. Smith and Lois G. Schermerhorn reviewed the content of certain sections of the book for readability. Bill Flynn, Sandra H. Stewart, and various members of the BTG Technical Forum provided helpful suggestions for some aspects of this book. Scott Henry from BTG provided us new insight in computer literature. Over the course of my work on this book, many engineers from the team at Mozilla.org were very helpful in answering my questions, and I commend them on the work that they have done on the Mozilla project.

It has been wonderful collaborating with the other authors of this book, Vaughn Bullard and Michael C. Daconta. It has truly been a pleasure working with them on this book and on the jXUL project. Emilie Herman from John Wiley & Sons was also a joy to work with, and she helped steer us through this project.

In addition to the people that I have mentioned, I would like to thank certain individuals who have had a profound impact on my growth as a software engineer: Carl A. Smith, Dr. Phil Kearns, Seth Bromberger, Kevin Moran, Matt Holmes, Darren Govoni, and Brian Williams. During the writing of this book, Ken and Myrtle Ruth Stockman allowed me to unwind by helping me restore a pickup truck in their driveway (www.geocities.com/trumantruck/), and believe it or not, that therapeutic activity inspired much of the content of this book. Finally, I would like to thank my mother, Linda S. Smith, who lost her battle with Lou Gehrig's disease two years ago. She taught me to write, and she would have loved reading this book.

—Kevin T. Smith

I would like to thank my wife, Lynne, who is the best partner anyone could hope for. Her patience with my continuous stream of projects is a blessing. I would also like to thank my children—CJ, Gregory, and Samantha—for sharing daddy with the computer.

Second, I would like to thank my coauthors, Vaughn and Kevin, for their professionalism and hard work throughout this project. They took all my criticisms and suggestions with an aggressive, positive, can-do attitude. Thanks for making this project a great collaborative effort! Great collaborations would not be complete without a great editorial team. Special thanks go to Bob Elliott and Emilie Herman for all their hard work in managing this project. If you want a good experience writing a book, you need to be with people who both understand the market and understand writers. Bob and Emilie fit the bill!

Third, I would like to thank all of my family and friends who support me and cheer for me. I would also like to thank my colleagues at McDonald Bradley, Inc., for their support and encouragement.

Lastly, I would like to thank the thousands of readers who send us feedback, encouragement, errata, and suggestions. You make the writer's life all worthwhile. Thanks!

—Michael C. Daconta

About the Authors

Vaughn Bullard is a Senior Principal Software Engineer with BTG, Inc. In this position, he acts as the Java/XML/UML evangelist and instructor for the Defense and Intelligence Systems Division for BTG, Inc. He teaches and develops curricula for software development technologies including XML, Java, and UML for both Learning Tree International and George Mason University.

Vaughn has more than 13 years of solid software engineering experience developing everything from complex FORTRAN applications to more recently XML-based online stock trading platforms. He has significant experience in Java and SGML-based technologies. He specializes in Human Machine Interface (HMI) development.

He also is chairman of Bullard Acquisitions and Holdings, Inc. (www.bullardaq.com), an incubator company dedicated to creating technological innovations in the areas of software development.

Kevin T. Smith is a Senior Principal Software Engineer at BTG, Inc., where he specializes in Java and XML solutions. At BTG, he has worked in the roles of Program Manager, Chief Architect, and Lead Engineer for various projects. During the past 10 years, he has focused his academic and professional research on object-oriented architectures, real-time collaboration, adaptable user interfaces, and information security.

Kevin received his Bachelor's degree in Computer Science from the College of William and Mary and a Master's degree in Computer Science from George Mason University, and he continues to pursue graduate coursework and research in information security. In the past, he has contributed to several papers and published works. In particular, he was a contributing author to *Java Application Frameworks* (Wiley 1999), and was a technical session speaker at JavaOne 1999.

Michael C. Daconta is the director of Web and technology services for McDonald Bradley, Inc. (www.mcbrad.com), where he conducts training seminars and develops advanced systems with Java, JavaScript, and XML.

Over the past 15 years, Daconta has held every major development position including chief scientist, technical director, chief developer, team leader, systems analyst, and programmer.

He is a Sun-certified Java programmer and coauthor of *Java Pitfalls* (John Wiley & Sons, 2000), *Java 2 and JavaScript for C and C++ Programmers* (John Wiley & Sons, 1999), and *XML Development with Java 2* (Sams Publishing, 2000). In addition, he is the author of *C++ Pointers and Dynamic Memory Management* (John Wiley & Sons, 1995).

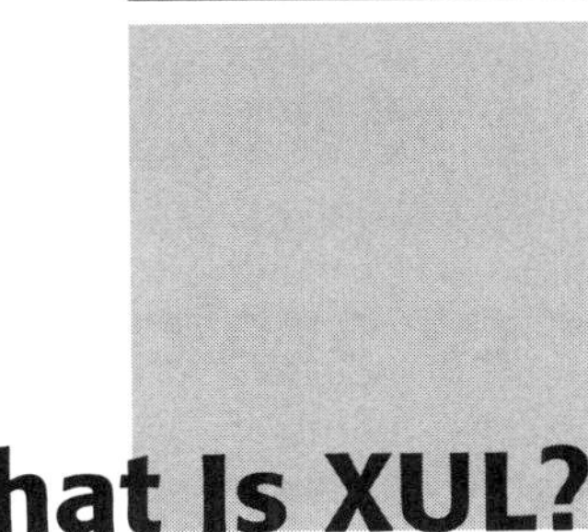

What Is XUL?

The interface is the part of a tool or technology with which the user interacts. For a screwdriver, it's the handle. For a bicycle, it's the seat, handlebars, pedals, and gear levers. For a web site, it's a crafted communication environment that houses the site's content and the navigation devices the user needs to get the content.

Jack Davis and Susan Merritt, *The Web Design Wow! Book*

What is XUL? You might conjure up thoughts of a famous Argentinean poet or even a character from a well-known ghost movie. However, the XUL that is the subject of this book refers to the user interface language for the eXtensible Markup Language (XML). It has gained momentum as *the* language Web developers and programmers should use for creating user interfaces. This is because XUL is easy to learn.

NOTE **For those who are phonetically challenged, XUL is pronounced "zool"—rhyming with cool. Those who lived through the 1980s might remember an anthemic movie where a bunch of guys wearing "proton packs" run around New York catching ghosts and destroying anything not nailed down to the floor. Many of the themes and the pronunciation of XUL were adopted tongue-in-cheek from the *Ghostbusters* movie. That's OK with us—a sense of humor is always a good thing. It reminds us in this "browser-eat-browser" world that we need to step back and take stock of our efforts.**

<colorpicker palettename="web"/>

Figure 1.1 A simple XUL component.

XUL, quite simply, is a presentation specification for creating lightweight, cross-platform, cross-device user interfaces. A XUL graphical user interface (GUI) can be lightweight in the sense that there are no huge libraries of widgets to download. XUL interfaces can be cross-platform because they are derived from a generic specification for user interfaces. XUL has the ability to run on different platforms on Internet-enabled devices. XUL enables you, the interface developer, to easily create an interface that is as simple or complex as you would like to make it. Figure 1.1 shows a simple XUL "colorpicker" component interface with its corresponding XUL markup. A more complex interface can be seen in Figure 1.2.

XUL is composed of widgets that are easy to use when building a complex user interface. XUL is so open in design that it could be ported easily as a GUI interface meta-library to other programming languages, such as Java or C++. In fact, this is done in Chapter 8, "The jXUL Open Source Project." Using XUL to describe any user interface in any programming language is possible. Someone just has to be willing to sacrifice his or her time to build a parser for a respective programming language. Luckily, the team at Mozilla.org developed a platform for XUL development and deployment, and they use XUL to create the user interface of their browser.

This chapter introduces you to the XUL language with a brief overview of its core features and a discussion of how it is implemented in the Mozilla browser.

It is not the intention of this chapter to be a summary of every aspect of the XUL language. The building blocks of XUL are discussed in detail in subsequent chapters.

In order to gain a complete perspective of XUL, it is necessary to discuss the origins of the language. The next section provides this historical perspective.

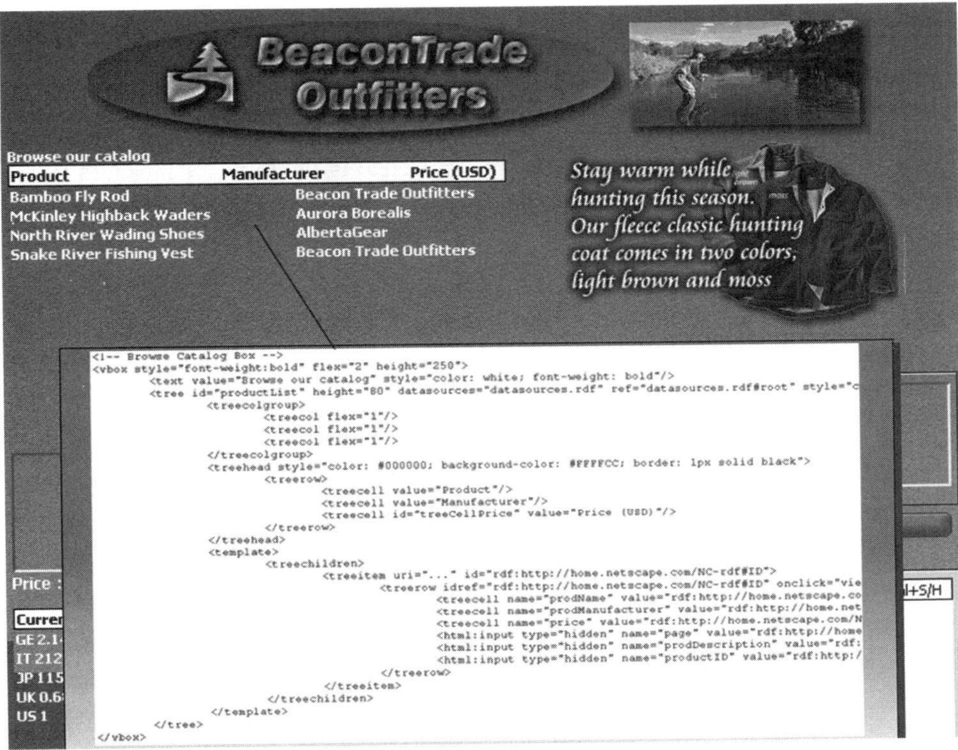

Figure 1.2 A more complex XUL interface.

The Origins of XUL

It is necessary to gain a historical knowledge of the Mozilla project to help you better understand the necessity of XUL.

On January 23, 1998, under pressure from the open source community and market conditions, Netscape Communications announced that the Netscape Communicator package and the source code would be free. After a little legal wrangling, Netscape released the developer source code on March 31, 1998.

The very nature of this type of release brought about a new organization called Mozilla.org, which is a virtual organization consisting of many developers working across the Internet developing source code for various projects, based on standards compliance, performance, and portability. Mozilla.org, a virtual phoenix on the Internet, rose out of the browser war ashes and made it possible for open source developers to work together to develop a new Internet browser and exciting related technologies. Several programming projects emerged.

Enter XUL. XUL emerged from Mozilla.org's Cross-Platform Front-End (XPFE) project, whose mission was "to make cross-platform user interfaces as easy to customize as Web pages."[1] This project, which is now called the XPToolkit project, established a development environment in which GUIs could be constructed from XML and JavaScript, eliminating hard-coded platform-specific user interfaces. XUL was created as an XML language, and the language was made of XML element tags that describe visual components. The components of the new Netscape/Mozilla browser were constructed out of the XUL language, and the browser's rendering engine, Gecko, parses XUL and creates the user interface on the fly. Gecko is the term for Mozilla's layout engine. It is an embeddable component and is designed to display user interfaces based on open standards languages.

As XUL has evolved, technologies have been added to complement its features. Cascading Style Sheets (CSS) are used to describe the "style" of XUL user interfaces, and JavaScript is used as the "glue" for event handling. The XML Binding Language (XBL), as covered in Chapter 7, "XUL Overlays and XBL," is used to create reusable composite widgets. New features have emerged, such as *downloadable chrome*, in which users can download themes to decorate the look and feel of their browser. As the language has evolved, developers have recognized that XUL has made user interface development easier. The team at Mozilla.org, operating in the "Bazaar" style of Eric Raymond's "The Cathedral and the Bazaar," created a powerful technology, and we feel that this is only the beginning.[2]

In 2001, the authors of this book created a new open source project, called jXUL, located at http://www.jxul.org, creating a Java library for translating XUL into Java-based user interfaces. At the same time, Mozilla.org is continuing to focus on XUL-based user interfaces and is influencing standards on the Internet. The future of XML-based user interfaces is here.

Leveraged Technologies in XUL

This section focuses on other standards and technologies that are used in conjunction with XUL to develop applications. XUL uses the following technologies as shown in Figure 1.3.

- XML
- CSS
- HTML
- XBL
- JavaScript
- RDF

In the following sections, we discuss each technology and how it is related to XUL.

XUL Is XML

XUL is an XML vocabulary, and thus adheres to the rules of XML. Code Listing 1.1 shows the structure of a XUL document, as it conforms to the XML standard.

Important items to note about Code Listing 1.1 are:

- Like all XML documents, XUL uses the XML declaration, shown in the first line.
- The namespace is http://www.mozilla.org/keymaster/gatekeeper/there.is.only.xul.
- The root element of a XUL document is always the <window> tag.

Figure 1.3 XUL and its leveraged technologies.

```
<?xml version="1.0"?>
<?xml-stylesheet href="chrome://navigator/skin/" type="text/css"?>
<window id="main-window" xmlns:html="http://www.w3.org/1999/xhtml"
xmlns="http://www.mozilla.org/keymaster/gatekeeper/there.is.only.xul">
  <!-XUL elements go here!! -->
</window>
```

Code Listing 1.1 A XUL document.

For those of you new to XML, Chapter 2, "An XML Primer," is an XML primer and focuses on XML from a XUL perspective. If you are proficient in XML, you may want to skip Chapter 2.

XUL Uses Cascading Style Sheets

XUL uses Cascading Style Sheets (CSS) to add style and behavior to its elements. In XML, you can change the presentation of a document with CSS and XSL style sheets. XUL uses only CSS and does not use XSL for styling documents. If you're familiar with CSS, you will be happy about the native support that XUL allows.

The difference between Cascading Style Sheets and XSL style sheets is the manner in which they operate. Cascading Style Sheets are event driven, which means that a browser steps through an XML document and creates styles based on the elements presented. An XSL style sheet works in much the same way as a procedural programming language works, step by step. Creating XSL style sheets enables you to program looping statements and create conditional operations. XSL is a more powerful language, but it is not event driven. This is the main advantage of using CSS over XSL. CSS is also easier to learn. For example, a highlight class in a cascading style sheet:

```
.highlight
{
    font-weight: bold;
    font-color: red;
}
```

Invoking the highlight class in an HTML document:

```
<p class="highlight">Example text</p>
```

When the HTML document is loaded, "Example text" is formatted according to the highlight class rules predefined in the Cascading Style Sheet. Cascading Style Sheets are in effect easier to learn and create. In this example, "Example text" is formatted in bold, and the color of the font is changed to red.

In line two of Code Listing 1.1, we show how a XUL document references a CSS style sheet to attach style to elements. Just as HTML documents use CSS to attach style, XUL can reference an external style sheet with a stylesheet declaration, or XUL elements can attach style by using the *style* attribute, as shown here:

```
<button id="whatever" style="background-color: red; " label="OK"/>
```

CSS is one of the most important technologies used with XUL. CSS is used to attach behavioral bindings to XML elements with XBL. Style sheets are also used in conjunction with the skinning of the Mozilla browser. Before XUL, the only control over the browser interface in a standards-based Web browser was in the document display area. XUL and CSS enable you to skin, or change, the whole look and feel of the browser—creating a Netscape theme. The menus, windows, and everything viewable to a user are easily modified in a Netscape theme. The potential for this is tremendous. In the future, imagine that a visitor to your music-oriented Web site sees a browser that transforms into something that looks like a stereo. You have total control! For those needing an introduction to style sheets, a CSS primer is contained within Chapter 3, "Using Cascading Sytle Sheets." Creating Netscape themes is covered in Chapter 5, "Creating Netscape Themes." Attachment of behavior to XUL elements with XBL and CSS is discussed in Chapter 7, "XUL Overlays and XBL."

XUL Uses "Well-Formed" HTML

HTML elements can be intermingled with XUL elements in an XUL interface. Because XUL is XML, it must adhere to XML's specifications for "well-formedness," and any HTML elements included should adhere to these rules as well. If you would like to put an HTML element in your XUL document, you would first declare the HTML namespace in the declaration of the root element and then reference that namespace in the HTML element. This is demonstrated in Code Listing 1.2.

Code Listing 1.2 uses the <a> tag to include a link to send mail to someone. Many XUL developers use HTML elements for formatting text in their user interfaces.

XBL Extends XUL Elements

The XBL is an XML language used to add anonymous content, properties, and implementation methods to XML elements. Used in tandem with XUL and CSS, XBL is used to create reusable composite widgets that can be used in a development project. CSS is used to bind XUL elements to bindings in an XBL document.

XBL can be used with XUL to add new content, properties, and methods—providing encapsulation (data hiding). This is quite useful when a software developer builds a complex widget made of smaller XUL elements. Because of data hiding, any developer can use the new widget without having to know the minute details of how the composite widget is implemented. Figure 1.4 shows an example of how XUL and XBL can be used together. In the figure, a node in the XBL file is bound via CSS to a binding that inserts new content, a property called *illuminated*, and a method called *selectIlluminatedItem()*. The result of this binding creates the new composite widget; the internal added content is hidden from the developer; and all the software developer needs to know are the public properties and methods on the new widget. When bindings are used to add properties and methods, a developer can use JavaScript to call these methods and reference these properties.

```
<?xml version="1.0"?>
<window
xmlns="http://www.mozilla.org/keymaster/gatekeeper/there.is.only.xul"
       xmlns:html="http://www.w3.org/TR/REC-html40"
>
   <html:a href="mailto:xul@mindspring.com">Keymaster</html:a>
</window>
```

Code Listing 1.2 Using HTML elements in XUL.

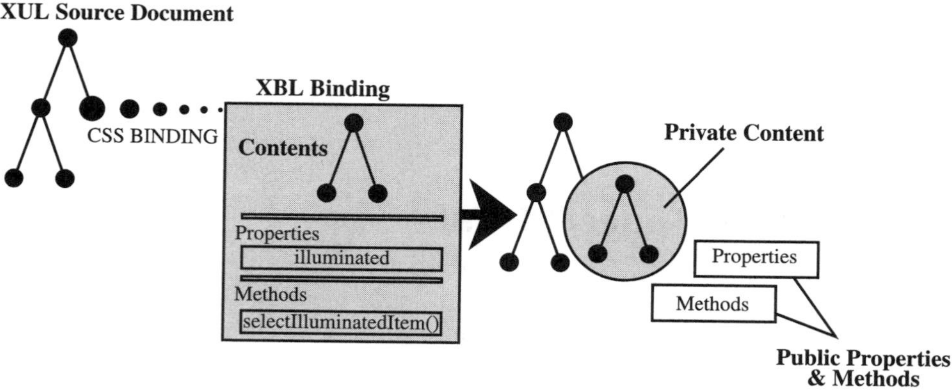

Figure 1.4 XBL and XUL.

By adding content and behavior to XUL elements, XBL provides the features of reusability and encapsulation. XBL is discussed in detail in Chapter 7, "XUL Overlays and XBL."

JavaScript Is Used in XUL

Every user interface needs event handling. This is accomplished in XUL with JavaScript. JavaScript is a browser and platform-independent scripting language. It enables you to build callbacks to events and to manipulate XUL user interface elements via the Document Object Model (DOM). In addition, some XUL elements may have JavaScript properties and methods that can be referenced and called by JavaScript.

To embed JavaScript, use the <script src=" "> tag in the same fashion as you would declare it in HTML. Embedding the JavaScript as an event handler is even more intuitive, as demonstrated in Code Listing 1.3.

```
closewindow.js

function closeThatWindow()
{
   this.window.close();
}
example.xul
<window>
   <script src="closewindow.js">
   <menuitem label="Close" accesskey="c"
oncommand="closeThatWindow();"/>
</window>
```

Code Listing 1.3 Event Handling in XUL with JavaScript.

When you select the menu item either by a mouse click or access key, it calls the JavaScript function closeThatWindow( ). Handling events through JavaScript is essentially the best way to manipulate XUL elements.

You can embed JavaScript right into the XUL document, although we recommend that you use a <script src="http://myserver/myJavaScript.js"> tag. The reasoning behind this is to ensure the proper nesting and termination of element tags. You may want to have a comparison operator in JavaScript to compare two numbers for example. If left in, it might cause the XUL document to not be properly parsed, resulting in no user interface whatsoever.

JavaScript is used in XUL examples throughout this book for event handling and for retrieving and manipulating XUL elements. Appendix A, "XUL Programmer's Reference," provides an excellent reference of XUL elements, listing each element's JavaScript methods and properties, as well as providing the API for the DOM. Used together, JavaScript and XUL provide a powerful mechanism for quickly creating applications and prototypes.

XUL Leverages RDF

The Resource Description Framework (RDF) is a framework for describing documents, files, or other data using meta data. XUL uses RDF to build user interfaces and templates that enable the user interface designer to embed and create dynamic content. They act as self-describing data containers. RDF files are used as little databases and are data containers for XUL elements. So if you had a list of 1000 customers, you could place those customers in an RDF file and then display them as a populated XUL <tree> element. If you are familiar with XML, this is similar to XSL Transformations (XSLT).

RDF files are also used in skinning the browser. Code Listing 1.4 shows how one would package a skin using the Mozilla/Netscape 6 Manifest.rdf file format. This file is used to describe to the Mozilla/Netscape 6 browser the format in which a skin is organized. These attributes include the author, the registry name, and subpackages in which the chrome is stored. Most notable are the global, communicator, editor, navigator, and messenger skins.

Chapter 5, "Creating Netscape Themes," discusses RDF's role for creating Netscape themes in more detail. Chapter 6, "RDF and XUL Templates," presents a more detailed introduction to RDF and shows how RDF is used to generate dynamic user interface content.

Types of XUL User Interface Widgets

XUL has an extensive set of easily modified user interface components. These include elements such as windows, toolbars, menus, dialogs, trees, labels, springs, boxes, progress meters, stacks, decks, bulletin board, and content panel components. These items can be extended in functionality beyond their existing capabilities.

```
<?xml version="1.0"?>

<RDF:RDF xmlns:RDF="http://www.w3.org/1999/02/22-rdf-syntax-ns#"
         xmlns:chrome="http://www.mozilla.org/rdf/chrome#">
  <!- List all the skins being supplied by this theme ->
  <RDF:Seq about="urn:mozilla:skin:root">
    <RDF:li resource="urn:mozilla:skin:vaughn/1.0" />
  </RDF:Seq>
  <!- Vaughn Information ->
  <RDF:Description about="urn:mozilla:skin:vaughn/1.0"
        chrome:displayName="vaughn"
        chrome:author="javant.com"
        chrome:name="vaughn/1.0">
    <chrome:packages>
      <RDF:Seq about="urn:mozilla:skin:vaughn/1.0:packages">
        <RDF:li
resource="urn:mozilla:skin:vaughn/1.0:communicator"/>
        <RDF:li resource="urn:mozilla:skin:vaughn/1.0:editor"/>
        <RDF:li resource="urn:mozilla:skin:vaughn/1.0:global"/>
        <RDF:li resource="urn:mozilla:skin:vaughn/1.0:messenger"/>
        <RDF:li resource="urn:mozilla:skin:vaughn/1.0:navigator"/>
      </RDF:Seq>
    </chrome:packages>
  </RDF:Description>
</RDF:RDF>
```

Code Listing 1.4 Netscape 6/Mozilla "skin" Manifest.rdf.

We will touch on what some of these elements will look like, along with their corresponding source code. These include windows, buttons, and trees, to name a few.

Windows

Windows are the base (root element) container for most XUL interfaces. This container is represented as the following code:

```
<window id="main-window" xmlns:html="http://www.w3.org/1999/xhtml"
xmlns="http://www.mozilla.org/keymaster/gatekeeper/there.is.only.xul"
class="dialog">
```

Buttons

Buttons are another essential user interface component. They can be placed anywhere on an XUL interface. The button in Figure 1.5 can be represented with the following code:

```
<button label="Sort Customers"/>
```

Figure 1.5 XUL button.

Trees

Trees are to XUL what tables are to HTML. The difference is that you can manipulate items within the tree. This is not possible in an HTML table. You are also able to collapse tree rows by clicking what is called a *twisty*. A twisty is an arrow that when clicked turns pointing down to indicate an open tree element or points to the right to indicate a closed tree element. As you can see from Code Listing 1.5, a tree widget is composed of many subelements. Figure 1.6 shows a graphical view of the tree.

We have shown you a relatively small sample of XUL elements, but it should give you an idea of the power of the language. In later chapters, you will learn about these elements in more detail. Appendix A, " XUL Programmer's Reference," provides an excellent reference for XUL elements.

XUL Features

In addition to being a markup language that is rich in user interface widgets, XUL has several key features that are discussed in detail throughout this book. This section provides a brief overview of some of these features.

Dynamic Content Generation

Although you can write static user interfaces, XUL uses templates in combination with RDF datasources to dynamically generate user interfaces. RDF allows a XUL element to cycle through the RDF datasource and populate the XUL element's child elements. This enables XUL user interfaces to be built dynamically, as shown in Figure 1.7. XUL templates are used to provide flexible interfaces that describe ever-changing user preferences, such as bookmarks and preferred online resources. Chapter 6, "RDF and XUL Templates," provides a detailed description of using XUL templates to build dynamic content.

Reusability

XUL incorporates a technology called "overlays" into the language. A XUL overlay is a separate XUL file that can be merged with content from a main XUL file at run time. Most XUL overlays are menus, toolbars, and dialogs that are used repeatedly in a software project. By using overlays, you can build reusable components. Figure 1.8 shows a graphical depiction of how an overlay can be used throughout a project. In the figure, XUL Document A and XUL Document B both reference the overlay in their respective

```
<tree id="assetList" flex="1" height="1" width="1">

  <treecolgroup>
    <treecol flex="1" />
    <treecol flex="1" />
    <treecol flex="1" />
  </treecolgroup>

  <treehead style="background-color: #FFFFCC; border: 1px solid
black">
    <treerow>
      <treecell label="Asset"/>
      <treecell label="Manufacturer"/>
      <treecell label="Value"/>
    </treerow>
  </treehead>
  <treechildren flex="1" >
    <treeitem container="true" open="true">
      <treerow>
        <treecell class="treecell-indent" label="Office 1"/>
      </treerow>

      <treechildren>
        <treeitem>
          <treerow>
            <treecell class="treecell-indent"
                      label="File Server"/>
            <treecell label="Compaq"/>
            <treecell label="7500.00"/>
          </treerow>
        </treeitem>
      </treechildren>
    </treeitem>

    <treeitem container="true" open="true">
      <treerow>
        <treecell class="treecell-indent" label="Warehouse"/>
      </treerow>

      <treechildren>
        <treeitem>
          <treerow>
            <treecell class="treecell-indent"
                      label="Server Rack"/>
            <treecell label="BBN Com"/>
            <treecell label="3775.00"/>
```

Code Listing 1.5 Tree elements.

```
          </treerow>
        </treeitem>
      </treechildren>
    </treeitem>

    <treeitem container="true" open="true">
      <treerow>
        <treecell class="treecell-indent"
                  label="San Jose Office"/>
      </treerow>
      <treechildren>
        <treeitem>
          <treerow>
            <treecell class="treecell-indent"
                      label="Color LaserJet"/>
            <treecell label="HP"/>
            <treecell label="2300.00"/>
          </treerow>
        </treeitem>
      </treechildren>
    </treeitem>
  </treechildren>
</tree>
```

Code Listing 1.5 Tree elements (Continued).

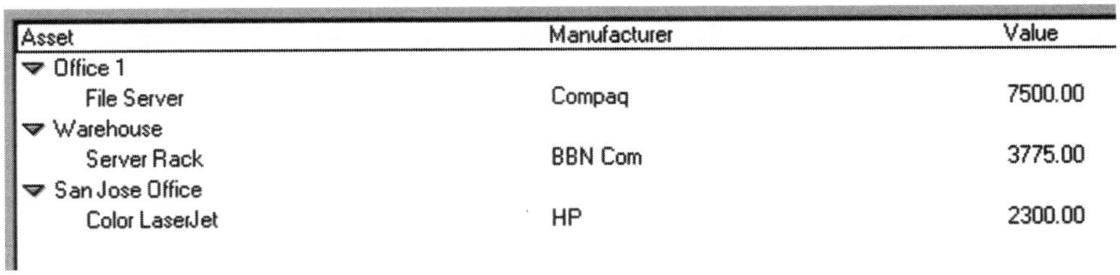

Asset	Manufacturer	Value
▾ Office 1		
File Server	Compaq	7500.00
▾ Warehouse		
Server Rack	BBN Com	3775.00
▾ San Jose Office		
Color LaserJet	HP	2300.00

Figure 1.6 Tree element.

files, and the resulting user interfaces for A and B benefit from the reusable code. Chapter 7 discusses XUL overlays in detail, and Chapter 9 gives a real-world example of how overlays are used in the Netscape/Mozilla browser.

Themes

The result of the modularization of the Netscape browser has made it very easy to change the look and feel of all or individual subcomponents. Netscape has formalized a

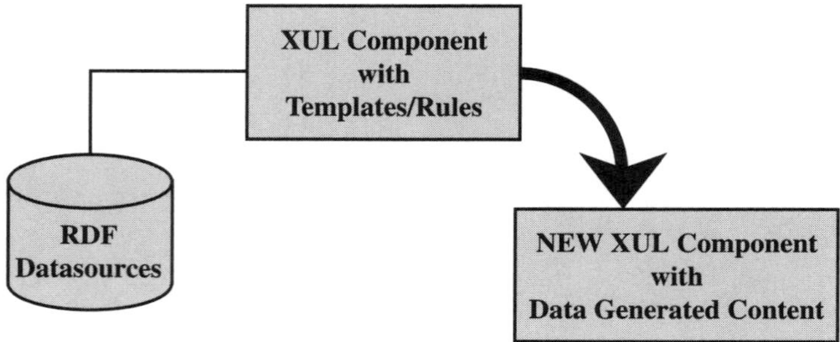

Figure 1.7 Dynamic Content Generation in XUL.

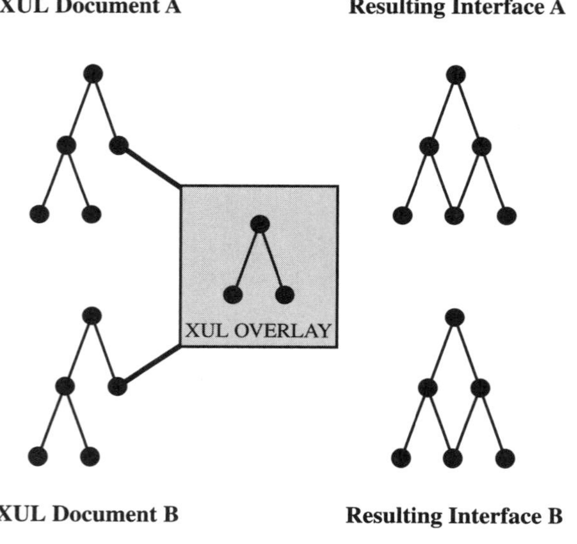

Figure 1.8 Overlays.

way to make global or local changes to the browser. This is called *theming* or *skinning* the browser. With themes, you can change the look and feel and the behavior of every element within the browser, providing yet another abstraction for customizable applications. Chapter 5 goes in depth on how to create your own theme.

Internationalization and Localization

Creating content based upon locality is also modularized. This is done through the replacement of entity references supplied in Document Type Definition (DTD) documents. You could develop an XUL user interface that is accessible to both your German users and your American users. Code Listing 1.6 demonstrates how you could do this.

```
DTD file for your German user
<!ENTITY goodBye.label "Auf Wiedersehen Geck!">
DTD file for your American User
<!ENTITY goodBye.label "Good Bye Dude! ">
In your XUL interface
<label id="goodByeMessage" value="&goodBye.label"/>
```

Code Listing 1.6 Localized content.

Implementing XUL

So far we have given a high-level overview of XUL, but we know that you are dying to see how the language works. In this section, we give you a brief look at a XUL application, and we discuss how the Netscape/Mozilla browser transforms this language into the user interface that we will see. This section does not get into the gritty details; details will be discussed later in this book.

What Does XUL Code Look Like?

Code Listing 1.7 shows a simple XUL document describing a button interface for a simple XUL interface. Like we discussed in earlier sections, the XUL file is an XML document and uses the XUL namespace, and we apply a stylesheet in the second line of the listing. The <window> element is always the root element of a XUL document. This example uses the <toolbox>, <button>, and <toolbar> XUL tags to describe a simple user interface.

Code Listing 1.7 also has an event handler associated with it, as defined by the JavaScript <script> tag. This example will create a toolbar, with a button on it called "Sort Customers." When the button is invoked, from either a key press or a mouse click, the message "You have clicked the Sort Customers button." is displayed within a JavaScript alert box. Figure 1.9 shows the resulting interface after it has been parsed in the Netscape 6.x browser.

NOTE **Throughout this book, we refer to the Netscape Browser as the Netscape 6.x browser. The underlying structure of XUL code in the Mozilla browser is the same for the Netscape browser, so all of the discussion of XUL and the design of its components are also relevant to both browsers. Some of the internal Netscape code that we show in this book may change as future versions of Netscape and Mozilla are enhanced, but the concepts presented and studied in this book will be the same. This book presents in-depth studies of how real-world solutions can be accomplished by using XUL and its companion technologies.**

As you can see, developing this user interface was quite simple, and it is reminiscent of Web programming. What makes XUL stand apart is the fact that when we write a

```
<?xml version="1.0"?>
<?xml-stylesheet href="chrome://navigator/skin/" type="text/css"?>

<window id="main-window"
xmlns="http://www.mozilla.org/keymaster/gatekeeper/there.is.only.xul"
class="dialog">
  <script language="JavaScript">
    function alertUser()
    {
      alert("You have clicked the\n\nSort Customers\n\nbutton.");
    }
  </script>
  <toolbox flex="1">
    <toolbar>
      <button class="dialog" label="Sort Customers"
              oncommand="alertUser();"/>
    </toolbar>
  </toolbox>
</window>
```

Code Listing 1.7 XUL code with an event handler.

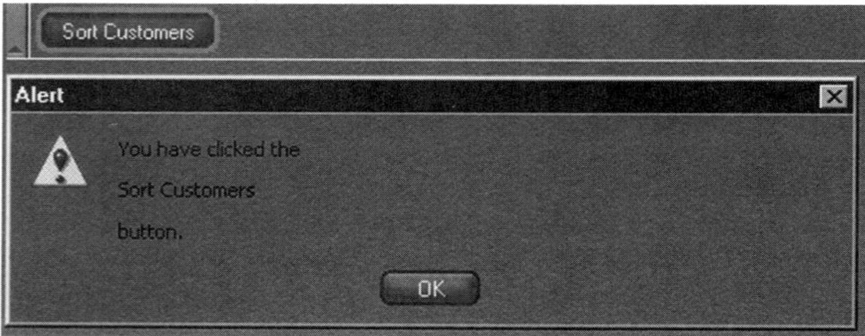

Figure 1.9 A JavaScript alert generated by a XUL button.

XUL document, we are describing the look and feel of a software application. By using XUL and its complementary technologies, Mozilla.org was able to build their entire browser, eliminating the need for porting the user interface code across multiple platforms and creating a user interface that can be easily changed by Web developers.

How Does Everything Work?

To create a XUL interface, you need only a text editor and a browser. Then you can create an XUL interface file and open it in Navigator or Mozilla to be parsed. The resulting

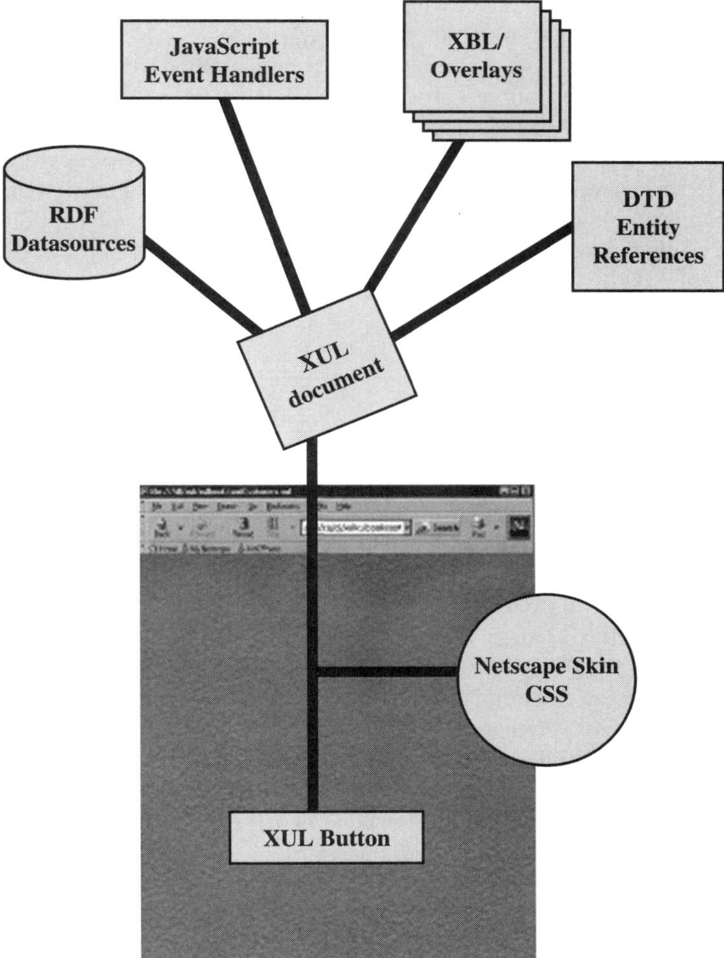

Figure 1.10 Parsing of a XUL interface.

parsed document creates an element-rich user interface. Buttons, scrollbars, menus, trees, tabbed panels, and other elements populate the interface. Figure 1.10 shows how all of the technologies and XUL work together to build a GUI. Netscape's rendering engine parses the XUL and creates the view.

When the browser loads a XUL file, multiple steps could occur before Netscape creates a user interface. The XUL document may call an internal stylesheet to create elements based upon the user's currently selected theme. XBL may be used to extend widgets in a XUL document. Overlays may be used to create additional modularized content. A DTD may be called for creating localizable or internationalized content. Any JavaScript source files may be included to create event-handling routines for the user interface. RDF datasources may be called by elements internal to the XUL document to create dynamic content. All of these technologies work together in a complimentary way, giving the user interface developer much flexibility.

XUL styles its documents according to the browser's currently applied theme. It then takes all these elements, parses them, and creates a new XUL Document Object Model (DOM) tree. This tree is then parsed and displayed in the browser.

This architecture is referred to as the XPToolkit architecture. Although development of user interfaces can be very simple, the design of the architecture that supports XUL is quite flexible and supports many open technologies. As the language evolves, perhaps new emerging technologies will be added to this architecture.

Summary

In this chapter, we introduced you to XUL by providing a high-level overview of its history, related complementary technologies, and the language's features. We showed you a very simple example of a XUL interface, and we have given you an idea of how XUL works together with other open standards in the Mozilla architecture.

As software developers, we face certain obstacles in software development projects. Sometimes, user interfaces are required to change as our customers' requirements evolve. When this happens, user interfaces that are hard-coded into our compiled programming languages are difficult to change. If a software project needs to support multiple platforms, this increases the complexity of our dilemma. With the technology of XUL, we can abstract the view of our application from the business logic of our systems. Because XUL is easy to write, change, and customize, we can focus more of our time on the critical logic of our applications. If we have a rendering engine like the Netscape browser that parses XUL into an application user interface, difficulties with cross-platform portability are diminished. Finally, because XUL is an XML language and interfaces with open standards, we are not stuck in the rut of proprietary code. As our quotation hinted at the beginning of this chapter, XUL takes advantage of its tightly integrated communication environment to provide a rich toolbox for software developers to use.

The simplicity of XUL is complemented by the complexity and strength of its advanced features. Although user interfaces, like our example in this chapter, can be easy to write, there is more "under the hood" that you as a software developer can take advantage of to create dynamic and extensible user interfaces.

The next two chapters are primers on XML and CSS that will help you understand the details and advanced features of XUL. If you feel comfortable with both subjects covered in the following two chapters, go ahead and skip to Chapter 4, "Building a Simple XUL Interface."

Notes

[1]Mozilla.org, "XPToolkit Project," www.mozilla.org/xpfe/

[2]Eric Raymond, "The Cathedral and the Bazaar," http://www.tuxedo.org/~esr/writings/cathedral-bazaar/cathedral-bazaar/, 2000.

CHAPTER 2

An XML Primer

In reality, XML just clears away some of the syntactical distractions so that we can get down to the big problem: How we arrive at common understandings about knowledge representation.

John Bosak

XUL files adhere to the syntactic rules specified by the eXtensible markup language (XML). This chapter starts by precisely defining XML and then proceeds to examine all the key components. After reading this chapter, you will be able to construct both well-formed and valid XUL files. The name eXtensible markup language is a misnomer, as it is not a language. A language has a vocabulary and a grammar—XML has neither. XML is a language specification, a set of rules for constructing markup languages. So, XML is a set of rules for defining a markup language. But, what is a markup language?

The most common markup language is Hypertext Markup Language (HTML), which defines a hypertext document. A hypertext document is a multimedia document that can include links to other documents. In order to specify the formatting and placement of content in the document, special tags are used that have specific meaning to an application program (called a hypertext browser), which renders the document. These tags are called markup. Code Listing 2.1 is a simple document that demonstrates the HTML markup language. Figure 2.1 shows xuluniverse.html in Netscape 6.

The important thing to note about Code Listing 2.2 is that it contains three parts: tags, a hierarchical structure, and content. If we were to separate the content out of the document it would look like Code Listing 2.2.

The purpose of a markup language is to separate the structure of a document from its content using tags and nesting. The structure of a document indicates purpose and semantic meaning while the content is one specific instance, among many, of that structure. So, Code Listing 2.1 would be formally called a document "instance" of the HTML document type.

```
<html>
     <head>
          <title> XUL Universe </title>
     </head>
     <body BGCOLOR="#DDDDDD">
     <h2> <center> XUL Universe </center> </h2>
     Here are some links to my <em>favorite</em> Xul sites! <br />
     <ul>
          <li> <a href="http://www.mozilla.org"> Mozilla </a> </li>
          <li> <a href="http://www.xulplanet.com"> Xul Planet </a>
</li>
          <li> <a href="http://www.jxul.org"> The JXUL project </a>
</li>
     </ul>
     </body>
</html>
```

Code Listing 2.1 xuluniverse.html.

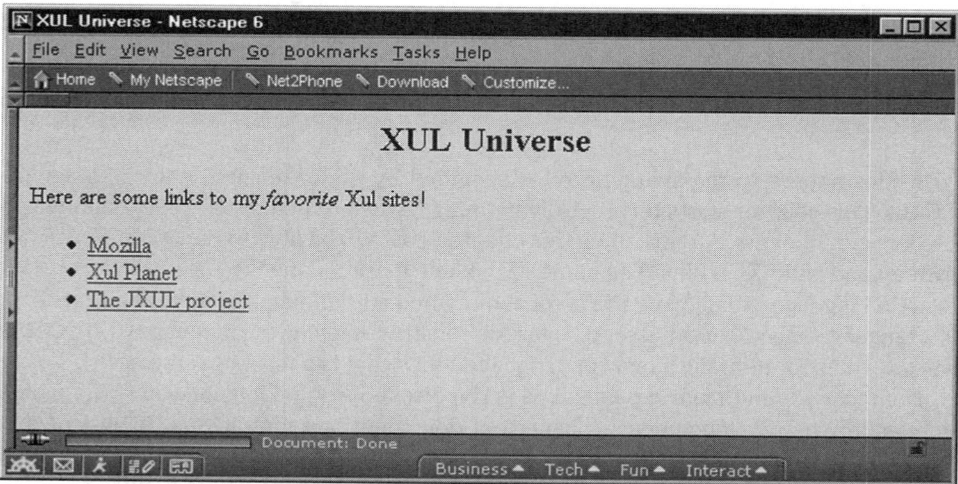

Figure 2.1 A simple HTML document.

```
XUL Universe
XUL Universe
Here are some links to my favorite Xul sites!
Mozilla
Xul Planet
The JXUL project
```

Code Listing 2.2 HTML document content.

NOTE Another way to express the purpose of a markup language is to separate the document data from the meta data. Meta data is defined as data about data. For example, in the sentence "My name is Mike," the word *name* is the meta data that describes the meaning of the word *Mike*. We could express the same information in a markup language like this: <name> Mike </name>

The rules for creating markup languages are specified in the XML 1.0 recommendation, available at http://www.w3.org/TR/REC-xml. The rules fall into two categories: syntactic and declarative. We'll first discuss syntactic components, and then we'll examine how to declare what is valid.

XML Syntax

Syntactic rules specify how you create markup and where you place it in a document. The declarative rules specify how you define your legal markup names and the legal nesting arrangement of your document. The key syntax rules to creating well-formed XUL are the XML declaration, elements, attributes, namespaces, comments, processing instructions, and the document type declaration. In the following sections, we will examine each in detail.

XML Declaration

XML documents have a simple order. An XML document starts with a prolog and then has a single root element that may contain other elements. Although all the items of a prolog are optional, we recommend that you include an XML declaration to specify the version of XML to which your document conforms. Here is a sample XML declaration:

```
<?xml version="1.0" ?>
```

An XML declaration starts with the literal characters "<?xml" and ends with "?>". The XML declaration is a type of XML processing instruction. The syntax of processing instructions will be discussed later in this chapter. If you add an XML declaration to your document, it must be the first thing in the document. Secondly, the minimum requirement for a proper XML declaration is to have a version attribute as shown here. Optionally, you may have an encoding declaration, a standalone document declaration, or both.

An encoding declaration specifies the character encoding used in the file. The character encoding is different than the character set used. The character set for XML files is the Unicode character set. Detailed information about the Unicode character set can be found at http://www.unicode.org. The character set defines the number to letter mappings for every letter in the languages represented in the character set. As an international character set, Unicode is large enough to map all the current languages and is formally called the Universal Character Set (UCS). A Unicode character has a position between 0 and 65,535. The encoding of a file is how you map the position of a character in a character set (which may occupy more than a single byte) in a binary file composed of a set of contiguous bytes. The default encoding of an XML file is either UTF-8 or UTF-16. UTF stands for UCS Transformation Format, and the appended number refers to the 8-bit or 16-bit version of the format. Other possible encoding formats are ISO-8859-6 (Arabic), ISO-2022-kr (Korean), and ISO-2022-jp (Japanese). Here is a sample of an XML declaration with an encoding declaration:

```
<?xml version="1.0" encoding="ISO-2022-jp" ?>
```

A standalone document declaration specifies whether the XML processor needs to process external references that will modify the XML document. The declaration is an attribute with the name standalone and a value of either yes or no. If the value is yes, no external references will affect the document. The default value of this attribute is no. Here is an example of a standalone document declaration:

```
<?xml version="1.0" standalone="yes" ?>
```

After the XML declaration is an optional document type declaration (discussed later) and then the root element. The document type declaration is used to declare a Document Type Definition (DTD), which specifies the legal elements and attributes. Elements and attributes are the two main XML components that make up your documents.

Elements

An element defines a structural part of a document by wrapping and labeling it. For example, you define the title of an HTML document by wrapping it in start and end tags that are labeled "title."

```
<title> My Super Web Site </title>
```

Notice that you can have freeform text contained within an element. The element starts at the start tag and ends with the end tag. A start tag begins with the less-than character (<), is followed by a label, and ends with the greater-than character (>). The end tag is the same as the start tag, except that the label is preceded with a forward slash (/). The name of an element must start with a letter or an underscore, followed by any number of letters, digits, hyphens, underscores, or periods. You can also have other elements contained inside an element. Code Listing 2.3 has three XUL elements: a window, a menubar, and a menu.

```
<window>
        <menubar>
             <menu />
        </menubar>
</window>
```

Code Listing 2.3 Three_XUL elements.

In Code Listing 2.3, the window element contains a menubar element, and the menubar element contains an empty menu element. Notice that the empty menu element is a start element with a forward slash before the enclosing greater-than symbol (>). We like to think of it as a start tag and end tag smashed together.

The end result of a document composed of elements containing other elements is a tree structure. The one root element can have any number of subelements, which, in turn, can also have any number of subelements, and so on. Part of defining the markup language is defining the shape of your tree, which is determined by specifying what each element will contain, known as its content model.

NOTE In an XML document, every start tag must have a corresponding end tag (unless it's an empty element).

Besides a content model, an element can have attributes. An element's attribute defines a specific characteristic of that element. An example of an attribute for a window element is width. Elements often represent real-world objects, and attributes define the characteristics of the object. XUL follows this model with the majority of its elements referring to GUI components such as window, menu, button, text, and checkboxes. The majority of XUL elements have attributes.

Attributes

An attribute is a name-value pair that qualifies an element. For example, the window element has 15 attributes:

align

height

id

ondraggesture

onload

onunload

persist

title

titlemenuseparator

titlemodified

width

windowtype

x

xmlns

y

Those are the names (or identifiers) of the attributes. To add an attribute to an element, you equate a value to the attribute name like this:

```
<window title="My Tic Tac Toe Game">
```

The value must be enclosed in either single or double quotes. You can specify multiple attributes for an element like this:

```
<window title="My Tic Tac Toe Game" width="600" height="400">
```

Attribute names follow the same rules as element names. The name must start with a letter or an underscore, followed by any number of letters, digits, hyphens, underscores, or periods. The colon character is reserved to specify a namespace for elements and attributes.

Namespaces

A namespace is a grouping mechanism that creates a collection of unique names. The namespace is identified by a Uniform Resource Identifier (URI). You use a namespace to ensure that the names of elements and attributes in your document type will not conflict with the names of elements and attributes in other document types. You add a namespace to your document by adding an attribute to the root element like this:

```
<window xmlns=
  "http://www.mozilla.org/keymaster/gatekeeper/there.is.only.xul">
```

There are two forms of the xmlns attribute. The declaration of the default namespace (shown previously) and the declaration of a namespace prefix like this:

```
<window xmlns:html="http://www.w3.org/TR/REC-html40">
```

The default namespace is declared by not specifying a prefix; thus all nonprefixed subelements belong to the default namespace. For namespaces declared with a prefix, the prefix precedes the element or attribute name. For example, "<html:title>." It is very important to understand that the URI value of the namespace is used to create *only* a unique name and is not used to access a resource. The URI should not reference anything.

You sometimes will use one or more namespaces in the same document. For example, with XUL, you routinely use both XUL and HTML as in Code Listing 2.4.

In Code Listing 2.4, the window, menubar, and menu elements belong to the default namespace, and the *a* element belongs to the html namespace. It is important to understand that the prefix is not the namespace; the prefix is merely shorthand for the URI it represents. The namespace prefix is replaced by the URI when the XML parser parses the document.

Namespaces have scope (an area of the document where the namespace has meaning). The scope of a namespace is the current element and all elements it contains. For

```
<window
xmlns="http://www.mozilla.org/keymaster/gatekeeper/there.is.only.xul"
        xmlns:html="http://www.w3.org/TR/REC-html40">
     <menubar>
           <menu />
         </menubar>
     <html:a href="mailto:joecoder@xulit.org"> Joe programmer
</html:a>
</window>
```

Code Listing 2.4 MultipleNamespaces.xul.

example, in Code Listing 2.4, the default XUL namespace is applied to the window, menubar, and menu element.

Lastly, namespace can apply to both elements and attributes. Here is an example of the HTML namespace applied to both an element and an attribute:

```
<html:applet html:width="400" html:height="300">
```

Comments

XML uses the same comment syntax as HTML. You create a comment in a XUL document like this:

```
<!-- This is the main window of the application. -->
```

Comments are freeform text used to explain parts of the documents to readers. A comment cannot contain -- (two hyphens) or the string -->, which ends a comment. Comments are stripped out of the document when parsed and not passed on to the application. Lastly, you can place comments before the document element, inside an element (but not inside a tag), or after the document element.

Processing Instructions

A processing instruction is a special command to a single application. The W3C has defined some special processing instructions for certain standard actions like the XML declaration and attaching style sheets to XML documents. We like to think of processing instructions as an escape hatch to enable you to add non-XML or nonlanguage specific syntax to a document. The syntax of the processing instruction takes the following general form:

```
<?application free-form-text ?>
```

For example:

```
<?EZformat font="helvetica" size="24" ?>
```

The most common processing instruction besides the XML declaration is the instruction to attach a stylesheet to an XML document. The format of the instruction to attach a stylesheet is:

```
<?xml:stylesheet href="http://www.xulit.org/cool.xsl"
                 type="text/xsl" ?>
```

The xml:stylesheet processing instruction is allowed only in the prolog of an XML document (must be before the root element). The psuedo attributes follow the exact syntax as the HTML link tag to associate stylesheets (<LINK REL="stylesheet">). The possible psuedo attributes are:

alternate

charset

href

media

title

type

Lastly, you can also use this processing instruction to attach stylesheets of type text/css.

Document Type Declaration

The Document Type (DOCTYPE) declaration is an optional part of the prolog of an XML document. The purpose of a DOCTYPE declaration is to specify the location (either internal, external, or both) of the Document Type Definition (DTD) for documents of this type. The DTD is a set of element and attribute declarations. If a DOCTYPE declaration exists, it must be after the XML declaration and before the root element of the document. Here is a sample of an external DOCTYPE declaration:

```
<?xml version="1.0" ?>
<!DOCTYPE window SYSTEM "http://www.xulbook.com/xul.dtd">
<window xmlns=" http://www.mozilla.org/keymaster/gatekeeper/
there.is.only.xul">
</window>
```

The DOCTYPE declaration takes four forms. The simplest is an internal DTD in which the element and attribute declarations are part of the XML instance:

```
<?xml version="1.0" ?>
<!DOCTYPE document-type-name [
```

```
<!-- Internal DTD declarations here -->
]>
```

The internal DTD declarations are referred to as the *internal subset*. An internal subset is part of the current document and, thus, it is internal. Notice that following the "<!DOCTYPE" keyword is the name of the document type that must correspond to the name of the root element. In the code example shown previously, the document-type-name and the root element are named window. You can declare an external DTD (also called an external subset) in two ways. The first external method is to refer to the external DTD via a URI. The external DTD resides in a separate file. Here is the form of the first external DTD declaration:

```
<!DOCTYPE document-type-name SYSTEM "uri-reference">
```

The SYSTEM keyword denotes that DTD will be referenced using a system identifier, which is the following URI. The second form of the external DTD declaration is to use a public identifier. Here is the general form:

```
<!DOCTYPE document-type-name PUBLIC "public-Id" "uri-reference">
```

A public identifier refers to a well-known location; however, if the processing software does not know the location, a URI is also provided. Lastly, you can also use the DOCTYPE declaration to refer to schema definitions. The URI will just point to a Schema file (usually with an .xsd extension) instead of a DTD file (usually with a .dtd extension).

Creating a Document Type Definition

The XML 1.0 specification borrowed the document definition syntax from the Standard Generalized Markup Language (SGML). The syntax is similar to the DOCTYPE tag and does not use XML start and end tags. Another form of DTD created by the W3C is called XML Schemas. These will be discussed in the next section, "Constructing a XUL DTD." The purpose of both Schemas and DTDs is to determine whether the document is valid. A document is well-formed if the XML is properly nested; all elements and attributes are properly named; and no illegal characters are used (in other words, if it follows the syntax rules). A document is valid if it is well-formed and adheres to the declarations in the DTD or Schema. Any element or attribute used in an XML document must have a corresponding declaration in the DTD or Schema.

Declaring Elements

An element declaration involves specifying the name of the element and its content model. The general form of an element declaration is:

```
<!ELEMENT elem-name content-model>
```

The element name is an XML name. As such, it must start with a letter or underscore and is followed by any number of letters, numbers, hyphens, underscores, or periods. The element's content model is where you describe what subelements may be contained in this element. First, there are four types of content-models:

Empty. This type specifies an empty element. Use the EMPTY keyword as the content model like this:

```
<!ELEMENT image EMPTY>
```

Any. This type specifies that the element can have any type of contents (elements, text, or none). This basically means that anything goes and is not recommended. Use the ANY keyword as the content model like this:

```
<!ELEMENT lenient ANY>
```

Element only. This type specifies that an element will have only subelements or child elements in its content (no text). This content model is the most common and the one that should be used to structure the container relationships in your document. Combine the child element names with a few simple symbols that represent order, existence, and repeatability. We will go over multiple examples of this content model in the ensuing paragraphs.

Mixed. This type specifies that an element can have only text or text and subelements. To specify text, use the keyword #PCDATA, which stands for Parsed Character Data. The only text form is much more common and looks like this:

```
<!ELEMENT name (#PCDATA)>
```

The element-only content model is the most important and most complex to understand, because there is not one simple form to follow. The element-only content model uses a simple expression syntax to enable you to combine your child elements in numerous ways. You can express child-element content in five ways: single elements, grouping elements, element groups, repeatable elements, and groups:

A single child element. This method is when your element contains only one child. You simply specify the name of the child element within parentheses like this:

```
<!ELEMENT slider (thumb)>
```

Grouping elements. This method is where you want multiple child elements. You have two operators to separate groups of child elements: a sequence operator (,) and a choice or logical OR operator (|). The sequence operator specifies a precise order in which one child must follow another. The OR operator allows only one child to be chosen from a set of many. Here are examples of a sequence and a choice:

```
<!ELEMENT group1 (childA, childB)>
```

This example states that the group1 element will have two children: one called childA followed by childB. The order is strict, and the presence of both childA and childB is mandatory.

```
<!ELEMENT group2 (childC | childD)>
```

This example states that group2 will have only one child element, and that child can be EITHER childC OR childD.

Element groups. This method describes how you act on an entire group of elements. In a content model, a group is called a content particle and is specified by wrapping it in parentheses. We have seen the parentheses used to express the entire content model, which you should think of as the outer-most group.

```
<!ELEMENT group3 ( (childA, childB) | (childC, childD) )>
```

The preceding example states that group3 will have either the first or second content particle. Both content particles are sequence content particles.

Repeatability. This method is how to specify whether elements can be repeated. There are three repeatability operators: the optional operator (?), the optional-and-repeatable operator (*), and the required-and-repeatable operator (+). A repeatability operator can be placed next to a child element or a group of elements.

```
<!ELEMENT group4 (childE?)>
<!ELEMENT group5 (childF*)>
<!ELEMENT group6 (childG+)>
```

It is very common to apply content operators to content particles. Here is how you would allow a set of three children in any order and any quantity:

```
<!ELEMENT group7 (childH | childI | childJ)*>
```

Declaring Attributes

Unlike elements in which you define one element at a time, you define attributes in an attribute list declaration. In an attribute list declaration, you can declare all the attributes that belong to a specific element. The general form of an attribute list declaration is:

```
<!ATTLIST elem-name
          att1-name att1-type att1-default-decl
          ...
          attN-name attN-type attN-default-decl>
```

The elem-name refers to the element name these attributes belong to. The element name is then followed by one or more attribute declarations. An attribute declaration has three parts: an attribute name, an attribute type, and a default declaration. Here is a sample attribute list declaration for the XUL tab element:

```
<!ATTLIST tab
     value CDATA #REQUIRED
     style CDATA #IMPLIED
     selected (true | false) "false"
     orient (vertical | horizontal) "vertical"
     autostretch (never | always) "never"
     oncommand CDATA #IMPLIED>
```

The attribute name has the same requirements as an element name (start with a character, etc.) There are nine possible attribute types: CDATA, enumerated type, ID, IDS, IDREF, IDREFS, NMTOKEN, NMTOKENS, and NOTATION. Table 2.1 defines the nine attribute types.

The default declaration of the attribute declaration can be a presence keyword, a default value, or both. Here are samples of those three variations:

Presence keywords. The three possible keywords are #REQUIRED, #IMPLIED, and #FIXED. #REQUIRED means that the attribute is mandatory. #IMPLIED means that the attribute is optional. #FIXED means the attribute's value will not change. The #FIXED keyword must be followed by the fixed value in quotes. Here is a sample declaration with a presence keyword:

```
value CDATA #REQUIRED
```

Default value. Instead of using #REQUIRED or #IMPLIED, you can specify a default value for the attribute. Here is a sample declaration with a default value:

```
selected (true | false) "true"
```

#FIXED. The #FIXED attribute uses both the presence keyword and a default value. Here is a sample of the #FIXED attribute:

```
version CDATA #FIXED "1.0"
```

Declaring attributes and elements will occupy the majority of your work on the DTD. Next we discuss two less common parts: entities and namespaces.

Declaring Entities

An entity is an abbreviation for some other data. There are different categories of entities. Figure 2.2 shows the category types of entities.

You can declare entities in five different ways:

General, internal, parsed entity. As Figure 2.2 states, general entities are for the abbreviation of data in XML instance documents. The simplest abbreviations are short text words that stand for larger text passages. For example, if you wanted to use your initials to abbreviate your full name:

```
<!ENTITY mcd "Michael C. Daconta">
```

After the keyword ENTITY, you have the entity name and then the replacement text (for internal entities, the replacement data is with the declaration). To use this entity in an XML document, you use the following format "%entity-name;" like this:

```
<bio>
    <p> My name Is %mcd;. blah blah blah. </p>
    <p> %mcd; was born... </p>
</bio>
```

General, external, parsed entity. You can also put markup in the replacement data. Think of using entities as automated cut and paste. If you have a large amount of replacement data, you may put it in an external file. For example, the

Table 2.1 Attribute Types

TYPE	DESCRIPTION	EXAMPLE
CDATA	Stands for character data. Free text values a (string type). This is the most common attribute type. Sample declaration: Name CDATA #REQUIRED	name = "Henry Ford"
Enumerate type	A choice of one from a specific list of name tokens. A name token is any set of name characters (letter, number, underscore, hyphen, and period). The characters of a name token may be in any order. Sample declaration: selected (true | false) #REQUIRED	selected = "true"
ID	An XML name that serves as a unique id for the element. The value of this id must be unique in the document. Sample declaration: productId ID #REQUIRED	productId = "pid-01"
IDREF	An attribute whose value is the ID of another element. Used so that one element can refer to another element in the same document. Sample declaration: orderedProduct IDREF #REQUIRED	ordered Product = "pid-01"
IDREFS	A list of multiple IDs to refer to multiple elements. Sample declaration: orderedProducts IDREFS #REQUIRED	ordered Products = "pid-01 pid-02"
NMTOKEN	An attribute whose value is a name token. A name token is any set of XML name characters. This enables you to make an XML value slightly more restrictive (although it is a far cry from Schema data types). Sample declaration: date NMTOKEN #REQUIRED	date = "12-12-2001"
NMTOKENS	A list of name tokens. Sample declaration: keyDates NMTOKENS #REQUIRED	keyDates = "12-12-01 12-25-01"
NOTATION	A attribute value that can be only a predeclared Notation type. Notations are declared with the <!NOTATION ...> declaration and stand for an external notation like an image format. Sample declaration: imgType NOTATION #REQUIRED	imgType = "gif"
ENTITY	An attribute value that can be only an external unparsed entity (a phrase that means a binary file). Entities are declared with the <!ENTITY ...> declaration. An image or audio file are examples of an external unparsed entity. The value of the attribute must be the entity name. Sample declaration: img ENTITY #REQUIRED	img = "folderIcon"
ENTITIES	A list of external unparsed entities. Sample declaration: Images ENTITIES #REQUIRED	images = "folderIcon bookIcon"

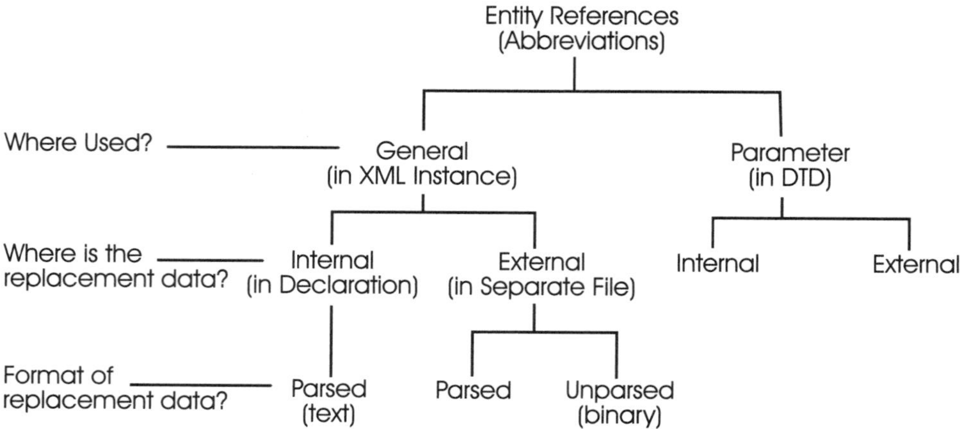

Figure 2.2 Entity reference hierarchy.

lawyers in your company may have a standard legal blurb that you must put at the bottom of every XML document. You can do that with a general, external parsed entity like this:

```
<!ENTITY legalese SYSTEM "http://www.your-company.com/legal.xml">
```

You should note that this is similar to the format of the DOCTYPE declaration. When this general entity is used in a document, the replacement text will be fetched from the URI.

General, external, unparsed entity. If the data you want to refer to is not XML, it is called an unparsed entity (an entity that should not be parsed). A common use for an unparsed entity is to refer to images or audio files. Here is an example of declaring an unparsed entity:

```
<!ENTITY logo SYSTEM "http://www.your-company.com/logo.gif" NDATA
GIF>
```

The difference between this entity and the external parsed entity is the two keywords at the end of the declaration. The NDATA keyword denotes this entity as an unparsed entity. The word following NDATA must be a previously declared notation. Here is an example of a NOTATION declaration:

```
<!NOTATION GIF SYSTEM "apps/Imgviewer.exe">
```

The format of the notation declaration is the NOTATION keyword, followed by the name of the notation, followed by the SYSTEM keyword, and ending with the freeform string that can refer to a helper application or some other user-defined description about the notation (like a list of file types for the notation).

Parameter, internal entity. As specified in Figure 2.2, you use parameter entities to abbreviate declarations in a DTD. Parameter entities cannot be used in an XML instance. In fact, parameter entities are clearly distinguished from general entities by starting with a percent symbol (%) instead of an ampersand (&). Here is an example of a parameter entity:

```
<!ENTITY % elem1 "<!ELEMENT foo (a, b, c)>">
%elem1;
```

You may think that the preceding declaration is silly because it is declared and then used. This would be an example of a legal declaration in an internal DTD subset. In an internal subset, you can have only parameter entities that refer to entire declarations. This restriction does not exist for an external DTD subset (DTD in an external file). Here is a more useful parameter entity:

```
<!ENTITY % Inherited "Id ID #IMPLIED
                      class CDATA #IMPLIED
                chromeclass CDATA #IMPLIED
                context CDATA #IMPLIED"
```

The preceding entity could be used to attach a set of inherited attributes to all elements in a DTD. Something similar to this will be used in the XUL DTD (discussed in the next section).

Parameter, external entity. An external parameter entity refers to a set of DTD declarations in a separate file referred to by a URI. This can be very useful when modularizing a large DTD in smaller functional components. That way a person can construct a new DTD by picking and choosing only the components in which they are interested. Here is an example of an external parameter entity:

```
<!ENTITY % frameset SYSTEM "http://www.your-co.org/dtd/
frameset.mod">
%frameset;
```

Now we have the necessary background to construct a DTD for the XUL elements and attributes.

Constructing a XUL DTD

Here is a portion of the XUL DTD. The complete DTD will be posted on `http://www.xulbook.com`. Notice how the DTD makes use of many of the features we discussed: element declarations, attribute list declarations, content models, entity references and attribute types.

```
<!-- This DTD was created by examining the XUL
Programmer's Reference found on mozilla.org -->
<!-- All Xul elements Inherit the following attributes:
     Id, class, chromeclass, context, style, persist, popup,
      popupanchor, popupalign, ondraggesture, ondragdrop, ondragover,
     ondragexit. -->
<!ENTITY % Inherited "id ID #IMPLIED
                      class CDATA #IMPLIED
                     chromeclass CDATA #IMPLIED
                     context CDATA #IMPLIED
                     style CDATA #IMPLIED
```

```
                    persist NMTOKENS #IMPLIED
                    popup IDREF #IMPLIED
                    popupanchor (none | topleft | topright | bottomleft
| bottomright) #IMPLIED
                    popupalign (none | topleft | topright | bottomleft |
bottomright) #IMPLIED
                    ondraggesture CDATA #IMPLIED
                    ondragdrop CDATA #IMPLIED
                    ondragover CDATA #IMPLIED
                    ondragexit CDATA #IMPLIED ">
<!ENTITY % allwidgets "arrowscrollbox | box | bulletinboard | button |
browser | checkbox | colorpicker | deck | editor | grid | hbox | iframe
| image | keyset | label | menu | menubar | menubutton | menulist |
menupopup | popup | popupset | progressmeter | radio | radiogroup |
scrollbox | separator | spring | stack | statusbar | tabpanel | textbox
| titledbox | toolbar | toolbox | tree | vbox">
<!-- Besides window, an overlay can be the root element of a
     XUL document; however, since every document must only have
     A single root element - see xuloverlay.dtd. -->
<!ELEMENT window (%allwidgets;)*>
<!ATTLIST window
     %Inherited;
     align (left | right | center | vertical | horizontal) #IMPLIED
     autostretch (never | always) "always"
     collapsed CDATA #IMPLIED
     crop (left | right | center | none) "none"
     debug CDATA #IMPLIED
     flex CDATA #IMPLIED
     height CDATA #IMPLIED
     left CDATA #IMPLIED
     onload CDATA #IMPLIED
     onunload CDATA #IMPLIED
     orient (horizontal | vertical) "horizontal"
     persist CDATA #IMPLIED
     title CDATA #IMPLIED
     titlemodifier CDATA #IMPLIED
     titlemenuseparator CDATA #IMPLIED
     top CDATA #IMPLIED
     valign (top | middle | bottom | baseline) "top"
     width CDATA #IMPLIED
     xmlns CDATA #FIXED
"http://www.mozilla.org/keymaster/gatekeeper/there.is.only.xul"
     xmlns:html CDATA #FIXED "http://www.w3.org/1999/xhtml"
     xmlns:rdf CDATA #FIXED "http://www.w3.org/1999/02/22-rdf-syntax-ns#">
<!ELEMENT arrowscrollbox (autorepeatbutton)>
<!ATTLIST arrowscrollbox
     %Inherited;
     autostretch (never | always) "always"
     collapsed CDATA #IMPLIED
     crop (left | right | center | none) "none"
     debug CDATA #IMPLIED
     flex CDATA #IMPLIED
```

```
     height CDATA #IMPLIED
     left CDATA #IMPLIED
     orient (horizontal | vertical) "horizontal"
     top CDATA #IMPLIED
     valign (top | middle | bottom | baseline) "top"
     width CDATA #IMPLIED>

<!ELEMENT autorepeatbutton EMPTY>
<!ATTLIST autorepeatbutton
     %Inherited;
     autostretch (never | always) "always"
     flex CDATA #IMPLIED
     height CDATA #IMPLIED
     src CDATA #IMPLIED
     width CDATA #IMPLIED>

<!ELEMENT box (%allwidgets;)*>
<!ATTLIST box
     %Inherited;
     autostretch (never | always) "always"
     collapsed CDATA #IMPLIED
     crop (left | right | center | none) "none"
     debug CDATA #IMPLIED
     flex CDATA #IMPLIED
     height CDATA #IMPLIED
     left CDATA #IMPLIED
     orient (horizontal | vertical) "horizontal"
     top CDATA #IMPLIED
     valign (top | middle | bottom | baseline) "top"
     width CDATA #IMPLIED>

<!ELEMENT broadcaster EMPTY>
<!ATTLIST broadcaster
     %Inherited;
     action CDATA #REQUIRED
     value CDATA #REQUIRED
     oncommand CDATA #IMPLIED>

<!ELEMENT bulletinboard (%allwidgets;)*>
<!ATTLIST bulletinboard
     %Inherited;
     debug CDATA #IMPLIED
     flex CDATA #IMPLIED
     height CDATA #IMPLIED
     left CDATA #IMPLIED
     top CDATA #IMPLIED
     width CDATA #IMPLIED>

<!ELEMENT button EMPTY>
<!ATTLIST button
     %Inherited;
     accesskey CDATA #IMPLIED
```

```
crop (left | right | center | none) "none"
default CDATA #IMPLIED
disabled CDATA #IMPLIED
flex CDATA #IMPLIED
height CDATA #IMPLIED
left CDATA #IMPLIED
orient CDATA #IMPLIED
src CDATA #IMPLIED
top CDATA #IMPLIED
tooltiptext CDATA #IMPLIED
toggled (0 | 1 | 2) #IMPLIED
value CDATA #IMPLIED
width CDATA #IMPLIED>
```

Creating a Schema

DTDs have been criticized for not conforming to XML syntax and because they lack strong data typing. To address these deficiencies, the W3C created an XML-based syntax to describe the structure of documents called *Schema*. Let's examine the basic rules for creating a Schema. For the complete set of rules examine the Schema specification at www.w3.org/TR/xmlschema-1.

Schema Prolog

Because a Schema is an XML document, it has a prolog just like every XML document. The Schema prolog is as follows:

```
<?xml version="1.0" ?>
<!DOCTYPE schema PUBLIC "-//W3C//DTD XMLSCHEMA 200010//EN"
"XMLSchema.dtd">
<schema xmlns='http://www.w3.org/2000/10/XMLSchema'
        xmlns:xsd='http://www.w3.org/2000/10/XMLSchema'>
```

The key parts of the prolog are the XML declaration (which is optional but recommended) and the DOCTYPE declaration. Also shown is the default namespace declaration in the root element, which is named schema.

Declaring Simple Elements

Schema is object oriented, so instead of just attaching a content model to an element name (and possibly repeating it for many others), you create a generic type and declare that a specific element is of that type. So, in order to declare elements, you first declare a type and then declare an element of that type. You have two categories of types: simple and complex. Simple types consist of primitive types or types derived from primitive types (for example, adding a range constraint). The primitive types correspond to primitive types in most programming languages (like int, float, string, etc.). If an element does not have a content model, you can declare it directly as being one of the simple types. Table 2.2 lists all of the simple types.

Table 2.2 Built-In Simple Types

SIMPLE TYPE	DESCRIPTION
String	A character string. Example: "Hello World"
CDATA	Derived from string. "Hello World"
Token	Derived from CDATA. Represents tokenized strings. The strings cannot contain a line-feed, tab, nor leading or trailing spaces. "Hello World"
Byte	Derived from short by setting maxInclusive to 127 and minInclusive to -128. Examples: -1, 28
UnsignedByte	Derived from unsignedShort by setting the value of maxInclusive to be 255. Examples: 0, 121
Binary	Arbitrary binary data. Cannot be used directly, only derived types (with an encoding) can be used in a schema.
integer	Derived from decimal. The value space is the infinite set of whole numbers. Examples: -1, 0, 1024
positiveInteger	Derived from nonNegativeInteger by setting the value of minInclusive to be 1.
negativeInteger	Derived from nonPositiveInteger by setting the value of maxInclusive to -1.
nonNegativeInteger	Derived from integer by setting the value of minInclusive to 0.
nonPositiveInteger	Derived from integer by setting the value of maxInclusive to be 0. Example: -2
Int	Derived from long by setting maxInclusive to 2147483647 and minInclusive to -2147483648.
unsignedInt	Derived from unsignedLong by setting the value of maxInclusive to 4294967295.
Long	Derived from integer by setting maxInclusive to 9223372036854775807 and minInclusive to -9223372036854774808.
unsignedLong	Derived from nonNegativeInteger by setting the value of maxInclusive to be 18446744073709551615.
short	Derived from int by setting maxInclusive to 32767 and minInclusive to -32768.
unsignedShort	Derived from unsignedInt by setting maxInclusive to be 65535.
decimal	Arbitrary precision decimal numbers. Example: 4.8
Float	IEEE single-precision 32-bit floating point type. Example: -1E4

continues

Table 2.2 Built-In Simple Types (Continued)

SIMPLE TYPE	DESCRIPTION
Double	IEEE double-precision 64-bit floating point type. Example: 1267.432E4
boolean	Supports binary logic with a value space of {true, false}.
time	An instance of time that recurs every day. The value space is the time of day values defined in ISO 8601. Derived from recurringDuration.
timeInstant	A specific instant of time. Derived from recurringDuration. The value space is a combination of date and time of day values defined in ISO 8601.
timePeriod	Represents a specific period of time with a given start and end. Derived from recurringDuration. The value space is the period of time as defined in ISO 8601.
timeDuration	A duration of time composed of six components: Gregorian year, month, day, hour, minute, and seconds. Example: P2Y1M3DT5H30M
date	A timePeriod that starts at midnight of a specified day and lasts until midnight of the following day. The value space is the set of Gregorian calendar dates as defined in ISO 8601. Example: 1999-10-26.
month	A timePeriod that starts at midnight the first day of the month and lasts until midnight the last day of the month. The value space is Gregorian calendar months as defined in ISO 8601. Example: 1999-10.
year	A timePeriod that starts at midnight of the first day of the year and ends at midnight of the last day of the year. The value space is Gregorian calendar years as defined in ISO 8601. Example: 1999
century	A timePeriod that starts at midnight the first day of the century and ends at midnight the last day of the century. The value space is the set of Gregorian calendar centuries as defined in ISO 8601. Example: 19.
recurringDay	A day of the month that recurs. Derived from recurringDuration. Example: —15
recurringDate	A day of the year that recurs. Derived from recurringDuration. Example: -12-02
recurringDuration	A period of time that repeats with a specific frequency. Example: 2001-02-01T09:08:23.12

Table 2.2 (Continued)

SIMPLE TYPE	DESCRIPTION
Name	An XML Name that matches the name production in the XML 1.0 recommendation. Example: "address"
QName	An XML Qualified Name. The value is a tuple that includes the namespace name and the local part. Example: html:title.
NCName	An XML noncolonized name. The value is all strings that match the NCName production in the Namespaces in XML specification. Informally, this is an XML name minus the colon:. For example: "title".
uriReference	A Uniform Resource Identifier (URI) as defined in RFC 2396 (and amended by RFC 2732). Example: http://www.foo.com/index.html
language	Natural language identifiers as defined in RFC 1766. Example: "en"
ID	XML 1.0 attribute type.
IDREF	XML 1.0 attribute type.
IDREFS	XML 1.0 attribute type.
ENTITY	XML 1.0 attribute type.
ENTITIES	XML 1.0 attribute type.
NOTATION	XML 1.0 attribute type.
NMTOKEN	XML 1.0 attribute type.
NMTOKENS	XML 1.0 attribute type.

Declaring an element of a primitive type takes the following general form:

```
<xsd:element name="elemName" type="xsd:typeName" />
```

So, defining a simple string element called LastName would look like this:

```
<xsd:element name="LastName" type="xsd:string" />
```

The key thing to understand about declaring an element is that you are associating an element name with a type. That type can be simple or complex. A simple type can either be built-in (like string) or user-defined. You create user-defined simple types by deriving new types (like adding a different legal range for a new integer type or a regular expression pattern for a new string type) from those listed in Table 2.2. You create a new simple type with the simpleType element. An interesting extension of a simple type is the list type. Here is an example of the declaration for a list type of integers.

```
<xsd:simpleType name="IntegerList">
  <xsd:list itemType="xsd:int"/>
</xsd:simpleType>
```

In addition to simple types, you can create complex types. A complex type can have attribute declarations and a content model (a set of children with an expressed order, repeatability, and presence). Before discussing complex types, let's examine how to declare attributes.

Declaring Attributes

An attribute is the association of a name to a simple type, occurrence information, and optionally a default value. The general (and most common) form of declaring an attribute is as follows:

```
<xsd:attribute name="attName" type="typeName" use="prohibited | optional
| required | default | fixed" />
```

Other attributes that are less common are specified in the Schema specification. Here is an example of declaring a required attribute called age.

```
<xsd:attribute name="age" type="xsd:int" use="required" />
```

If the value of the use attribute is default or fixed, then you include the "value" attribute with the default or fixed value, respectively. Here is an example of a fixed attribute:

```
<xsd:attribute name="country" type="xsd:string" use="fixed" value="US"/>
```

Declaring Complex Elements

An element with a complex type is an element that can have attached attributes and a content model. You define new complex types with the complexType element. Because we just discussed declaring attributes, let's create a complex type called "windowType" with attributes for "height" and "width." You include attribute elements as child elements of the complexType:

```
<xsd:complexType name="windowType">
     <xsd:attribute name="width" type="xsd:int" />
     <xsd:attribute name="height" type="xsd:int" />
</xsd:complexType>
```

Schemas also have the ability to create a named attribute group that can be used in many Schemas. Examples of this feature are in the schema specification (Part 0, Primer). Besides adding attributes, you can create content models to describe the order, presence, and repeatability of child elements. To specify order, you need to create a group of elements. There are three types of groups: a sequential set (sequence), a set of alternatives (choice), and a connected set (all). The sequence and choice groups correspond exactly to their DTD counterparts. In the all set, all particles (child element or another group) may exist either 0 or 1 time. Also, elements in an all set may be in any order. Let's look at examples of all three groups:

```
<xsd:complexType name="demo">
     <xsd:sequence>
          <xsd:element name="one" type="xsd:string" />
          <xsd:element name="two" type="xsd:string" />
     </xsd:sequence>
     <xsd:choice>
          <xsd:element name="first" type="xsd:string" />
          <xsd:element name="second" type="xsd:string" />
     </xsd:choice>
     <xsd:all>
          <xsd:element name="harry" type="xsd:string" />
          <xsd:element name="george" type="xsd:string" />
     </xsd:all>
</xsd:complexType>
<xsd:element name="MyDemo" type="demo" />
```

Now let's examine a legal instance of the MyDemo element that conforms to the demo type:

```
<MyDemo>
     <one> </one>
     <two> </two>
     <first> </first>
     <george> </george>
     <harry> </harry>
</MyDemo>
```

To determine repeatability of a group or a single element, you attach the "minOccurs" and "maxOccurs" attributes to either the "element" or any of the particles (sequence, choice, or all). Here is an example of specifying a child element as repeatable:

```
<xsd:complexType name="Folder">
     <xsd:element name="bookmark" type="bookmarkType" minOccurs="1"
maxOccurs = "unbounded" />
</xsd:complexType>
```

The Folder type would allow one or more bookmark elements in the Folder type. Another interesting feature related to groups is *named element groups*. Just like named attribute groups, you can create named particle groups with the xsd:group element. More information on this can be found in the XML schema specification. To make an element optional, you would set minOccurs equal to "0" and maxOccurs equal to "1."

If an element has no children, it is said to have an *empty* content model. To specify empty content, you create a type with no children. Here is an example of an empty Image element.

```
<complexType name="imageType">
     <xsd:attribute name="href" type="xsd:string" />
</complexType>
```

One last interesting feature of Schemas is the ability to specify a wildcard particle. A wildcard particle allows you to describe content that can hold any set of elements or attributes. Although there are several variations of wildcards, the simplest is the any element. Here is an example that allows any XHTML element as a child element in a type:

```
<xsd:complexType name="wildcardType" mixed="true">
  <xsd:sequence>
    <xsd:any namespace="http://www.w3.org/1999/xhtml"
      minOccurs="0" maxOccurs="unbounded"
      processContents="skip"/>
  </xsd:sequence>
x</xsd:complexType>
```

Notice that the wildcardType uses two attributes we have not yet seen: mixed and processContents. The `mixed` element allows mixed content (elements and character data). The `processContents` attribute specifies the action an XML processor should take when validating the children elements. The legal values for the `processContents` attribute are "skip," "lax," or "strict," which mean ignore, validate if possible, and strictly validate, respectively. The Schema specification includes other features like annotations, defining your own `simpleContent` or `complexContent`, nullable fields, keys, and substitution groups that are outside the scope of this book. Refer to the Schema specification at http://www.w3.org/TR for the complete specification and primer.

A XUL Schema

Now we are ready to examine a partial schema definition for the window element. Although the output is more than a page, it describes (and not completely) only a single element. It is clear that a Schema is more verbose than a DTD. A useful exercise would be to compare some of this declaration to the corresponding window declaration in the DTD. The complete Schema will be posted on http://www.xulbook.com.

```
<?xml version="1.0" ?>
<!DOCTYPE schema PUBLIC "-//W3C//DTD XMLSCHEMA 200010//EN"
"XMLSchema.dtd">
<xsd:schema xmlns='http://www.w3.org/2000/10/XMLSchema'
xmlns:xsd='http://www.w3.org/2000/10/XMLSchema'
targetNamespace =
"http://www.mozilla.org/keymaster/gatekeeper/there.is.only.xul">
<xsd:complexType name="windowType" content="elementOnly">
          <xsd:choice minOccurs="0" maxOccurs="unbounded">
                   <xsd:element name="arrowscrollbox"
                   type="arrowscrollboxType"/>
               <xsd:element name="box" type="boxType"/>
               <xsd:element name="bulletinboard"
                    type="bulletinboardType"/>
               <xsd:element name="button" type="buttonType"/>
```

```
        <xsd:element name="browser" type="browserType"/>
        <xsd:element name="checkbox" type="checkboxType"/>
        <xsd:element name="colorpicker" type="colorpickerType"/>
        <xsd:element name="deck" type="deckType"/>
        <xsd:element name="editor" type="editorType"/>
        <xsd:element name="grid" type="gridType"/>
        <xsd:element name="hbox" type="hboxType"/>
        <xsd:element name="iframe" type="iframeType"/>
        <xsd:element name="image" type="imageType"/>
        <xsd:element name="keyset" type="keysetType"/>
        <xsd:element name="label" type="labelType"/>
        <xsd:element name="menu" type="menuType"/>
        <xsd:element name="menubar" type="menubarType"/>
        <xsd:element name="menubutton" type="menubuttonType"/>
        <xsd:element name="menulist" type="menulistType"/>
        <xsd:element name="menupopup" type="menupopupType"/>
        <xsd:element name="popup" type="popupType"/>
             <xsd:element name="popupset" type="popupsetType"/>
             <xsd:element name="progressmeter"
             type="progressmeterType"/>
        <xsd:element name="radio" type="radioType"/>
        <xsd:element name="radiogroup" type="radiogroupType"/>
        <xsd:element name="scrollbox" type="scrollboxType"/>
        <xsd:element name="separator" type="separatorType"/>
        <xsd:element name="spring" type="springType"/>
        <xsd:element name="stack" type="stackType"/>
        <xsd:element name="statusbar" type="statusbarType"/>
        <xsd:element name="tabpanel" type="tabpanelType"/>
        <xsd:element name="textbox" type="textboxType"/>
        <xsd:element name="titledbox" type="titledboxType"/>
        <xsd:element name="toolbar" type="toolbarType"/>
        <xsd:element name="toolbox" type="toolboxType"/>
        <xsd:element name="tree" type="treeType"/>
        <xsd:element name="vbox" type="vboxType"/>
   </xsd:choice>
   <xsd:attribute name="id" type="xsd:ID"/>
   <xsd:attribute name="class" type="xsd:string"/>
   <xsd:attribute name="chromeclass" type="xsd:string"/>
   <xsd:attribute name="context" type="xsd:string"/>
   <xsd:attribute name="style" type="xsd:string"/>
   <xsd:attribute name="persist" type="xsd:NMTOKENS"/>
   <xsd:attribute name="popup" type="xsd:IDREF"/>
   <xsd:attribute name="popupanchor">
        <xsd:simpleType base="xsd:NMTOKEN">
             <xsd:enumeration value="none"/>
             <xsd:enumeration value="topleft"/>
             <xsd:enumeration value="topright"/>
             <xsd:enumeration value="bottomleft"/>
             <xsd:enumeration value="bottomright"/>
        </xsd:simpleType>
   </xsd:attribute>
   ... (some window attributes deleted for brevity)
```

```
        </xsd:complexType>
...
</xsd:schema>
```

Take special note of the following key parts of the Schema:

- The creation of elements in a Schema has a different pattern than for a DTD. In a Schema, you first create a type and then declare an element of that type. Although there are ways to declare anonymous types, explicitly declaring types will lead to better reuse. The convention used in the XUL schema is for a type to have the same name as the element with the word Type appended to the end. So, in the preceding example, we declare the element "button" of type "buttonType."
- The built-in types like xsd:string, xsd:int, and xsd:float will allow unambiguous validation. This feature, all by itself, is worth upgrading to Schemas!
- It should be evident that schemas are much more verbose than DTDs. Although that is true, they are also easier to read and use the same syntax as XML instance documents. Standardizing on a single, syntax for all markup languages (including document definitions) outweighs the initial learning curve.
- Notice that the popupanchor element defines its type as an enumerated type. This is an example of an anonymous declaration of a simpleType. It is linked to the popupanchor element by its containment. It would be better to declare the type separately (and explicitly with its own name) if many attributes plan on reusing the same type.

That concludes our discussion of Schema. You can use the XUL Schema on the book's Web site http://www.wiley.com/compbooks/bullard to validate your XUL documents.

The Document Object Model

The Document Object Model (DOM) is a standard representation of a document as a set of objects in memory. The DOM is defined in several W3C standards categorized by levels. There are currently three DOM levels (1, 2, and 3). You can find the W3C DOM specifications at http://www.w3c.org/TR. The W3C defines DOM bindings in three languages: ECMAScript (standard JavaScript), Java, and the CORBA Interface Definition Language (IDL). Here are some of the objects standardized by the DOM specifications:

Document. Represents a single HTML or XML document. Also has methods to create and insert new elements, attributes, text nodes, comments, and processing instructions.

Element. An element is a node that has attributes and can contain children nodes. Every document has a single root element.

Node. A generic representation of any object that can be part of an XML or HTML document. As such, it can contain children nodes. This is the simplest way to view a DOM.

What does it mean to standardize an object? The two parts of an object standardized are the properties (or characteristics) of the object and the operations (or methods) that can be called on the object. Here are some of the properties of a node:

nodeName. The name of the node like "text," "element," etc.

nodeType. The type of node as a number from 1 to 12. One is element, 2 is attribute, and 3 is Text Node. The DOM Level 1 specification contains the mapping from numbers to object types.

Here are some of the operations on a node:

hasChildNodes(). This operation returns "true" or "false" based on whether the current node contains any children.

removeChild(Node oldChild). This operation removes a node from the tree of nodes.

Why is it important to standardize a document as a set of objects? The DOM is supported in all major browsers including IE, Netscape, Mozilla, and Opera. This enables you to write cross-browser ECMA Script, plugins, and applets that manipulate (or dynamically modify) documents inside the browser.

To incorporate a wide variety of programming languages, you can access a DOM in two ways: as a tree of plain vanilla objects or as flavored objects. The plain view is where every object is an instance of a node. So all you have is a tree of nodes. This is often called the flattened view. The other way to view a DOM is based on inheritance and a variety of types (referred to previously as different flavors). In this view, you have a document, elements, text nodes, comment nodes, etc. Figure 2.3 depicts one document in the two different ways to access it.

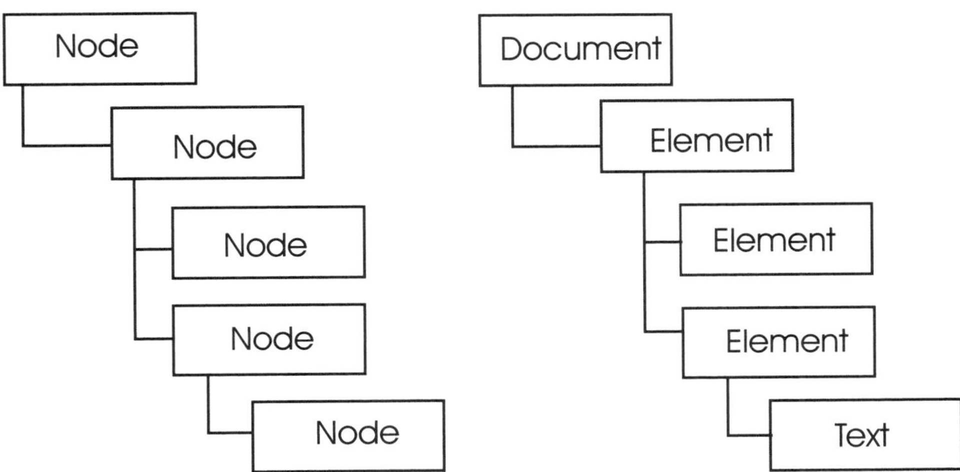

Figure 2.3 Flattened and hierarchical views of DOM.

```
<html>
<head>
<title> DOM Test </title>
<style type="text/css">
     #imgDiv { visibility: hidden; }
</style>

<script language="javascript">

function showImage()
{
    var node = document.getElementById("imgDiv");
    node.style["visibility"] = "visible";
}
function hideImage()
{
    var node = document.getElementById("imgDiv");
    node.style["visibility"] = "hidden";
}
</script>
</head>
<body onload="window.defaultStatus='hello world';return true;">
<h2> DOM TEST </h2>
<script language="javascript">
     document.writeln("root element name: " + document.nodeName + "<br
/>");
     document.writeln("children? " + document.hasChildNodes());
</script>
<div ID="imgDiv">
     <img src="apple.gif" />
</div>

<form>
     <input type="button" value="show image" onClick="showImage();" />
     <input type="button" value="hide image" onClick="hideImage();" />
</form>
</body>
</html>
```

Code Listing 2.5 dom-test.html.

What does this have to do with XUL? XUL extends the DOM, and you use the XUL document and JavaScript to control your user interface. You manipulate the DOM with JavaScript by accessing the properties and invoking the methods on the objects. Let's examine a simple example that uses JavaScript to manipulate the DOM. Code Listing 2.5 is an HTML document that displays some of the DOM properties and modifies the style attribute of elements in the DOM to turn on and off the display of an image.

Figure 2.4 Accessing the DOM via JavaScript.

When we run Code Listing 2.5 in the Netscape 6 browser, we see Figure 2.4. You may also run this simple DOM application from your Web browser at http://www.xulbook.com/dom-test.html.

Code Listing 2.5 uses JavaScript to access objects in the DOM. Here are the key points to note about Code Listing 2.5:

- In the body of the document, you see a JavaScript script that accesses a property and method of the document object. The property is document.nodeName, which holds the value "#document." The method invoked is called hasChildNodes(), and it returns a "true." The dot operator denotes a member of the object. A member can be either a property or method.
- The rest of the HTML document consists of an image surrounded by a <div> element, which hides it and a simple form with two buttons. The form invokes either the showImage() or hideImage() method depending on which button is clicked. Both methods are nearly identical. The first invokes a method of the

document object called getElementById(), which searches the entire DOM for an element with an ID attribute that matches the value passed in. That method returns a node. We then access the style property of the node (which is an array) and set the visibility property to either hidden or visible.

At this point, you know the basics of the Document Object Model. From here, all you need to do is learn more of the properties and methods that you have access to and that are available in the W3C specifications. Now you are ready to set your XUL user interfaces in motion and have them respond to events.

Summary

This chapter introduced you to the syntax, validation languages, and object model of XML. The syntax includes declarations, elements, attributes, namespaces, comments, processing instructions, and the document type declaration. Of those components, the far most common and important are the elements and attributes. It is sometimes helpful to think of elements as nouns and attributes to be characteristics of those elements. For example, a window is an element that has a width and height attribute.

After learning the markup elements, we learned how to declare the legal elements and attributes in the document by creating a Document Type Definition (DTD). The discussion covered declaring elements, declaring attributes, and declaring entities and culminated with a XUL DTD. Declaring elements was covered extensively with numerous examples of various content models. We covered how to specify a sequence or choice, content particles, and repeatability operators like ?, +, and *. Declaring attributes also included numerous examples that revealed how to declare an attribute type and a default declaration.

Besides the DTD, we learned an alternative document definition language called Schema. Designed to overcome the deficiencies of DTDs and to use the XML syntax, Schema development included defining a prolog, creating simple elements, learning the built-in types, declaring attributes, and declaring complex types. The discussion culminated with a portion of a XUL Schema. Although Schema is more verbose than DTDs, it encourages type reuse, has robust validation with numerous built-in types and the ability to create custom types, and uses the familiar XML syntax.

The chapter concluded with a discussion of the basic concepts of the Document Object Model (DOM). The DOM is the representation of an XML or HTML document as a standard set of objects. Via multiple programming languages, developers have access to the properties and methods of the standard objects. Developers can choose one of two ways to access the DOM: the flattened or hierarchical view. The chapter finished with an example of JavaScript methods accessing methods and properties of objects in the DOM.

Using Cascading Style Sheets

At the moment, there is no more profound expression of the power of XML and CSS combined.[1]

Eric Meyer, "What Makes CSS So Great"

XML is designed to separate a document's data content from the way it is displayed. Because of this, there are mechanisms for displaying the presentation of the XML document—style sheets. Two types of style sheet languages are available for displaying XML: eXtensible Stylesheet Language (XSL) and Cascading Style Sheets (CSS). Because the World Wide Web Consortium (W3C) developed both languages, programmers sometimes are confused about their uses.

XSL is a language for transforming XML into new XML documents—XSL Transformations (XSLT)—and provides an XML vocabulary for formatting objects. An XSL processor takes a two-phase approach: first transforming a source document into a new tree and then applying formatting style rules to the resulting document.[2] XSL is a very powerful and complex language and is being developed by the W3C in two different drafts: XSL (for formatting) and XSLT (for transformations). CSS is a much simpler language and is used only for formatting the display of HTML and XML document elements. A CSS processor traverses a document tree and adds styles to each element in the tree. This chapter focuses on CSS because it is the style sheet language used for formatting properties of XUL elements.

CSS version 1 (CSS1) was introduced as a W3C Recommendation in 1996 to enhance the presentation of HTML documents without adding new tags to the HTML language. Without style sheets, Web authoring was difficult because so many versions of the same HTML code existed—Netscape, Microsoft, frames, and text-only. Web authors struggled to resolve content versus design issues by maintaining multiple versions of the same

HTML documents. CSS enables authors to override existing style properties rendered by HTML browsers and to give pages a unique and consistent design. In both HTML and XML, CSS enable the Web designer to separate text content and style by assigning different style rules to individual elements in a document within a style sheet. The rendering application—sometimes referred to as the browser, user agent, or rendering agent—follows or cascades through these style rules and must use the style that is given priority according to the CSS Specification.

As you can imagine, Cascading Style Sheets play a major role in XUL. Because the goal of XUL is to provide a language that describes user interfaces, you can gain an enormous benefit by using style sheets to describe the style of elements in a user interface. This chapter is a primer chapter on CSS, and it covers the basic concepts of CSS—syntax, selector types, different types of CSS properties, and how developers can apply CSS rules. At the end of this chapter, we briefly focus on how CSS is used with XUL. For those of you already familiar with CSS, you should know that it is used in XUL the same way that HTML or XML uses CSS. By the end of this chapter, you will be ready to apply CSS rules to the XUL language.

A Simple CSS Example

Before we hose you down with syntax and basic data types, let us first give you a few examples of how Cascading Style Sheets work. Because you should be familiar with

THE ROLE OF THE W3C IN CSS

The W3C has promoted the use of style sheets on the Internet, led by the W3C User Interface Domain group. The mission of this group is to improve the technology that enables users to effectively perceive and express information. The Style Sheets Activity is a part of this group and has been responsible for the development of the CSS specification. CSS has now been through a number of stages of development. CSS1, developed in 1996, introduced the core language and addressed relatively simple style sheet functions such as colors and fonts. CSS2, developed in 1998, extended CSS1 to include more sophisticated features, such as dealing with page-based layout, support for downloadable fonts, the definition of chapters, and new media types for target devices that support functionality, such as Braille feedback, handheld devices, and aural speech synthesizers. By the time this book is published, CSS3 will be completed. CSS3 will bring modularization, Scalable Vector Graphics (SVG) for styling graphics, behavioral extensions describing style changes associated with events, and much more.

Although the W3C is currently focusing on CSS3, Web browsers are always a bit behind. To keep up to date, we recommend that you check documentation on compliance at http://www.w3.org/Style/CSS/#browsers. Throughout this chapter, we will provide XML examples and show how they are rendered, using the Microsoft Internet Explorer browser and the Netscape 6.x browser. Both browsers support XML rendering, and they support most of the stylesheet properties discussed in this chapter.

For more information on the style sheets and the W3C Style Sheets Activity, visit them on the Web at http://www.w3.org/Style/.

```
<!DOCTYPE HTML PUBLIC "-//W3C//DTD HTML 4.0//EN">
<HTML>
  <HEAD>
    <TITLE>Restoring Old Chevy Trucks</TITLE>
  </HEAD>
  <BODY>
     <CENTER>
       <H1>Restoring Old Chevy Trucks</H1>
       This page will describe how to restore old Chevy
       Trucks, using a 1967 C-10 truck as an example.
     </CENTER>
   </BODY>
</HTML>
```

Code Listing 3.1 A simple HTML file.

HTML, we will present an example using a simple Web page. Code Listing 3.1 shows a simple HTML file that we will build upon using CSS.

What type of style rules could we apply to this page? Perhaps we would like the color of the <H1> element to be red. Perhaps we would like to make the font of H1 different from the rest of the page. In order to do this, we must apply a CSS rule to the element H1 in the document. A CSS rule could be included in the HTML document itself, or we could have the documents reference a style sheet with the rules.

A rule is composed of a *selector* and a *declaration*. A selector denotes the element to which you are applying a rule. In this case, the selector will be <H1>. A declaration consists of the property you are describing, followed by the value of that property. In the case of assigning the font size to 80 points, the declaration would be "font-size: 80pt." This rule can be shown simply, as:

```
H1 {font-size: 80pt}
```

Now that we've created our first CSS rule, how can we apply it? In HTML, the <LINK> element assigns the style sheet to the document, as shown in Code Listing 3.2. The stylesheet, referenced by the LINK element of Code Listing 3.2, is simply one line:

```
H1 {font-size: 80pt}
```

Figure 3.1 shows what the applied style sheet looks like, using the Mozilla browser.

Now that you have applied a style sheet to HTML, what would be different in an XML document? Instead of using the <LINK> tag, you would use the <?xml-stylesheet> processing instruction in the following manner:

```
<?xml-stylesheet href="ex1.css" type="text/css"?>
```

Now that we've seen a quick example, let's go deeper into the rules and syntax of CSS to see how we can apply them to real-world applications. Because CSS is used

```
<!DOCTYPE HTML PUBLIC "-//W3C//DTD HTML 4.0//EN">
<HTML>
  <HEAD>
    <TITLE>Restoring Old Chevy Trucks</TITLE>
    <LINK rel="stylesheet" href="ex1.css" type="text/css">
  </HEAD>
  <BODY>
     <CENTER>
       <H1>Restoring Old Chevy Trucks</H1>
       This page will describe how to restore old Chevy
       Trucks, using a 1967 C-10 truck as an example.
     </CENTER>
   </BODY>
</HTML>
```

Code Listing 3.2 A simple HTML file with style sheet link.

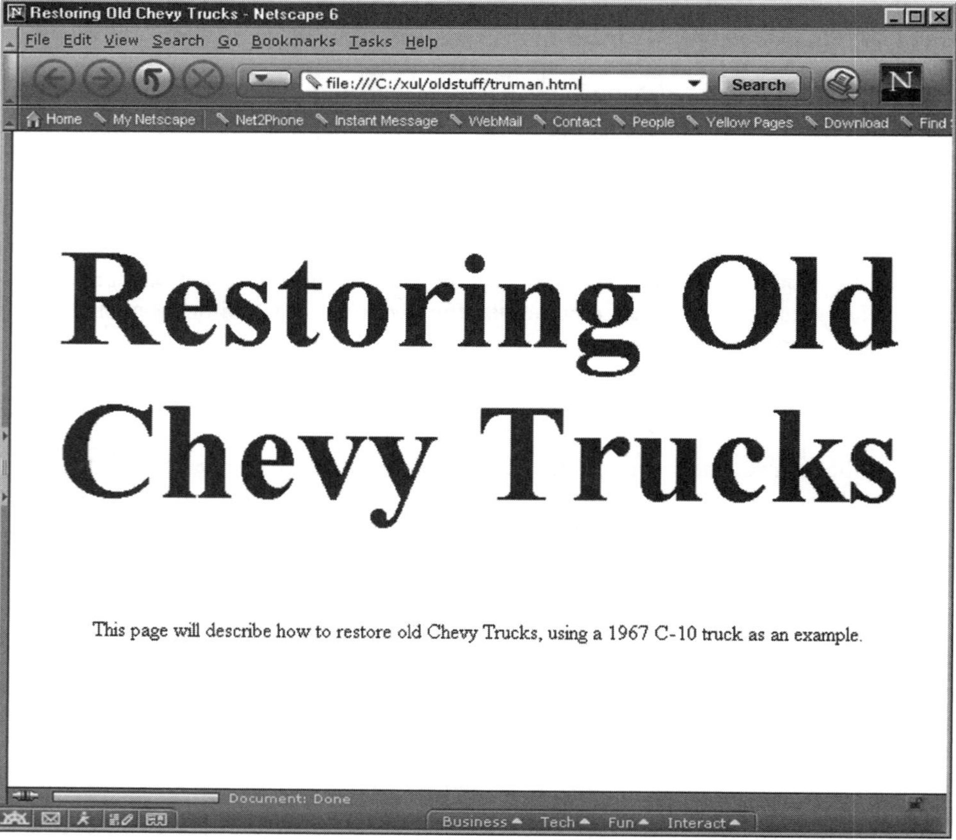

Figure 3.1 Example of an applied style sheet in HTML.

heavily in XUL, which is an XML language, we will be using XML examples for the rest of this chapter.

CSS Fundamentals

This section focuses on the fundamentals of CSS, namely:

"CSS Syntax Overview." In this section, we will define the basic syntax for CSS files.

"Choosing the Right Selector." We will define different types of selectors in this section.

"Changing Your Element's Properties." In this section, we will focus on some of the more common properties to which CSS rules are applied.

"Cascading Rules." In this section, we discuss the "C" in Cascading Style sheets and the rules involved.

Throughout these sections, we will step through examples to prepare you for using CSS with XUL.

CSS Syntax Overview

Selectors and declarations make up CSS rules. The selector is always to the left of the declaration, and the declaration—consisting of a property: value pair—is always included in the curly braces as shown in the following example. The left and right curly brace, respectively, denote the beginning and the end of the style rules described for the selector. Here, H1 is the selector, and "color: red" is the declaration.

```
H1 {color:red}
```

Of course, more than one declaration can be associated with an element type (or selector). Because of this, we can group the declarations that relate to the same selector. In this example, we can assign a font style, a color, and text alignment to all of the H1 elements in that document. To achieve this, our CSS rule could be:

```
H1 {
      color: red;
      font-style: italics;
      text-align: center;
   }
```

The semicolon separates the declarations in a CSS rule.

TIP Don't forget to separate each declaration with a semicolon. Although most Web browsers support CSS, some are more likely to skip the rest of the declarations if you leave out a semicolon in the middle of your rule.

Selectors and declarations, with their related properties and value types, are the building blocks of CSS. In the next few sections, we discuss the different classes of selectors, properties, and value types.

Choosing the Right Selector

The selector is a link between a document element and its style. To give the application designer more power in determining to which elements a style can be applied, CSS2 supports four selector schemes: type, attributes, the context in which the element is used, and external information about the element. These selector schemes are shown in Table 3.1 and are defined in-depth in this section.

Type Selectors

A type selector is the simplest kind of selector and applies a style sheet property to a specific element. The element "type" is denoted by the element name. In our previous examples, we have been using type selectors to apply different properties to the H1 element. Following is a good example of a set of rules that apply the color green to the elements TITLE, AUTHOR, and PUBLISHER.

```
TITLE {color: green}
AUTHOR {color: green}
PUBLISHER {color: green}
```

Although listing the type selectors separately is syntactically correct, they can be grouped together if the same property value is to be applied. This rule combines the TITLE, AUTHOR, and PUBLISHER to accomplish the same goal:

```
TITLE, AUTHOR, PUBLISHER { color: green}
```

Attribute Selectors

Using Attribute Selectors can be very powerful for the XML designer, because they enable designers to match elements by their attributes. You can use the many types of attribute selectors in various ways:

By attribute name. Causes a selection to be matched when an element has a certain attribute. (For example, match all anchor elements <A> that have an "HREF" attribute and apply a certain property.)

```
EX: A[HREF] {color:red}
```

By attribute value. Causes a selection to be matched when an element's attribute has a certain value. (For example, match all anchor elements <A> that have an HREF value of www.xulguide.com.)

```
EX: A[HREF=http://www.xulguide.com/] {color: red}
```

Table 3.1 Types of Selectors with Their Declarations

SELECTOR TYPE	SYNTAX	EXAMPLE
Type	EL{P:V}	K {color: red} *Matches:* <K>hello!</K>
Attribute	EL[ATT] {P:V} EL[ATT=VAL]	A[HREF] {color: red} *Matches:* <A HREF=www.cnn.com>click</A> <A HREF="xul.html">click</A> --- A[HREF=mozilla.org] {color: red} *Matches:* <A HREF=mozilla.org>click</A>
ID	#UNIQUEID {P:V}	#mm{color: red} Matches: <K id="mm">foo</K>
Class	.CLASSNAME {P:V}	.low{color: red} *Matches:* <K class="low">hi!</K> <R class="low">hi!</K>
Child	EL1 > EL2 {P:V}	Body > A {color: red} *Matches:* A if it is a child of Body
Descendant	EL1 EL2 {P:V}	Body A {color: red} *Matches:* A if it is a descendant of Body
Adjacent	EL1 + EL2 {P:V}	Body + A {color: red} *Matches:* A if it is a sibling of the Body element
Universal	* {P:V}	* {color: red} *Matches:* Every element
Pseudo Class	EL:PSEUDO-CLASS{P:V} :PSEUDO-CLASS{P:V}	A:VISITED{color: purple} :hover {color: purple}
Pseudo-Element	EL:PSEUDO- ELEMENT{P:V} EL.CLASS.PSEUDO- ELEMENT{P:V}	TEXT.first-letter {color: red} TEXT.first-line {font-style: bold} BOOK.TEXT.first-letter{color: red}

By multiple attributes. Causes a selection to be matched when multiple attributes of an element has certain values. (For example, match all <BOOK> elements that have attributes title="Tom Sawyer" and author="Twain".)

```
EX: BOOK[title="Tom Sawyer][author="Twain"] {color: red}
```

In two special cases of attribute selectors—ID selectors and CLASS selectors—the syntax is quite different. ID selectors enable the selection to occur on the unique identifier (attribute "id") of the element. CLASS selectors, on the other hand, enable the selection to occur on the class attribute (attribute "class") of the element. ID selector syntax is different, because it begins with a # sign. The syntax for an ID selector is:

```
#idref {property: value} <!-- id selector -->
```

For example, if an XML element is <BOOK ID="12345">Tom Sawyer</BOOK>, the rule "#12345 {color: red}" would match it. A class selector has a different syntax. Instead of beginning with the # sign, it begins with a dot (.). The syntax for a class selector is as follows:

```
.classname {property: value} <!--class selector -->
```

For example, if an XML element was <P class="foo">here is a paragraph</P>, a rule such as ".foo {font-size=20px}" would match.

Contextual Selectors

An element's context is formed by its position in relation to other elements in an XML document. An XML document, with its hierarchical structure, can be viewed as a tree, in which someone can pinpoint adjacent nodes, child nodes, and descendent nodes. When you want to attach a certain style to nodes depending on their relationship in the XML document (for example, "All descendents of <box> should have a border"), you should use contextual selectors. Adjacent, child, and descendent selectors are contextual selectors that enable the designer to name a specific sibling, child, or descendant.

Figure 3.2 contains a tree-like representation of an XML document, describing a very small library with one book and one magazine. Every node in the XML document is a *descendent* of the LIBRARY element. LIBRARY has a child that is element BOOK, and a child that is element MAGAZINE. Because MAGAZINE and BOOK are on the same level in the tree, they are called *adjacent* or *sibling nodes.*

An *adjacent selector* is sometimes called the sibling selector. The syntax for matching an element B that is adjacent to another element A is the following:

```
A + B {property: value}
```

A good example of a sibling selector in the library example would be the following:

```
chapter1 + chapter2 {color: red}
```

This would perform a color selection on all chapter2s that are siblings of chapter1.

A *child selector* is a contextual selector that performs a specific selection on a node B if it is a child of node A. The syntax of such a selection is:

```
A > B {property:value}
```

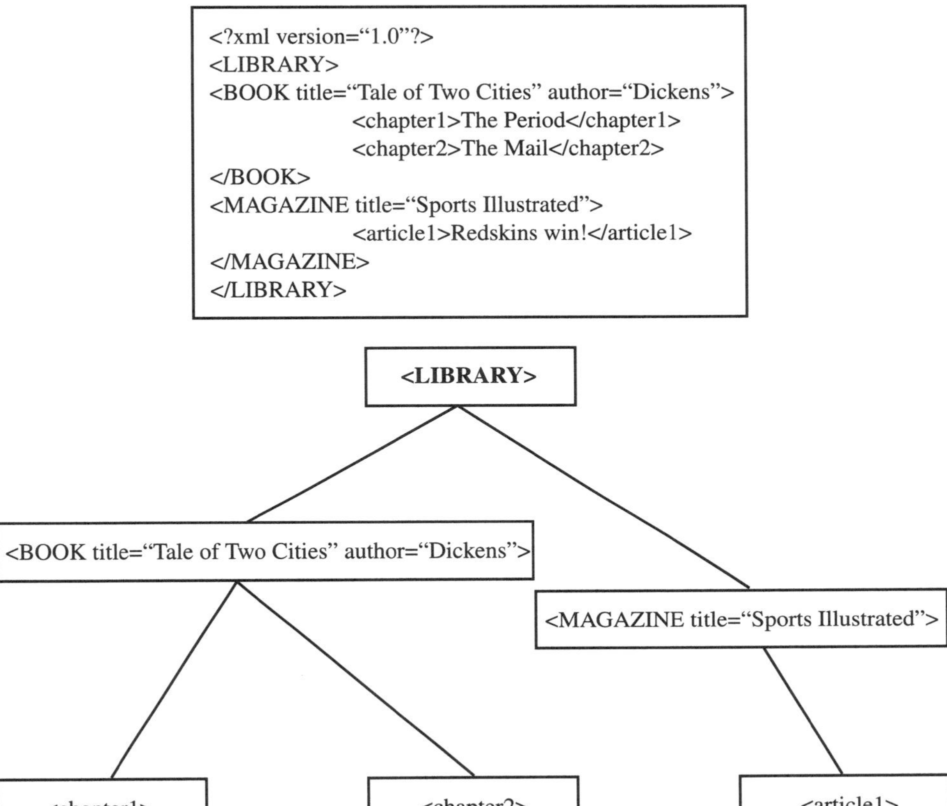
<?xml version="1.0"?>
<LIBRARY>
<BOOK title="Tale of Two Cities" author="Dickens">
<chapter1>The Period</chapter1>
<chapter2>The Mail</chapter2>
</BOOK>
<MAGAZINE title="Sports Illustrated">
<article1>Redskins win!</article1>
</MAGAZINE>
</LIBRARY>
<LIBRARY>
<BOOK title="Tale of Two Cities" author="Dickens">
<MAGAZINE title="Sports Illustrated">
<chapter1>
<chapter2>
<article1>

Figure 3.2 Tree representation of XML.

An example of a child selector in the library example would be to select an element BOOK if it is a child of LIBRARY. In this case, the syntax would be:

```
LIBRARY > BOOK {color:red}
```

A *descendent selector* performs a specific selection on a node B if it is a descendent from an element A. The syntax of a descendent selector is:

```
A B {property:value}
```

In the library example, the following will select the <article> element, which is a descendant of LIBRARY.

```
LIBRARY article {color:red}
```

The contextual selectors can be used in combination with each other. For example, if you wanted to select any chapter1 element whose parent is BOOK, which is a descendent of LIBRARY, your selector would be:

```
LIBRARY BOOK > chapter1
```

Universal Selectors

Universal selectors let the designer use the wildcard operator (*) to select elements within its scope. These selectors can be used in combination with other types of selectors. They are often called the *any* selectors. Keeping with the same LIBRARY example, the following will select every node in the tree and apply the color red:

```
* {color:red}
```

Universal selectors are quite useful for combining with other selectors. In certain cases, the element name does not matter. For instance, the following CSS rule applies the universal selector to an attribute selector, applying a bold font style to any element with the attribute NAME.

```
*[NAME] {font-weight: bold]
```

Pseudo-Classes and Pseudo-Elements

Pseudo-classes and *pseudo-elements* apply style to elements based on information that is held in the rendering application but that does not exist in the source document itself.[3] For example, a designer might want the first word of a sentence to be capitalized, or he may want to apply a style to a link that has been visited. This information isn't in the source HTML or XML itself, but it is held by the Web browser. Pseudo-classes classify elements on characteristics other than their attributes. Pseudo-elements create abstractions about the document tree beyond those specified by the document language. Using pseudo-classes in HTML, you could change the color of a document's link if the link has already been visited. Using pseudo-elements, you can change the style of the first letter of an element.

A pseudo-class is not directly listed in the source but is supported by the document renderer. For example, HTML has "Anchor" pseudo-classes that describe certain things about the <A> class. Whether or not the user has clicked on that link before is not listed in the HTML source as an attribute of the anchor element; instead, it is a pseudo-class called *visited*. The catch is that the document renderer (Web browser) will understand what we are doing when we make a selector on the pseudo-class VISITED of the anchor tag. In the following example, A is the element type; VISITED is the pseudo-class, separated by a flag character (colon); and this style rule will make all visited links have the color purple.

```
A:VISITED {color:purple}
```

Standard pseudo-classes are listed in Table 3.2.

Table 3.2 Standard Pseudo-Classes

PSEUDO-CLASS	DESCRIPTION	EXAMPLE
first-child	Matches an element that is the first child of some other element	P:first-child {color: red}
link	Matches a link that hasn't been visited	:link { color: red}
visited	Matches a link that has been visited	:visited { color: green}
lang	Matches an element based on its language to add language-specific style guidelines (such as German umlauts, French quotation marks, and so on)	:lang(fr) {att: val}
active	Matches an element while it is being activated by the user	A:active {color: red}
focus	Matches an element when it is in focus	A:focus {color: yellow}
hover	Matches an element while the mouse is over it	A:hover {color: green}

Like a pseudo-class, a pseudo-element isn't specifically listed in the source XML but is understood by the document renderer. For example, the first letter of a chapter might be very large and could be written in bold and italics. In this case, the following CSS code could be used:

```
CHAPTER { display: block}
CHAPTER:first-letter {
                    font-size: 200%;
                    font-style: italic;
                    font-weight: bold;
                 }
```

In the previous CSS rules, CHAPTER is the element to be matched, and first-letter is the pseudo-element. Code Listing 3.3 shows an example of using pseudo-elements, using the opening words from Charles Dickens' *A Tale of Two Cities*. Figure 3.3 shows the rendering of the XML in Code Listing 3.3. Standard pseudo-elements are shown in Table 3.3.

NOTE As with many aspects of CSS, the rendering of the document depends on how well the standard is supported by the browser. Check with your browser vendor to see the level of its CSS compliance.

Table 3.1 gives a listing of the types of selectors with their declarations. Next, we discuss the different types of properties that we can use with these selectors.

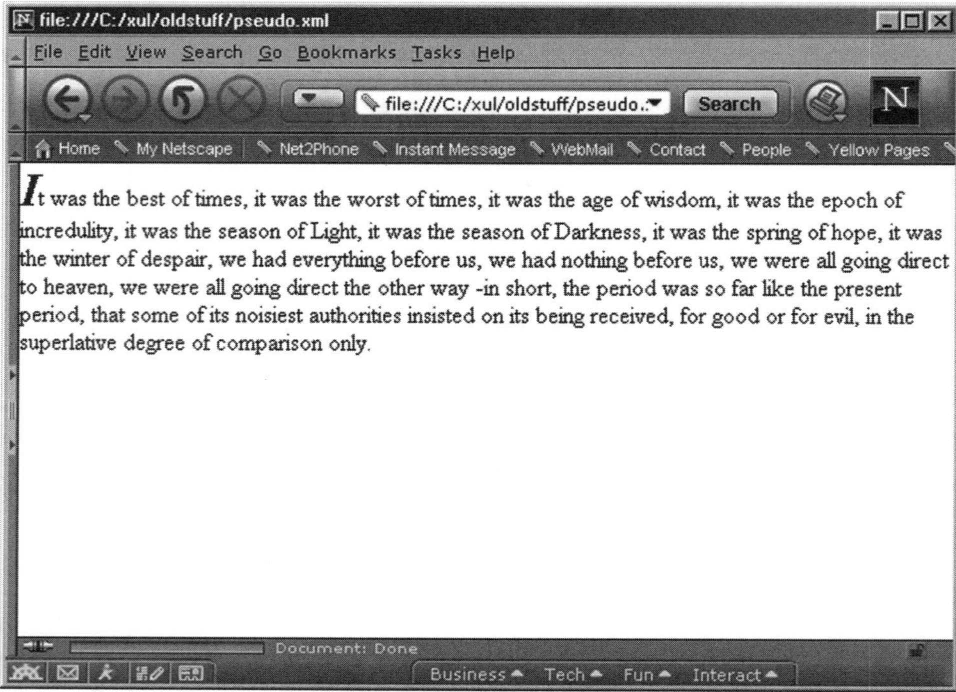

Figure 3.3 Rendering of "first-letter" pseudo-element.

```
<?xml version="1.0"?>
<?xml-stylesheet href="ch4ex2.css" type="text/css"?>
<BOOK name="A Tale of Two Cities">
<CHAPTER number='1'>
It was the best of times, it was the worst of times, it was the age of
wisdom, it was the epoch of incredulity, it was the season of Light,
it was the season of Darkness, it was the spring of hope, it was the
winter of despair, we had everything before us, we had nothing before
us, we were all going direct to heaven, we were all going direct the
other way-in short, the period was so far like the present period,
that some of its noisiest authorities insisted on its being received,
for good or for evil, in the superlative degree of comparison only.[4]
</CHAPTER>
</BOOK>
```

Code Listing 3.3 XML for demonstrating pseudo-element.

Changing Your Element's Properties

Properties determine the tangible characteristics of how selectors are formatted. Most properties have easily recognized characteristics such as width, height, color, back-

Table 3.3 Table of Pseudo-Elements

PSEUDO-ELEMENT	DESCRIPTION	USAGE
first-letter	Matches the first letter of an element	P:first-letter {color: red}
first-line	Matches the first line of an element as it is rendered in the application	P:first-line {color: red}
Before	Matches the area before an element in order to generate content	P:before {content: "BEFORE P"}
After	Matches the area after an element in order to generate content	P:after {content: "AFTER P"}

ground-color, and font-width. The CSS Web site at the W3C, www.w3c.org/Style/CSS/, includes resources that list all of the CSS properties, and the book, *Cascading Style Sheets: Designing for the Web* by Håkon Wium Lie and Bert Bos contains a great quick reference for CSS properties. Instead of giving you an exhaustive list containing the most intuitive property types, this chapter covers some of the least intuitive property types. Most of these properties are related to element display and positioning, as well as object alignment, borders, and margins.

Before we get into the individual properties, however, we should mention the concept of *inheritance*. When no rule exists to set a property value in an element, the element may inherit that property from its parent element, if the property is *inheritable*. When a designer wants to make certain that an element inherits a property from its parent, he can use the inherit keyword to make certain, as in " H3 {font-size: inherit}".

The Display Property

The display property renders the basic shapes of elements. With this property, the Web designer can specify whether an element is displayed as a block of text, a part of a line of text, a list item, or not at all. Following are valid values of the display property: block, inline, list-item, run-in, compact, marker, table, inline-table, table-row-group, table-header-group, table-footer-group, table-row, table-column-group, table-column, table-cell, table-caption, and none. As you can see, the display property has many possibilities!

When an element has a *block* display value, it starts on and ends on a new line. For example, the <P> element in HTML has a block display value. When the element has an *inline* display value, it is displayed on the same line. In XML, all elements are inline, unless they are specified.

The *list-item* display property displays an element as a label in a list. When this value is set, it is used in tandem with the list-style-type, list-style-image, and list-style-position properties, which specify many characteristics of the list. With the list-item property, a list can have images, bullets, roman numerals, and various other types next to each item.

When the element has a *run-in* display property, the element will start on a new line but will not end on a new line. A *compact* display value puts an element in the margin of the next block. A value of *marker* allows list items to be counted and numbered accordingly. A *none* value makes the element invisible.

Some of the other possible values of display involve tables and are beyond the scope of this book. For more information, go to the CSS Web site at the W3C: www.w3c.org/Style/CSS/. An example of using the display property for block-formatted text is shown in Code Listing 3.5.

The Position Property

The position property tells the rendering application how to position an element in the document. Some possible values for the position property are absolute, relative, fixed, and static:

- When the position property is *absolute*, the element will be placed in the absolute positioning on the X- and Y-axis, starting at (0,0) from the top left corner of a window.
- When the value of the position property is *relative*, the position of the element is dependent on other elements in the document. A typical use of using relative positioning is to move elements away from their customary position (for example, text animation).
- When the value of the position property is *fixed*, the element will always remain on-screen, even if scrolling occurs in the document. Sometimes, using a fixed position allows someone to break a document into multiple parts.
- When the value of the position property is *static*, the element uses no positioning at all. Static elements are placed relative to their parents and to elements that precede them. All nonstatic elements use the top, left, bottom, and right properties to specify positioning.

Using these position properties, the designer can have complete control over the way an element is displayed on-screen. For example, let's look at Code Listing 3.4. This

```
<?xml version="1.0"?>
<?xml-stylesheet href="absolutepos.css" type="text/css"?>
<MAGAZINE>
     <TITLE>The XUL Express</TITLE>
     <ARTICLE>
       <CONTENT>XUL uses Cascading Style sheets to
                 control the look-and-feel of objects'
                 properties!
       </CONTENT>
     </ARTICLE>
</MAGAZINE>
```

Code Listing 3.4 xulmagazine.xml.

```
MAGAZINE { display: block;
           background-color: green;
           width: 800px;
           height: 600px;
           font-size:60px;
           color: white;
         }
ARTICLE {
         display: block;
         position: absolute;
         top: 80px;
         left: 50px;
         background-color: yellow;
         font-size: 30px;
         color: green;
         width: 500px;
         height: 300px;
        }
```

Code Listing 3.5 absolutepos.css.

contains a simple XML file containing the code for a magazine called the *XUL Express*. It is formatted by referencing absolutepos.css, listed in Code Listing 3.5.

Notice in Code Listing 3.5 that we did not specify positioning for the MAGAZINE element and that we used a display property to specify block display. Not giving positioning properties here should make the magazine element begin in the upper-left corner of the browser in the style sheet code in Code Listing 3.4. In this case, MAGAZINE is a block with a background color of green; it has a 800 × 600 pixel area; and all text listed in the element will have a font-size of 60 pixels and a font color of white. The style sheet contains values for the ARTICLE element, which is set to be displayed in block mode, has a background color of yellow, and has dimensions of 500 × 300. Notice that the ARTICLE element uses absolute positioning, which is specified by the top and left properties.

Figure 3.4 shows how a browser would render this XML. Because the MAGAZINE element mentions no positioning, the upper-left corner of that element is set to (0,0), and it takes up 800 × 600 of the entire page. ARTICLE, on the other hand, specifies absolute positioning, so its upper-left corner is set to (50,80). In a real-world scenario, this style sheet would probably not be best. Why? Because the absolute positioning specified in the ARTICLE element should really be dependent on the font size of the text in the magazine's TITLE element. If this style sheet was longer and more complex, it might be easy to overlook the font-size property in MAGAZINE and have the ARTICLE block be formatted over the text.

For this reason, our position property should probably have the value of "static," as shown in Code Listing 3.6. Using this positioning technique, the ARTICLE and other MAGAZINE elements (in this case, TITLE) cannot overlap, showing a rendering style in

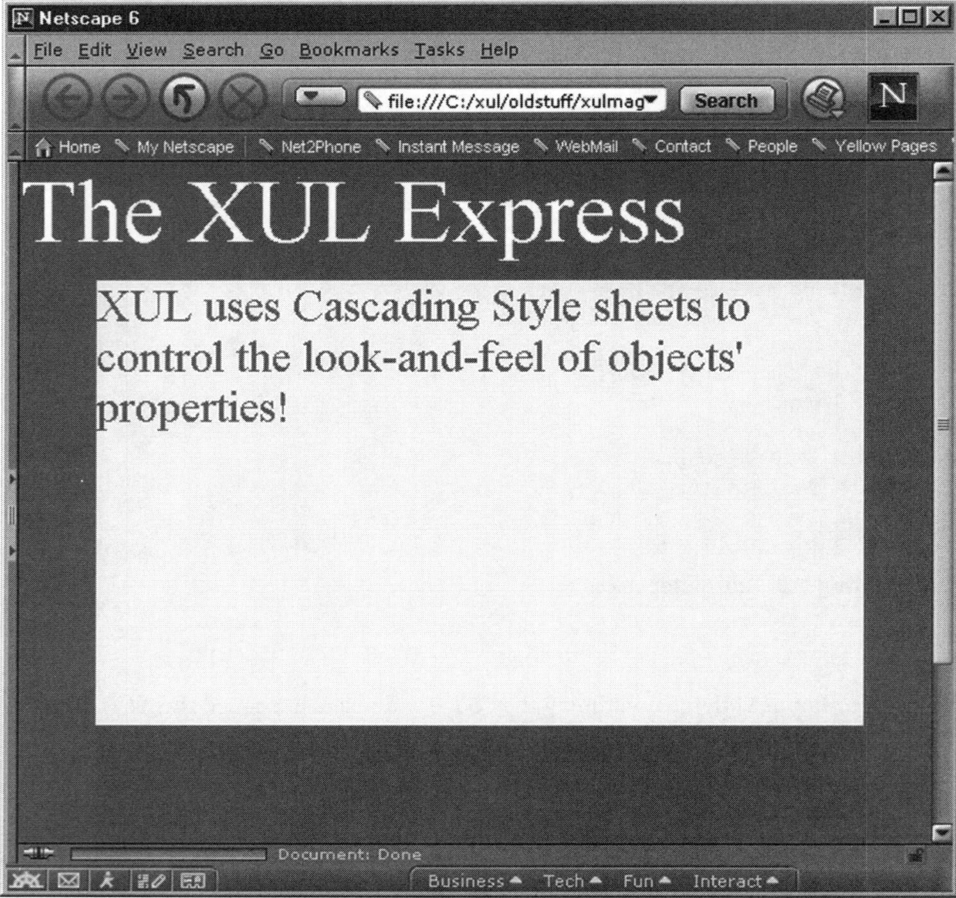

Figure 3.4 Absolute positioning.

Figure 3.5. Note that the left side is now at x coordinate 0, because we are no longer using absolute positioning. Figure 3.5 shows a rendering of static positioning.

Margin, Padding, and Border Properties

Margin, padding, and border properties are similar in that they all offer space around elements. The *margin* properties (margin-top, margin-right, margin-bottom, and margin-left) control the amount of space existing outside the edge of an element. The *padding* properties (padding-top, padding-right, padding-bottom, and padding-left) add space between elements. The *border* properties (border-width, border-color, border-style, border-width, and border-length) enable the designer to manage the look and feel of borders around elements. Figure 3.6 shows a graphical display of these properties.

```
MAGAZINE { display: block;
           background-color: green;
           width: 800px;
           height: 600px;
           font-size:60px;
           color: white;
          }
ARTICLE {
          display: block;
          position: static;
          background-color: yellow;
          font-size: 30px;
          color: green;
          width: 500px;
          height: 300px;
         }
```

Code Listing 3.6 static.css.

As shown in Figure 3.6, the padding property consists of the amount of space between the text and the box around it in a block-formatted text area. The border represents the area between that block of text and the margin. The margin, of course, represents the amount of space between the text border and the side of the page.

Margin, border, and padding can actually apply to all four sides of an element. In order to specify these values correctly, the designer needs to follow the following syntax:

- To make these properties apply to all slides, you can specify one value, as in:

  ```
  H1 { margin: 2em}
  ```

- To make the top and bottom properties apply, you can specify two values, as in:

  ```
  H1 {border: 3em 1 em}
  ```

- To only assign top, right, and left properties (in that order), specify the following:

  ```
  H1 {padding: 2em 1em 3em}
  ```

- To assign them different properties in the order of top, right, bottom, and left, specify:

  ```
  H1 {border: 3em 1em 2em 4em}
  ```

If you think that was important to remember, you're right! Because of this, the authors of CSS created multiple properties for margins, borders, and padding. The properties are:

- Margin-top, margin-bottom, margin-left, and margin-right
- Padding-top, padding-bottom, padding-left, and padding-right
- Border -top, border-bottom, border-left, and border-right

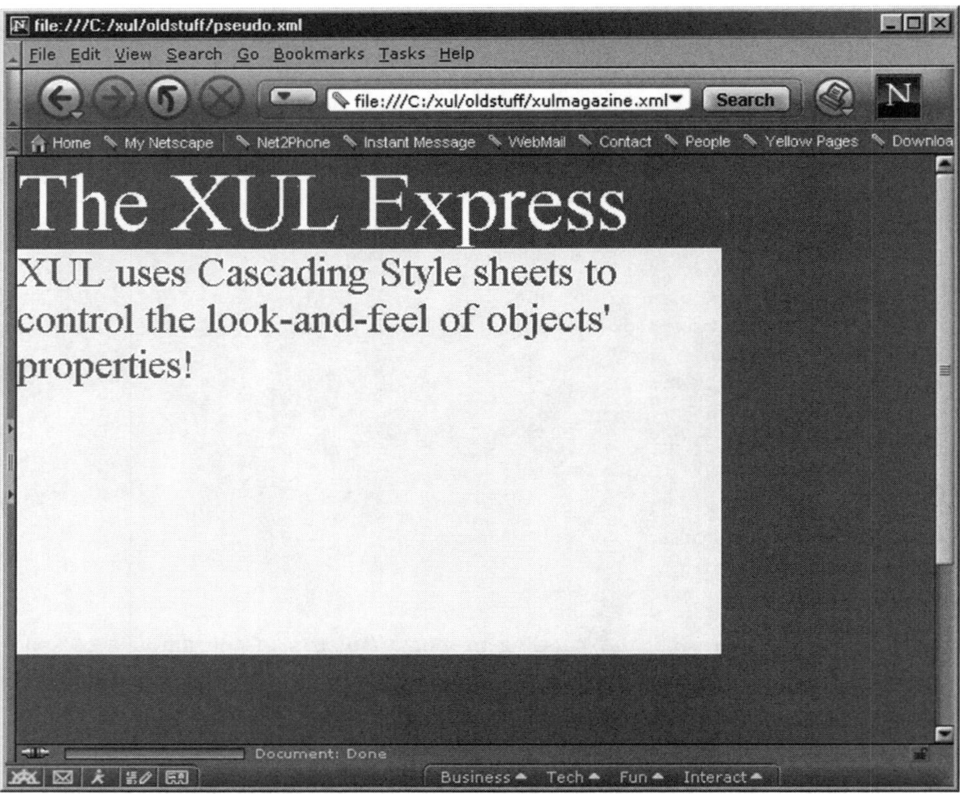

Figure 3.5 Rendering of static positioning.

As you can see, there are many ways to assign these properties. A common use of the margin property is to indent a paragraph to set it apart from the rest of the text. Code Listing 3.7 shows an XML with a standout tag that we would like to make indented in a document to draw attention to it. We do this with the stylesheet in Code Listing 3.8, and the result appears in Figure 3.7.

The *border* property, which is the amount of space wedged between the element's padding and margin, is a way to highlight an element. Including the positional border properties that we mentioned before, there are actually 20 different border properties. These properties are easy to understand, so for the sake of space constraints, we will leave out most experimentation with these properties. One of the most interesting border properties is the border-style property. This property enables the designer to set the appearance of the border, with the following possible values:

solid. A solid line

dotted. A dotted line

dashed. A dashed line

double. A double line, with the border-width property between the two lines

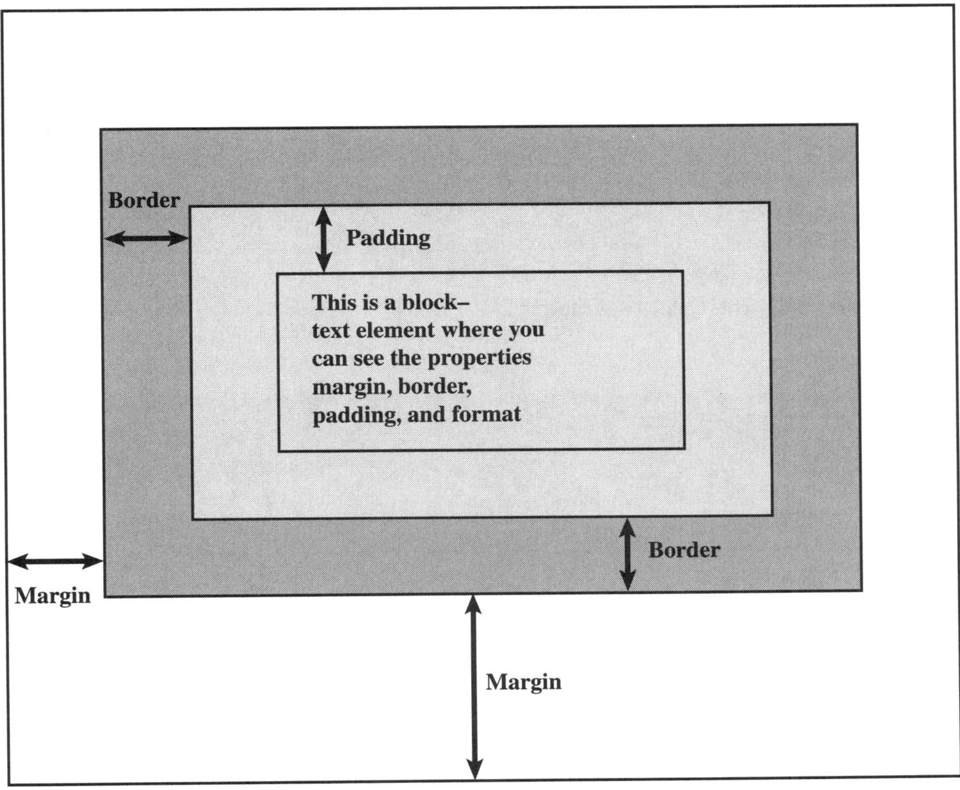

Figure 3.6 Margin, padding, and border properties.

```
<?xml version="1.0"?>
<?xml-stylesheet href="margin.css" type="text/css"?>
<DOC>
   This is a good example of how margins can be used.
   In a situation where you might want to let an area
   of text stand out:
   <standout>
      You may set the margins of the area of the
      text to differentiate it from the rest of the document.
   </standout>
   If we did it correctly, you should be able to tell
   which block of text had the margin around it in this
   example.
</DOC>
```

Code Listing 3.7 XML for showing margins.

```
DOC {
      display: block;
      background-color: yellow;
    }
standout {
        display: block;
        margin: 2em;
        }
```

Code Listing 3.8 The CSS to set margins.

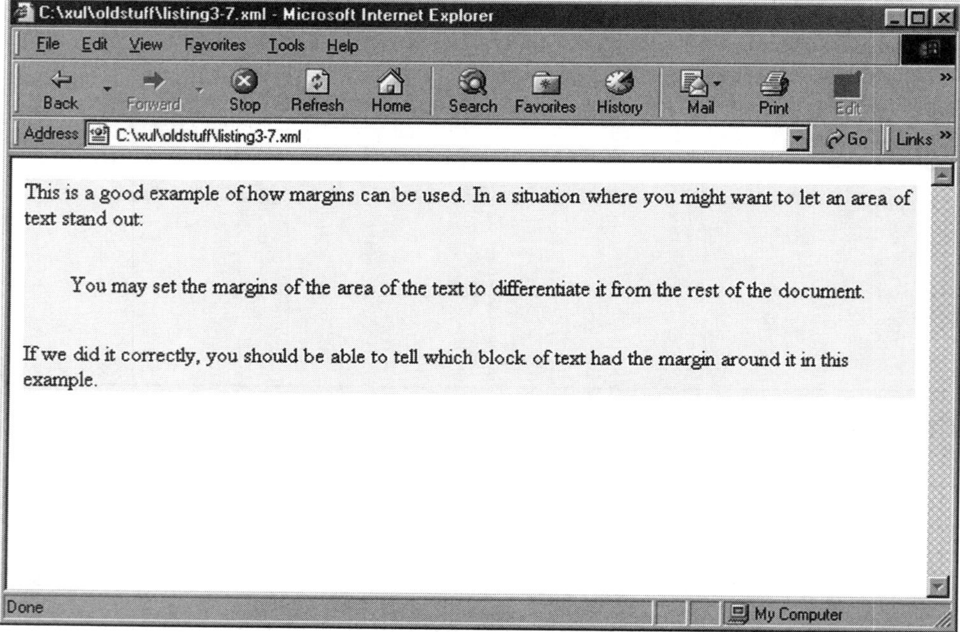

Figure 3.7 Presentation of margin text.

groove. A three-dimensional inward groove

ridge. A three-dimensional outward ridge

inset. Having the property of being pressed inward

outset. Having the property of being pressed outward

As an example, let's add a double-lined border around the standout element that we used to demonstrate margins. Code Listing 3.9 shows that we added a border of length one em and used the border-style double, so that we can actually see the width of our border. Figure 3.8 shows the result using the Netscape browser.

```
DOC {
      font-style: Roman;
      display: block;
      background-color: yellow;
    }
standout {
          display: block;
          border: 1em;
          border-style: double;
          margin: 2em;
          }
```

Code Listing 3.9 Adding a border to our style sheet.

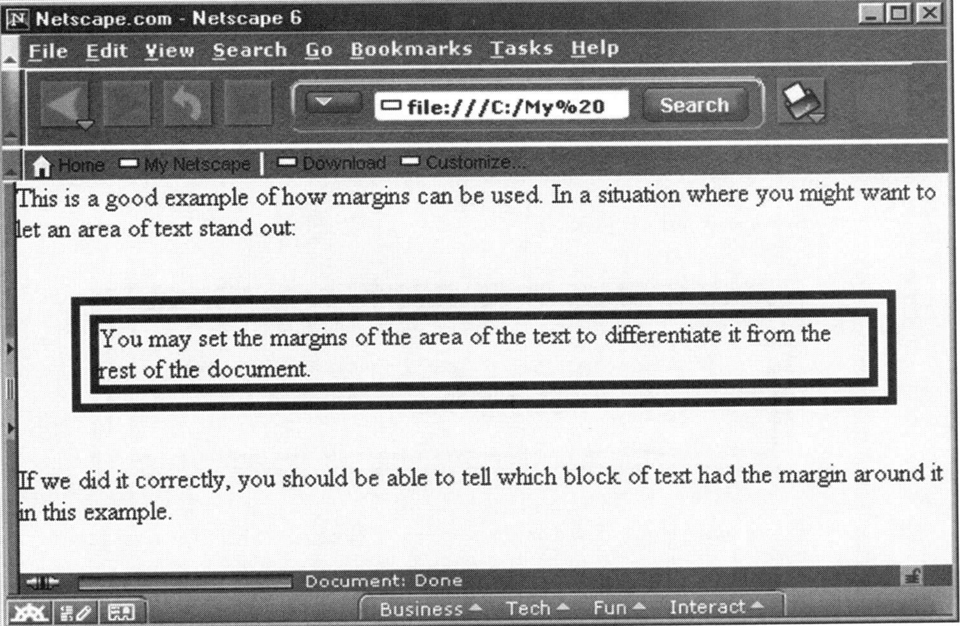

Figure 3.8 Result of adding a double border.

The *padding* property is the space between an element and its margin or between and element and its border. Let's set a padding of two em to the standout element for this section's example by making the change shown in Code Listing 3.10. Figure 3.9 shows the result of adding the padding property to the standout element. As you can see, there is much more space in between the text and the double-lined border than there was in Figure 3.8.

```
DOC {
            font-style: Roman;
            display: block;
            background-color: yellow;
    }
standout {
            display: block;
            border: 1em;
            border-style: double;
            padding: 2em;
            margin: 2em;
          }
```

Code Listing 3.10 Adding the padding property.

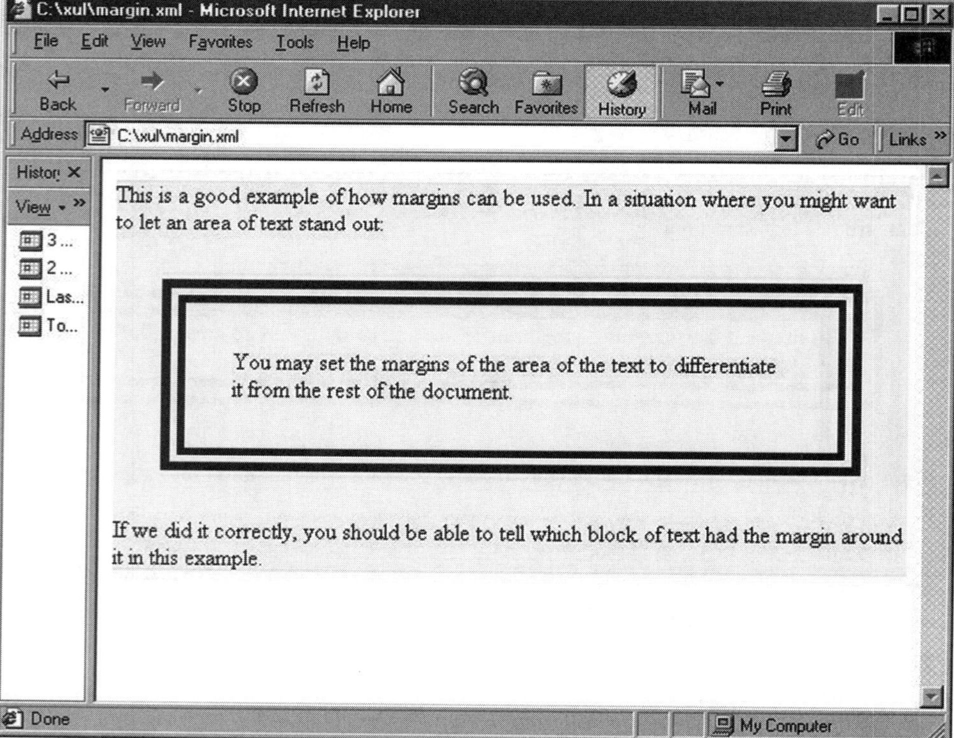

Figure 3.9 Adding the padding property.

Text Display Properties

Without text, style sheets would probably be meaningless. As you have seen throughout this chapter, most of the properties have a lot to do with blocks of text. Specifying text display properties is the most common use of style sheets.

Common properties that developers specify to control text are the following:

text-align. For setting the way lines are adjusted horizontally. This property enables you to align a paragraph to the left, right, or centered.

text-indent. For indenting the beginning of a paragraph.

text-decoration. For adding strikeouts, underlining, or blinking to text.

text-transform. For transforming text elements into uppercase or lowercase or for capitalizing the first letter of each word.

line-height. For specifying the distance between lines in a paragraph.

word-spacing. For adjusting the amount of spacing between words.

letter-spacing. For adjusting the amount of space between letters.

vertical-align. For raising or lowering letters above or below the baseline of the text.

Code Listing 3.11 shows XML that demonstrates some of these text display properties. We apply the CSS in Code Listing 3.12, which applies the text display properties of text-align, text-transform, text-decoration, and text-indent. Just for fun, we've added a few of the border-style property values that we discussed earlier.

```
<?xml version="1.0"?>
<?xml-stylesheet href="textprop.css" type="text/css"?>
<DOC>
<first>
This is a good example of a lot of different text properties.
We will set the text-transform property to make this all upper case,
and we would like this to be centered.
</first>
<right>
We would like to align this text to the right. We can also
add a text decoration property to show a strikeout of all the
<mistake>mistrakes</mistake> mistakes we've made. At the
same time, let's set the line-height property.
</right>
<indent>
Let's make this text indented! If I put a lot of text in this element,
we will see how the line wraps.
</indent>
</DOC>
```

Code Listing 3.11 XML example for text display properties.

```
DOC { display: block }

first {
        display: block;
        text-transform: uppercase;
        text-align: center;
        border-style: outset;
      }
right {
       display: block;
       border: 1.2em;
       border-style: double;
       text-align: right;
       word-spacing: 3em;
       background-color: yellow;
       line-height: 2em;
      }
mistake {
        text-decoration: line-through;
        }
indent {
        text-indent: 10%;
        border: 1.5em;
        border-style: groove;
        display: block;
        vertical-align: bottom;
       }
```

Code Listing 3.12 CSS for text display property example.

One of the things that you might notice about this example is that we used a percentage to describe the value of text-indent. Whenever there is a percentage for this property value, the amount of indentation will be proportional to the size of the first line of the block of text. This way, if you resize the rendering application, the indentation size will always change in relation to the rest of the text.

Figure 3.10 shows the rendering of the XML using the Mozilla browser. As you can see, the text blocks were displayed as we intended.

In the next section, we will discuss important properties that also have an impact on the display of text: font properties. We will also build on the XML and CSS found in Code Listing 3.11 and Code Listing 3.12 to demonstrate some of the different types of font properties.

Font Properties

Fonts are an important part of text formatting. Because there are so many different properties related to fonts, we decided to have a separate section dedicated to them. The font properties are:

font-family. This property describes what family or group the font comes from. Examples are serif, Arial, Helvetica, and Times.

font-size. This property describes the size of the font.

font-style. This property describes the text as italic, normal, or oblique.

font-weight. This property describes the weight, or the amount of lightness or darkness of the text.

font-variant. This property enables you to specify a small-caps style within the current font family.

font-stretch. The font-stretched property enables you to describe how stretched or condensed a text element may be.

font-size-adjust. This property enables you to adjust the font to a size related to another font.

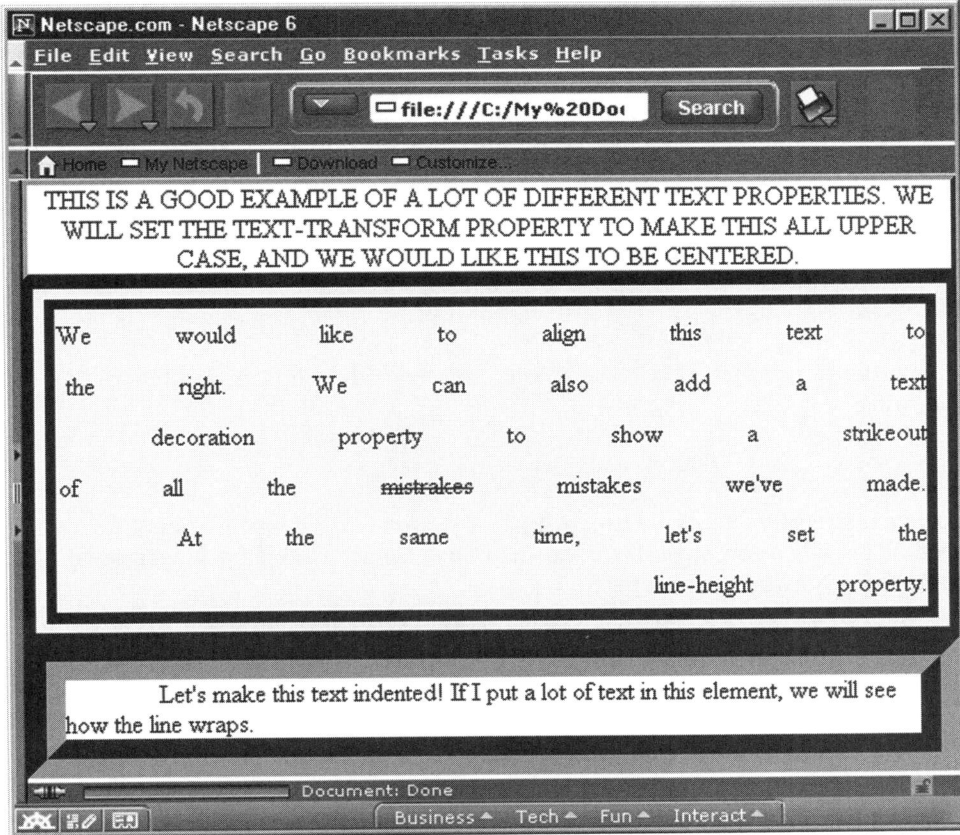

Figure 3.10 Text properties.

Fonts are measured in the following units:

em. This unit is a general unit for measuring length, based on the pitch size, or the width of the letter m of the current font.

px. This unit is the size in number of pixels.

ex. This unit is a general unit for measuring length, based on the font's x character.

pt. This unit represents the size in points.

pc. This unit represents the size in picas.

The most interesting of these units are the em and the ex unit. Both can be powerful tools in style sheet design because they are relative units for measuring length. Sometimes, an application will allow you to enlarge or shrink the size of the text. In the case of such customization, a style sheet that describes absolute sizes may impair the look of the application. Because of this, most designers make it a point to use only em units to describe font sizes, because this allows fonts to be independent of the program that is rendering the document. In fact, em units and ex units are not only used to describe fonts; they can also be used in describing horizontal and vertical length properties of text (as listed in the previous section).

Note that some of the possible values of fonts may not be supported by some applications. There is a very long list of possible fonts, and certain systems and applications may not support them all. For this reason, CSS2 introduced the concept of *WebFonts*, which are fonts that browsers can automatically download. In order for this to happen, you must list font descriptions that tell the browser how to download them. A font description always begins with the @font-face sign, as can be seen here:

```
@font-face{
    font-family: "Chicken Scratch";
    src: url(http://www.fonts.com/chicken-scratch);
 }
```

In order to use this, a style sheet could reference the Chicken Scratch font by the following:

```
P { font-family: "Chicken Scratch", serif; }
```

To demonstrate how fonts are used with CSS, we will expand on the example of the last section, provide a new style sheet, shown in Code Listing 3.13, and apply this style sheet to the same XML in Code Listing 3.11.

Figure 3.11 shows the result in Internet Explorer when we apply these properties.

Cascading Rules

Cascading refers to the cascade of style sheets from different sources, which may influence the presentation of a document.[5] Because a document can be influenced by more than one style sheet, you might think that there would be rule conflicts—for example, a

```
DOC { display: block }
first { display: block;
        text-transform: uppercase;
        text-align: center;
        font-family: serif;
        font-stretch: wider;
        font-size: 1.3em;
        border-style: outset;
      }
right {
       display: block;
       border: 1.2em;
       border-style: double;
       text-align: right;
       font-family: helvetica;
       font-size: 2em;
       background-color: yellow;
      }
mistake {
         text-decoration: line-through
         font-family: monaco;
         font-weight: 900;
        }
indent {
        text-indent: 10%;
        border: 1.5em;
        border-style: groove;
        display: block;
        font-size: 2em;
        font-family: andy;
       }
```

Code Listing 3.13 Adding font properties to the CSS.

designer's style sheet, a user's style sheet, and an application's (browser's) style sheet may include conflicting rules. Because of this, a rule-based mechanism was put in place for CSS:

- Designer style sheets override user style sheets.
- The **!important** tag carries extra weight and can be a tie breaker in the event of a set of conflicting rules.
- The most specific rule overrides the least specific rule.
- Order is important; the later a rule is specified, the greater weight it is given.
- Inheritance rules apply after cascading rules.

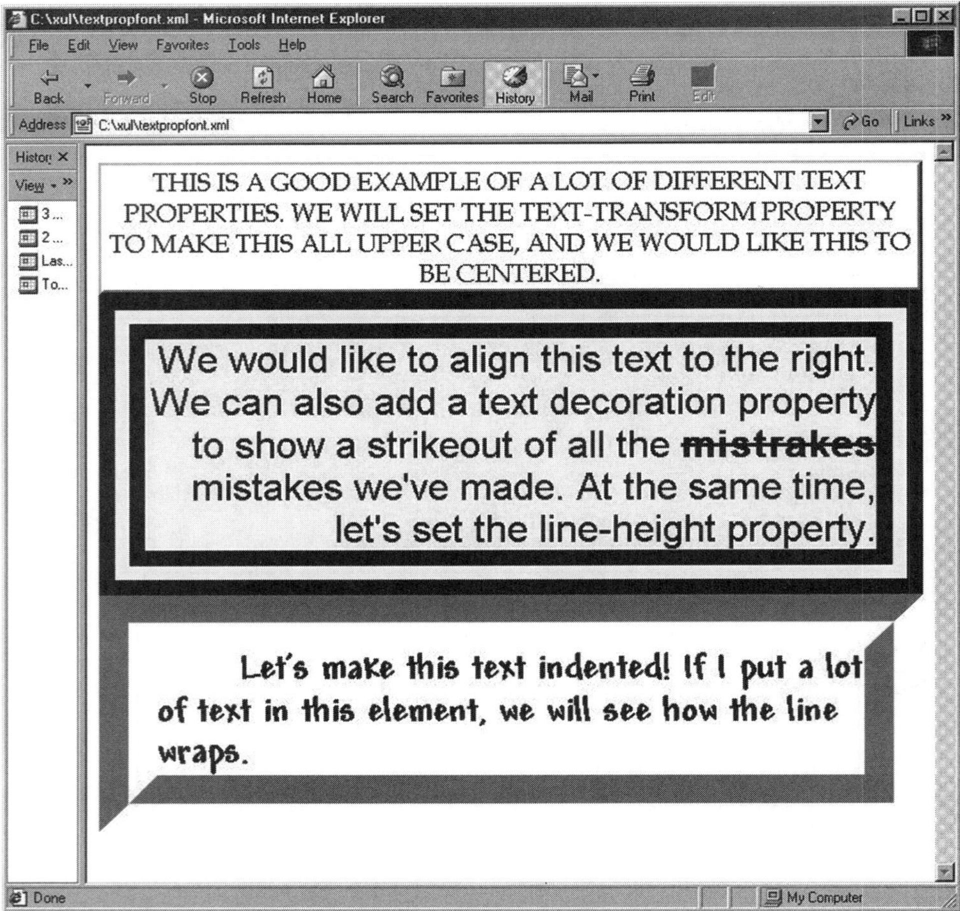

Figure 3.11 Applying fonts to the document.

Following these rules, a browser resolves conflicts between the various style sheets. Most of the time, the designer's style sheet has priority, but the user does have a say in specifying which rules are important by using the !important tag.

Using CSS with XUL

Developers use CSS to describe the style of XUL elements. Every XUL element has a *style* attribute where CSS rules may be applied, but it is more common to reference external CSS style sheets for every XUL file. Because the user interface of the Netscape 6.x browser is written in XUL, there are CSS style sheets for the navigator, its Web browser; the messenger, its mail client; and its other components. The browser has global style sheets that apply to all of Netscape's XUL components. Because Netscape engineers have developed detailed CSS files to give nice styles to their browser components, many developers of XUL applications re-use these CSS files in their own XUL applications.

Code Listing 3.14 shows a snapshot of the browser's global.css file. This file is the style sheet that describes the CSS properties of XUL elements of the browser. By this point, the file should look familiar to you!

Netscape 6.x enables you to customize properties in the browser by editing these style sheets. XUL developers can re-use these style sheets, or they can write their own. You can enhance the browser's performance by using certain CSS style guidelines. The browser's CSS implementation matches rules by starting with the rightmost selector and moving to the left. If there is a mismatch or a typo, the processor will terminate processing. Because of this, it is very important to:

Make sure to use valid CSS syntax. This first guideline may seem self-explanatory, but it is very important. A break in the syntax of your CSS could cause undesirable effects. Some of the worst problems seen to date by the Mozilla team have been caused by syntactically incorrect CSS.

Filter out rules for each element. The fewer rules that the processor has to check for each element, the faster the CSS will be processed. This involves some good design sense when you are writing your CSS.

TIP **The mozilla.org XPToolkit project has an excellent guide to writing efficient CSS. The project recommends avoiding using universal rules, descendant selectors, and to rely on inheritance. For more information, please visit David Hyatt's "Writing Efficient CSS" at http://www.mozilla.org/xpfe/goodcss.html.**

XUL files reference CSS files to describe the style of their elements. During the rest of this book, you will see many examples of CSS being used in XUL applications.

Summary

We cannot emphasize enough how important knowing CSS is to XUL programming. In this chapter, we discussed the syntax and types of selectors and matching rules that are used in CSS. As we have shown you, it is quite simple to get started in using them with XML and HTML documents. Finally, we have given you a peek at what Netscape's style sheets look like, and we have given you a taste of what is involved in using CSS in the real world.

In the next few chapters, you will see how to apply this knowledge to XUL and see how the use of style sheet rules can quickly customize the look and feel of XUL-based applications.

```
/**
 * XXX-DEBUG: HTML namespace/titledbutton striping.
 **/
  html|*
    {
      border                 : 1px solid green !important;
    }

  html|form
    {
      border                 : none !important;
    }

  titledbutton
    {
      border                 : 1px solid purple !important;
    }

/**
 * XUL <window> element
 **/
  window
    {
      background-color       : threedface;
      color                  : windowtext;
      padding                : 0px;
      font                   : dialog;
    }

  window[wait-cursor]
    {
      cursor                 : wait !important;
    }

  window.dialog
    {
      background-color       : threedface;
      padding                : 7px 5px 5px 5px;
    }
```

Code Listing 3.14 Part of Netscape's global.css file.

Notes

[1]*The O'Reilly Network*, 7/21/2000, www.oreillynet.com/pub/a/network/2000/07/21/magazine/css_intro.html, referring to the implementation of the Mozilla browser.

[2]*W3C Working Group on Extensible Stylesheet Language*, Version 1.0, W3C Recommendation, www.w3.org/TR/xsl/, 2000.

[3]Håkon Lie, and Bert Bos. *Cascading Style Sheets: Designing for the Web*, Harlow, England: Addison-Wesley, 1999.

[4]Charles Dickens, *A Tale of Two Cities*, 1859.

[5]Lie, 1999.

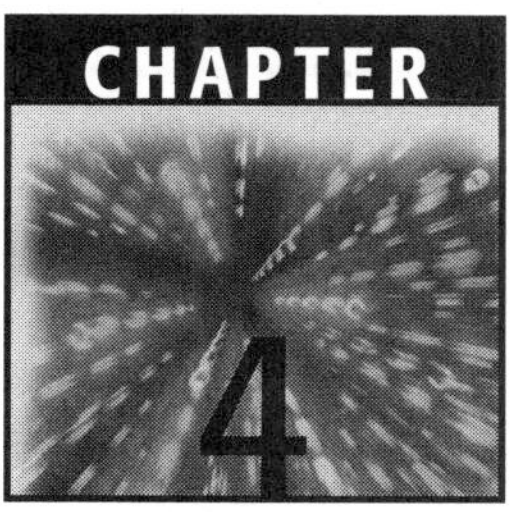

Building a Simple XUL Interface

Always design a thing by considering it in its next larger context—a chair in a room, a room in a house, a house in an environment, an environment in a city plan.

Eliel Saarinen, *Time*, July 2, 1956

After brushing up on XML and Cascading Style Sheets, you should now be ready to jump right into building your first XUL interface. We will build an easy application using simple XUL interface components to give you an idea of how XUL interface components are created and then displayed. You will find that when building our application we use most of the common XUL elements. We will also show you how XUL, HTML, and JavaScript interact within our XUL application.

Our application is a business asset management program. This type of application is used to store information about assets, such as computers, that are bought for a business. Typical data sets that could be stored are the manufacturer, model, serial number, and cost. This sort of information is needed when justifying the tax liability for a business. It is also a prime example of a user interface because we may incorporate text fields, radio buttons, checkboxes, menus, and drop-down lists. Figure 4.1 shows the main interface for our application.

In Chapter 9, "Case Study: Creating a Customizable Browser Portal," and Chapter 10, "Case Study: Building an E-Commerce User Interface with XUL," we will build more complex XUL interfaces, including a customized browser portal and an e-commerce interface.

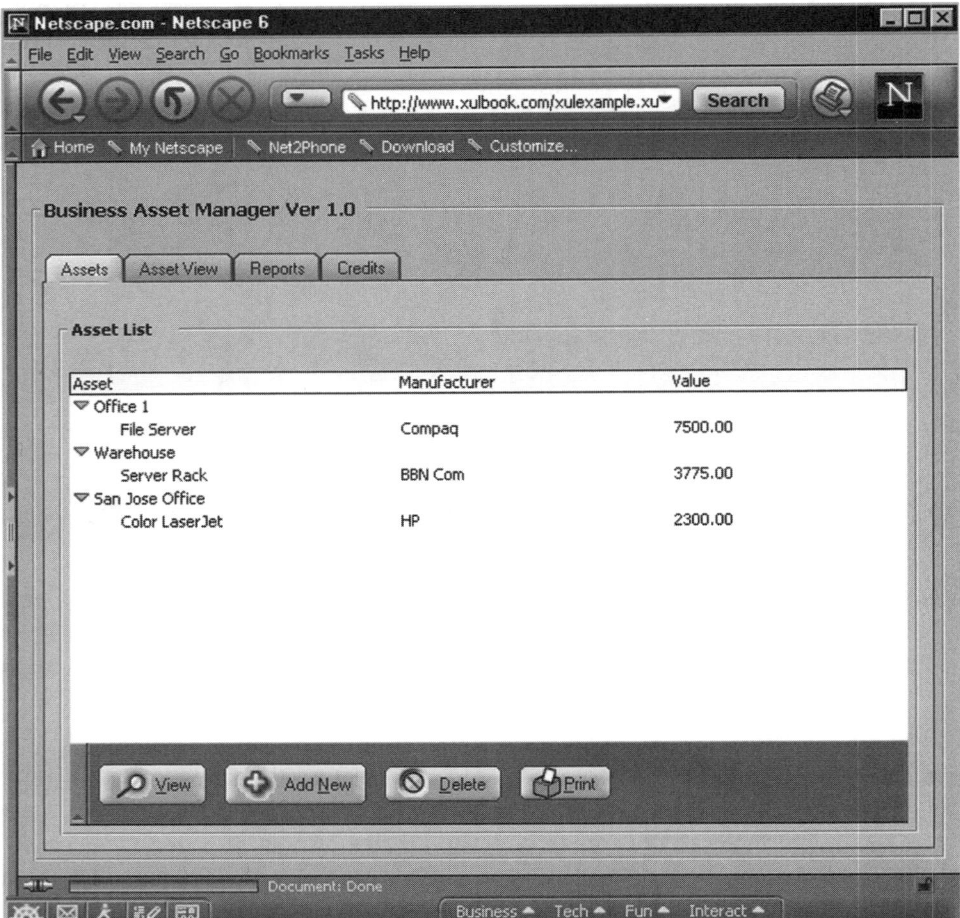

Figure 4.1 The Business Asset Manager Ver 1.0 screen layout.

> **CHOOSING AN EDITOR**
>
> **You will need a text editor to create a XUL application. One of our favorites is XMLSpy, which you can download from http://www.xmlspy.com. This editor contains many great features of more powerful editors without the associated cost. You may load our example within Netscape Navigator 6 in its entirety from http://www.xulbook.com/xulexample.xul. For a complete list of XML/XUL editors, please go to the companion Web site from http://www.xulbook.com.**

Building a XUL Application

Any application starts with an intelligent, top-down approach to design. First, we will need several views for our application, so we incorporate the use of tabs and tab panels to separate the views with their corresponding content. We will have a tab for a list of assets, an asset view, a report view, and credits. It is an application that is simple but is extensible enough to exemplify the most common XUL elements.

In writing your XUL application, keep several things in mind. Because a XUL document is also an XML document, the syntactical structure of the XUL document is very important. That means you will have to make sure that you always close your tags, for example <tag></tag>. The following rules apply just as they do in XML:

- All elements, events, and attributes must be in lowercase, for example, <**window title**="win1">.
- All strings must be in double quotes.
- Attributes if named must have a value associated and must be in, for example <window **title=**"win1">.

With these simple rules in mind, we can create our document by declaring that it is indeed an XML document.

```
<?xml version="1.0"?>
<?xml-stylesheet href="chrome://navigator/skin/" type="text/css"?>
```

First, we declare that the document we have created is an XML document and assign the version attribute to be "1.0." Second, we declare an XML-stylesheet element. We simply use Netscape Navigator's built-in stylesheets, called chromes.

A *chrome* is the Netscape internal reference for a theme. A *theme* is a collection of skins. Themes are style sheet packages stored in a Java archive (JAR) file and filed away in a *user's* chrome folder of Netscape Navigator 6. You may change the complete look and feel of the browser with a chrome.

We declare this style sheet to be a local style sheet. For more information on changing the look and feel of your Netscape Navigator, refer to Chapter 5, "Creating Netscape Themes."

In a XUL document unlike an XML document, there is no support for a Document Type Definition (DTD). We created a DTD for XUL, and it is included, in draft form in Chapter 8, "The jXUL Open Source Project." Nevertheless, this is supposed to be an XML document, and that means more rules. These declarations form the basis for which the XUL parser built into Netscape Navigator will handle our XUL interface.

Laying the Foundation

Now that we've covered the basics, we will declare a window element. As a good coding habit—one that will reduce errors later on—go ahead and close the element with a </window> close tag :

```
<window align="left"
 xmlns:html="http://www.w3.org/TR/REC-html40"

 xmlns="http://www.mozilla.org/keymaster/gatekeeper/there.is.only.xul">
</window>
```

In order to start placing interface components on the page, we need to have a container for those elements. The window just happens to be the root element for placing those elements on the interface. So let's talk about the window interface. Its first attribute is the ALIGN attribute. All subcomponents will be displayed with whatever orientation you have defined for them in the ALIGN attribute. In this case, we will lay the subcomponents out left-justified within this interface.

There is an additional tag called *orient* that specifies vertical or horizontal orientation. This means that any child elements of the tag specifying the orientation will be displayed in accordance to the *orient* tag.

Our next attribute will be the XMLNS:HTML attribute. XMLNS is an acronym for XML Name Space. This unique identifier enables you to separate differing document types. We also will be using HTML tags along with XUL tags. This allows the XUL parser in Netscape Navigator to properly reference the document type for a certain tag. It is especially useful should XUL incorporate an element with the same name as an HTML tag. For instance, both HTML and XUL documents have a <title> element. By predefining these elements using XML namespaces, this element allows the browser to choose the correct parser for the specified document type. One thing to note is that the HTML namespace in XUL may be deprecated in the future.

Therefore, in our XMLNS:HTML namespace tag, we reference the World Wide Web Consortium's (W3C) specification recommendation for the HyperText Markup Language (HTML). All HTML tags that we use in our document will derive their behaviors from the namespace specification. The namespace tag, when envisioned, was meant to be a means by which the parser could validate that document type's structure, similar to a DTD. Most XML parsers, including Netscape's XUL parser, reference only the namespace tag as an internal namespace and do not actually load the URI specified in the attribute's value. This seems to be a widespread problem in most XML parsers and not specific to Netscape.

Our third attribute will be the XML namespace for XUL. At the current time, the DTD is a work in progress and will not be recognized outside of the Netscape Navigator browser. The information currently held there is just a dummy value and is only there for the well-formed and valid rules of XML.

We now have our base window component into which we will lay out our subcomponents.

Adding Subcomponents

In Figure 4.2 you can see the box that reads "Business Asset Manager Ver 1.0." This component is a *titledbox*. Code Listing 4.1 demonstrates the <titlebox> element.

The titledbox in this example has the ability to flex up to 100 percent of the <window> tag using the flex="1" attribute. This means that it will take 100 percent of the parent element no matter what the size of the parent element may be. This attribute's value is only a ratio between sibling components. This is relative positioning and in our opinion is better UI design.

```
<titledbox flex="1">
    <label value="Business Asset Manager Ver 1.0">

</titledbox>
```

Code Listing 4.1 The titledbox.

Figure 4.2 The titledbox.

> **ABSOLUTE VERSUS RELATIVE UI POSITIONING**
>
> **Two schools of thought about user interface design persist. One school uses absolute positioning, whereby a UI designer specifies where everything is laid out with absolute pixel positioning. For example, a window's dialog box is displayed only from the current position of 100,200 and is only 200 pixels high by 200 pixels wide. Absolute positioning can be tricky because if you do not know your user's screen size, your application may run off the screen. Relative positioning, on the other hand, does not assume that the application has knowledge of a user's screen size.**

Furthermore, we would like give this box a title, so we enclose "Business Asset Manager Ver1.0" in a <label> tag. Whatever text we insert in this tag will then be displayed as if it was embedded into the line of the titledbox. We give it the title *Business Asset Manager Ver 1.0*. Because this is an XML document, we must properly format this tag.

Adding the Tabpanel

Now we can add a tabbed panel to separate the views of our application. Please refer to Figure 4.3, which shows what our layout will look like. Our views were the Assets, Asset View, Reports, and Credits. The tabbed panel consists of many different child elements that modify the control and structure. These elements are further explained in the following sections.

The <tabbox>

To start building our tabpanel, we must first add a <tabbox> element. Please reference the <tabbox> element in Code Listing 4.2. The <tabcontrol> element is simply the top-level container for our tabbed pages. Insert the following code between the <titledbox> and </titledbox> tags. Doing this properly nests these elements as subcomponents of our titledbox, which has two children elements called <tabs> and <tabpanel>. These

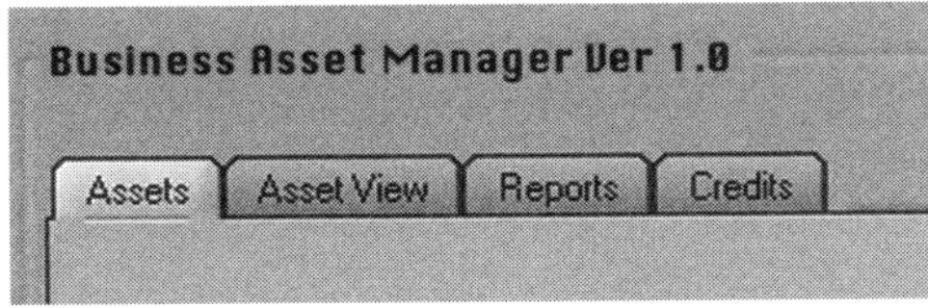

Figure 4.3 The tabbed panel with tabs.

children elements must be included, or your XUL interface might display incorrectly. The order in which the subcomponent elements are laid out is also important. You must first perform the layout of the tabs, which contains the corresponding <tab> elements. Then lay out the tabpanel. The tabpanel will contain an ordered set of elements. This order must reflect the same number of tabs as <tabbox> subcomponents. This means that if you have four tabs, you must have four elements in your tabpanel. These elements can be a box, titledbox, or any other XUL element, but they must always have the same amount of corresponding tabs. We can't tell you how many times we have seen our XUL interface crash the browser because we didn't have the proper amount of corresponding tabs and elements. So XUL hackers beware.

The <tabbox> and <tabs>

Our tabbox is a container for our tabs. These tabs include the Assets, Asset View, Reports, and Credits tab. Please reference the <tabbox> element in Figure 4.4. The <tabbox> has a default left-justification alignment. This means that the <tabs> and <tab> subcomponents will actually layout left justified. Notice that we assign an element id to our second tab. Assigning your element a unique id gives you more control when using the Document Object Model. We will demonstrate this later in "Adding Event Handlers with JavaScript."

We also add a value of 1 to the flex attribute. We do this so it will take up 100 percent of the parent element. Flex is an attribute passed down from XULElement, the root element of all XUL documents. Values for the <flex> element are only ratios. This means that if two elements lying side by side were displayed in an XUL document—the first element with a flex value of 1, and the second element with a flex value of 2—the second element would grow at ratio twice the size of the first element. This flex attribute has its advantages when laying out elements upon a XUL interface because one may specify relative layout and not absolute positioning. This allows the elements within your interface to grow or shrink dependent upon the parent element's size. In our opinion, Netscape Navigator has given us adverse reactions to displaying the flex attribute properly.

```
<tabbox>
   <tabs align="left">
      <tab id="assetListTab" selected="true" label="Assets"/>
      <tab id="assetViewTab" label="Asset View"/>
      <tab id="assetReptTab" label="Reports"/>
      <tab id="assetCrdtTab" label="Credits"/>
      <spring flex="1"/>
   </tabs>
</tabbox>
```

Code Listing 4.2 Setting up tabs.

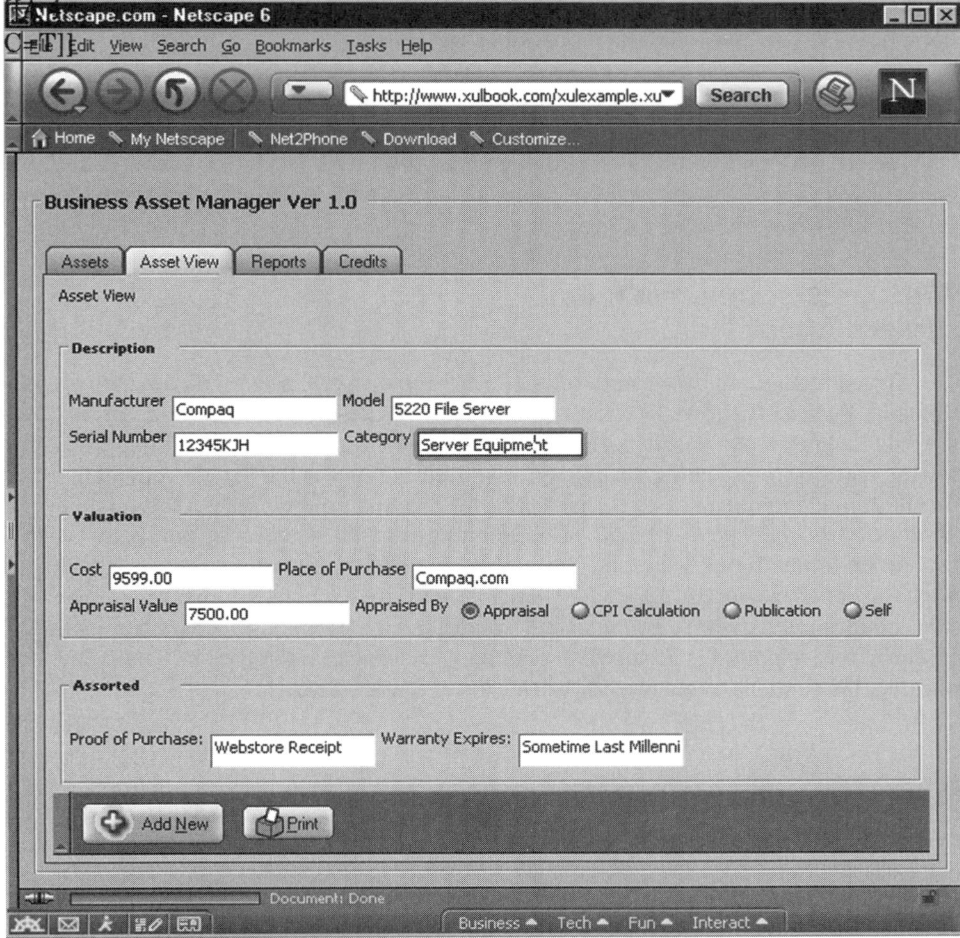

Figure 4.4 The asset view panel.

The <spring>

The spring was introduced to put spacing into a window. The <spring> element has only one attribute, the flex attribute. In our example, we add a spring because it allows us to fill the space between the end of the tabs and the end of the <tabbox> to 100 percent of the parent container's size.

The <tabpanel>

The <tabpanel> element is the next element in our interface (see Code Listing 4.3). The <tabpanel> element should have four elements to reflect the four tabs (Assets, Asset View, Reports, and Credits) that we set up in our <tabs> element.

What is displayed is a tabbed panel group nested within a titledbox. This titledbox is then nested in the root element <window>.

These elements set up our framework for which we will layout our user interface components. Next, we will layout our Asset List Panel.

Building the Asset List Panel

Our Asset List Panel consists of two elements, the <tree> and <toolbar>. The <tree> element is a versatile component as you may lay out data in a tabular way, similar to an HTML table but with major differences.

The <tree>, <treeitem>, and <treechildren>

The <tree> element allows you to take information and give related data a defined relationship. Figure 4.1 shows an asset list tree. These assets belong to some location. Each asset is a child of the parent location; therefore, we reflect this in the code in the following way. In Code Listing 4.4, notice how a <treeitem> is the top level container and its children elements are a <treerow> element (see the bold type)? On the same level is another <treechildren> element. This element allows us to nest our actual assets tabbed underneath our location. These elements can be hidden from view by clicking what is called a *twisty* (a small triangle) next to each location. This causes the <treechildren> element to collapse underneath the location, obscuring it from view.

The <tree> element is great when dealing with large tabulated lists. Netscape incorporates this element frequently in the Edit/Preferences dialog box.

```
<tabpanel autostretch="always" flex="1" >

      <!-- tab 1 -->
      <box align="left" flex="1">
         <label value="Asset List Panel">

      </box>
      <!-- tab2 -->
      <box align="left" flex="1">
         <label value="Asset View">

      </box>
      <!-- tab3 -->
      <titledbox align="horizontal" flex="1">
         <label value="Asset Reports">

      </titledbox>

      <!-- tab4 -->
      <titledbox align="vertical" flex="1">
         <label value="Credits View">
      </titledbox>
</tabpanel>
```

Code Listing 4.3 Setting up a tabpanel.

```
<tree id="assetList" flex="1" height="1" width="1">

   <treecolgroup>

      <treecol flex="1" />
      <treecol flex="1" />
      <treecol flex="1" />
   </treecolgroup>

   <treehead style="background-color: #FFFFCC; border: 1px solid
     black">
      <treerow>
         <treecell label="Asset"/>
         <treecell label="Manufacturer"/>
         <treecell label="Value"/>
      </treerow>
   </treehead>

   <treechildren flex="1" >
      <treeitem container="true" open="true">
         <treerow>
            <treecell class="treecell-indent" label="Office 1"/>
         </treerow>

         <treechildren>
           <treeitem>
              <treerow>
                 <treecell class="treecell-indent" label="File
                   Server"/>
                 <treecell label="Compaq"/>
                 <treecell label="7500.00"/>
              </treerow>
           </treeitem>
         </treechildren>
      </treeitem>

      <treeitem container="true" open="true">
         <treerow>
            <treecell class="treecell-indent" label="Warehouse"/>
         </treerow>

         <treechildren>
            <treeitem>
               <treerow>
                  <treecell class="treecell-indent" label="Server
                    Rack"/>
                  <treecell label="BBN Com"/>
```

continues

Code Listing 4.4 Building the asset list tree.

```
                <treecell label="3775.00"/>
            </treerow>
        </treeitem>
    </treechildren>
</treeitem>

<treeitem container="true" open="true">
    <treerow>
        <treecell class="treecell-indent" label="San Jose
          Office"/>
    </treerow>

    <treechildren>
        <treeitem>
            <treerow>
                <treecell class="treecell-indent" label="Color
                  LaserJet"/>
                <treecell label="HP"/>
                <treecell label="2300.00"/>
            </treerow>
        </treeitem>
    </treechildren>
</treeitem>
</treechildren>
</tree>
```

Code Listing 4.4 Building the asset list tree (Continued).

Building a Toolbar

Now let's build a toolbar to add a row of buttons, such as a print, add new item, view item, and a delete item button, to perform some nifty little functions for us. We must insert our <toolbox> container; see Code Listing 4.5.

The <toolbox> and <toolbar>

Within our <toolbox> element, we will layout a <toolbar>. The <toolbar> is the parent container for the buttons we will add. <toolbar> also has an align attribute, in which we place a value of *horizontal*. This value forces the buttons to be laid out horizontally.

The <button>

We want to add four buttons to the <toolbar> element. The element <button> has quite a few attributes but generally needs only two or three attributes to actually work. Those of you familiar with the HTML input type of button should have no problem recognizing the commonality between the HTML button and a XUL button. As we build the View button, we assign it an *ID*. This attribute, as a good coding habit, should always be pre-

```
<toolbox align="horizontal">
   <toolbar align="horizontal">
      <button id="view-button" align="right" imgalign="center"
        src="view.gif" class="dialog" value="View"
        oncommand="viewItem()" accesskey="v"/>
      <button id="new-button" align="right" imgalign="center"
         src="addnew.gif" class="dialog" value="Add New" accesskey="n"
         oncommand="newItem()"/>
      <button id="delete-button" align="right" imgalign="center"
         src="delete.gif" class="dialog" value="Delete" accesskey="d"
         oncommand="deleteItem()"/>
      <button id="print1-button" align="right" imgalign="center"
         src="print.gif" class="dialog" value="Print" accesskey="p"
         oncommand="printButton()"/>
   </toolbar>
</toolbox>
```

Code Listing 4.5 Toolbars, toolboxes, and buttons.

sent. It is the unique identifier of that certain element within your document. By doing so, it allows JavaScript under the Document Object Model (DOM), to control the behavior of user interface components within our XUL document. It's also a good coding habit in the XML world.

Our next attribute is the *align* attribute, which we assign it with a value of right. This aligns the text within the button to the *right of the embedded image*. Because we are adding an image to our button, we add an *imgalign* attribute with a value of center. That's right. We can now add images within our buttons! The *imgalign* attribute allows us to force the alignment of the image to be laid out in the center of the button. Our next attribute is the *src* attribute. The value for the *src* attribute is the actual relative or absolute URI of the image we will place on our button.

Next we want to define the *class* attribute. Our button is derived from the dialog button class. Now we add a value to this button by changing the value of the *value* attribute. The value is the actual text of the button.

Those of you who program event handler actions on your Web pages via an *onclick* method or attribute should be aware that this method might go the way of the Dodo. This is because buttons may be invoked by actions other than a mouse click, such as a key press. The solution to this is the *oncommand* method.

One of the actions that could invoke a button could be a keystroke. This is another attribute for our button, the *accesskey* attribute. Whatever key we assign to the button should be a letter that is contained within the value of the button, for example, v for View. Otherwise, the key will not be recognized by your user. This button can now be invoked using the <ALT> and <V> key pressed at the same time. We will discuss the ability to bind our keys and the ability to redefine them in Chapter 10, "Building an E-Commerce Site." If we place an onclick method to handle the event, the only event the event listener will pick up is a mouse click event for that element. This is why the oncommand method is better, and the onclick method will more than likely be deprecated in the future.

Building the Asset View Panel

This asset view will have new elements that we haven't used yet. These include the <label>, <textbox>, <menu>, and <radiogroup> elements. In Code Listing 4.6, we nested these elements in between the <tabpanel> and </tabpanel> elements after the `<!-- tab2 -->` comment line. Figure 4.4 shows the Asset View Panel display.

```
<!-- tab2 -->
   <tabpanel>
      <titledbox id="assetView" align="left" flex="1"
        orient="vertical">
         <label value="Asset View"/>

         <!-- descriptionBox -->
            <titledbox align="left" flex="1" >
               <label value="Description"/>
               <box flex="1" align="left">
                  <box flex="1">
                     <label value="Manufacturer"/>

                     <textbox id="manufacturer" value="Compaq"/>
                     <label value="Model"/>
                     <textbox id="model" value="5220 File Server"/>
                  </box>

                  <box flex="1">
                     <label value="Serial Number"/>
                     <textbox id="serialNumber" value="12345KJH"/>
                     <label value="Category"/>

                     <box style="background: #FFFFCC;font-color:
                       #000000;font-weight: bold">
                        <menu id="selectedEquipment" label="Type
                          Equipment" style="background:
                          #FFFFCC;font-color: #000000;font-weight:
                          bold">
                           <menupopup>
                              <menuitem label="Server Equipment"
                                oncommand="selectItem('Server
                                Equipment')"/>
                              <menuitem label="Storage"
                                oncommand="selectItem('Storage')"/>

                              <menuitem label="Client Equipment"
                                oncommand="selectItem('Client
                                Equipment')"/>
                              <menuitem label="Networking"

                              oncommand="selectItem('Networking')"/>
```

Code Listing 4.6 Asset view panel code.

```
                        </menupopup>
                    </menu>
                </box>
            </box>
        </box>
    </titledbox>
</tabpanel>
```

Code Listing 4.6 Asset view panel code (Continued).

To build our asset view, we want to logically break the data up into three divergent views. Data such as manufacturer, model, serial number, and category should be organized into a box called Description. Data such as the cost, place of purchase, appraisal value, and appraised by should be organized into a Valuation box. Finally, our other miscellaneous data can be lumped together in our Assorted box.

In our Description box, we introduce the <label>, <textbox>, <menu>, <menupopup>, and <menuitem> elements. The description box contains the general descriptive elements of our asset such as its manufacturer, model, serial number, and category. The manufacturer, model, and serial number we have determined to be simple text values. We will represent these with <textbox> elements.

The <label> and <textbox>

Notice in Figure 4.4 that we want to display the word “Manufacturer” and then put a text field next to it. To do this, we use the element <label> with an attribute called *value* with a value of “Manufacturer”:

```
<label value="Manufacturer"/>
<textbox id="manufacturer" value="Compaq"/>
```

We won’t forget to close out the tag by putting a / character before the greater-than sign. Then to create our text field, we use the <textbox> element. This has the attribute called id, its unique namespace identifier, and the attribute called value. We would use the *id* attribute in very much the same way as we use the *name* attribute for an input type in an HTML form. We assign our *value* attribute the value of “Compaq.” Id is an XML attribute.

The <menu>

Our next data element would be our category. Because we need to have a list of predefined categories, this would be a perfect example of using a popup menu to select the category we want. First, we must define a container for the elements. The <menu> is that container.

The <menupopup> and <menuitem>

Because we want our menu to be a popup menu, we add the <menupopup> element as the subcontainer. In that, we add our <menuitem> elements:

```
<menu id="selectedEquipment" label="Type Equipment"
style="background: #FFFFCC;font-color: #000000;font-weight: bold">
   <menupopup>
      <menuitem label="Server Equipment"
         oncommand="selectItem('Server Equipment')"/>
      <menuitem label="Storage" oncommand="selectItem('Storage')"/>
      <menuitem label="Client Equipment"
         oncommand="selectItem('Client Equipment')"/>
      <menuitem label="Networking"
         oncommand="selectItem('Networking')"/>
   </menupopup>
</menu>
```

We close the element tags and start designing our next box.

In our Valuation box, we introduce the <radiogroup> and <radio> elements. Of course we have also some <label> and <textbox> elements before that. For the sake of simplicity, we didn't think that presenting these elements over again would keep you interested, so we venture forth.

The <radiogroup> and <radio>

To present a radio group, we have only one parent container called <radiogroup>. We then nest our <radio> elements under <radiogroup>. By default, these <radio> elements will not need a name as in the previous <menuitem> example. They are automatically grouped via the <radiogroup> parent element. You should however use an id attribute within the <radiogroup> element to group them according to the DOM. By default, <radiogroup> elements will automatically assume the orientation of the <radiogroup>'s parent's *orient* attribute. In our example, they will assume the orientation of the <radiogroup> parent, <box>. This just happens to be horizontal. The following code demonstrates the <radiogroup> and <radio> elements:

```
<radiogroup id="appraisal">
   <radio checked="true" value="Appraisal"/>
```

In our Assorted box is assorted data that we put in here for the sake of looking cool to the rest of our readers. Don't we want to present a complete solution? If we did that, we might have to start commenting code. Good-bye job security!

Again, we add another toolbox. This time we take out two of the buttons, because they would not be needed in this view. We leave our Add New Item and Print Buttons.

Building the Reports Panel

A simpler panel (see Figure 4.5) than our previous panels, the reports panel allows us to insert inline frames into our user interface components with the use of the iframe tag This element may be deprecated in the future with the implementation of a new <page> element. We insert the following code in between our <tabpanel> and </tabpanel> elements after the `<!-- tab3 -->` comment line:

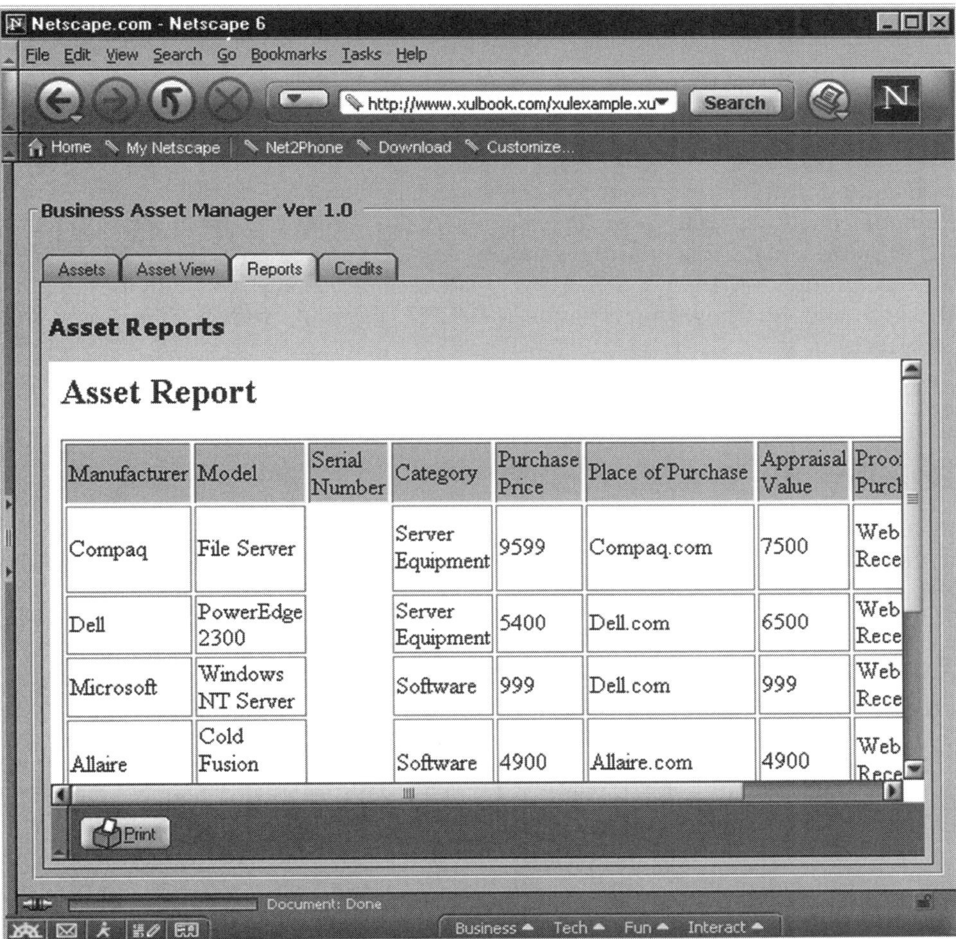

Figure 4.5 The Reports panel.

```
<!-- tab3 -->
<tabpanel>
     <box id="assetReportView" align="left" flex="80%">
                    <label>Asset Reports</label>
               <iframe id="web-frame1"
                 src="http://www.xulbook.com/assets.cfm?view=ID"
                 flex="1"/>
            <toolbox align="left">
                    <toolbar flex="2" align="left">
                      <button id="print1-button" align="right"
                        imgalign="center" src="print.gif"
                        class="dialog" label="Print" accesskey="p"
                        oncommand="printButton()"/>
                    </toolbar>
            </toolbox>
```

```
    </box>
</tabpanel>
```

The noticeable thing that we do differently here is that we add an <iframe> element. We give this element a *flex* attribute so that it stretches to the full width and height of the parent container.

In our iframe element, our *src* attribute has an absolute URI of http://www.xulbook.com/assets.cfm?view=ID. This is actually a Cold Fusion Markup Language (CFML) Web page that we are running on the xulbook.com Web site. It pulls all the information from a SQL Server database. This page was simply designed to show how one might incorporate their XUL interface with their existing Web architecture.

Again, we build another toolbar at the bottom. This time we need only a Print button.

Building the Credits Panel

Finally, we get to the Credits panel (see Figure 4.6), which are three boxes with the authors' names. Again, we create another toolbar exactly like the one we built for our Reports Panel.

Adding Event Handlers with JavaScript

The user interface is nice, but how does it interact with the user? To answer that, we must incorporate JavaScript. If you're not familiar with JavaScript, here is a quick and dirty tutorial for you.

JavaScript is also a Netscape-created technology. It is both a server-side and client-side platform-independent scripting language. It is already used within the confines of HTML. It is used extensively within the Web development industry to do great things such as create dynamic page content, perform those nifty little roll-over button effects, and more extensively, for form validation.

JavaScript is easy to learn. A downside to programming in this language is the fact that it doesn't support strong data typing. That means when you assign a value to a variable, it can be a Boolean, integer, string, or null value.

As a user, you might have seen JavaScript in action on various Web sites like Yahoo.com or Successtrade.com when you filled out a form and got an alert dialog like the one shown in Figure 4.7. This script would be embedded into the HTML file and called when an HTML-driven event has occurred within the browser, such as a form submission or an input validation. Code Listing 4.7 shows how a JavaScript script could have generated the alert in Figure 4.7.

In our XUL document, we load the JavaScript file eventhandlers.js through the following command. We insert it after the window element has been defined. By doing this, we associate the <window> root element to the functions contained within the JavaScript file.

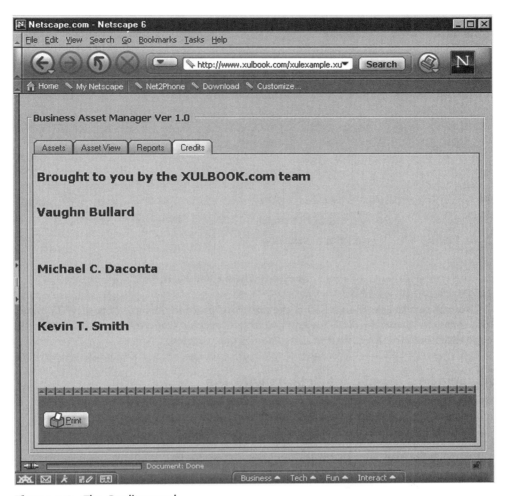

Figure 4.6 The Credits panel.

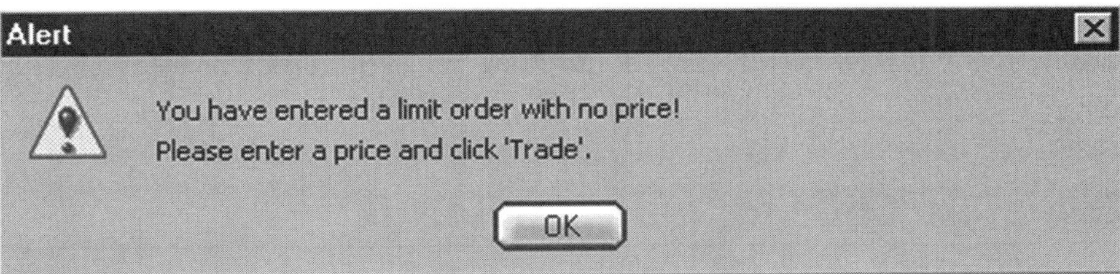

Figure 4.7 A JavaScript alert dialog.

```
<script language="JavaScript">
function notifyUser(form)
{
     if(form.orderType.value == "Limit")
     {
          if(form.price.value == null)
               alert("You have entered a limit order with no
               price!\n\nPlease enter a price and click 'Trade'.");
   else
               form.submit();
     }
}
</script>
```

Code Listing 4.7 A JavaScript alert dialog.

```
< script language="javascript" src="eventhandlers.js"/>
```

Loading this file through a URI is the preferred method because of reserved characters that may cause the XUL file to not parse correctly. One could put the JavaScript code directly in the XUL file, but it is *strongly* discouraged.

Associating JavaScript Actions with the Buttons

When we added our toolbar buttons to the bottom of our tabbed panels we associated a JavaScript action with each of the oncommand attributes. In this section, we show you easy examples of JavaScript. The idea is not to confuse you but to give you the idea of how powerful this language really is. Please note that in HTML, you would call a command with *onCommand* attribute. XUL is case-sensitive so you would have to declare a command with the *oncommand* attribute. Note the difference in capitalization. There were many times, that we declared onCommand out of habit. You may need to break yourself of that habit if you are an avid HTML programmer.

We associated our Print button with the JavaScript function printButton(). The print button when invoked, via a key command or button click, calls the JavaScript function printButton(). It then tells the browser to bring up a Print dialog box. Pressing OK causes the browser to print out the page in the current window.

Complete Code for xulexample.xul

The Code Listing 4.8 represents the entirety of our simple XUL interface. Reference this when building a user interface. You may view this application at http://www.xulbook.com/xulexample2.xul.

```
<?xml version="1.0"?>
<?xml-stylesheet href="chrome://navigator/skin/" type="text/css"?>

<window align="left"
  xmlns:html="http://www.w3.org/TR/REC-html40"

xmlns="http://www.mozilla.org/keymaster/gatekeeper/there.is.only.xul"

  class="dialog" flex="1">
  <script language="javascript" src="eventhandlers.js"/>
  <titledbox flex="1" align="left">
     <label value="Business Asset Manager Ver 1.0"/>
    <tabbox>

      <tabs align="left">
        <tab id="assetListTab" selected="true" label="Assets"/>
        <tab id="assetViewTab" label="Asset View"/>
        <tab id="assetReptTab" label="Reports"/>
        <tab id="assetCrdtTab" label="Credits"/>
        <spring flex="1"/>
      </tabs>

      <tabpanels>
        <tabpanel autostretch="always" flex="1">

           <!-- tab 1 -->
           <box id="assetListView" align="left" flex="1" >

          <titledbox align="left" flex="1" >
              <label value="Asset List"/>
             <box align="left" flex="80%">
              <tree id="assetList" flex="1" height="1" width="1">

                   <treecolgroup>
                      <treecol flex="1" />
                      <treecol flex="1" />
                      <treecol flex="1" />
                   </treecolgroup>

                   <treehead style="background-color: #FFFFCC;
                     border: 1px solid black">
                        <treerow>
                           <treecell label="Asset"/>
                           <treecell label="Manufacturer"/>
                           <treecell label="Value"/>
                        </treerow>
                   </treehead>
```

continues

Code Listing 4.8 A simple XUL interface.

```
        <treechildren flex="1" >
          <treeitem container="true" open="true">
            <treerow>
              <treecell class="treecell-indent"
                label="Office 1"/>
            </treerow>
            <treechildren>
              <treeitem>
                <treerow>
                   <treecell class="treecell-indent"
                     label="File Server"/>
                   <treecell label="Compaq"/>
                    <treecell label="7500.00"/>
                </treerow>
               </treeitem>
            </treechildren>
        </treeitem>

          <treeitem container="true" open="true">
            <treerow>
              <treecell class="treecell-indent"
                label="Warehouse"/>
            </treerow>
            <treechildren>
              <treeitem>
                  <treerow>
                     <treecell class="treecell-indent"
                       label="Server Rack"/>
                     <treecell label="BBN Com"/>
                     <treecell label="3775.00"/>
                  </treerow>
              </treeitem>
            </treechildren>
        </treeitem>

          <treeitem container="true" open="true">
            <treerow>
              <treecell class="treecell-indent"
                label="San Jose Office"/>
            </treerow>
            <treechildren>
              <treeitem>
                  <treerow>
                     <treecell class="treecell-indent"
                       label="Color LaserJet"/>
                     <treecell label="HP"/>
                     <treecell label="2300.00"/>
```

Code Listing 4.8 A simple XUL interface (Continued).

```
                    </treerow>
                  </treeitem>
                </treechildren>
              </treeitem>
            </treechildren>

          </tree>

        </box>
         <box align="left" flex="5%">
        <toolbox flex="20%" align="left">
          <toolbar flex="20%" align="left">
            <button id="view-button" align="right"
              imgalign="center"
              src="view.gif" class="dialog" label="View"
              oncommand="viewItem()" accesskey="v"/>
            <button id="new-button" align="right"
              imgalign="center"
              src="addnew.gif" class="dialog" label="Add New"
              accesskey="n" oncommand="newItem()"/>
            <button id="delete-button" align="right"
              imgalign="center" src="delete.gif" class="dialog"
              label="Delete" accesskey="d"
              oncommand="deleteItem()"/>
            <button id="print1-button" align="right"
              imgalign="center" src="print.gif" class="dialog"
              label="Print" accesskey="p"
              oncommand="printButton()"/>
          </toolbar>
        </toolbox>


        </box>
      </titledbox>
    </box>
  </tabpanel>

  <!-- tab2 -->
  <tabpanel>
    <titledbox id="assetView" align="left" flex="1"
      orient="vertical">
      <label value="Asset View"/>
      <!-- descriptionBox -->
      <titledbox align="left" flex="1" >
          <label value="Description"/>
```

continues

Code Listing 4.8 A simple XUL interface (Continued).

```
        <box flex="1" align="left">
          <box flex="1">
            <label value="Manufacturer"/>
            <textbox id="manufacturer" value="Compaq"/>
            <label value="Model"/>
            <textbox id="model" value="5220 File Server"/>
          </box>
          <box flex="1">
            <label value="Serial Number"/>
            <textbox id="serialNumber" value="12345KJH"/>
            <label value="Category"/>
            <box style="background: #FFFFCC;font-color: #000000;
              font-weight: bold">
            <menu id="selectedEquipment" label="Type Equipment"
              style="background: #FFFFCC;font-color: #000000;
              font-weight: bold">
              <menupopup>
                <menuitem label="Server Equipment"
                  oncommand="selectItem('Server Equipment')"/>
                <menuitem label="Storage"
                  oncommand="selectItem('Storage')"/>
                <menuitem label="Client Equipment"
                  oncommand="selectItem('Client Equipment')"/>
                <menuitem label="Networking"
                  oncommand="selectItem('Networking')"/>
              </menupopup>
            </menu>
            </box>
          </box>
        </box>

      </titledbox>

      <!-- valuationBox -->
      <titledbox align="left" flex="1" >
        <label value="Valuation"/>
        <box flex="1" align="left">
          <box flex="1" align="left">
            <label value="Cost"/>
            <textbox id="assetCost" value="9599.00"/>
            <label value="Place of Purchase"/>
            <textbox id="purchasePlace" value="Compaq.com"/>
          </box>
          <box flex="1" align="left">
            <label value="Appraisal Value"/>
            <textbox id="appraisalValue" value="7500.00"/>
            <label value="Appraised By"/>
            <radiogroup>
```

Code Listing 4.8 A simple XUL interface (Continued).

```
              <radio id="appraisal" checked="true"
                label="Appraisal"/>
              <radio id="cpiCalculation" checked="false"
                label="CPI Calculation"/>
              <radio id="publication" check="false"
                label="Publication"/>
              <radio id="self" check="false" label="Self"/>
            </radiogroup>
          </box>

        </box>
      </titledbox>

      <!-- assortedBox -->
      <titledbox align="left" flex="80%" >
        <label value="Assorted"/>

        <box flex="1" align="horizontal">
          <label value="Proof of Purchase:"/>
          <textbox id="purchaseProof" value="Webstore Receipt"/>
          <label value="Warranty Expires:"/>
          <textbox id="warrantyExpiration"
            value="Sometime Last Millennium"/>
        </box>
      </titledbox>

          <toolbox flex="20%" align="left">
          <toolbar flex="20%" align="left">
            <button id="new-button" align="right"
              imgalign="center"
              src="addnew.gif" class="dialog" label="Add New"
              accesskey="n" oncommand="newItem()"/>
            <button id="print1-button" align="right"
              imgalign="center" src="print.gif" class="dialog"
              label="Print" accesskey="p"
              oncommand="printButton()"/>
          </toolbar>
          </toolbox>
    </titledbox>
  </tabpanel>

  <!-- tab3 -->
  <tabpanel>
    <box id="assetReportView" align="left" flex="80%">
          <label>Asset Reports</label>
              <iframe id="web-frame1"
```

continues

Code Listing 4.8 A simple XUL interface (Continued).

```
                src="http://www.xulbook.com/assets.cfm?view=ID"
                flex="1"/>
            <toolbox align="left">
              <toolbar flex="20%" align="left">
                <button id="print1-button" align="right"
                  imgalign="center" src="print.gif" class="dialog"
                  label="Print" accesskey="p"
                  oncommand="printButton()"/>
              </toolbar>
            </toolbox>

        </box>
      </tabpanel>

      <!-- tab4 -->
      <tabpanel>
        <titledbox id="creditsView" align="left" flex="1">
              <label value="Brought to you by the XULBOOK.com team"/>
            <titledbox flex="20%" align="center">
            <label value="Vaughn Bullard"/>
            <label value="Bullard AQH Inc., http://www.bullardaq.com"/>
            </titledbox>
            <titledbox flex="20%" align="center">
            <label value="Kevin T. Smith"/>
            <label value="Rebuilding the Truman,
               http://www.geocities.com/trumantruck/"/>
            </titledbox>
            <titledbox flex="20%" align="center">
            <label value="Michael C. Daconta"/>
            <label value="McDonald Bradley, http://www.mcbrad.com"/>
            </titledbox>
            <toolbox align="left">
              <toolbar flex="20%" align="left">
                <button id="print1-button" align="right"
                   imgalign="center" src="print.gif" class="dialog"
                   label="Print" accesskey="p"
                   oncommand="printButton()"/>
              </toolbar>
            </toolbox>
        </titledbox>

      </tabpanel>
    </tabpanels>

    </tabbox>
  </titledbox>
</window>
```

Code Listing 4.8 A simple XUL interface (Continued).

Complete Code for eventhandlers.js

The Code Listing 4.9 is for the JavaScript event handlers for our simple XUL inter- face. If you would like to download this code, you may do that at http://www.xulbook.com/eventhandlers.js.

```
function printButton()
{
     this.window.print();
}
function selectItem(selectedEquip)
{

document.getElementById('selectedEquipment').setAttribute('label',
selectedEquip);
}
function newItem()
{
     alert("Add New Item");
}
function noItems()
{
     alert("You have no items selected.");
}
function deleteItem()
{
     if(confirm('Would you like to delete this item?'))
     {
          var tree     = document.getElementById('assetList');

          var items     = tree.selectedItems;
          if(items.length==0)
          {
               noItems();
          }else
           {

alert(items[0].firstChild.firstChild.getAttribute('label'));

items[0].firstChild.firstChild.setAttribute('label','');

items[0].firstChild.firstChild.nextSibling.setAttribute('label','');
               items[0].firstChild.lastChild.setAttribute('label','');
           }
     }
```

continues

Code Listing 4.9 JavaScript event handlers.

```
}
function viewItem()
{
  var tree=document.getElementById('assetList');

  var items=tree.selectedItems;
  if (items.length==0) alert("No items are selected.");
  else {
    txt="You have selected:\n\n";
    for (t=0;t<items.length;t++){
      txt+=items[t].firstChild.firstChild.getAttribute('label')+'\n';
    }
    alert(txt);
  }
}
```

Code Listing 4.9 JavaScript event handlers (Continued).

Summary

In this chapter, you have learned how to build an application using XUL. Not only was it easy to build this user interface, but you created a user interface that is viewable both cross-platform and cross device. How many user interface languages can sing that mantra? Only one can prove it—XUL.

You also learned how to incorporate JavaScript into your XUL interface to provide some form of user interaction. This chapter was just a brief introduction to the most common XUL elements. The next chapter, "Creating Netscape Themes," teaches you how to create Netscape themes with XUL and CSS. The succeeding chapters will discuss the more advanced features of XUL.

CHAPTER 5

Creating Netscape Themes

The very essence of the creative is its novelty, and hence we have no standard by which to judge it.

Carl R. Rogers, *On Becoming a Person*

Now that you've learned how to use XUL elements in a larger user interface, we will discuss the largest XUL interface, the Netscape browser. Huh? Yes, the entire browser is built using the XPCOM Toolkit. This is done through *Netscape Themes*, which are collections of skins that define the look and feel of each Netscape Navigator component.

The Netscape browser is a wonderfully done XUL interface. One way to get your hand in the cookie jar, so to speak, is to create your own theme. A theme is a collection of skins. Skins are individual implementations of interface elements using cascading style sheets, which you learned about in Chapter 3, "Using Cascading Style Sheets." Theme structures reflect the components of the Netscape Navigator Package, including AOL Instant Messenger, Communicator, Composer (Editor), Messenger, Navigator, and Global.

How are Themes used in Netscape? You can change the default theme by going to the ***Edit*** menu and then by selecting the ***Preferences*** menu item. Up will pop the Preferences dialog box. Under the Appearance twisty is the Themes tab. Select Themes and you will see a list of installed Themes. The default-installed Themes are Modern and Classic. You can download themes from several sites but the most notable is Netscape's Theme Park at http://home.netscape.com/themes. If you can't find a theme that suits you, you can create your own. Creating your own theme enables you full control over every little aspect of the browser.

In this chapter, you will learn how to create themes by first exploring the types of tools you can use to make and structure themes. We accomplish this by creating a theme and then stepping you through the process of creating a collection of skins.

Gathering Your Tools

You will need a few tools to create your theme. The first is a text editor. A text editor enables you to edit the cascading style sheets, which lay out the style for all the components, and the manifest.rdf file. The manifest.rdf file is a meta data file for the Theme. It describes to the Netscape browser the components that the Theme will cover. We tend to use WinEdit or TextPad, two very popular Windows editors. If you are working on a Mac, you might want to try BBEdit, a great text editing tool.

Second, you will need an image or paint program. What we used is a combination of Adobe ImageStyler and Adobe PhotoShop. We used ImageStyler for creating and manipulating icons, textures, and images. We used PhotoShop for the exact triangulation and exporting of transparent GIFs. We used these tools because PhotoShop is a companywide standard that we use. Any image and editing program with the ability to save as GIF or JPG will do fine.

Third, you will need an archival and extraction tool. Most of these on the Windows platform are based on the PKZip libraries. The best application on the windows platform we have found is WinZip. This tool is used for the packaging and extraction of files within a Theme. You can download this program from http://www.winzip.com. For a list of other archiving programs, please visit the http://www.xulbook.com Web site.

Last but not least, you will need a combination of creativity, ingenuity, and determination. Trying to imagine what looks good sometimes turns out to look like the inside of a goat's stomach! Jokes aside, careful planning coupled with successive rounds of experimenting probably will get you the Theme you want. With more than 800 files that can be edited, however, you will definitely need determination. We know because we have been there. It's not hard to create a Theme, but it can be tedious.

TIP **Make sure that you use good tools. We used a combination of Adobe GoLive, Adobe PhotoShop, and Adobe ImageStyler. Professional applications always help with the small details.**

Downloading a Template

Now that you have your tools successfully installed, it is time to download a template from which to base your Theme. You can download a template from Netscape called modern_template.jar or from this book's companion Web site at http://www.xulbook.com. From the Chapter 5 link, you will find a list of Themes that you can download for free.

If you download via an install, which is the easiest method you can find the file in the chrome directory of your user directory. If you download modern_template.jar, you should see it in the \Program Files\Netscape\Users50\yourprofile\ directory.

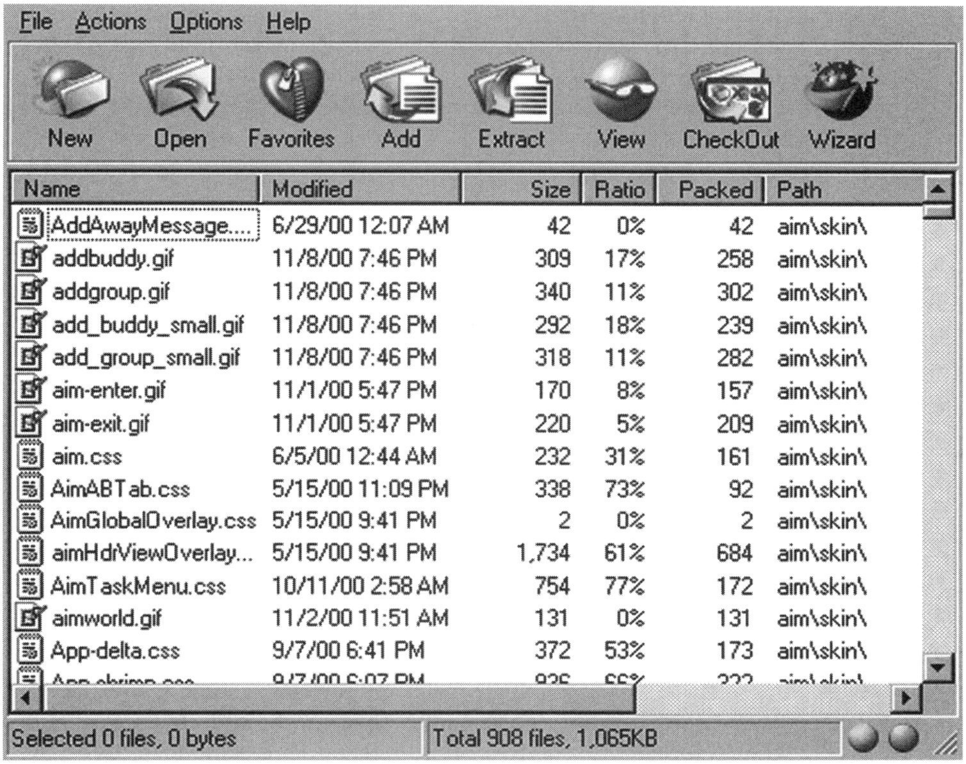

Figure 5.1 Netscape Theme structure.

Viewing the Structure of a Theme

After you have located your template, you will need to open it up in your Zip program. Here you will see a list of files. As demonstrated in Figure 5.1, these files are basically organized into five directories, each with a skin/ subdirectory with files that are used for each Netscape Navigator component:

- The aim/skin/ subdirectory holds the files for the AOL Instant Messenger (AIM) service built into the sidebar of Netscape Navigator. This subdirectory contains approximately 51 cascading style sheets describing the AIM interfaces. This skin/ subdirectory contains the most cascading style sheets. It also contains 124 images that are used throughout the AOL Instant Messenger. All of these files are congregated into one component package to create the AOL Instant Messenger user interface.
- The communicator/skin/ subdirectory holds the interface files for the Netscape Navigator browser. Twelve cascading style sheets describe the browser interface. Twenty-seven images are used to define and populate the user interface. An XML file, menuButtonBindings.xml, defines the binding, or

extended behavior, of the menuButton class. In addition, nine subdirectories reflect in structure the components of the Netscape Navigator browser. These components are bookmarks, directory, help, profile, reviewer, related, search, sidebar, and xpinstall. To modify these user interface elements, you can edit the cascading style sheets and images in each one of these directories. The communicator/ subdirectory has the largest number of subdirectories. Note that the communicator component refers to all of the Web browser components within the Netscape Navigator package.

- The editor/skin/ subdirectory holds the interface files for Composer, Netscape Navigator's Web page editing tool. Five cascading style sheets describe this interface. The editor/skin/ has a subdirectory called images/. These images are grouped in this subdirectory because of an inheritance issue. The images/ subdirectory has 134 images.
- The global/skin/ subdirectory contains the files for the top-level definition of Netscape Navigator components. As such, it contains the most files, 278 files, 22 cascading style sheets, and 256 images. All cascading style sheets within a Theme derive their attributes and behaviors from this directory. The global.css file within this subdirectory contains all the skin attributes for *all* packages within the entire Netscape Navigator package.
- The messenger/skin/ subdirectory holds the interface files for Messenger, Netscape Navigator's E-Mail component. This subdirectory is the second largest component in stature of all the Netscape Navigator components. Its subdirectory contains 124 files, 11 cascading style sheets, and 113 images. It also has two subdirectories called addressbook/ and messengercompose/. The addressbook/, appropriately named, is the skin directory for Messenger's address book component. Messengercompose/ is the skin directory for new mail window. This is invoked when Messenger is run and New Mail or New Post is clicked.
- The navigator/skin/ subdirectory contains the files necessary to skin just the browser window. This subdirectory contains only 25 files, 1 cascading style sheet, and 24 images. You can modify these files if you wanted to skin only the browser window.

For a more detailed reference on the structure of Netscape Navigator Themes, visit the companion Web site at http://www.xulbook.com or turn to Appendix B, which includes a detailed listing of all the cascading style sheets and images that are used.

Navigating the New Navigator

The new Netscape Navigator package offers a level of abstraction that affords the Web programmer extensibility and modularity. They do this by tying components together with English-like languages, such as XUL and Cascading Style Sheets. The benefits, such as event-driven interfaces, are great, but you should also approach with caution.

Managing the assembly of styles, Themes, widgets, and other components can be a massive undertaking. For example, let's take the Modern Mozillium Theme created by

Netscape. In this theme alone are 895 files that you can edit. Of these files, 112 are cascading style sheets; the rest are images. This is why changing or creating a Theme can be as difficult or as easy as you want to make it.

In Chapter 2, "An XML Primer," you learned to separate data by structure, content, and presentation. Netscape has taken a similar approach in developing Navigator. Three technologies form the core components of the Netscape user interface:

CSS. Impacts the look and feel of the user interface.

JavaScript. Guides the behavior between elements.

XUL. Defines the structure of the user interface.

Cascading style sheets were discussed extensively in Chapter 3, "Using Cascading Style Sheets." Cascading style sheets and Images, as a Theme, sit at the top level of user interface presentation.

XUL is used extensively throughout Navigator to affect the browser's look and feel. It is easier to change the look and feel through a few lines in a XUL text file than it is to modify the existing code, compile, and then test on multiple platforms. It simply reduces the time to market for your product.

JavaScript is a client- and server-side scripting language used mainly for form validation and interaction and to create dynamic pages. It is also used for animation effects used by many graphical sites. JavaScript, although similar sounding to Java, is structurally different. Java is a programming language where programs are compiled as byte code. JavaScript is a scripting language that is not compiled. Netscape enables you to use JavaScript by selecting it in the Preferences dialog box. You can use a JavaScript function to run through elements of the Document Object Model (DOM). This would allow you to get an individual element's attributes within that document. Code Listing 5.1 demonstrates how you would use JavaScript to do this.

The programmer may use different DOM calls to manipulate data within the structure of the document. In Code Listing 5.1, the changeTradeNumber( ) function gathers, through the DOM, the current value of the tradeRefNo document element. It then increments that value by one and assigns it to a JavaScript variable called tradeRefNo. The document element tradeRefNo is then reassigned the value of the JavaScript variable tradeRefNo.

Using JavaScript for interactivity between XUL elements, Web pages, and other browser functions is just natural. If you haven't already experienced programming in

```
function changeTradeNumber()
{
var tradeRefNo      =
document.getElementById("tradeRefNo").getAttribute("label");
tradeRefNo++;
document.getElementById("tradeRefNo").setAttribute("tradeRefNo",
tradeRefNo);
}
```

Code Listing 5.1 A JavaScript/DOM example.

JavaScript, check out Danny Goodman's book, *JavaScript Bible*, published by IDG books. JavaScript is such an integral part to how you may interact between your document and the browser.

Looking at Figure 5.2, you will see the modularity of the Netscape Navigator. This is at the highest level of abstraction. The application core is the foundation. On top of that sits the XUL/user interface structure. And, on top of the XUL/user interface structure sits the Themes and user interface presentation. XUL follows the XML mantra of separation of a data set's content from its structure and from its presentation.

Developing Your Netscape Theme

Netscape says that you have four ways to develop Themes: starting from scratch, migrating previous Themes (NS6PR2 to NS6), skinning a single component, and touching up a Theme. In our estimation, touching up a Theme and then modifying it to what you want it to look like will be the easiest to learn. We downloaded the Modern Mozillium Theme from the Netscape Web site. We did this because we didn't want to change the modern and classic Themes that we had already installed. It will be more professional looking if you incrementally build this Theme.

Download the Modern Mozillium Theme from the Netscape Theme Park home page. After downloading, locate your .jar file in your user's profile directory. In this directory, you will see a chrome subdirectory. In the chrome directory, you will see a list of .jar files including modern.jar, classic.jar, and the Theme we will modify, modern_mozillium.jar. A JAR file is a Java archive. See Chapter 9 for more information on Java archives. If you open the .jar file in an archive program, such as WinZip, you will see a hierarchical list of files, sorted by their skin affiliation. Figure 5.3 explains the correlation and inheritance model that comprises the Netscape Navigator browser.

Now, extract this archive to a directory that we will call XULisCool. Where you decide to place this directory is really of no consequence until we ZIP up the Theme when we are finished. We are simply extracting these files so that we may edit them to create our new Theme. In your XULisCool directory, you will see six subdirectories: aim, communicator, editor, global, messenger, and navigator. Underneath each one of

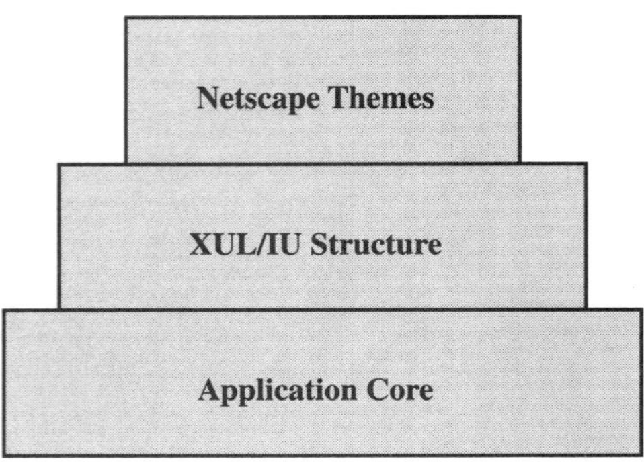

Figure 5.2 Netscape Navigator 6 component modularity.

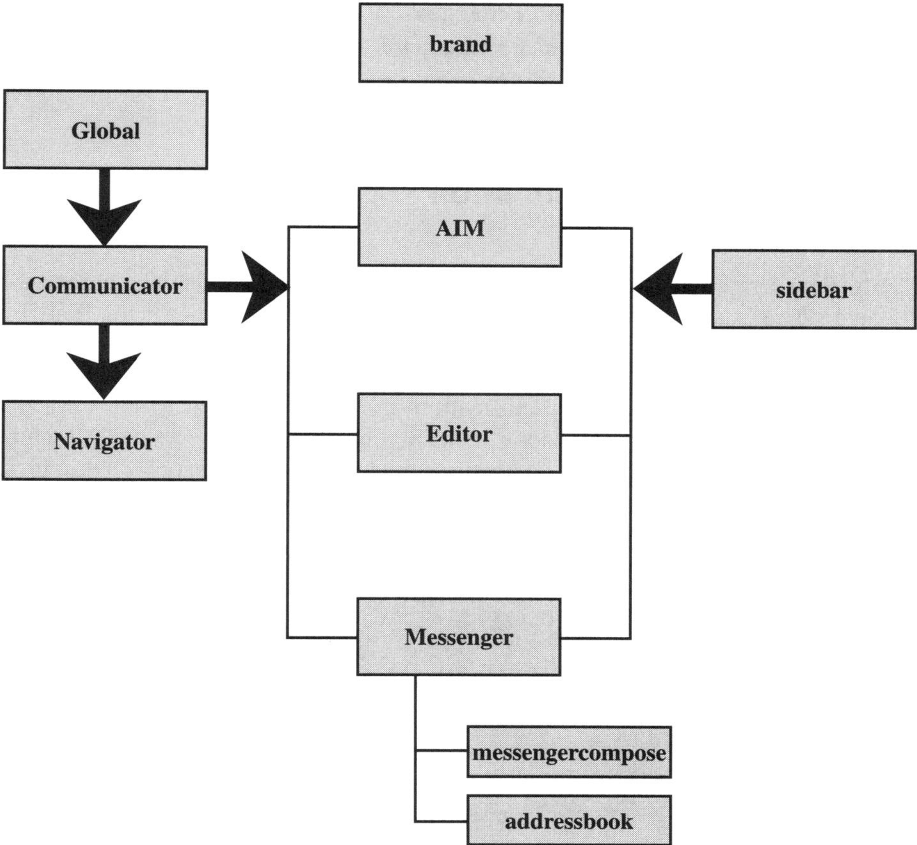

Figure 5.3 Netscape Skin inheritance model.

these six subdirectories, you will find a skin subdirectory. Each one of these skin subdirectories contains the files necessary for styling the individual Netscape component.

To start reskinning our first Theme, it is important to know about skin inheritance and how it will affect the development of your Theme. The global skin, at the top level, passes its styling to the communicator skin. The communicator skin then passes its styling to the aim, editor, and messenger skins. Figure 5.3 shows how the hierarchy of skin inheritance is structured. Notice that the sidebar skin is more of a peer to the communicator skin. That's because the sidebar skin actually passes, or imports, its skin information at the same level as the communicator skin. The aim, editor, and messenger skins all have a sidebar element. This means that the communicator and sidebar skins must basically sit at the same level.

TIP **Save time by choosing a Theme that is already registered in your profile. Simply copy your .jar file out to a separate directory and then unpack it into an unarchived directory. Now you're ready to modify the Theme components.**

When you're ready to check out your changes, ZIP your archive and then replace it in the directory from which you copied. Make sure that Netscape Navigator is closed when you do this to avoid causing a sharing violation in the operating system.

Step 1: Changing the Activation Splash Screen

The activation screen, as seen in Figure 5.4, is used to serve as a splash screen for your Theme. This is a 400 × 400 pixel, 256-color image. This does not mean that you have to use only 256 colors. Go hog wild here if you're going to create a catchy graphic. Just remember, users don't want to sit around waiting too long for a graphic whose only purpose is the personal edification of the Theme creator. What we did was create a 400 × 400 image in Adobe ImageStyler. This gave us the exact area in which to work. Adobe ImageStyler is a great product in which to create Web graphics. So what we did was add a few items of text explaining who created this product and

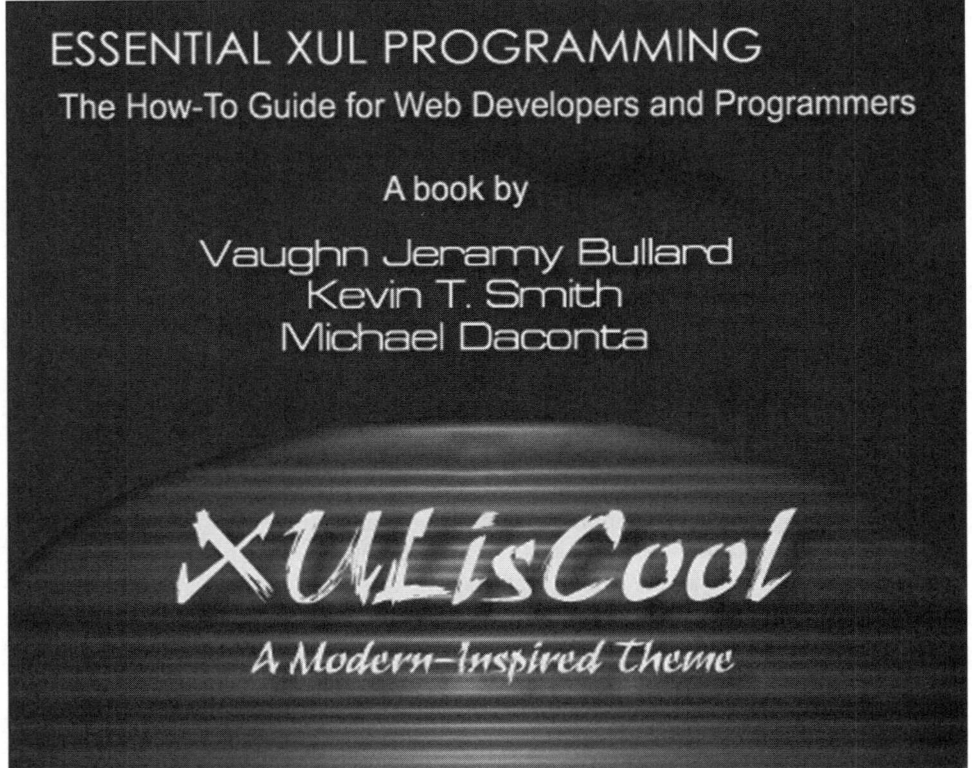

Figure 5.4 Activation splash screen.

the Theme name, as demonstrated in Figure 5.4. We then saved this file, under your Theme directory as /communicator/skin/profile.activation.gif. This activation splash screen will be displayed when we package, install, and then use our Theme.

Step 2: Branding the Browser

Now we will brand the browser or change the icon in the upper right-hand corner. We can also change the look and feel of this area of the browser. Why would you want to? A company may want to change the brand of the browser to fit its corporate identity, which is useful for marketing internally to employees or externally to customers or suppliers.

We really have to worry about two states. The first one is the wait state. The image used for this is animthrob_single.gif. This image is what you see when no Web pages or messages are available to download. Animthrob_single.gif is a 30 × 30 pixel, 256-color image. These images are collectively called the Throbber.

The second state is the busy or hover state. The image used for this is animthrob.gif. This image is an animated image in GIF/89A format. If you are unfamiliar with these type of images, they are pretty simple to understand. The image is a formatted collection of images done in much the same way a cartoon animator draws multiple cels to create an animation. A Web designer would create this image with a program, such as GIF Animator from Ulead Systems, Inc. You can download this program at http://www.ulead.com. It has great features, such as an animation wizard, and optimization features that make it one of the better image animation programs.

The way the branding works is that when a Web page is loaded, the wait state image is swapped out for the hover state image. It gives the user a visual clue through the user interface that the browser is busy. When the Web page has finished downloading, the hover state image is then swapped out for the wait state image. Again this gives you a visual clue that the browser is finished with downloading.

We started editing the first image in Adobe PhotoShop. This image, animthrob_single.gif, is in the /global/skin/ subdirectory. We took everything in the image and painted it over with a purple paintbrush. We created this as a transparent GIF/89 and then saved the file.

In the second image, we edited it with a combination of Adobe PhotoShop and Ulead GIF Animator. This image is a bit more complicated to create. Our busy/hover state image will flash the letters *XUL is Cool*. We want the image to flash one letter at a time, like X U L i s C o o l. To do this, we have to create nine images. All these images will be 30- × 30-pixel, 256-color images. For each image, we created a black background, then inserted a different letter atop each background—for example, X for image one; U for image two; L for image three. We saved these files in the /global/skin/ subdirectory, giving them a common format name (anim-frame1.gif, anim-frame2.gif, anim-frame3.gif, and so forth). This is shown in Figure 5.5.

In the Ulead GIF Animator, animation wizard combined all these images into a single file. We then saved this file as animthrob.gif under the /global/skin/ subdirectory.

We now have four images to edit, which will border our brand image. They are in order: throbber-groove-bottom.gif, throbber-groove-top.gif, throbber-groove-left.gif, and throbber-groove-right.gif. These files are under the /communicator/skin/ subdirectory. Because

Figure 5.5 Creating the animation frames.

Figure 5.6 Branding the browser.

we were designing our Theme around a blue marble-inspired browser color, we wanted to give these images a blue hue. We opened these images, edited them to be blue, and then saved them. In Figure 5.6, you will notice the structure of the branding area of the browser.

Next we move onto editing our first cascading style sheet within this extensive Theme structure. Because we are touching up a Theme instead of creating a new one, we don't have to change this. However, you may find yourself experimenting with different sizes of throbber images. It then will be necessary to change some spacing attributes in your cascading style sheets.

We are going to edit the brand.css file located in the /communicator/skin/ subdirectory. In Code Listing 5.2 is the full text of brand.css. We have added some comments into the code to show you where to modify. Our comments are noted by //.

Under the #navigator-throbber heading you may notice that it has a XUL binding associated with this throbber. That XUL binding is pulled from /global/skin/globalBindings.xml#throbber. This URL reference tells the browser what type of XUL element the throbber is. If you look at the entry in the XML file as shown in Code Listing 5.3, you will see that the throbber area is simply a collection of XUL widgets.

Save all of your files, and you are finished with branding the browser component of our Netscape Navigator theme.

Step 3: Skinning the Menus

Understanding the XUL Widget model for a menu, we can break it down into the following elements. First, we should have a menubar. In that menubar, we will place a menu. In that menu, we can place menu items. These menu items can be checkable, or they can pop up new menus (menupopup). To better understand how you can redesign the menus, think of the ways in which you've seen other menus built. Figure 5.7 describes the menu components.

We have created a blue-marbled background and saved it as navbar-bg.gif. We will use this file as a background for many components within the navigator component of

```
Brand.css
// This is considered the "branding area"
// There are three states in which throbber image will exist.  The
static wait
// state, the busy state, and the hover state.
#navigator-throbber
  {
    -moz-binding          :
url("chrome://global/skin/globalBindings.xml#throbber");
    margin                : 2px 1px 6px 8px;
    border                : 0px;
    padding               : 0px;
    min-width             : 0px;
    background-color      : transparent;
    list-style-image      :
url("chrome://global/skin/animthrob_single.gif");
    text-align            : center;
    cursor                : pointer;
    -moz-user-focus       : ignore;
  }
// These are the throbber's attributes when the browser is out
searching for a web
// page or downloading messages.  It simply swaps the default image
animthrob_single
// for the image animthrob, which is the animated image
#navigator-throbber[busy="true"]
  {
    list-style-image      : url("chrome://global/skin/animthrob.gif");
  }
// You can change this to also give a busy state.  This is best
demonstrated by the Sky
// Pilot theme.  When a mouse pointer is placed over the area, the
animated image "plays"
#navigator-throbber:hover:active
  {
    margin                : 2px 1px 6px 8px;
//  Added the following line of code, so when the mouse pointer is
hovering, the animated
//  image will play
    list-style-image      : url("chrome://global/skin/animthrob.gif");
  }
.throbber-icon
  {
    margin             : 0px;
    background-color: #637D94;
```

continues

Code Listing 5.2 Brand.css.

```
  }
// This is the left side border of the throbber
.throbber-groove-left  {
    width              : 2px;
    height             : 36px;
    background         : url(chrome://communicator/skin/throbber-
groove-left.gif) no-repeat;
  }
// This is the right side border of the throbber
.throbber-groove-right
  {
       width              : 2px;
       height             : 36px;
       background : url(chrome://communicator/skin/throbber-groove-
right.gif) no-repeat;
  }
// This is the top border of the throbber
.throbber-groove-top
  {
       height             : 2px;
       background : url(chrome://communicator/skin/throbber-groove-
top.gif) repeat-x;
  }
// This is the bottom border of the throbber
.throbber-groove-bottom
  {
       height             : 2px;
       background : url(chrome://communicator/skin/throbber-groove-
bottom.gif) repeat-x;
  }
```

Code Listing 5.2 Brand.css (Continued).

our Theme, including the menus. Because we want this background to be inherited down the Theme structure, we will modify the menu cascading style sheet within the global package of our Theme. To start, open the menu.css stylesheet file.

In this file are many predefined classes. In these classes are the behaviors for all of the Netscape menu components. Changing the attributes and values of these classes will, in effect, trickle down the component hierarchy. The main visual components of the menu that you should be concerned about are the menubar, menu, popup menu, icons within the menus, and the hover actions of the menus.

Our first component is the menubar. To change this component, go to the following line:

```
menubar
  {
  }
```

```
<binding id="throbber"
extends="chrome://global/content/xulBindings.xml#basetext">
       <content>
          <xul:spring class="throbber-groove-left"/>
         <xul:box flex="1" class="throbber-middle" orient="vertical">
           <xul:spring class="throbber-groove-top"/>
              <xul:image flex="1" class="throbber-icon" inherits="src"
              autostretch="never"/>
              <xul:spring class="throbber-groove-bottom"/>
         </xul:box>
         <xul:spring class="throbber-groove-right"/>
    </content>
  </binding>
```

Code Listing 5.3 Binding example from globalBindings.xml.

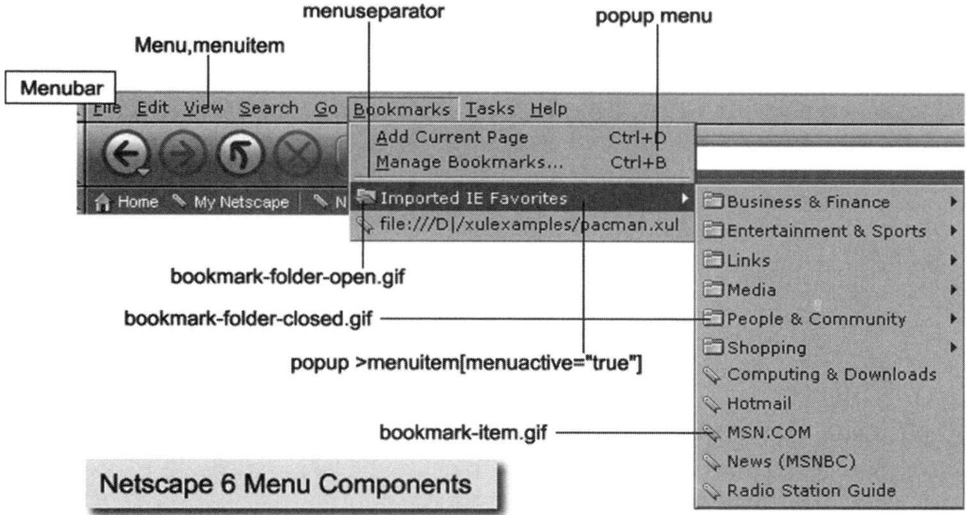

Figure 5.7 Netscape 6 menu components.

We will change the class to reflect the following attributes and values: make the background color on the menubar blue, make the text white and bold, and place our marbled background as the background image. We chose white bold text because it would contrast better for the blue marbled background that we created:

```
background-color       : #296eb3;
color                  : #FFFFFF;
```

```
font-weight              : bold;
background-image         : url("chrome://global/skin/navbar-bg.gif");
```

Our second component is the menuitem itself. This component has values like File, Edit, View, Window, and Help. A menuitem can be any selectable item on the menu. This class is found under the heading:

```
menu, menuitem
  {
  }
```

We changed this class to reflect the following attributes and values. What this does is make our text bold and change its color to white. Because we want the component centered, we use the vertical-align: middle attribute.

```
color                    : #FFFFFF;
font-weight              : bold;
vertical-align           : middle;
```

Our third component is our disabled menuitems. These components are unselectable because of user interface rules created by Navigator designers. An example of this might be when you first start Netscape Navigator. Selecting the Go menu and then trying to select Forward will not work because you have not gone anywhere yet; hence it is a deselected item. Meaning this menu item is not enabled until you have gone to another Web page. To modify this class, go to the following class line:

```
menu[disabled="true"], menuitem[disabled="true"],
menu[menuactive="true"][disabled="true"],
menuitem[menuactive="true"][disabled="true"]
  {
}
```

We want to change only the background color of this text. A good color to go with bold, white text and a blue marbled background would be gray text. We create this by adding the following attribute and value to our class:

```
color                    : #444444;
```

Our fourth component is our popup menu. Popup menus are essentially the same thing as drop-down menus. When a menuitem such as the File menu is selected, instead of it invoking a drop-down menu, it invokes a popup menu at the File menuitem's x,y position. This nifty little user interface idea was a great idea of component reuse. To modify this class, go to the heading:

```
menupopup, popup
  {
  }
```

In this class, we want the background color to be blue. We also want a border around our menu to allow some kind of visual separation of the popup menu from the main menu component. We give this a 1-pixel white colored border. Keeping in line with our color scheme, we continue by giving our text a white color and a bold attribute.

We also use our blue marbled background with the background-image attribute. A new attribute you will see is the background-repeat attribute. We tell the browser to repeat this background vertically by telling it repeat-y, vertically, or by telling it to repeat-x, horizontally. We also pad the menu by 1 pixel horizontally. Padding's attribute values are formatted as padding: x, y. We insert the following attributes and values into our disabled menuitem class:

```
background-color      : #296eb3;
border                : 1px solid #FFFFFF;
color                 : #FFFFFF;
font-weight           : bold;
background-image      : url("chrome://global/skin/navbar-bg.gif");
background-repeat     : repeat-y;
padding               : 1px 0px;
```

Our fifth component is our menuseparator. The menuseparator functions as just that; a separator for menuitem components. This component enables you, as an interface designer, to logically group menuitems according to their associated functions. An example of this would be the cut, copy, paste group in the Edit menu. It is separated by the menuseparator from other menuitem components. This class is listed under the menuseparator heading:

```
menuseparator
  {
      border-top              : 1px solid #FFFFFF;
      border-bottom           : 1px solid #FFFFFF;
      margin                  : 2px 3px;
  }
```

In this class we introduce three new attributes and values: border-top, border-bottom, and margin. We give the first two attributes a 1-pixel sizing and white color. To create a three-dimensional effect for our menuseparator, we could give our border-top attribute a white color and the border-bottom attribute a color like dark gray. Because we think three-dimensional is sometimes overdone and for simplicity's sake here, we color both attributes white. The margin attribute follows the format of the padding attribute previously explained; we format it like margin: x, y. What the margin attribute does here is give the menuseparator a 2-pixel horizontal margin and 3-pixel vertical margin on each side of the menuseparator component.

Our sixth component is the popup menuitem. This item is selected when you have a menu open and are basically hovering over a menuitem with your mouse. The hovering layer is a layer above our blue marbled background. We would like our hovering layer to give us some of kind of visual clue that the menuitem is currently selected. Find the following heading in the menu.css file:

```
popup > menuitem[menuactive="true"]
  {
      background-color       : #296eb3;
      background-image       : url("chrome://global/skin/menuhover-
yellow.gif");
      background-repeat      : repeat-y;
      color                  : #FFFFFF;
      font-weight            : bold;
  }
```

We choose the background-color attribute to be the blue that we have chosen before. We define a background-image attribute and tell Navigator to repeat it vertically. Our text color is defined as white and bold.

In Adobe PhotoShop, we want to create a background image for the selected menu item. We don't know what size our menuitem will be, so we give the image a pixel height of only one. We give the image a pixel width of 20. Although not the full size of most menuitem components, the image is just a visual clue. (This will not work in all cases.) In this image we created a yellow gradient. The color range goes from yellow to white, left to right. We then exported this image as a transparent GIF/89 image. We selected white and related lighter colors as transparent alpha colors. We saved this image as menuhover-yellow.gif in the /global/skin/ subdirectory. When viewed in the browser, the image will appear to hover over our blue marbled background. Because we chose a blue background, our yellow transparent gradient will appear to run from yellow to a brighter blue. You will not see the blue marbled background when the menuitem is selected. Because we also classified the background-repeat attribute to repeat vertically, it is repeated for however many pixels high the menuitem takes. This essentially gives the menuitem a focused, visual cue. Not only that, we happen to think it looks sharp!

An important thing to note is that the height is generally not an easily understood variable. This means that the height can change because a user may select a different font face and size for the browser's system font. The menu will adjust to the new font size or font face values. Therefore, if you had a fixed value background image that was not repeating, you might run into several design issues. One way you may get around this issue is by creating an image with a height value of one and then repeating it vertically (repeat-y) as we did.

Our seventh component of the menu is the tooltip feature. The tooltip is essentially a popup menu that is not selectable. Its purpose is to serve as an informational popup box. As you go over an item within a user interface, a tooltip may appear over that user interface element. This is especially helpful if you want to give a user information about that particular user interface component. Find the following class heading:

```
.tooltip
  {
     background-color       : #296eb3;
     border                 : 1px solid #FFFFFF;
     color                  : #FFFFFF;
     font-weight            : bold;
     font-size              : 10px;
```

```
    padding              : 2px;
    padding-right        : 3px;
  }
```

In our tooltip, we will declare our background color to be our oh-so-familiar blue. We will also define a 1-pixel, white border. The text will be bold and white. We further define the text to be 10 pixels high, because tooltips shouldn't take up the entire user interface. We define a small fixed width for the tooltip text.

The next thing we do is go through our menu cascading style sheet, ensuring that the style sheet is in the proper format. Every class, attribute, and value should fall in the following format. If it does not, then Netscape Navigator may not run or display the page correctly when confronted with parsing a malformed style sheet. Good form when writing style sheets will pay off when Netscape Navigator actually runs.

```
class
{
   attribute: value;
}
```

As you are scanning this file, make sure that you change any color attribute to white. Rogue components may exist that some developer has decided to change! Then save the file. Now it's time to change some of the icon components, like the bookmark folder icons, of our menu. When selecting a bookmark folder, the static closed bookmark folder is replaced with an open bookmark folder. There are also components for actual bookmarks. These icons can also be replaced with other images, if needed, to simulate a hover effect.

The following images can be found in the /communicator/skin/bookmarks/ directory:

```
Bookmark-folder-closed.gif
Bookmark-folder-open.gif
Bookmark-item.gif
Bookmark-item-hover.gif
Home.gif
Personal-folder-closed.gif
Personal-folder-open.gif
```

We then opened the bookmark-folder-closed.gif file. This image file is used in the non-hover state of the bookmark menuitem. When the bookmarks menu is opened, all bookmark folder menuitems are populated with the bookmark-folder-closed.gif file. When a bookmark menuitem is selected, the icon for the closed bookmark folder is replaced with an open bookmark folder. This file is called bookmark-folder-open.gif. What we ended up doing is cannibalizing the same icons. We painted them with colors that contrasted very well with the blue marbled background. We then colored the closed folder a gradient of bright yellow and the open folder a gradient of bright purple. We repeated this process with the icons, personal-folder-closed.gif and personal-folder-open.gif.

For our bookmark items, we did not cannibalize the same icons. We created two simple rectangles. The first image, bookmark-item.gif, is a white rectangle with a black border. The second image, bookmark-item-hover.gif, is a black rectangle with a white

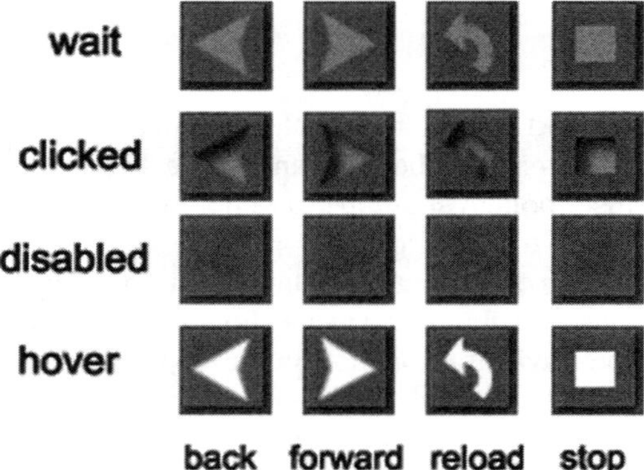

Figure 5. 8 Navigation bar subcomponents.

border. When a bookmark item is highlighted, the bookmark-item.gif is replaced with the hover state icon, bookmark-item-hover.gif.

We have another image in this directory—home.gif. This file is the little house icon in the right side of the personal toolbar. We polished this image in Adobe PhotoShop with a gold gradient rather than recreate such a familiar icon.

This is how you would skin the menu. The learning curve on this is really low. When you first do it, you might think that there are a lot of little steps to skin the menu, but over time, you will become so familiar with developing Netscape Themes that it essentially becomes second nature. (We know because we have developed many Themes.)

Step 4: Skinning the Navigation Bar

The navigation bar is the Netscape Navigator component with the back, forward, reload, URL field, search, and print buttons. The navigation bar consists of many buttons and states and, as such, requires an extra amount of due diligence in creation.

Start in the /navigator/skin/ directory. We need to be concerned with four buttons: back, forward, reload, and stop. Each of these buttons has four states, in order of operation: regular wait state, clicked, disabled, and hover. The naming convention for these buttons is shown in Table 5.1.

Netscape Navigator is distributed with its Themes with the names in this format. We use the names in this format because it's easier. For information on how to change this in navigator.css, see Appendix C, "Netscape Theme Reference." In this appendix is a section on changing Navigator components. Figure 5.8 shows how we created our buttons.

These images are all 32 × 32 pixels, 256-color images. We want these buttons to contrast well against the blue marbled background, because in the modern template, the files are a bright blue. Keeping that in mind, we created our new images with a pale blue background. We chose a simple square shape for all images in all states.

Table 5.1 Naming Conventions

BACK BUTTON	FORWARD BUTTON
Back.gif	Forward.gif
Back-clicked.gif	Forward-clicked.gif
Back-disabled.gif	Forward-disabled.gif
Back-hover.gif	Forward-hover.gif
RELOAD BUTTON	**STOP BUTTON**
Reload.gif	Stop.gif
Reload-clicked.gif	Stop-clicked.gif
Reload-disabled.gif	Stop-disabled.gif
Reload-hover.gif	Stop-hover.gif

We created these files in Adobe ImageStyler, although other packages, such as Adobe GoLive, allow you to create JavaScript rollover effects. These effects are great to test, because you can't easily iteratively develop rollover images for a Netscape Navigator Theme; you must package them up and reload the browser each time.

We formatted the images with the following scheme:

Regular wait state (or enabled). Pale blue background with lighter blue arrow

Clicked state. Pale blue background with inset white arrow

Disabled state. Pale blue background with gray arrow

Hover state. Pale blue background with white arrow

We then saved these files using Adobe PhotoShop to reduce the image colors and file size. Our next navigation bar button is the print button. The print button is not in the same directory location as the back, forward, reload, and stop buttons. Because the print button is more than just a navigator component, meaning it can be used in other locations, it is placed in the /global/skin/ subdirectory.

We opened the print buttons. In Adobe PhotoShop we designed a similar 32 × 32 pixel, 256-color image with all the states: enabled, clicked, disabled, and hover. We then saved the files back into the /global/skin/ subdirectory.

To change the cascading style sheets and format of the print button, modify the /global/skin/global.css cascading style sheet file. Then go the heading #print-button and modify the classes as in Code Listing 5.4.

As you can see, the print button, similar to branding the browser we mentioned in Step 1, uses an XML binding to further define the attributes of the print button area. When looking at the menubuttonBindings.xml file, which is located in the /communicator/ skin/subdirectory, we notice the bindings for the print button area underneath the

```
#print-button
  {
    -moz-binding          :
url("chrome://communicator/skin/menubuttonBindings.xml#menubutton-
dual-foo");
    list-style-image       : url("chrome://global/skin/print.gif");
     margin                : 6px 6px 10px 6px;
  }
#print-button[disabled="true"],
#print-button[disabled="true"]:hover,
#print-button[disabled="true"]:hover:active,
#print-button[disabled="true"] > .menubutton-dual-stack > .menubutton-
dual-button,
#print-button[disabled="true"] > .menubutton-dual-stack > .menubutton-
dual-button:hover,
#print-button[disabled="true"] > .menubutton-dual-stack > .menubutton-
dual-button:hover:active
  {
    list-style-image      : url("chrome://global/skin/print-
disabled.gif");
  }
#print-button > .menubutton-dual-stack > .menubutton-dual-button:hover
  {
    list-style-image      : url("chrome://global/skin/print-
hover.gif");
  }
#print-button > .menubutton-dual-stack > .menubutton-dual-
button:hover:active
  {
    list-style-image      : url("chrome://global/skin/print-
clicked.gif");
  }
#print-button > .menubutton-dual-stack > .menubutton-dual-dropmarker-
box
  {
    margin-left             : 19px;
    margin-top               : 22px;
  }
```

Code Listing 5.4 Editing the print button attributes.

#menubutton-dual-foo heading. Code Listing 5.5 shows how to edit the menu button bindings.

This binding is essentially a menubutton that has a stack laid upon it. The stack enables us to create layers. For the print button, we want to layout a drop-down menu from the print button. This is similar to the back and forward buttons having drop-down menus for the URI history. So, in the XML binding one layer exists for the print button, and another layer exists for a dropmarker (an image indicated by a down-pointing

```
<binding id="menubutton-dual-foo">
    <content includes="menupopup">
      <xul:stack class="menubutton-dual-stack">
        <xul:button class="menubutton-dual-button button-toolbar-1
top" allowevents="true"
inherits="tooltiptext=buttontooltiptext,oncommand=buttonaction,src,
value,crop,accesskey,disabled"/>
       <xul:box class="menubutton-dual-dropmarker-box" autostretch=
"never" flex="1">
          <xul:image class="menubutton-dual-dropmarker" inherits=
"disabled"/>
       </xul:box>
    </xul:stack>
  </content>
</binding>
```

Code Listing 5.5 Editing the menu button bindings.

white arrow). The dropmarker is actually a white arrow indicating further choices are underneath this print button.

Generally, you will need only these components to skin the navigation bar. Again, make sure that you have all classes, attributes, and XML elements correctly nested and terminated.

Step 5: Packaging Your Theme

You are finally at the final stages of Theme development. Well, we've developed our Theme, but we need to package it to make it deliverable. Netscape Themes are essentially ZIP files in which the file extension has been changed to .jar—indicating a Java Archive. Java Archives are not ZIP files. They are, however, structured such that you may archive or extract .jar files with an archive utility such as WinZip. JAR files are, in its most basic form, ZIP files with a manifest.rdf file in the top level of the archive. Netscape uses this format because it can deliver such a file via the SmartUpdate utility, considering it was developed to deliver .jar files.

The first thing you have to do is edit the manifest.rdf file. This file will sit at the top level of your Theme structure with the subdirectories, /aim/, /communicator/, /editor/, /global/, /messenger/, and /navigator/. The open the file will look like Code Listing 5.6.

We will change the manifest.rdf file to reflect a new name for our Theme. Keeping in the spirit with our book, we called it XULisCool. So, we did a search and replace for "modern" in our manifest.rdf file. We replaced "modern" with the word "xuliscool," which is reflected throughout our manifest.rdf file. The RDF file acts as a sort of ship's manifest to tell the SmartUpdate Utility to update the profile's registry with that Theme's packages, such as aim, communicator, editor, global, messenger, and navigator. It also updates the registry with a description of our installed theme. In Code Listing 5.7, you will find the changes reflected in our new manifest.rdf file.

```
<?xml version="1.0"?>

<RDF:RDF xmlns:RDF="http://www.w3.org/1999/02/22-rdf-syntax-ns#"
         xmlns:chrome="http://www.mozilla.org/rdf/chrome#">

  <!-- List all the skins being supplied by this theme -->
  <RDF:Seq about="urn:mozilla:skin:root">
    <RDF:li resource="urn:mozilla:skin:modern/1.0" />
  </RDF:Seq>
  <!-- modern-mzl Information -->
  <RDF:Description about="urn:mozilla:skin:modern/1.0"
        chrome:displayName="Modern"
        chrome:author="Netscape"
        chrome:description="This Modern theme is the default for
Netscape 6."
        chrome:name="modern/1.0"

chrome:image="jar:resource:///chrome/modern.jar!/skin/modern/global/
preview.gif">
    <chrome:packages>
      <RDF:Seq about="urn:mozilla:skin:modern/1.0:packages">
        <RDF:li resource="urn:mozilla:skin:modern/1.0:aim"/>
        <RDF:li resource="urn:mozilla:skin:modern/1.0:communicator"/>
        <RDF:li resource="urn:mozilla:skin:modern/1.0:editor"/>
        <RDF:li resource="urn:mozilla:skin:modern/1.0:global"/>
        <RDF:li resource="urn:mozilla:skin:modern/1.0:messenger"/>
        <RDF:li resource="urn:mozilla:skin:modern/1.0:navigator"/>
      </RDF:Seq>
    </chrome:packages>
  </RDF:Description>
</RDF:RDF>
```

Code Listing 5.6 Original manifest.rdf file.

We then save the file as manifest.rdf in text format. Our next step involves creating our Java Archive, essentially packaging our Theme. To do this, we run WinZip, our archiving and ZIPping program. In Figure 5.9, we create an archive called xuliscool.jar. The name must be the same as what is written in the manifest.rdf file that we just modified. After clicking the OK button, you are prompted to add files to the archive. The secret with this is that you must click the button Add With Wildcards. This selection allows you to add all files and their recursive directory structure. Don't forget to include subfolders in the Folders dialog box. Figure 5.9 shows what your directory structure should look like.

Now we have to deliver our theme.

Step 6: Delivering and Installing Our Theme

Now that you have your bags packed, so to speak, it is time to hop on the train and get to our destination. This is delivering our Theme. To do so, you will have to create an

```
<?xml version="1.0"?>
<RDF:RDF xmlns:RDF="http://www.w3.org/1999/02/22-rdf-syntax-ns#"
         xmlns:chrome="http://www.mozilla.org/rdf/chrome#">
  <!-- List all the skins being supplied by this theme -->
  <RDF:Seq about="urn:mozilla:skin:root">
    <RDF:li resource="urn:mozilla:skin:xuliscool/1.0" />
  </RDF:Seq>
  <!-- xuliscool-mzl Information -->
  <RDF:Description about="urn:mozilla:skin:xuliscool/1.0"
        chrome:displayName="Xuliscool"
        chrome:author="XULBook.com"
        chrome:description="XULisCool is a modern inspired theme
created by authors of Essential XUL Programming: The How-To Guide for
Web Developers and Programmers."
        chrome:name="xuliscool/1.0"

chrome:image="jar:resource:///chrome/xuliscool.jar!/skin/xuliscool/
global/preview.gif">
    <chrome:packages>
      <RDF:Seq about="urn:mozilla:skin:xuliscool/1.0:packages">
        <RDF:li resource="urn:mozilla:skin:xuliscool/1.0:aim"/>
        <RDF:li
resource="urn:mozilla:skin:xuliscool/1.0:communicator"/>
        <RDF:li resource="urn:mozilla:skin:xuliscool/1.0:editor"/>
        <RDF:li resource="urn:mozilla:skin:xuliscool/1.0:global"/>
        <RDF:li resource="urn:mozilla:skin:xuliscool/1.0:messenger"/>
        <RDF:li resource="urn:mozilla:skin:xuliscool/1.0:navigator"/>
      </RDF:Seq>
    </chrome:packages>
  </RDF:Description>
</RDF:RDF>
```

Code Listing 5.7 New manifest.rdf file.

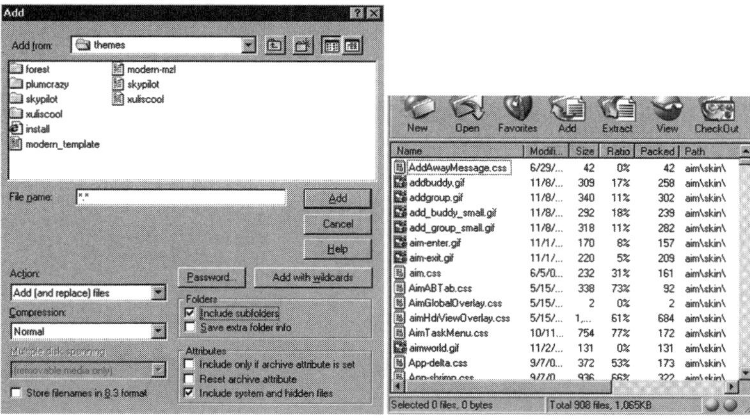

Figure 5.9 Creating a Java Archive.

installation script. This installation script is written in our familiar scripting language, JavaScript.

We will walk step-by-step through the Web page's JavaScript code, shown in Code Listing 5.8.

This HTML file will be in the same directory as our Theme. What we have created is an installTheme method. This method takes the following form:

```
installTheme(filename,registryName/version);
```

The filename can be an absolute (i.e., http://server/theme.jar) or relative (i.e., subdirectory/theme.jar) URI. The registry name argument creates a registry entry under the profile in which the Theme is registered. It then adds the version number of the registered Theme. Essentially, this is just a namespace. This is in case you decide to deliver a newer version of your Theme. When registering your revised Theme, it won't have a namespace conflict with the older version.

```
<HTML>
<HEAD>
<SCRIPT LANGUAGE="JavaScript">
function installTheme(fname,tname)
{
InstallTrigger.installChrome(InstallTrigger.SKIN, fname, tname);
}
</SCRIPT>
</HEAD>
<BODY BGCOLOR=#FFFFFF>
<FORM METHOD=POST>
<input type=button name="gardenerfive" value="Install Gardener Five"
onClick="triggerURL('http://www.javant.com/themes/gardenerfive.xpi',
"gardenerfive/1.0");">
<input type=button name="plumcrazy" value="Install !Plum Crazy!"
onClick="triggerURL('http://www.javant.com/themes/plumcrazy.jar');">
<input type=button name="plumcrazy" value="Install !Plum Crazy!"
onClick="triggerURL('http://www.javant.com/themes/plumcrazy.jar','plum
crazy/1.0')">
<input type=button name="sky" value="Install SkyPilot"
onClick="javascript:installTheme('skypilot.jar','skypilot/2.2');">
<input type=button name="Modern Mozillium" value="Install Modern
Mozillium" onClick="javascript:installTheme('modern-mzl.jar','modern-
mzl/1.0');">
<input type=button name="XULisCool" value="Install XULisCool"
onClick="javascript:installTheme('xuliscool.jar','xuliscool/1.0');">
</FORM>
</BODY>
```

Code Listing 5.8 Install HTML page.

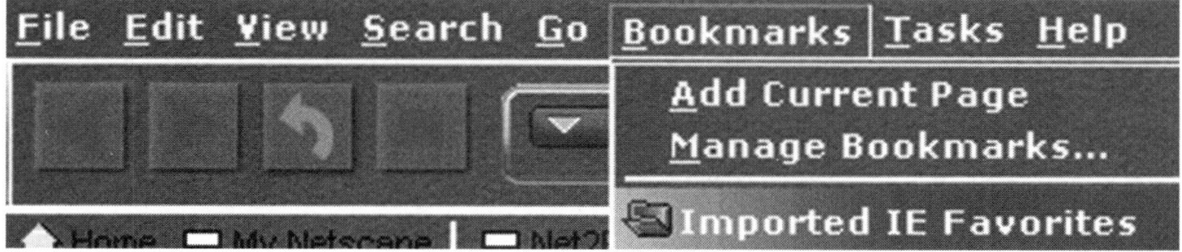

Figure 5.10 XUL is cool Theme.

When the form button is clicked, it invokes the installTheme( ) method. Then JavaScript invokes the following method:

```
InstallTrigger.installChrome(InstallTrigger.SKIN, fname, tname);
```

TIP Don't change the filenames unless it is a new file; otherwise you'll have to modify your cascading style sheet, which is unnecessary work.

InstallTrigger is an internal Netscape Navigator class that invokes the SmartUpdate Utility. We tell the InstallTrigger that we want to invoke the installChrome( ) method. It then takes the InstallTrigger.SKIN, filename and registryName namespace arguments. When invoked, this method will prompt you, "Install this theme?" You would then click the OK button to have a SmartUpdate box appear with a progress meter. InstallTrigger then downloads the Theme into your profile's chrome folder.

You then click the menu View/Apply Theme/XULisCool. Voila! You now have created your first Theme (Figure 5.10). It really wasn't that bad, was it?

Summary

We did not change the entire interface for Netscape Navigator in this chapter. However, you can change individual components by going into component subdirectories and changing. However, you can change the skin of each sub-component of Netscape Navigator by going into their respective subdirectory and changing the cascading style sheets and images. We also developed a few Themes that you may download "for your own spiritual enlightenment" at www.xulbook.com. Themes will be extremely useful when Netscape Navigator allows the browser's look and feel to change based on the page the user is viewing. Imagine a browser environment that changes for a Web site such as Amazon.com. This would be especially useful when trying to brand a company's product. As you can see, skinning Netscape Navigator is a perfect example of the ultimate XUL interface.

In the following chapter, you will learn a more advanced topic of XUL: RDF and XUL Templates.

RDF and XUL Templates

To build an apple pie from scratch, you must first invent the universe.

Carl Sagan, *Cosmos*

The past few chapters introduced the key concepts of XUL, and hopefully your mind is full of ideas on the language's potential. If you use a XUL-capable Web browser, you can change the browser's look and feel, and you can design and develop an application within the browser itself. Up to this point, all of the XUL examples that we have presented have been static. As we have been discussing XUL elements and building XUL files, we have been placing static data into the XUL files. This chapter will discuss approaches to including dynamic data sources into a XUL application using XUL templates with Resource Description Framework (RDF) data sources.

RDF is a W3C standard for representing information using XML as an interchange syntax.[1] RDF uses XML to exchange descriptions of Web resources in a portable way. Put simply, RDF is used to describe different resources and how they relate with one another. RDF emphasizes facilities to enable automated processing of Web resources in many interesting areas, such as cataloging search engines, promoting knowledge management between intelligent software agents, and expressing privacy policies for Web sites and users on the Internet. An RDF model is often discussed as an RDF graph because it can be represented as a hierarchical tree-like structure.

The developers of the Mozilla XPToolkit use RDF and XUL together as the framework for the Application Object Model (AOM) of the Netscape 6.x browser. A XUL template is the mechanism for creating dynamic user interfaces, and a template is directly related to one or more RDF data sources. Using this mechanism, XUL files can reference RDF data sources that represent constantly changing data instead of simply representing static information. XUL templates can aggregate multiple RDF datasources—that is, they can take data from different sources, both local and remote, and merge them. A visual representation of bookmarks, mail items, or user preferences could be loaded into a user interface at run-time.

This chapter presents a brief overview of RDF data sources and gives a comprehensive overview of building XUL templates for constructing dynamic data. We will demonstrate the main concepts with several examples. For testing purposes, we recommend that you use the latest version of the Mozilla browser. All of the code will also be available for download on our companion Web site, www.xulbook.com/.

The RDF Model and Syntax

As mentioned in the introduction to this chapter, RDF is a standard facility for describing Internet resources. The foundation of RDF is a model for representing properties and values. An RDF data model consists of three types of objects: *resources, properties, and statements.*[2] A resource is something that is being described. A property is a characteristic used to describe a resource, and an RDF statement ties a resource to a named property. A statement consists of a resource, property, and property value. Any resource being described is the *subject*. The property being described is the *predicate*. The property value, which is usually a number or a string literal, is the *object*. As an example, we can dissect the following sentence into RDF syntax: "Kevin Smith is the author of the Web page http://www.geocities.com/trumantruck/." The main resource of this sentence is the Web page, so "http://www.geocities.com/trumantruck" is the subject. The property being described is "author," so that will be the predicate. Finally, the property value of "author" is "Kevin Smith," so that value is the object. In the sentence, the subject is the Web page, the predicate is the author, and the object is "Kevin Smith." An example RDF graph for that sentence is shown in Figure 6.1.

NOTE **In our high school English classes, we were used to diagramming sentences a little differently—for this reason, the terms "subject", "predicate", and "object" may be a bit confusing to you, especially when looking at the example just described. In order to understand RDF data sources, it is important to recognize that subject refers to a resource—not the subject of the sentence. Understanding this concept is important, and it is important to refer to relationships**

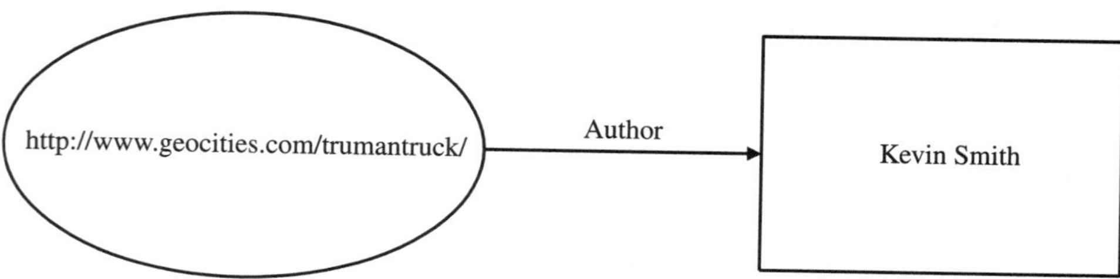

Figure 6.1 Example RDF graph.

in RDF in terms of subjects, predicates, and objects because this is how XUL refers to these relationships.

Using XML as the interchange format, the RDF syntax for the graph in Figure 6.1 is:

```
<?xml version="1.0"?>
<rdf:RDF>
 xmlns:rdf="http://www.w3.org/1999/02/22-rdf-syntax-ns#"
 xmlns:nsexample="http://www.xulbook.com/schemaExample#">
 <rdf:Description about="http://www.geocities.com/trumantruck/">
  <nsexample:author>Kevin Smith</nsexample:author>
 </rdf:Description>
</rdf:RDF>
```

The previous example used the fictitious namespace "nsexample" to show how RDF would describe this sentence. It is a good example of how a simple RDF statement can be shown in XML. As you can see, RDF uses the XML namespace facility to differentiate diverse elements in the document. You can write and use many types of schemas with RDF. The Dublin Core metadata standard is one of these, and it was designed to provide a common language to facilitate the discovery of electronic resources. We will not be focusing on individual schemas in this chapter, but you can go to http://www.purl.org/dc/ for more information on the Dublin Core Metadata Initiative.

RDF XML Syntax

The RDF XML syntax is often called the *serialization syntax*. The simplest RDF/XML document can have an RDF begin tag, an RDF description, and an end tag as shown in the previous example. The Description tag contains all descriptive elements that hold the identification of the resource being described.

Basic Elements

The following tags play a very important role in the RDF XML Syntax. As these tags are listed, we are referencing the RDF namespace by including "rdf:" before each tag. We could have simply listed the tag name, but it is good practice to precede the tag names with "rdf:":

<rdf:RDF>. This tag encloses the entire RDF document.

<rdf:Description>. This tag describes a datasource. Any number of RDF datasources can be in an RDF document. Optional attributes included in the Description tag are the ID attribute and the about attribute. The difference between these two tags is that the ID attribute lists a symbol identifier, and the about attribute lists the URI-reference. XUL templates usually reference the about attribute when first locating resources by a URI. Neither the ID nor the about attribute is required; they are used only if an application needs to reference the datasource by its ID or URI.

Property elements. Within <rdf:Description> tags for a resource are property elements that provide data descriptions for properties of the datasource. The description of the property can be included within the property elements (for example, "<property name>value</propertyname>"), or the description can be referenced by the URI of the resource (for example, <propertyname resource= "#uri reference"/>.

Remember these major tags when looking at the basic syntax of an RDF/XML document. Code Listing 6.1 provides an example of using these basic structures.

Code Listing 6.1 shows an RDF file that uses the elements of RDF as we have defined them so far and describes two resources. The most important thing to realize when looking at the syntax of an XML RDF document is that an RDF file can describe several different resources, and each resource is described between <rdf:Description> tags. At this point, we have given simple examples of datasources. However, aren't there cases where properties could contain a list of values? Answering this question leads us to the next section.

RDF Container Elements

Containers are a collection of resources, and they provide the opportunity to give items a list of values. These elements always fall underneath the <rdf:Description> element. RDF defines three types of container objects:

<rdf:Bag>. *A bag container* is an unordered list of property values. The bag container is used to convey the fact that an object has a bunch of property values but that the order is not relevant (serial numbers of computer equipment, for example).

```
<?xml version="1.0"?>
<rdf:RDF>
 xmlns:rdf='http://www.w3.org/1999/02/22-rdf-syntax-ns#'
 xmlns:dog="http://www.xulbook.com/schema/dog#'
 xmlns:cat="http://www.xulbook.com/schema/cat#'>
 <rdf:Description about="fox">
  <dog:Name>Fox</dog:Name>
  <dog:age>4</dog:age>
  <dog:weight>26lbs</dog:weight>
  <dog:sibling resource="#malory"/>
 </rdf:Description>
<rdf:Description about="malory">
  <cat:Name>Malory</cat:Name>
  <cat:age>7</cat:age>
  <cat:weight>14lbs<cat:weight/>
</rdf:Description>
</rdf:RDF>
```

Code Listing 6.1 Example of basic syntax.

<rdf:Seq>. *A sequence container* is an ordered list of property values. The sequence container is used to convey the fact that a resource has a sequence of values (an alphabetical list, for example).

<rdf:Alt>. *An alternative container* is a list of possible values that a resource may have. The alternative container contains a list of "or values." A light, for example, can have the value "on" or "off".

Bag containers, sequence containers, and alternative containers list items by using the <rdf:li> (list item) tag, and the <rdf:li> tag can be used as an inline item (for example, <rdf:li>value</rdf:li>) or as a referenced item (for example, rdf:li resource= "#resource uri"/>).

Let's look at an example. We could use an RDF file to represent a user's bookmarks. In this example, let's create a representation of a user's bookmarks. In the example shown in Code Listing 6.2, we show someone with the bookmarks http://www.xml.com/, http://www.btg.com/, http://www.xulportal.com/, and http://www.yahoo.com/. Because the bookmarks are in no particular order, we can use the Bag Container by using the rdf:Bag tag. If we really wanted to show sequence, we could use the rdf:Seq tag to describe this. As you can see, we have referenced two namespaces with this RDF document—one is the RDF namespace at http://www. w3.org/1999/02/22-rdf-syntax-ns#. This is the namespace that will be used for all RDF documents. The other namespace references a namespace at http://home.netscape. com/NC-rdf#.

```
<?xml version="1.0"?>
<rdf:RDF xmlns:rdf="http://www.w3.org/1999/02/22-rdf-syntax-ns#"
         xmlns:nc="http://home.netscape.com/NC-rdf#">
<rdf:Description about="urn:root">
   <nc:links>
    <rdf:Bag>
      <rdf:li>
           <rdf:Description nc:name="http://www.xml.com/"/>
      </rdf:li>
      <rdf:li>
           <rdf:Description nc:name="http://www.btg.com/"/>
      </rdf:li>
      <rdf:li>
           <rdf:Description  nc:name="http://www.xulportal.com/"/>
      </rdf:li>
      <rdf:li>
           <rdf:Description nc:name="http://www.yahoo.com/"/>
     </rdf:li>
    </rdf:Bag>
   </nc:links>
</rdf:Description>
</rdf:RDF>
```

Code Listing 6.2 Example bookmark RDF file.

We will be coming back to this example later in the chapter, as we discuss creating RDF graphs for visualizing RDF datasources, and we will also show how this bookmark file can be used with XUL in a real-world example.

To help summarize RDF/XML syntax, we have provided Table 6.1 as a reference for the tags that are used in RDF files.

RDF Graphs

Developers sometimes find it easier to develop RDF graphs—sometimes called *node and arc diagrams*—to visually represent RDF datasources. Knowing how to diagram RDF files in graph form will come in handy when you are looking at very complex RDF files and are trying to develop XUL templates. A basic syntax exists for drawing these diagrams:

- Nodes that are ovals represent resources. Resources, as we discussed in the last section, are designated by the <rdf:Description> tags and are referred to as the subject of a relationship. They can also be direct objects of other relationships but are always subjects.
- Nodes that are rectangular represent the object of the relationship and are represented in an RDF file as a text value of a node or as an attribute value.

Table 6.1 RDF/XML Element Reference

ELEMENT	ATTRIBUTES	CHILD OF	NOTES
<rdf:RDF>	None	None	Begins/ends the RDF/XML file
<rdf:Description>	about="uri" ID="identifier"	<rdf:RDF>, <rdf:li>	Describes a resource; can be multiple rdf:Description tags in a document
Property element (any XML tag) <namespace: propertyname>	ID or resource	<rdf:Description>	Describes properties of a resource, for example: <ns:age>12</ns:age> <ns:friend reference= "#bob"/>
<rdf:Seq>	ID	Property element	Sequential list
<rdf:Bag>	ID	Property element	Unordered list
<rdf:Alt>	ID	Property element	Alternative list
<rdf:li>	Resource	Container element (<rdf:Seq> or <rdf:Bag> or <rdf:Alt>)	List item; can reference resources inline or by reference, for example: <rdf:li><rdf Description nc:name="Gwen"/> </rdf:li> or <rdf:li resource="#gwen"/>

- Arcs begin at the subject, and they point at the direct object of the statement, describing a property value. The arc represents the predicate of the relationship and is represented in an RDF file as a tag contained within the <rdf:Description> element.

When we diagrammed our first example in Figure 6.1, we used these rules. By looking at an RDF graph, it is easy to determine the subject, predicate, and object of a relationship. Figure 6.2 shows a graphical depiction of these rules.

In the first example at the beginning of this section, we diagrammed a simple sentence into an RDF graph. The URL of the Web site was an oval resource node, and the value of the creator property was a rectangular string node. Graphs can get quite complex. For example, Figure 6.3 diagrams the sentence, "The author of http://www.geocities.com/trumantruck/ has the name Kevin T. Smith, email address xul@mindspring.com, and shoe size 10."

In that sentence, we know that the resource http://www.geocities.com/trumantruck/ is the subject, and the predicate is "Author." The direct object is represented by someone who is described by the predicates "name," "email address," and "shoe size," and which have the objects "Kevin T. Smith," "xul@mindspring.com," and "10," respectively.

The result of the diagram in Figure 6.3 shows an empty node, which is called an *anonymous resource*. This is because we did not specify a value for this resource. If, however, our sentence was "The author of http://www.geocities.com/trumantruck/ is a resource referred to by 'Employee 1819', and has the name 'Kevin T. Smith', the email address 'xul@mindspring.com' and the Shoe Size 10," then the value in the empty Circle would be "Employee 1819." In that case, Employee 1819 would be called the *identifier* and would probably be referenced in the RDF by the about attribute.

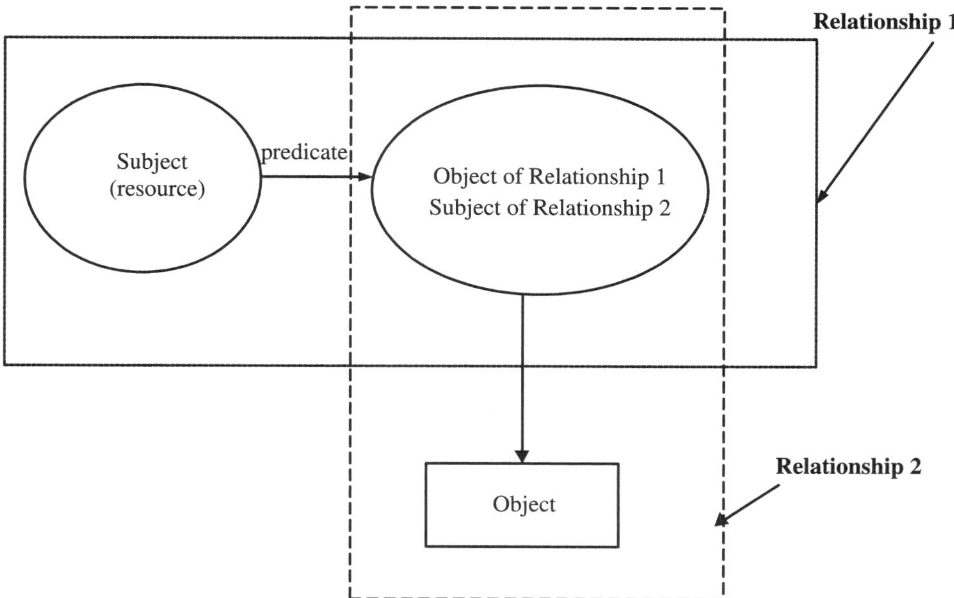

Figure 6.2 RDF graph rules.

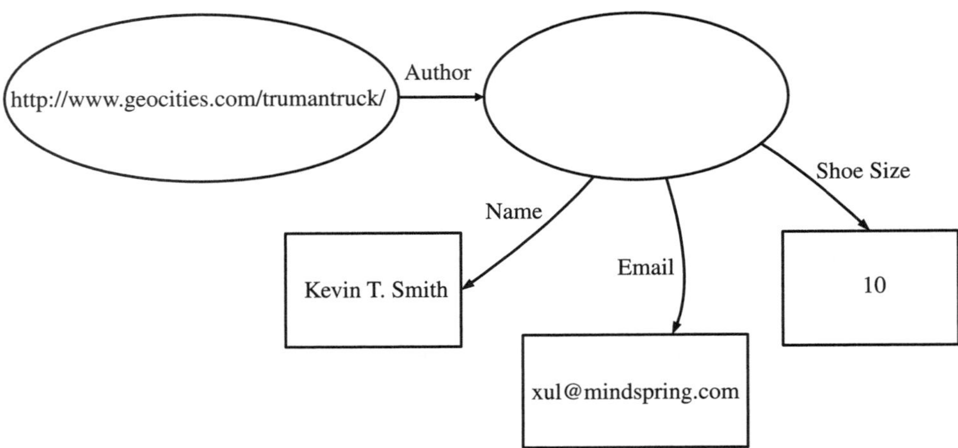

Figure 6.3 RDF graph example.

Now that we have diagrammed a simple sentence, let's diagram a graph for an example RDF/XML document. Code Listing 6.3 shows an example RDF file that is a datasource representing many of the chapters of a book.

Figure 6.4 shows how the RDF graph is drawn for the RDF file. Notice that the IDs are drawn with the # sign, and these are the resources described in the ovals. For the sake of reducing the complexity in our graphs, we did not write out the entire URI of the predicates and subjects. Instead, we referenced each by its namespace, which was defined in the RDF file. For example, instead of labeling the arcs "http://home.netscape.com/NC-rdf#name", we instead labeled them "nc:name". Instead of labeling the Sequence container by its fully qualified name "http://www.w3.org/1999/02/22-rdf-syntax-ns#Seq, we labeled the object "rdf:Seq". This can make graphs a lot easier to read. However, both are syntactically correct.

As you can see, RDF graphs can get complicated. However, they can be quite useful when creating XUL templates, as we will see in our next section, "Building and Using XUL Templates."

In Figure 6.4, why do we see the "A" resource, and the "rdf_1", "rdf_2", and "rdf_3" predicates when we don't see them in the RDF file? We mentioned before that there could be anonymous resources in an RDF file. Unless we specifically want to reference these resources by name, we don't really need to give them an ID or an about attribute. As we graph RDF files, we give these anonymous subjects temporary identifiers, so that we can describe them more clearly. Whenever a container relationship exists between subjects and objects, we usually give the predicate the value of rdf_1, rdf_2, rdf_3, and so on. In this example, the subject of the container relationship is anonymous as well, because the entire file is described as this sequence of books and chapters, and chances are, the developer knows what the file describes.

Of course, ID tags for references are not mandatory and sometimes are not used. An example of an RDF file that does not use ID tags is in our bookmark example in Code

```
<?xml version="1.0"?>
<!-- This file shows information about the first two chapters in each
book
     of Charles Dickens' "A Tale of Two Cities".
  -->
<rdf:RDF xmlns:rdf="http://www.w3.org/1999/02/22-rdf-syntax-ns#"
         xmlns:nc="http://home.netscape.com/NC-rdf#">
  <rdf:Description about="urn:root">
    <nc:hierarchy>
      <rdf:Seq>
        <rdf:li>
           <rdf:Description ID="book1" nc:name="Recalled To Life">
              <nc:chapter>
                 <rdf:Description ID="B1C1" nc:name="The Period"
                      nc:numpages="30"/>
                 <rdf:Description ID="B1C2" nc:name="The Mail"
                      nc:numpages="10"/>
              </nc:chapter>
           </rdf:Description>
        </rdf:li>
        <rdf:li>
           <rdf:Description ID="book2" nc:name="The Golden Thread">
           <nc:chapter>
             <rdf:Description ID="B2C1"
                  nc:name="Five Years Later"/>
             <rdf:Description ID="B2C2"
                  nc:name="A Sight" nc:numpages="30"/>
           </nc:chapter>
           </rdf:Description>
        </rdf:li>
        <rdf:li>
            <rdf:Description ID="book3" nc:name="The Track of A
              Storm">
               <!--we can reference the chapters this way, too! -->
               <nc:chapter resource="#B3C1"/>
               <nc:chapter resource="#B3C2"/>
            </rdf:Description>
        </rdf:li>
      </rdf:Seq>
    </nc:hierarchy>
</rdf:Description>
<rdf:Description ID="B3C1" nc:name="In Secret"
        nc:numpages="10"/>
  <rdf:Description ID="B3C2" nc:name="The GrindStone" />
</rdf:RDF>
```

Code Listing 6.3 RDF/XML for the organization of a book.

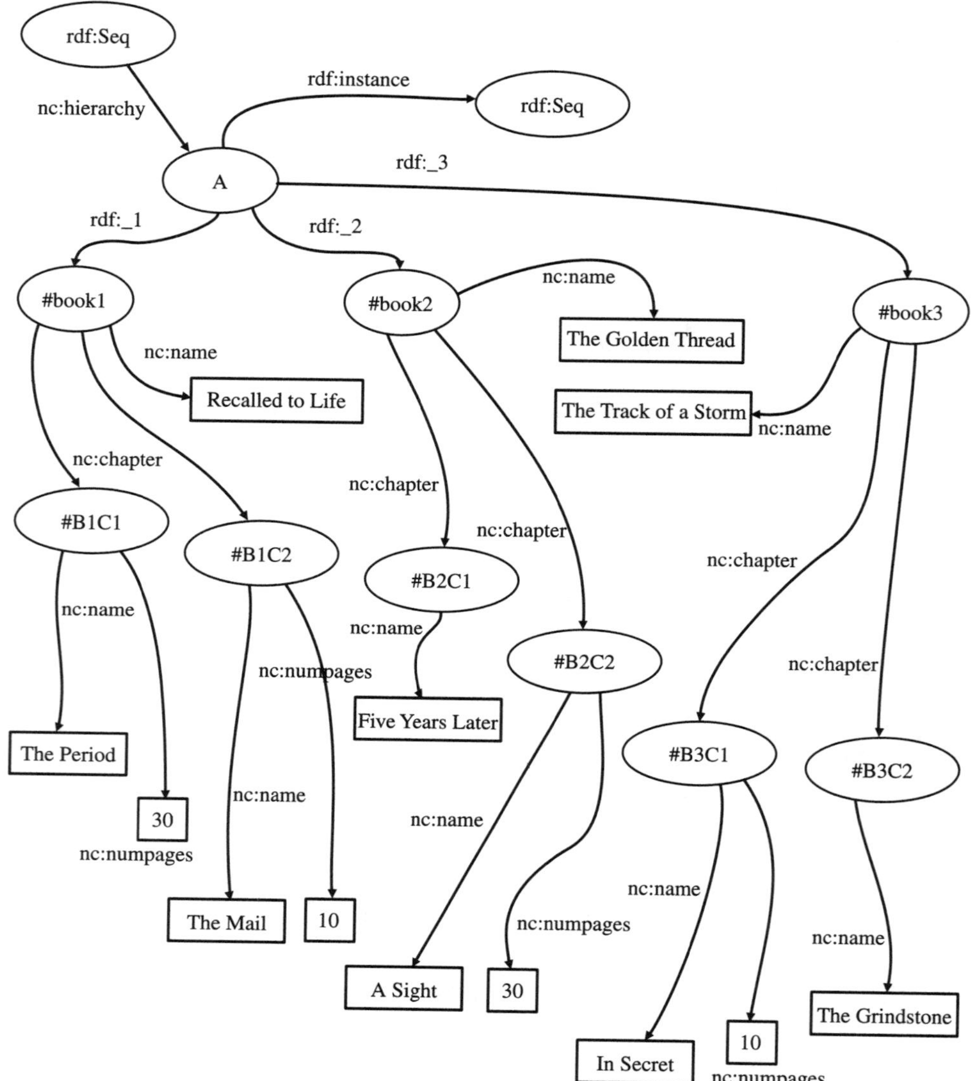

Figure 6.4 RDF graph for book organization.

Listing 6.2. In the case of not using identifiers, we will label the resources alphabetically. Figure 6.5 shows the RDF graph for the bookmark example.

Now that we have presented some of the basic information about RDF, we will dive into building XUL templates. RDF is a standard for which an entire book could be dedicated, and although we have not gone in depth, we do believe that RDF is important and deserves much more attention. For more information on RDF, see the RDF page at the W3C Web site, http://www.w3c.org/RDF/.

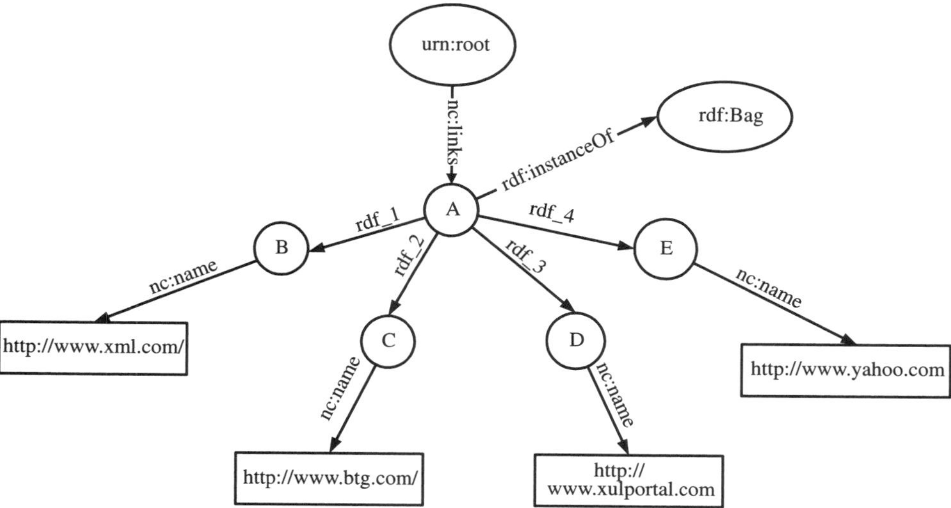

Figure 6.5 Graphical version of bookmark RDF file.

Building and Using XUL Templates

Because XUL's content tree structure for a window is represented as a hierarchical set of objects, it is often referred to as the Application Object Model (AOM), just like an XML document can be referred to as the DOM. A key part of building the AOM is by using RDF data sources to dynamically create XUL content. A XUL template is a collection of rules that uses RDF sources to build this content.[3] A template shows the content model pattern and serves as a template for dynamically building XUL, thus importing live data into the application. The Mozilla and Netscape browsers use RDF with XUL templates for many things: referencing email messages, bookmarks, views of local files, and maps to other sites. Using RDF with XUL templates is a very practical way to create dynamic, adaptable user interfaces that change along with the data that an application represents and references.

NOTE **In this section, we will use several examples from earlier in the chapter to build XUL templates for dynamic content. The examples that we will use are the bookmark RDF example from Code Listing 6.2 and Figure 6.5, as well as the book organization example from Code Listing 6.3, graphed in Figure 6.4. Building XUL templates for these two examples can be done very differently.**

XUL Template Syntax

To build user interface content from an RDF data source, the developer must first map a XUL element to an RDF data source. This XUL element is often called the *datasource element*.[4] You specify immediately within that element one or more templates that are made up of rules and actions applied on that element.

The datasources Attribute

The *datasources* attribute can be added to any XUL element, and it can be added to any number of elements in a XUL file. Attaching this attribute to a XUL element creates a *composite datasource* that can aggregate many RDF datasources. The form of this attribute is the following:

```
<anyxulelement datasources="rdf-datasource-list" >
...
 </anyxul element>
```

The "rdf-datasource-list" can be one or more datasource identifiers, which can be *contract identifiers*, a *local file name*, or an *URL*. When the datasource identifier references a "contract id" it is considered to be a built-in datasource and references a component in the Netscape 6.x browser. If the datasource ID references an URL, it is referred to as a remote datasource. Of course, if the ID references a filename, it is referred to as a local datasource. Table 6.2 shows the types of datasources and examples.

The key thing to know is that an element can reference multiple datasources. This could be helpful, for example, if you would like a pull-down menu to keep track of local bookmarks, mail messages, news messages, and perhaps remote news information.

An example could be if we wanted to create a menu to reference the bookmarks in our earlier bookmark example, shown in Code Listing 6.2 and Figure 6.5. If we wanted to use the bookmark RDF file to populate the menu, we would create the tag, "<menu datasources='bookmarks.rdf'>".

Table 6.2 Types of Attribute Values for the datasource Attribute

TYPE	DESCRIPTION	EXAMPLE
Contract ID	References a component internal to Netscape, followed by the @ sign	<tree datasources="@mozilla.org/rdf/datasource;1?name=mail">
Filename	References a local datasource	<tree datasources="rdf/stuff.rdf">
URL	References a remote datasource	<menu datasource="http://www.xulbook.com/rdf/test.rdf">
Combination	References multiple datasources at the same time	<tree datasources="apples.rdf oranges.rdf http://www.xulbook.com/bananas.rdf">

The ref Attribute

The ref attribute is included in the element referencing the datasource to reference a starting point resource in an RDF document. In our bookmark example in Code Listing 6.2, the RDF document describes the resource as urn:root. If we were going to reference this in our menu, we would build on our menu tag to include the ref attribute in the following manner:

```
<menu datasources="bookmarks.rdf" ref="urn:root">
```

The <template> Element

Add the template element directly beneath the element that references the datasource. The XML code that is written between the <template> and </template> is the magic of XUL templates and is not rendered by the application. Instead, the application processes the rules beneath the <template> tag, to serve as the logic for rendering information from the RDF datasources. Optionally, *container* and *member* attributes to the template can exist, to specify the containerhood and membership of the rules beneath the tag. Use these attributes when more than one rule exists.

In our bookmark example, we would place the <template> tag as a direct descendant of the menu tag, which references the bookmark file. In our next section, "Using XUL Templates," we will do just that.

The <rule>, <conditions>, and <action> Elements

These elements establish the procedure for how information is retrieved from the RDF file and how it is translated into the XUL application. The <rule> element is a direct descendent of a template element, and multiple rules can be in a template. For each rule, there are conditions, and for every condition, there is an action. If a condition does not match, the rule fails, and the action is not performed. The <conditions> and <action> elements are direct descendents of the <rule> element and always exist with each rule element. The syntax is shown in Code Listing 6.4.

We put the pattern-matching logic in the <conditions> section, and we put the results of the matching logic in the <action> section. For example, if we were to create a menu with menuitems that represent the names of the bookmarks from the bookmark.rdf file, we will put the logic to match the bookmark names in the <condition> section. In the <action> section, we will actually build the menuitem with the result of the matches.

Test Elements: <content>, <triple>, and <member>

These elements are the pattern-matching elements that can be children of the <conditions> element. The <content> element is used for matching a URI or a reference to the

```
<!-- beginning of XUL document skipped -->
<template>
      <rule>
         <conditions>
             <!--conditions will be here.. -->
         </conditions>
         <action>
             <!--the action that is performed by the XUL application
                 is placed here!
             -->
         </action>
      </rule>
      <rule>
         <conditions>...</conditions>
         <action>...</action>
      <rule>
         <conditions>...</conditions>
         <action>...</action>
      </rule>
      <!--more rules could be listed here-->
</template>
<!--ending of XUL document skipped-->
```

Code Listing 6.4 Rule-conditions-action syntax.

main datasource. The <triple> element is used to match a subject-predicate-object pair, and in fact, contains the attributes subject, predicate, and object. The <member> element is used for matching containment (or children).

These elements are usually referred to as *tests* or *test elements*. As rules match these tests, new variables are bound to the result of the match in the RDF graph, and these variables are used in the <action> section of the XUL template. Variables are preceded by a question mark, and are populated by using the <content>, <triple>, and <member> elements. Table 6.3 lists these elements, gives a description of each, and gives an example.

Table 6.3 is a good reference for the <content>, <triple>, and <member> elements. These elements are used to build variable bindings that will be used in the <action> section of a XUL template.

An example of using these elements together is shown in Code Listing 6.5. In that code listing, the variables "?uri", "?links", "?child", and "?name" are created as they match information in the RDF template. The first <content> test matches the URI of the RDF resource and creates a variable called uri. The next <triple> test looks for the subject-predicate-object pair that begins with the uri variable and sets up a new links variable, which is the result of that test. The <member> test creates a new variable child, which is the descendant of what was returned in the links variable. The final <triple> test then creates the name variable from the subject-predicate object triple.

Table 6.3 The <content>, <triple>, and <member> Elements

TEST ELEMENT	DESCRIPTION	EXAMPLE
<content>	Maps to a main datasource URI referenced by the XUL template element. The result is the population of the variable in the uri attribute.	<content uri="?uri"> In this example, the "?uri" variable is populated by the datasource that we are referencing. This variable is calculated by looking at the datasources and ref or about an attribute of the XUL element that we are populating.
<triple>	Matches a subject-predicate pair, resulting in the population of the object variable.	<triple subject="?uri" predicate= "http://xulbook.com/rdf#links" object ="?linkresult" In this example, we are testing against an already populated "?uri" variable, we are using a predicate http://xulbook.com/rdf#links, and we are populating a new variable "?linkresult".
<member>	Finds the child of an object	<member container="?linkresult" child "?kidofresult"> // This test finds the child (or children) of the "?linkresult" variable and populates the "?kidofresult" variable.

```
<!--beginning of XUL file cut-->
<conditions>
    <content uri=?uri"/>
    <triple subject="?uri"/>
            predicate="http://home.netscape.com/NC-rdf#links"
            object="?links"/>
    <member container="?links" child="?child">
    <triple subject="?child"
            predicate="http://home.netscape.com/NC-rdf#Name"
            object="?name">
</condition>
<!--end of XUL file cut-->
```

Code Listing 6.5 The pattern matching section.

If this confuses you, you're not the first. This syntax is very similar to rule matching in OPS-5 and Prolog. This is where drawing RDF graphs comes in very handy. The next section, "Using XUL Templates," will focus primarily on using these test elements in pattern matching.

```
<!-- beginning of XUL file cut-->
<rule>
    <conditions>
        <!--match patterns, binding the ?location variable -->
    </conditions>
    <bindings>
        <binding subject="?location"
                 predicate="http://home.netscape.com/NC-
rdf#neigborhood"
                 object="?neighborhood">
        <binding subject="?neighborhood"
                 predicate="http://home.netscape.com/NC-
rdf#streetaddress"
                 object="?streetaddress">
    </bindings>
    <action>..</action>
</rule>
<!-- ending of XUL file cut -->
```

Code Listing 6.6 <bindings>...<binding> syntax.

Creating Extra Variables: <bindings> and <binding>

The bindings and binding elements allow for additional variable bindings. The <bindings> element is a direct descendant of the <rule> element, and the <binding> element is a direct descendent of the <bindings> element. These bindings can be used along with the variables that were bound to information in the <conditions> section.

For a rule to execute an action, the conditions must be met. Although the <bindings> element is a child of the <rule> element, it is not in the <conditions> section, and therefore, a binding does not need to match in order for the action to be performed. This may be useful when you are trying to collect optional information.

A <binding> element consists of subject, predicate, and object attributes and works exactly the same as the <triple> element does. Given a subject and a predicate, the <binding> element populates a variable that is listed in its object attribute. Any number of <binding> elements may exist as descendents of the <bindings> element, and they are subject-predicate-object triples. An example syntax is shown in Code Listing 6.6.

As you can see by looking at Code Listing 6.6, bindings continue to create additional variables and bind them to information in the RDF file. From that example, you can see how it maps additional neighborhood and streetaddress variables to what we presume was created in the <conditions> section. Binding additional variables can be quite useful, especially when creating these variables is not dependent on the conditions of the rule executing.

NOTE **You may be asking yourself, "What is the difference between binding variables in the <bindings> section and assigning them in the <conditions>**

section?" Remember, in order for the <action> to execute, the rules must match in the <conditions> section. However, if you have optional variable bindings that you want to make *that may not match*, this is where the <bindings> section comes in handy. In the following section, we will show how this is quite useful.

Creating XUL Templates

In order to create XUL templates, you must understand how the XUL content model is created before it is rendered by the Web browser. In the last section, we presented the syntax of elements and attributes used in XUL templates and gave a high-level overview of the concepts of rules, conditions, and pattern matching. This section explains different pattern-matching styles by example and how to put this information to use in the Netscape 6.x and Mozilla browsers.

Simple Pattern Matching: The Bookmark Example

In the last section, we used the bookmark example from Code Listing 6.2 and Figure 6.5 to give examples of how some of the elements and attributes for XUL templates could be used. Because the bookmark RDF file is quite simple, this will be a good starting point to discuss *singular rules*. A XUL template can have multiple rules, but the easiest case to understand is a XUL file with one rule. Code Listing 6.7 shows a XUL file that we have built to create a bookmark menu based on the RDF datasource listed in Code Listing 6.2.

In Code Listing 6.7, you can see that we are associating the XUL "menubar" element with one datasource, "bookmarks.rdf" and that we are mapping the menubar element to the resource specified in the RDF file with "urn:root". Of course, there is only one resource in the RDF file, but you can see that that resource is tagged with the <rdf:Description about="urn:root"> element. We know that the menubar element is tied to that resource.

As we have discussed, the <template> element is the direct descendant of the <menubar> element because the menubar is now tied to that datasource. In the <conditions> section, pattern-matching rules create new variable bindings. For each match to those rules, an <action> is performed to create a menuitem. Let's go through those pattern-matching rules in detail:

<content uri="?uri"> creates a new variable binding and binds the uri variable to the URI of the resource to which menubar is tied. Of course, the URI is urn:root, so this begins a set of one match:

```
{(?uri=urn:root)}
```

The next <triple> test looks for a relationship in the RDF graph where the uri variable is in the subject, looks for the "http://home.netscape.com/NC-rdf#links" predicate, and where there is an object that will be bound to the "links" variable. This is where mapping RDF files into graphs really helps. Looking at Figure 6.5, you can see that such

```
<?xml version="1.0"?>
<?xml-stylesheet href="chrome://global/skin" type="text/css"?>
<window xmlns:html="http://www.w3.org/xhtml"

xmlns="http://www.mozilla.org/keymaster/gatekeeper/there.is.only.xul"
        align="vertical">
  <menubar>
  <menu label="Bookmarks">
  <menupopup datasources="bookmarks.rdf" ref="urn:root">
     <template>
       <rule>
         <conditions>
            <content uri="?uri" />
            <triple subject="?uri"
                    predicate="http://home.netscape.com/NC-rdf#links"
                    object="?links"/>
            <member container="?links" child="?child" />
            <triple subject="?child"
                    predicate="http://home.netscape.com/NC-rdf#name"
                    object="?name"/>
         </conditions>
         <action>
                  <menuitem uri="?child" label="?name"/>
         </action>
       </rule>
     </template>
    </menupopup>
   </menu>
  </menubar>
</window>
```

Code Listing 6.7 A XUL file for creating a bookmark menu.

a relationship exists between "urn:root", and node "A". Our list of values is now the following set:

```
{(?uri=urn:root)(?links= A )}
```

The next <member> test looks for a direct descendent of "?links" and is putting the result in variable "?child". We have built a value for "?links" in our result set, so this rule returns any number of sets that satisfies the test. In this case, there are three. Looking at the RDF graph in Figure 6.5, you find that nodes B, C, D, and E satisfy this rule. We now have four result sets:

```
{(?uri=urn:root)(?links=A)(?child=B)}
{(?uri=urn:root)(?links=A)(?child=C)}
{(?uri=urn:root)(?links=A)(?child=D)}
{(?uri=urn:root)(?links=A)(?child=E)}
```

The final <triple> test looks for the relation where "?child" is the subject, "http://home.netscape.com/NC-rdf#name" is the predicate, and a new variable, "?name," is the object. Because we have four result sets, we must apply this rule to each; there is a different value of "?child" in each. Looking at the RDF graph, the results that satisfy this test are:

```
{(?uri=urn:root)(?links=A)(?child=B)(?name="http://www.xml.com/")}
{(?uri=urn:root)(?links=A)(?child=C)(?name="http://www.btg.com/")}
{(?uri=urn:root)(?links=A)(?child=D)
  (?name="http://www.xulportal.com/")}
{(?uri=urn:root)(?links=A)(?child=E)
  (?name="http://www.yahoo.com/")}
```

Now that we do have those four result sets, we must apply each to the <action> section in the XUL template. If we apply each result set to the action section, we generate the following XUL:

```
<menuitem id="B" label="http://www.xml.com/"/> <!-- from first set-->
<menuitem id="C" label="http://www.btg.com/"/> <!-- from 2nd set -->
<menuitem id="D" label="http://www.xulportal.com/"/> <!-- from 3rd-->
<menuitem id="E" label="http://www.yahoo.com/"/>  <!-- from 4th set -->
```

The only difference is that when "uri" is specified in the XUL template action section, the XUL that is created is ID. Code Listing 6.8 shows the final, outputted XUL that is dynamically generated.

Because this is a simple example, we can load it in the Mozilla browser. Figure 6.6 shows the result of clicking on the Bookmarks menu. The menu items pop up. We could

```
<?xml version="1.0"?>
<?xml-stylesheet href="chrome://global/skin" type="text/css"?>
<window

xmlns="http://www.mozilla.org/keymaster/gatekeeper/there.is.only.xul"
      align="vertical">
  <menubar>
     <menu label="Bookmarks">
       <menupopup>
          <menuitem id="B" label="http://www.xml.com/"/>
          <menuitem id="C" label="http://www.btg.com/"/>
          <menuitem id="D" label="http://www.xulportal.com/"/>
          <menuitem id="E" label="http://www.yahoo.com/"/>
       </menupopup>
     </menu>
  </menubar>
</window>
```

Code Listing 6.8 Generated XUL output for bookmarks.

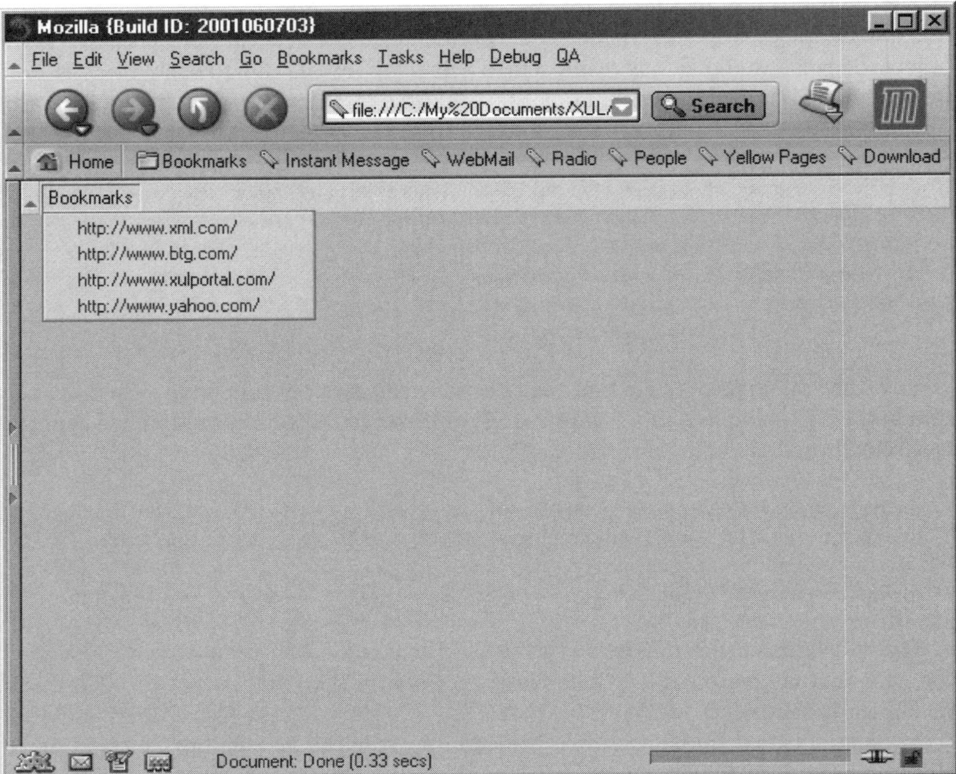

Figure 6.6 Loading the Bookmark example.

have certainly changed the main menu of the browser, but for debugging purposes, sometimes it is best to load it in the browser without changing the GUI.

Using Multiple Rules: The Book Example

As we have seen from the bookmark example, understanding the syntax of RDF datasources is important, and it is especially important to be able to draw an RDF graph from an RDF file. That way, identifying the subject-predicate-object triples for building the logic of your XUL template becomes much easier. Now, we will give an example of using multiple rules for pattern matching, using an RDF file presented earlier in the chapter in Code Listing 6.3 and graphed in Figure 6.4. Because we are familiar with the XUL objects for menus and menuitems, we will create an example that shows the books and chapters from the RDF file as menuitems.

Code Listing 6.9 presents the XUL for information from the RDF file. Notice that directly beneath the <template> element are two sets of rules. How does XUL handle this? We'll step through the XUL template and find out.

```
<?xml version="1.0"?>
<?xml-stylesheet href="chrome://global/skin" type="text/css"?>
<window xmlns:html="http://www.w3.org/xhtml"
      xmlns="http://www.mozilla.org/keymaster/gatekeeper/
there.is.only.xul"
      align="vertical">
  <menubar>
  <menu label="A Tale of Two Cities">

  <menupopup datasources="dickens.rdf" ref="urn:root">
     <template>
       <rule>
         <conditions>
            <content uri="?uri" />
            <triple subject="?uri"
                    predicate="http://home.netscape.com/NC-
                      rdf#hierarchy"
                    object="?hierarchy"/>
            <member container="?hierarchy" child="?child" />
            <triple subject="?child"
                    predicate="http://home.netscape.com/NC-rdf#name"
                    object="?name"/>
            <triple subject="?child"
                    predicate="http://home.netscape.com/NC-
                      rdf#chapter"
                    object="?chapter"/>
            <triple subject="?chapter"
                    predicate="http://home.netscape.com/NC-rdf#name"
                    object="?chname"/>
            <triple subject="?chapter"
                    predicate="http://home.netscape.com/NC-
                      rdf#numpages"
                    object="?numpages"/>
         </conditions>
         <action>
              <menuitem uri="?chapter"
                        label="?name -> ?chname - ?numpages pages"/>
         </action>
       </rule>
       <rule>
          <conditions>
            <content uri="?uri" />
            <triple subject="?uri"
                    predicate="http://home.netscape.com/NC-
                      rdf#hierarchy"
                    object="?hierarchy"/>
```

continues

Code Listing 6.9 A XUL file for presenting a book.

```
            <member container="?hierarchy" child="?book" />
            <triple subject="?book"
                    predicate="http://home.netscape.com/NC-rdf#name"
                    object="?name"/>
            <triple subject="?book"
                    predicate="http://home.netscape.com/NC-
                      rdf#chapter"
                    object="?chapter"/>
            <triple subject="?chapter"
                    predicate="http://home.netscape.com/NC-rdf#name"
                    object="?chname"/>
         </conditions>
         <action>
              <!-- note: in the value attribute of menuitem,
                   anything that is not a variable (i.e not
                   preceded by a question mark) is raw text
                -->
              <menuitem uri="?chapter"
                        label="?name -> ?chname -unknown # pages"/>
         </action>
       </rule>
      </template>
     </menupopup>
    </menu>
  </menubar>
</window>
```

Code Listing 6.9 A XUL file for presenting a book (Continued).

First of all, notice that our XUL file creates a menubar with a menu that has the value of "A Tale of Two Cities". We then map the menupopup element to the resource in the RDF file to the element that has the "urn:root" reference. Because two rule sets exist, we will break the building of the resulting set tree into two parts: Rule Set 1 and Rule Set 2.

Generating Results from Rule Set 1

In our conditions section, the <content> test binds the *?uri* variable to the resource "urn:root". Our result set begins with the following:

```
{(?uri=urn:root)}
```

The next <triple> test searches for the relationship beginning with "urn:root", using the predicate "nc:hierarchy" (short for http://home.netscape.com/NC-rdf#hierarchy/), and a binding variable ?hierarchy. As we look at the graph in Figure 6.4, we see that the relationship between "urn:root" and anonymous resource, "A", satisfies that relationship, binding the ?hierarchy variable to A. Our result set is now:

```
{(?uri=urn:root)(?hierarchy=A)}
```

The next <member> test looks for a descendant of "?hierarchy", which we know is bound to A by looking at our last result set. The <member> test binds the result to the ?book variable. If we look at the graph in Figure 6.2, we see that three nodes satisfy this relationship, creating three result sets:

```
{(?uri=urn:root)(?hierarchy=A)(?book=book1)}
{(?uri=urn:root)(?hierarchy=A)(?book=book2)}
{(?uri=urn:root)(?hierarchy=A)(?book=book3)}
```

The next <triple> test looks for the relationship defined by "?book" being the subject, "nc:name" being the predicate, and ?name being the object. Because we have solved for ?book from the result of the last test, we look in the RDF graph for the ?name that solves this relation for each of our three result sets. Because there is such a relationship between the book1 resource and "Recalled To Life," the book2 resource and "The Golden Thread," and the book3 resource and "The Track of A Storm," our result sets are shown below:

```
{(?uri=urn:root)(?hierarchy=A)(?book=book1)(?name="Recalled To Life")}
{(?uri=urn:root)(?hierarchy=A)(?book=book2)(?name="The Golden Thread")}
{(?uri=urn:root)(?hierarchy=A)(?book=book3)
  (?name="The Track of A Storm")}
```

The next <triple> test looks for a relationship with ?book being the subject, nc:chapter being the predicate, and with ?chapter being the new variable that is bound to the object. Because we have already solved for ?book, it is easy to see that we have six sets. Each ?book variable has two relationships that satisfy this test. For the purpose of brevity, we will only list a portion of the result set:

```
{.. (?chapter=B1C1)},{..(?chapter=B1C2)},{..(?chapter="B2C1")}
{.. (?chapter=B2C2)},{..(?chapter=B3C1)},{..(?chapter="B3C2")}
```

The next <triple> test looks for the relationship with ?chapter being the subject, nc:name being the predicate, and a new variable called ?chname. Because we do have six result sets, we apply this rule to each, adding the following to each result set:

```
(?chname="The Period"),(?chname="The Mail"),(?chname="Five Years Later")
(?chname="A Sight"),(?chname="In Secret"),(?chname="The Grindstone")
```

The final <triple> test in the first rule set looks for the relationship between the ?chapter variable having the predicate "nc:numpages". The result variable is ?numpages. Looking at our six result sets and looking at the RDF graph in Figure 6.4, we can see only four result sets from this, because two chapters do not have a nc:numpages predicate. We now

```
   RESULT SET 1:
{(?uri=urn:root)(?hierarchy=A)(?book=book1)(?name="Recalled To Life")
 (?chapter=B1C1)(?chname="The Period")(?numpages="30")}
RESULT SET 2:
{(?uri=urn:root)(?hierarchy=A)(?book=book1)(?name="Recalled To Life")
 (?chapter=B1C2)(?chname="The Mail")(?numpages="10")}
RESULT SET 3:
{(?uri=urn:root)(?hierarchy=A)(?book=book2)(?name="The Golden Thread")
 (?chapter=B2C2)(?chname="A Sight")(?numpages="30")}
RESULT SET 4:
{(?uri=urn:root)(?hierarchy=A)(?book=book3)
   (?name="The Track of A Storm")(?chapter=B3C1)(?chname="In Secret")
   (?numpages="10")}
```

Code Listing 6.10 Result sets from Rule Set 1.

have only four result sets, eliminating two. The final result set from this rule segment is shown in Code Listing 6.10.

Why were two result sets eliminated? Well, as we trace down the condition tests, if one result set does not match, it goes away. Using the result sets, let's populate the <action> section from Code Listing 6.9. We will show the result of this in Code Listing 6.11.

Generating Results from Rule Set 2

Now, let's look at the second rule set in Code Listing 6.9. The rules are actually the same, except that the last triple that was in Rule Set 1 is not in the second rule set. Because this is the case and we stepped through this process in Rule Set 1, we will list the value of this rule set in Code Listing 6.12. If you recall, before the final rule was executed in Rule Set 1, there were six result sets.

```
<menuitem id="B1C1"
          label="Recalled To Life --> The Period - 30 pages"/>
<menuitem id="B1C2"
          label="Recalled To Life --> The Mail - 10 pages"/>
<menuitem id="B2C2"
          label="The Golden Thread --> A Sight - 30 pages"/>
<menuitem id="B3C1"
          label="The Track of A Storm --> In Secret - 10 pages"/>
```

Code Listing 6.11 Populated <action> content from Rule Set 1.

```
RESULT SET 1:
{(?uri=urn:root)(?hierarchy=A)(?book=book1)(?name="Recalled To Life")
 (?chapter=B1C1)(?chname="The Period")}

RESULT SET 2:
{(?uri=urn:root)(?hierarchy=A)(?book=book1)(?name="Recalled To Life")
 (?chapter=B1C2)(?chname="The Mail")}

RESULT SET 3:
{(?uri=urn:root)(?hierarchy=A)(?book=book2)(?name="The Golden Thread")
 (?chapter=B2C1(?chname="Five Years Later")}

RESULT SET 4:
{(?uri=urn:root)(?hierarchy=A)(?book=book2)(?name="The Golden Thread")
 (?chapter=B2C2)(?chname="A Sight")}

RESULT SET 5:
{(?uri=urn:root)(?hierarchy=A)(?book=book2)
 (?name="The Track of A Storm")(?chapter=B3C1)(?chname="In Secret")}
RESULT SET 6:
{(?uri=urn:root)(?hierarchy=A)(?book=book2)
 (?name="The Track of A Storm")(?chapter=B3C1)
 (?chname="The Grindstonea)}
```

Code Listing 6.12 Results from Rule Set 2.

Now that we have generated the results from Rule Set 2, let's generate the action content, shown in Code Listing 6.13. In order to do this, look at the XUL Code Listing 6.9. For each rule set, the action section creates a menuitem and puts multiple things in the value attribute, saying that each chapter has an unknown amount of pages.

Merging Content

Well, now that we have populated action content from both rules, what do we do? Because identifiers in a XUL document (or XML document, for that matter) must be unique, we must somehow merge the populated content. The guidance for building XUL content is quite simple; even though one rule might match for a particular container/member pair, only one rule set for that element is allowed to build content.[5] The selection process picks the populated action content produced by the first rule set (in this case, the populated content from Rule Set 1 shown in Code Listing 6.11) and masks it with the populated action content from the following rule sets (in this case, the populated content in Code Listing 6.12). The result of this merge produces the action content in Code Listing 6.14.

Finally, after the action content is populated, we see the end result in Code Listing 6.15, which describes a menubar with the chapters from our book example. As you can

```
<menuitem id="B1C1"
          label="Recalled To Life --> The Period -unknown pages"/>
<menuitem id="B1C2"
          label="Recalled To Life --> The Mail -unknown pages"/>
<menuitem id="B2C1"
          label="The Golden Thread --> Five Years Later -unknown
pages"/>
<menuitem id="B2C2"
          label="The Golden Thread --> A Sight -unknown pages"/>
<menuitem id="B3C1"
          label="The Track of A Storm --> In Secret -unknown pages"/>
<menuitem id="B3C2"
         label="The Track of A Storm --> The Grindstone -unknown
pages"/>
```

Code Listing 6.13 Populated <action> content from Rule Set 2.

```
<menuitem id="B1C1"
          label="Recalled To Life --> The Period - 30 pages"/>
<menuitem id="B1C2"
          label="Recalled To Life --> The Mail - 10 pages"/>
<menuitem id="B2C2"
          label="The Golden Thread --> A Sight - 30 pages"/>
<menuitem id="B3C1"
          label="The Track of A Storm --> In Secret - 10 pages"/>
<menuitem id="B2C1"
          label="The Golden Thread --> Five Years Later -unknown
pages"/>
<menuitem id="B3C2"
         label="The Track of A Storm --> The Grindstone -unknown
pages"/>
```

Code Listing 6.14 Merged <action> populated content.

see, the result of our <action> content was placed beneath the menupopup element. The dynamically generated content in the Mozilla browser is shown in Figure 6.7.

Using Binding: Modifying the Book Example

Binding enables us to create optional variable bindings that do not affect the match. As you saw in the last section, the tests in the first rule eliminated two of the six sets,

```
<?xml version="1.0"?>
<?xml-stylesheet href="chrome://global/skin" type="text/css"?>
<window xmlns:html="http://www.w3.org/xhtml"
        xmlns="http://www.mozilla.org/keymaster/gatekeeper/
there.is.only.xul"
        align="vertical">
  <menubar>
  <menu label="A Tale of Two Cities">
  <menupopup>
      <menuitem id="B1C1"
          label="Recalled To Life --> The Period - 30 pages"/>
      <menuitem id="B1C2"
          label="Recalled To Life --> The Mail - 10 pages"/>
      <menuitem id="B2C2"
          label="The Golden Thread --> A Sight - 30 pages"/>
      <menuitem id="B3C1"
          label="The Track of A Storm --> In Secret - 10 pages"/>
      <menuitem id="B2C1"
          label="The Golden Thread --> Five Years Later -unknown
pages"/>
      <menuitem id="B3C2"
         label="The Track of A Storm --> The Grindstone -unknown
pages"/>
  </menupopup>
  </menu>
  </menubar>
</window>
```

Code Listing 6.15 Final generated output for book example.

because those sets did not have a chapter with the "nc:numpages" predicate. The last <triple> tests in the first rule set caused this to happen. Rule Set 2 in the book example from Code Listing 6.9 had all tests, with the final <triple> test eliminated. For the purposes of demonstrating bindings, we will use one rule set (Rule Set 2) from the book example, but we will use bindings to bind the ?numpages variable, creating a match like we did in the final <triple> test from Rule Set 1. Code Listing 6.16 shows the result of modifying the XUL file to create this.

If you look closely at the XUL template code in Code Listing 6.16, you will notice that the <conditions> section produces six result sets. Luckily, we have already listed these result sets in our previous example, in Code Listing 6.12.

The <bindings> section of the code creates optional variable bindings. After we have created result sets from the conditions section, we are ready to add our bindings from the bindings section. This is shown in Code Listing 6.17.

Looking at Code Listing 6.17, notice that Result Set 2 and Result Set 6 do not have a binding for ?numpages, but these result sets still exist. We have just demonstrated the

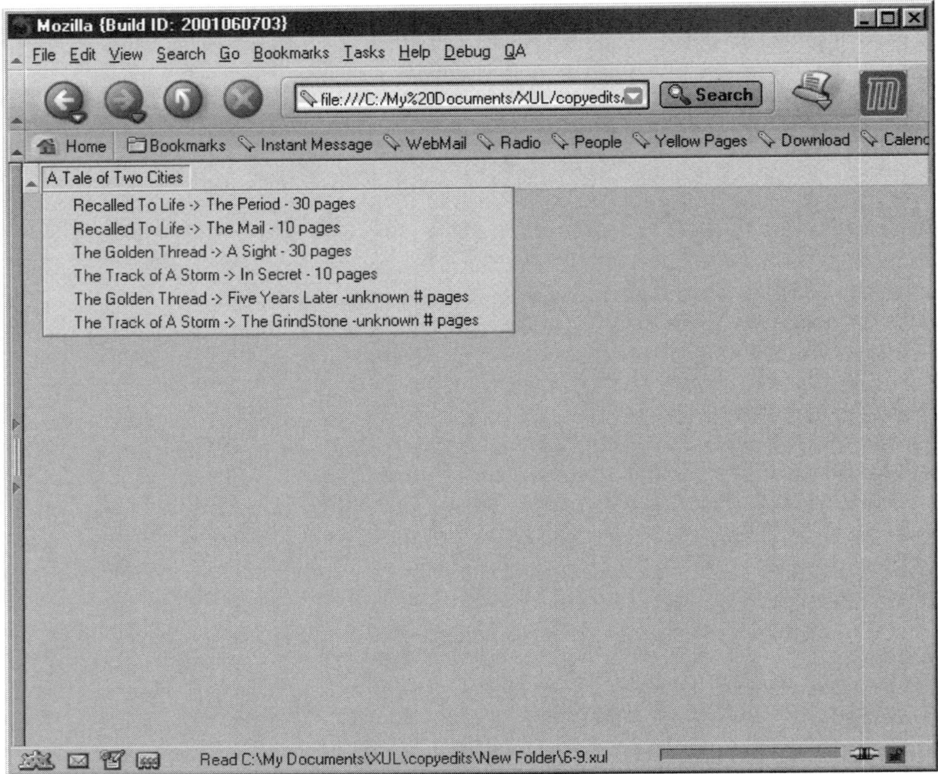

Figure 6.7 Loading the book example.

difference between tests in the <conditions> section and tests in the <bindings> section. Using these result sets, we are now ready to apply the <action> section to each result set, and the dynamically generated content is shown in Code Listing 6.18.

Because a ?numpages variable does not exist in two of the result sets, the <action> section ignores the ?numpages variable for those cases. After loading the XUL file into the Mozilla browser and clicking on the "A Tale Of Two Cities" menu, Figure 6.8 shows the result.

NOTE **What if the binding section did not exist in this example? If there were no binding section in Code Listing 6.16, there would not be a ?numpages variable. If, instead, we created a <triple> test to create the ?numpages variable in the <conditions> section, there would only be four result sets, because two result sets do not match the pattern. What the <bindings> section buys us here is another variable. Although the test for the ?numpages variable may not always match in the <bindings> section, a nonmatch does not nullify a result set.**

```
<?xml version="1.0"?>
<?xml-stylesheet href="chrome://global/skin" type="text/css"?>
<window xmlns:html="http://www.w3.org/xhtml"
        xmlns="http://www.mozilla.org/keymaster/gatekeeper/
          there.is.only.xul"
        align="vertical">
  <menubar>
  <menu label="A Tale of Two Cities">
  <menupopup datasources="dickens.rdf" ref="urn:root">
     <template>
       <rule>
         <conditions>
            <content uri="?uri" />
            <triple subject="?uri"
                    predicate="http://home.netscape.com/NC-
                      rdf#hierarchy"
                    object="?hierarchy"/>
            <member container="?hierarchy" child="?child" />
            <triple subject="?child"
                    predicate="http://home.netscape.com/NC-rdf#name"
                    object="?name"/>
            <triple subject="?child"
                    predicate="http://home.netscape.com/NC-
                      rdf#chapter"
                    object="?chapter"/>
            <triple subject="?chapter"
                    predicate="http://home.netscape.com/NC-rdf#name"
                    object="?chname"/>
         </conditions>
         <bindings>
            <!-- this is the original triple test that eliminated
                 2 result sets in our Book Example. However, bindings
                 are NOT conditions - they eliminate nothing!
              -->
            <binding subject="?chapter"
                     predicate="http://home.netscape.com/NC-
                      rdf#numpages"
                     object="?numpages"/>
         </bindings>
         <action>
              <menuitem uri="?chapter"
                        label="?name --> ?chname - ?numpages pages"/>
         </action>
       </rule>
    </template>
```

continues

Code Listing 6.16 Modifying the book example to use bindings,

```
    </menupopup>
    </menu>
   </menubar>
  </window>
```

Code Listing 6.16 Modifying the book example to use bindings (Continued).

```
RESULT SET 1:
{(?uri=urn:root)(?hierarchy=A)(?book=book1)(?name="Recalled To Life")
 (?chapter=B1C1)(?chname="The Period")(?numpages="30)}

RESULT SET 2:
{(?uri=urn:root)(?hierarchy=A)(?book=book1)(?name="Recalled To Life")
 (?chapter=B1C2)(?chname="The Mail")(?numpages="10")}
RESULT SET 3:
{(?uri=urn:root)(?hierarchy=A)(?book=book2)(?name="The Golden Thread")
 (?chapter=B2C1(?chname="Five Years Later")}
RESULT SET 4:
{(?uri=urn:root)(?hierarchy=A)(?book=book2)(?name="The Golden Thread")
 (?chapter=B2C2)(?chname="A Sight")(?numpages="30")}
RESULT SET 5:
{(?uri=urn:root)(?hierarchy=A)(?book=book2)
 (?name="The Track of A Storm")(?chapter=B3C1)(?chname="In Secret")
 (?numpages="10")}
RESULT SET 6:
{(?uri=urn:root)(?hierarchy=A)(?book=book2)
 (?name="The Track of A Storm")(?chapter=B3C1)
 (?chname="The Grindstone")}
```

Code Listing 6.17 Result set after the <bindings> section.

Using and Testing XUL Templates in Mozilla and Netscape 6.x

As we have built the examples in this chapter, we have screen shots of simply loading the XUL files in the Mozilla browser. The latest version of Netscape 6.x should be able to load them as well. Of course, we don't always intend for the XUL application content to appear in the document portion of the browser, but it is often helpful when testing each XUL module at a time. At the time the book was written, the browser does syntax checking on the XUL file itself. If the XUL file is not well-formed, the browser will report the exact position of the error in the file. However, it does not check for syntax on the RDF file that is being loaded into the XUL template. The browser also does not display the dynamically generated XUL, so it is often difficult to determine whether your rules were successful. It is for this reason that it is very important for XUL authors

```
<?xml version="1.0"?>
<?xml-stylesheet href="chrome://global/skin" type="text/css"?>
<window xmlns:html="http://www.w3.org/xhtml"
        xmlns="http://www.mozilla.org/keymaster/gatekeeper/
there.is.only.xul"
        align="vertical">
  <menubar>
  <menu label="A Tale of Two Cities">
  <menupopup>
      <menuitem id="B1C1"
          label="Recalled To Life --> The Period - 30 pages"/>
      <menuitem id="B1C2"
          label="Recalled To Life --> The Mail - 10 pages"/>
      <menuitem id="B2C1"
          label="The Golden Thread --> Five Years Later - pages"/>
      <menuitem id="B2C2"
          label="The Golden Thread --> A Sight - 30 pages"/>
      <menuitem id="B3C1"
          label="The Track of A Storm --> In Secret - 10 pages"/>
      <menuitem id="B3C2"
          label="The Track of A Storm --> The Grindstone - pages"/>
  </menupopup>
  </menu>
  </menubar>
</window>
```

Code Listing 6.18 Final generated output for binding.

to know how to build graphs from RDF files to be able to step-through the template rules as they are writing them. We found that it was helpful to start from a very simple template that works and incrementally add content. We also found that it was helpful to save backup versions of the files that worked.

After you have authored some content using RDF and XUL templates and tested them in the browser, you are ready to add these new windows to other elements of the browser by changing some of the main application XUL files and inserting your new content.

Summary

This chapter presented a brief overview of Resource Description Framework (RDF), described how to graph RDF files, and discussed how Internet resources can be described using this syntax. We showed how XUL templates can use RDF datasources to dynamically build content. We introduced you to XUL templates and gave real-world examples of how to build them. As the chapter progressed, we created simple rule-based pattern-matching templates and provided more complex examples, showing the

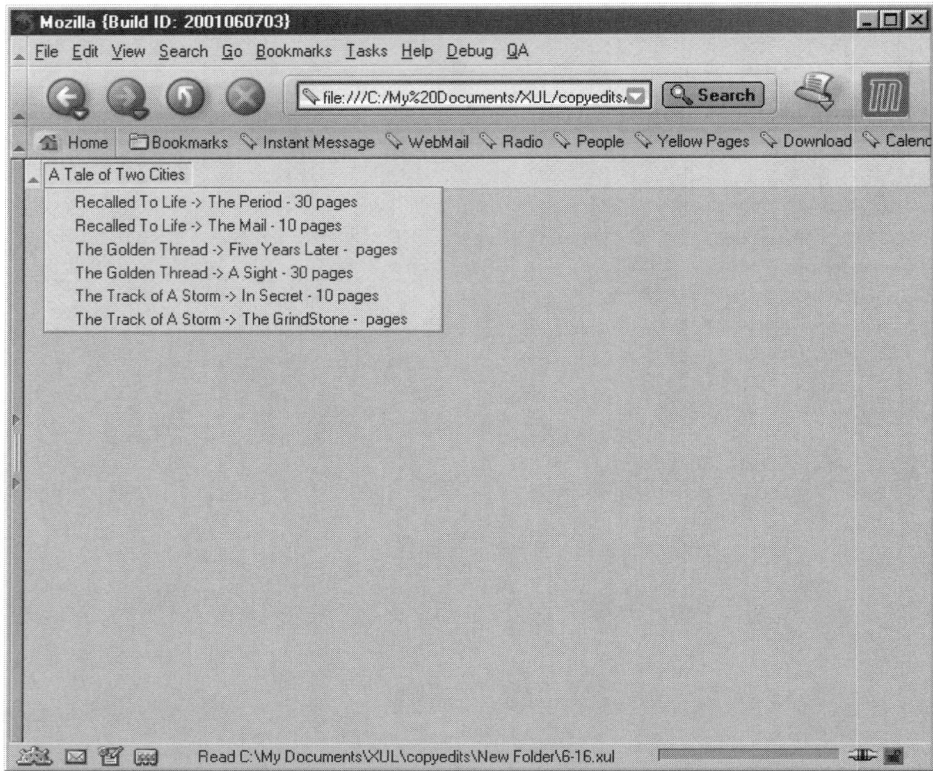

Figure 6.8 Looking at the binding example.

effects of multiple rules and bindings in XUL templates. We used the Netscape 6.x browser to test and present the dynamically generated content from our examples, and finally, we gave tips on how to successfully use the browser to test your code.

XUL templates give the programmer flexibility for displaying changing content, and RDF files provide the mechanism for describing this content. Using these technologies with XUL elements provides maximum flexibility for dynamic and adaptable user interfaces.

Chapter 9 will demonstrate XUL templates being put to use in a practical example, and Chapter 10 will also offer a case study where XUL loads RDF data sources. As XUL templates provide flexibility for generating XUL content, our next chapter will focus on the technologies that XUL uses to offer you extensibility in creating new interfaces.

Notes

[1]W3C Metadata Activity, *Resource Description Framework*, http://www.w3.org/RDF/, 2000.

[2]W3C Metadata Activity, *Resource Description Framework (RDF) Model and Syntax Specification, W3C Recommendation*, http://www.w3.org/TR/REC-rdf-syntax/, February 22, 1999.

[3]Chris Waterson, "XUL Template Primer," Mozilla.org, http://www.mozilla.org/docs/xul/xulnotes/template-primer.html, 1999.

[4]Hyatt, Churchill, and Waterson, "XUL <template> reference," Mozilla.org, http://www.mozilla.org/doc/xul-template-reference.html, 2000.

[5]Chris Waterson, "XUL Template Primer—Multiple Rules," Mozilla.org, http://www.mozilla.org/docs/xul/xulnotes/template-multi.html, 2000.

XUL Overlays and XBL

If you build systems and then reflect on what you build, you will see patterns in what you do.

Gamma, Helm, Johnson, Vlissides, *Design Patterns*

In software projects, the development of reusable components into modular software libraries helps save development time. Reusability and extensibility are important concepts that can be used to make a software system flexible and less complex in the software development cycle. This chapter introduces how these concepts of code reuse and extensibility are applied to the XUL language with XUL overlays and the XML Binding Language (XBL).

XUL overlays are part of the core XUL language, and these files contain XUL content that can be reused by different XUL-based applications. When a XUL file references an overlay file, XUL content from that overlay file is dynamically inserted into that XUL application. Typically, a XUL overlay file contains things that are used and shared repeatedly in many XUL applications, like toolbars with common buttons, menus with common menu items, and other widgets with common characteristics. By using XUL overlays, you can write XUL content once, so that it can be used repeatedly in an application.

Unlike XUL overlays, XBL is a separate language not dependent on XUL. XBL stands for the XML Binding Language, and it is a markup language for describing bindings that can be used to add to the behavior of elements in any XML document. An XBL document can describe bindings that add new properties, methods, event handlers, and content, which can be attached to XUL elements. When a XUL element is attached to a binding described in an XBL file, that element is extended to include this new data and behavior. Bindings can be reused throughout the code base of an application or between applications, promoting the concepts of both reuse and extensibility in XML-based software projects. Although the XBL language is not limited to XUL, it is used repeatedly in the code for the Mozilla and Netscape 6.x browser, and it is an exciting technology for dynamically changing document content.

Both XUL overlays and XBL can be used to create reusable software modules in XUL applications. In this chapter, we describe the syntax of XUL overlays and XBL, and we provide examples and demonstrations of how these mechanisms work. Both XUL overlays and XBL are easy to learn, and they can be valuable in any XUL project.

Using XUL Overlays

Every application contains widgets, menus, toolbars, and buttons that are used repeatedly. Usually, a menu bar has File, Edit, and Help menus, with menu items like Open, Save, Cut, Copy, and Paste. Toolbars may have common buttons in them, which many dialogs in your application will want to use. In XUL, as a developer, you have a choice to build these items in XUL from scratch every time you use them, or you can use XUL overlays to share functionality throughout your XUL code library. This section discusses the syntax of XUL overlays and gives you examples of how to use them.

XUL Overlay Syntax and Rules

A XUL overlay is a self-contained overlay file that contains XUL content which will be placed over content from a base window. The syntax for XUL overlay files is quite simple: The <overlay> tag is the root element of the document, and all subcontent is XUL content. All XUL content referenced should be uniquely identified by the id attribute. This syntax is demonstrated by the overlay skeleton code shown in Code Listing 7.1.

Any XUL content can be placed in an overlay XUL file, but because the content will be referenced by another XUL file, elements that will be reused should have their id attribute specified. A XUL file that wants to use an overlay file must specify it by using

```
<?xml version="1.0"?>
<!--xuloverlaysyntax.xul-->
<overlay id="myoverlay"

  xmlns="http://www.mozilla.org/keymaster/gatekeeper/there.is.only.
    xul">

<!-- Any XUL content can go here, but any content you want to pull into
     another XUL document should have an id attribute!
 -->

</overlay>
```

Code Listing 7.1 XUL overlay file syntax.

the <?xul-overlay> directive, specifying the overlay file with the href attribute, as is shown in the following line of code.

```
<?xul-overlay href="overlayfile.xul"?>
```

When a main XUL file references an overlay file with the <?xul-overlay> directive, elements in that main XUL file can reference overlay content by id. If a XUL element in the overlay file has the same id as a XUL element in the main XUL file, the matching XUL overlay content and its children will be *overlayed* (placed on top of) the element in the main XUL file with that id. When the referencing element in the main XUL file has content, and the overlay element with the same id has content, the resulting content is merged. Let's look at a simple example that demonstrates how the overlay works.

Code Listing 7.2 shows an example overlay file, in which we have a simple box with the id of "testbox", which contains four buttons with values "This", "is", "a", and "Test." In this listing, notice that the only element with a unique identifier is the box with the id of testbox. This means that when we want this box to overlay another component, we will be referencing only the box in the base window content.

Code Listing 7.3 demonstrates the basic syntax of a XUL file referencing overlays. As you can see, the code listing has a directive referencing the overlay file, and it includes a box with no content with the same id as the box in the overlay file. Whenever an element in a XUL file has the same id as an element in a XUL overlay file, the element listed in the overlay will be placed over the content in the main XUL file. This process results in the generated content seen in Code Listing 7.4.

Code Listing 7.4 shows the resulting content. Although the base class referenced an empty box with the same id as the box in the overlay file, the content from the box in the overlay file was merged with the XUL content of the box in the main XUL file.

If the preceding example has you wondering what would happen if the box in the main XUL file already contained content, you are on the right track. Rules are associated with merging by using XUL overlays, and these rules revolve around attributes that

```
<?xml version="1.0"?>
<overlay

  xmlns="http://www.mozilla.org/keymaster/gatekeeper/there.is.only.
    xul">
    <box id="testbox" style="background-color:white" flex="1">
         <button style="background-color:yellow" label="This"/>
         <button label="is"/>
         <button style="background-color:lightblue" label="a"/>
         <button style="background-color:lightgreen"
              label="Test"/>
     </box>
</overlay>
```

Code Listing 7.2. Example overlay file.

```
<?xml version="1.0"?>
<window
  xmlns="http://www.mozilla.org/keymaster/gatekeeper/there.is.only.
    xul">
<?xul-overlay href="overlayex.xul"?>

<box id="testbox" flex="1"/>

</window>
```

Code Listing 7.3 XUL file using the overlay file.

```
<?xml version="1.0"?>
<window
  xmlns="http://www.mozilla.org/keymaster/gatekeeper/there.is.only.
    xul">
<?xul-overlay href="overlaysyntax.xul"?>

     <box id="testbox" style="background-color:white" flex="1">
          <button style="background-color:yellow" label="This"/>
          <button label="is"/>
          <button style="background-color:lightblue" label="a"/>
          <button style="background-color:lightgreen"
               label="Test!"/>
     </box>

</window>
```

Code Listing 7.4 Resulting XUL content.

can be in the elements in a XUL overlay file. Table 7.1 shows a list of these attributes along with their descriptions.

Elements in an overlay file may have the attributes described in Table 7.1. When a window is using an overlay to overlay content, it looks for id matches. For each element in the main XUL file that matches the id of an overlay element, the following rules are used:

- Attributes from the overlay element will be added to the element that matches its id.
- If the overlay element contains an insertafter attribute that matches a node in the referencing XUL file, the overlay element will be added as the next sibling of the matched element.
- If the overlay element contains an insertbefore attribute that matches a node in the referencing XUL file, the overlay element will be added as the previous sibling of the matched element.

Table 7.1 Attributes Used in Overlays for Positioning

ATTRIBUTE	DESCRIPTION
insertafter	This attribute is optional and can be specified in an element in an overlay file. It is set to an id that matches an element in the main XUL file (the main file referencing the overlay). When an overlay element with this attribute matches an element in the main XUL file, the overlay element will be inserted *after* the matched node in the main XUL file.
insertbefore	This attribute is optional and can be specified in an element in an overlay file. It is set to an id that matches an element in the main XUL file (the main file referencing the overlay). When an overlay element with this attribute matches an element in the main XUL file, the overlay element will be inserted *before* the matched node in the main XUL file.
position	This attribute is optional and can be specified in an element in an overlay file. It is set to a *one-based position number* of the element in its container. When this attribute is set, the element is added at this index in its container. For example, when an overlay element has the *position* attribute set to "1", the element will always be the first element in the container when content from the overlay is generated in a main XUL file.

- If the overlay element contains a position attribute, the overlay element will be placed in this one-based index in its container.
- If the overlay element has none of the attributes specified in Table 7.1, it will be added as the last element.

An important thing to notice is that the element in the main XUL file referencing the overlay has priority. If the overlay elements do not specifically denote their positioning, they will be added at the end of the list, so that the children of the main element have priority. What happens when elements in a XUL file do not match any id values of a referenced overlay file? In that case, the overlay file is ignored. In "XUL Overlay Example," we give a detailed example of how these rules are used.

TIP **If a developer would like to reuse a XUL overlay, should overlay elements really have an insertafter or an insertbefore attribute? That's a good question. If you would like to create generic elements that could be used repeatedly, using the position attribute might be a better alternative, because you do not tie the overlay code to a specific main XUL file. However, the insertafter and the insertbefore attributes can be quite useful when you are using JavaScript to manipulate the XUL DOM. Instead of setting those specific attributes in the overlay file, you could have a JavaScript function called by a main XUL file set the insertafter and insertbefore attributes on the XUL overlay elements before the main XUL file is loaded. This way, your overlays can be truly generic.**

XUL Overlay Example

At this point, we have discussed rules and syntax, and we have showed you the basic format of XUL overlay files. Now, we will show you a real-world example. As we discussed in the introduction of this chapter, you may find it useful to create XUL overlays to promote code reuse in a project. Graphical items that are often used throughout XUL applications are <menu> and <menuitem> elements that share functionality. This example demonstrates using overlays for menus.

In Code Listing 7.5, we see that our overlay file contains a listing of generic <menupopup> elements which contain some of the functionality that most menus should have. Menu items that are common in most applications are the frequently seen File->Open, File->Exit, Edit-Cut, Edit->Copy, Edit->Paste, Help->About, Help->Contents, and Help->Search for Help On . . . menu items. We have placed all of these items in our overlay in Code Listing 7.5. In our example, both <menupopup> and <menuitem> elements have id attributes so that they can be uniquely referenced from a calling XUL file.

```
<?xml version="1.0"?>
<!-- This is a good example of how overlays work.
    This file lists a bunch of generic menu popups
    that we can use with many XUL files!
-->
<overlay id="generic-menuoverlay"
xmlns="http://www.mozilla.org/keymaster/gatekeeper/there.is.only.xul">
 <!--Generic File Menu Popup -->

    <menupopup id="generic-filepopup">
     <menuitem id="genericfile-open"
           label="Open..."
           accesskey="o"
           oncommand="fileOpen()"/>
     <menuitem id="genericfile-exit"
           label="Exit"
           accesskey="x"
           oncommand="fileExit()"/>
    </menupopup>

 <!-- Generic Edit Menu Popup-->

    <menupopup id="generic-editpopup">
     <menuitem id="genericedit-cut"
           label="Cut"
           accesskey="t"
           oncommand="editCut()"/>
     <menuitem id="genericedit-copy"
           label="Copy"
           accesskey="c"
           oncommand="editCopy()"/>
```

Code Listing 7.5 An overlay for generic menu popups.

```
      <menuitem id="genericedit-paste"
            label="Paste"
            accesskey="p"
            oncommand="editPaste()"/>
    </menupopup>

  <!-- Generic Help Menu Popup -->
  <!-- note that we put the position # in
    each menuitem, so that these menuitems
    appear before the other menuitems in the
    XUL file. Otherwise, all of these would
    appear last!
    -->
    <menupopup id="generic-helppopup">
  <menuitem id="generichelp-about"
            label="About..."
            accesskey="a"
            position="1"
            oncommand="helpAbout()"/>
    <menuitem id="generichelp-contents"
            label="Contents..."
            accesskey="n"
            position="2"
            oncommand="helpContents()"/>
    <menuitem id="generichelp-search"
            label="Search For Help On..."
            accesskey="s"
            position="3"
                  oncommand="helpSearch()"/>
    </menupopup>
  </overlay>
```

Code Listing 7.5 An overlay for generic menu popups.

When the XUL file references this overlay file, it may have <menupopup> elements and <menuitem> elements matching the ids of the overlay elements, resulting in a merge of the elements from the two files. Notice that in our overlay file in Code Listing 7.5, we set the position attribute on the <menuitem> elements in the generic Help menu. Because the position attributes on those elements are "1", "2", and "3", we know that these <menuitem> elements will always come first in the Help menu. Because we did not specify any other positioning attributes in any of the other menus in the overlay file, those menu items will always appear last when they are referenced by a XUL file.

See the XUL overlay file in Code Listing 7.6, a simple application that requires menus. The main XUL file creates three menus: File, Edit, and Help, which reference <menupopup> elements that match elements in the overlay file. In the case of the File and Help menus, the main XUL file in Code Listing 7.6 adds a <menuitem>. We add a File->New, and a Help->Search the Internet . . . menu item to the File menu and Help menu.

The resulting content is an XML merge between the main XUL file and the overlay file. In the case of the File menu, the new <menuitem> element is added before the elements from the overlay, because this is the default condition. In the case of the Help menu, the new <menuitem> is added last, because the help menuitems in the overlay file have set their absolute (one-based) positioning with the position attribute. The result of each of these merged <menupopup> elements can be seen in Figure 7.1, where we have included three screen shots of each menu's drop-down options.

Using XUL overlays is a great way to create a modular code base of graphical components. As we have shown you, it is not too difficult to get started. In our next section, we discuss XBL, and how it can be used to extend XUL components.

Using XML Binding Language (XBL)

Although not specifically tied to the XUL markup language, the XML Binding Language (XBL) is a language for describing behavior and content that can be attached to XML elements and is often used with XUL elements. Like overlays, bindings can be used repeatedly in XML-based software projects to extend the behavior of elements. XBL also introduces the concept of encapsulation: by using bindings, you can create a black-box widget, allowing objects to interact with it without knowing the tedious implementation details.

NOTE Although XBL was originally developed and deployed at Mozilla.org, the XBL 1.0 specification became a W3C Note in February 2001, residing on the Web at www.w3.org/TR/xbl/. The note was submitted to the W3C with the intention that they use it as a basis for furthering the work on Behavioral Extensions to CSS (BECSS). The actual implementation of XBL with Mozilla is different from the specification. This chapter focuses on the implementation of XBL as it pertains to XUL in the Mozilla.org implementation.

Figure 7.1 Resulting menus from overlay example.

```
<?xml version="1.0"?>
<!-- This is a good example of how we can use XUL overlays.
   We will take the menupopups from the menuoverlay.xul file
   and we will add other menuitems to the menupopups.
-->

<window id="main-window"
xmlns="http://www.mozilla.org/keymaster/gatekeeper/there.is.only.xul">
 <?xul-overlay href="menuoverlay.xul"?>

 <menubar>

   <!-- File Menu: We add a menuitem to the menupopup-->
   <menu id="filemenu" label="File" accesskey="f">
    <menupopup id="generic-filepopup">
     <!-- In our example, this should be the
         first menuitem on the list -->

     <menuitem label="New"
               accesskey="n"
               oncommand="filenew()"/>
    </menupopup>
   </menu>

   <!-- Edit Menu : We take everything from the overlay!-->
   <menu id="editmenu" label="Edit" accesskey="e">
    <menupopup id="generic-editpopup"/>
   </menu>

   <!-- Help Menu: We add a menuitem to the popup-->
   <menu id="helpmenu" label="Help" accesskey="h">
    <menupopup id="generic-helppopup">
    <!-- In our example, this should be the last
         menuitem on the list because the overlay
         specified the positioning.
    -->
      <menuitem label="Search the Internet..."
            accesskey="e"
            oncommand="searchNet()"/>
    </menupopup>
   </menu>
 </menubar>
</window>
```

Code Listing 7.6 A XUL file using the menu overlay.

In describing XBL throughout this section, we describe a binding as being new content or behavior added to an XML element. The element that is extended with this new content or behavior is referred to as the bound element. Bindings can contain new JavaScript methods, properties, and event handlers, which can be a registered element. Bindings can also add content that is inserted in or around an element.[1]

We refer to XBL content as *anonymous content*. Elements that appear in a normal XML file are referred to as *explicit content*, because they are visible throughout the document and can be manipulated and viewed via the DOM API. Elements that are added to a bound element with XBL are called *anonymous* nodes because after they are bound to an element, they are not visible to their parent element in the main XML file. Content bound to an element with XBL is hidden and can't be accessed by normal DOM methods, such as getElementById(). When we combine this mechanism of information hiding with the addition of new properties and methods through XBL, we can create composite widgets, which can be treated as black boxes with known inputs and outputs.

Using XBL gives the XUL developer flexibility to add behavior to multiple XUL elements and to create composite GUI widgets, which can be treated as a black box. In this section, we discuss the syntax of XBL; we define the XBL elements; we show how to generate content with XBL; and we show how to add properties and methods with XBL. Throughout this section, we discuss XBL from a XUL perspective.

XBL Syntax

An XBL file is an XML file with the root tag <bindings>, which is currently defined in the namespace "http://www.mozilla.org/xbl/". The <bindings> tag contains a collection of <binding> elements that describe element behavior. Each <binding> can include the <content> tag, which is used to describe anonymous content that can be inserted around a bound element, an <implementation> tag that can describe new properties and methods, and a <handlers> tag that can describe event handlers that can be bound to an element. Code Listing 7.7 shows skeleton XBL describing the XBL file syntax.

As you can see from Code Listing 7.7, each binding should have a unique id that can be referenced to bind an element to the behavior. How can we bind elements to a particular binding? We can do this by adding a binding property to an element using CSS.

CSS Binding Syntax

By using CSS, we can set an element's "-moz-binding" property to a certain URI. The following piece of CSS code should give you a good idea of how this is done:

```
menubutton.button-toolbar-4
 {
    -moz-binding:
url("http://xulbook.com/bindings/menu.xml#menubutton");
  }
```

```
<?xml version="1.0"?>
<bindings xmlns="http://www.mozilla.org/xbl/">
  <binding id="firstbinding">
    <content>
     <!-- "Anonymous" XUL content can go here! -->
    </content>
    <implementation>
     <!-- New Properties and Methods can go here!-->
    </implementation>
    <handlers>
      <!-- New Event Handlers can go here! -->
    </handlers>
  </binding>
  <binding id="secondbinding">
   <!-- add code here! -->
  </binding>
  <binding id="thirdbinding">
   <!-- add code here! -->
  </binding>
</bindings>
```

Code Listing 7.7 XBL file syntax.

Using CSS is an easy way to bind elements in a XUL document. As long as an element matches the style rule in the CSS, the binding will remain attached to a bound element. When an element is removed from a document, the binding will be detached.

DOM XBL Methods

By using a DOM API that supports XBL, you can call certain JavaScript methods on your document. DOM documents that support XBL implement the DocumentXBL interface, which means that they support the JavaScript methods shown in Table 7.2.

As you can see from Table 7.2, using the DOM API gives you access to add bindings, remove bindings, and to get binding information about the entire XML document. When the DOM API is used to add a binding, the bindingattached event is fired. When a binding is removed, a bindingdetached event is fired. Using JavaScript, you can add handlers to listen to these events.

In the next section, we describe the syntax of the elements of XBL. Before we do that, we would like to show you a simple example to get you thinking about how XBL works. In our example, we will build a window with an opinion poll. In any survey or poll, multiple types of questions are asked. Some are Yes/No questions; some are multiple-choice questions; and some require the user to fill in the blank. For our simple example, we have two types: Yes/No and I agree/I disagree. We will assign a <toolbar> element

Table 7.2 Methods in DocumentXBL Interface

PROPERTY/METHOD	DESCRIPTION
getAnonymousNodes(element)	This returns the anonymous content of an element after the insertion points have been applied.
addBinding(element, URI)	This JavaScript method adds a binding to an element, given the URI parameter.
removeBinding(element, URI)	This JavaScript method removes a binding from an element, given the URI parameter.
getBindingParent(element)	This JavaScript method returns the bound element's parent, if the element was placed underneath an insertion point.
loadBindingDocument(url)	This method is used to obtain an XBL document for use within the current XML document. This JavaScript method returns the XBL document.

two different types of classes; we will create bindings for each type of the classes; and we will use a CSS to bind the different types of toolbar classes to the right bindings. Code Listing 7.8 shows our XUL source code for our main example.

In listing 7.8, we have two toolbars with different classes: "yesnotoolbar" and "agreeprompt". We will want to create bindings for each of these types of classes. For our "yesnotoolbar" class, we would like to have three buttons designating "Yes", "No", and "I don't understand". For our "agreeprompt" toolbar class, we would like to have three buttons designating "I agree", "I disagree", and "I don't care". Code Listing 7.9 shows an XBL file that creates content for these bindings.

```
<?xml version="1.0"?>
<?xml-stylesheet href="promptstyles.css" type="text/css"?>

<!-- This is a simple example of using XBL to hide the
    implementation details of different classes of
    XUL widgets - in this case, the contents of our toolbars!
-->

<window
  xmlns="http://www.mozilla.org/keymaster/gatekeeper/there.is.only.
    xul"
  xmlns:html="http://www.w3.org/1999/xhtml"
  align="vertical">
```

Code Listing 7.8 XUL file for opinion poll

```
  <html:center>
   <html:h1>
    Opinion Poll!
   </html:h1>
  </html:center>

  <box id="promptbox"  align="vertical">
   <html:h2>Question 1</html:h2>
   <label value="Would you like to play a game?"/>
   <toolbar class="yesnotoolbar"/>
  </box>

  <box id="opinionpoll" align="vertical" flex="1">
   <html:h2>Question 2</html:h2>
   <label
      value="4 out of 5 dentists surveyed prefer eating rocks to
        eating nails."/>
    <label value="What do you think? Do you agree? Vote now!"/>
    <toolbar class="agreeprompt" valign="middle"/>
  </box>
</window>
```

Code Listing 7.8 XUL file for opinion poll

In our XBL listing, we use the <content> tag to designate anonymous content that will be added to a bound element. In Code Listing 7.9, we have two bindings: “yesnoprompt” and “agreeprompt”. Next, we need to bind the toolbars in the main XUL file from Code Listing 7.8 to these bindings. We add anonymous content to the toolbars via the CSS in Code Listing 7.10.

```
<?xml version="1.0"?>
<!-- This file is a demonstration file
    of different types of prompts that
    toolbars can have.
-->
<bindings xmlns="http://www.mozilla.org/xbl"
xmlns:xul="http://www.mozilla.org/keymaster/gatekeeper/there.is.only.
  xul">
 <binding id="yesnoprompt">
  <content>
    <xul:button label="Click Here for Yes"/>
    <xul:button label="Click Here for No"/>
    <xul:button label="Huh? What are you talking about?"/>
```

continued

Code Listing 7.9 XBL file containing prompt bindings.

```
    </content>
  </binding>

  <binding id="agreeprompt">
    <content>
      <xul:button label="I agree with that opinion."/>
      <xul:button label="I disagree with that opinion."/>
      <xul:button label="I could care less!"/>
    </content>
  </binding>
</bindings>
```

Code Listing 7.9 XBL file containing prompt bindings (Continued).

```
/*
  promptstyles.css – This is a simple example
  of how we can use bindings to designate "classes"
  of toolbars that can have anonymous button content
  generated in them.
 */

/* basic styles for XUL widgets */
box
{
  border : 2px solid black;
    padding: 2px;
}

button
{
   background-color: yellow;
}

/* Bindings for our classes of toolbars! */
toolbar.yesnotoolbar
{
  -moz-binding: url(promptbindings.xml#yesnoprompt);
}

toolbar.agreeprompt
{
    -moz-binding: url(promptbindings.xml#agreeprompt);
}
```

Code Listing 7.10 CSS for opinion poll.

In Code Listing 7.10, we use CSS to bind the two bindings to toolbars with class yesnotoolbar and toolbars with class agreeprompt. Figure 7.2 shows the result of this simple example.

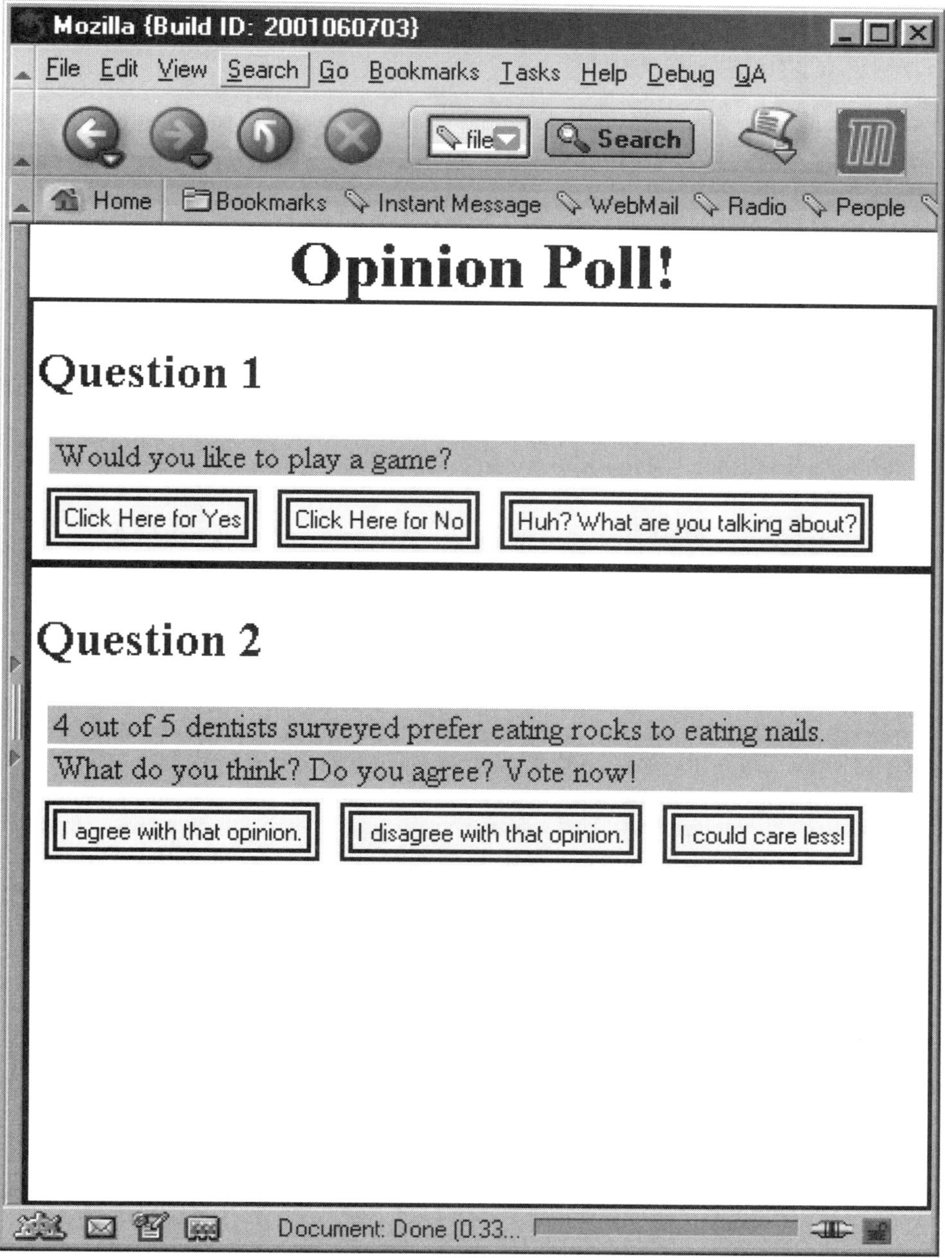

Figure 7.2 Screen shot of opinion poll.

Now, we have shown an easy example of using XBL to generate anonymous content. It is, however, only the tip of the iceberg of what XBL can do. In our next section, we go over the syntax of all of the XBL elements in detail. If you would like to continue with the tutorial, you might want to skip over this next section and come back for reference.

Syntax of XBL Elements

In this section, we will go through an alphabetical listing of XBL elements as they are used in the Mozilla.org implementation of XBL. Here, we discuss each element, providing tables with the following format:

Contained by. If the XBL element is usually a child of a certain element, this item will be listed in the table. If the contained by section is not listed, you are to assume that it could be contained by any element.

Contains. If the XBL element usually contains specific children related to its functionality, this will be listed in the table. If the contains section is not listed for an element, you are to assume that it may contain any element.

Attributes. If the XBL element contains attributes, these will be listed. If an important attribute relates to the element, this will be denoted in the text before the table.

See Also. If the element is related to another XBL element, they will be listed in this section.

<binding>

Used to describe a binding that dynamically binds new information to other documents in an XML document, this element can contain <content>, <implementation>, and <handlers> elements to specify content around the bound element, to specify additional methods and properties, and to specify new event handlers, respectively.

The id attribute is mandatory, because each <binding> needs to be unique. The extends attribute specifies the URL of another <binding> from which this <binding> could inherit. The applyauthorstyles attribute is a Boolean attribute that will specify whether the style sheets referenced by the original bound element's document applies to the content of the bindings. The styleexplicitcontent attribute is a Boolean attribute that will specify whether the style sheets loaded by the XBL document will apply to the bound element's children.

Contains	<content>, <implementation>, <handlers>
Contained by	<bindings>
Attributes	id, extends, display, applyauthorstyles, styleexplicitcontent

<bindings>

The root element of an XBL document, this element serves as a container for <binding> elements. It can contain <script> elements that can be referenced by the <binding> elements in the document. As in all XML elements, its id attribute is a unique identifier. Its type attribute is used to specify the scripting language used by the bindings in the document.

Contains	0 to many <binding> elements
Attributes	id, type

<body>

The <body> element contains the implementation script for a method. The <body> element usually contains JavaScript.

Contained by	<method>
Contains	Script text (usually JavaScript)
Attributes	id
See Also	<parameter>, <method>

<content>

The <content> element of an XBL document contains elements that can be inserted into the bound element. The nodes contained in this section are called anonymous content.

Contains	Any content, including <children> elements
Contained by	<binding>

<children>

The <children> element of an XBL document contains elements that can be inserted around the bound element. The nodes contained in this section are sometimes called anonymous content. The includes attribute is optional and uses an XPath description to list what of this content should be placed around the bound element.

Contained by	<content>
Attributes	id, includes,

<getter>

A child of the <property> element, a <getter> element contains executable script (usually JavaScript) that will execute when an element's property value is accessed. The type attribute is an optional attribute used to denote what scripting language is used.

Contains	Executable script
Contained by	<property>
Attributes	id, type
See Also	<setter>, <property>

<handler>

A child of the <handlers> element, a <handler> element contains executable script (usually JavaScript) that will execute when an element's event handler is called. As with all XML elements, the id attribute of <handler> is used as a unique identifier, but it is not mandatory. Instead, the mandatory field is the event attribute, which describes the event to which the handler is listening.

The action attribute contains script that is invoked when the <handler> is triggered. The phase attribute describes the phase of the event flow—capturing, bubbling, or target—and if the phase attribute is not explicitly listed, it will default to bubbling. The attachto attribute specifies the receiver with which the handler should be registered, and it has three possible values: element, document, or window. If the attachto attribute is not listed, it attaches itself to the bound element.

The button, charcode, keycode, and modifiers attributes are used to apply filters on the handler. The button attribute is used for mouse handlers to only trigger the handler if the label on the button equals a value of this attribute. When the charcode attribute exists, the handler is only executed if the charcode attribute of the event object matches this value. When the keycode attribute exists, it is used for key handlers to execute only the handler if the keycode attribute of the event objects equals this attribute. The modifiers attribute is a filter also used for key handlers, and it is similar to the modifiers attribute in the XUL <textbox> element.

Contains	Executable script
Contained by	<property>
Attributes	id, event, action, phase, attachto, button, modifiers, keycode, charcode, type.
See Also	<setter>, <property> , XUL <textbox>

<handlers>

A container for <handler> elements denoting the event handlers that can be bound to an element, this element can contain two optional attributes, id and type. As with all XML elements, the id attribute is used as a unique identifier. Its type attribute is used to specify the scripting language used, and it can be used to override the type attribute in its descendent elements.

Contains	<handler>
Contained by	<binding>
Attributes	id, type

<implementation>

The <implementation> section of a <binding> lists the methods and properties that can be bound to an external element. As with all XML elements, the id attribute is used as a unique identifier. The name attribute is an optional name for the implementation and can be used as a reference along with the id attribute. The implements attribute is an optional attribute that could list a set of space-separated interfaces that are implemented by the binding. Its type attribute is used to specify the scripting language used, and it can be used to override the type attribute in the <bindings> element.

Contains	<method>, <property>
Contained by	<binding>
Attributes	id, name, implements, type

<method>

The <method> element is used to describe a new method, or function, that can be applied to the bound element. It can contain 0 (zero) or many <parameter> elements that specify the parameters to the function, and it can contain a <body> element that describes the <body> of the function (usually in JavaScript). The mandatory name attribute is the name of the method that is invoked, and the optional type attribute is used to specify the language used in the body of the method.

Contains	<parameter>, <body>
Contained by	<implementation>
Attributes	id, name, type

<parameter>

The <parameter> method lists a single parameter for a method. Its name attribute is required, and it specifies the name of the parameter that is passed in.

Contained by	<method>
Attributes	id, name

<property>

The <property> element is a child of the <implementation> element, and it can contain getter and setter functions. The name attribute is mandatory, because it is the name used to reference the property on the bound element. The readonly attribute is Boolean and can be set to true or false, denoting whether or not the property can be set. (If it is read-only, the property cannot be changed by a JavaScript function.)

The onget attribute is an event attribute that references a JavaScript function, which executes when the property is requested. The onset attribute is an event attribute that executes when the property's value is being altered. As in many of the XBL elements, the type attribute is used to denote the scripting language used to describe the getters and setters.

When the <property> element has the attributes element, property, and attribute, the <property> tag can be used to tie together elements that were generated (the anonymous content). The element attribute is an id reference to an anonymous element generated by one of the bindings. If this attribute is set, whenever the property is set on the bound element, it will also be set on the anonymous element. Whenever this property is retrieved, it is obtained from the corresponding property on the anonymous element.

The property attribute is used in tandem with the element attribute to denote this corresponding property. The attribute attribute links the attribute of the anonymous element to the property, and when the property is set, the attribute denoted will be set.

Contains	<getter>, <setter>
Contained by	<implementation>
Attributes	id, name, readonly, onget, onset, element, attribute, property, type

<setter>

A child of the <property> element, a <setter> element contains executable script (usually JavaScript) that will execute when an element's property value is changed. The type attribute is an optional attribute used to denote what scripting language is used.

Contains	Executable script
Contained by	<property>
Attributes	id, type
See Also	<getter>, <property>

Adding Anonymous Content with XBL

Now that we have discussed the syntax of XBL, we will discuss how to generate content in a bound element. In our earlier example in Code Listing 7.8, Code Listing 7.9, Code Listing 7.10, and Figure 7.2, we showed that XBL can be useful for creating widgets that are made up of inner widgets and introduced you to the concepts of anonymous and explicit content. In our example, we had to reference only the outer widget, and anonymous content was added. Code Listing 7.11 shows skeleton XBL code for a binding for adding content. As you can see, the <content> section is where we add our anonymous content.

```
<?xml version="1.0"?>

<bindings xmlns="http://www.mozilla.org/xbl"
xmlns:xul="http://www.mozilla.org/keymaster/gatekeeper/there.is.only.
  xul">
  <binding id="binding1">
    <content>
     <!-- anonymous content goes here -->
    </content>
</bindings>
```

Code Listing 7.11 Skeleton XBL code for adding content.

Our earlier example of adding content was quite trivial because the bound element had no explicit children. Using XBL, we can add anonymous content in many ways, and like XUL overlays, rules are associated with adding content to a node that already has children. When bindings are attached to an element, anonymous content could be generated or destroyed.[2] Because several bindings could be attached to an element, the element's current bindings are checked for conflicts. When this happens, the following occurs:

- If a bound element has no explicit children, the new anonymous content is generated.
- If a bound element has explicit children, new anonymous content is added only if insertion points that refer to the explicit content are defined in the XBL. Otherwise, the new anonymous content is ignored.

The second rule is the most important. We must specify the insertion point in relation to all of the children of the bound element, or no content will be generated. How can we specify an insertion point if the bound element in question has explicit children? We can do this with the <children> element, which was defined in the last section.

Specifying an Insertion Point

When you want both the XBL content and the explicit content to be displayed, you must specify the placement of the explicit nodes with the <children> tag. The <children> tag represents the children of the bound node, and the <children> tag must be contained by an element in the <content> section.

Consider the simple example of a main XUL file shown in Code Listing 7.12. Our main XUL content consists of a box that contains two buttons and one text element.

Perhaps we would like to insert anonymous content around the children of the <box> element. In order to do so, we need to create an XBL binding to the <box> element in Code Listing 7.12. We provide such an example in Code Listing 7.13. In our binding, we must create a container for the <children> of the bound element, and we place the <children> tag in that container. By using the <children> tag shown in Code Listing 7.13, we specify the positioning of the explicit content.

```
<?xml version="1.0"?>
<window
  xmlns="http://www.mozilla.org/keymaster/gatekeeper/there.is.only.
    xul">
 <box id="includesbox">
   <button id="button1" label="button1"/>
   <button id="button1" label="button2"/>
   <text label="I am explicit content!"/>
 </box>
</window>
```

Code Listing 7.12 explicit.xul.

```
<bindings xmlns="http://www.mozilla.org/xbl"
xmlns:xul="http://www.mozilla.org/keymaster/gatekeeper/there.is.only.
  xul">
 <binding id="includestest">
  <content>
    <xul:text label="I am anonymous content"/>
    <xul:box>
     <children/>
    </xul:box>
    <xul:button label="I am an XBL-generated button"/>
  </content>
 </binding>
</bindings>
```

Code Listing 7.13 Simple <children> insertion.

In Code Listing 7.13, we place a text item and a button on either side of a box containing the children of the bound element. The resulting content is shown in Code Listing 7.14.

You can use the includes attribute on the <children> element to dictate exactly each element type that should be added. The value of the includes attribute can be set to a single tag name or to a list of tags separated by the | symbol. Using the includes attribute with the <children> tag enables you to state where different types of explicit content can go. In our example in Code Listing 7.14, we showed that we could put all of the explicit children in one place. By using the includes tag with children, you could actually break up the content by tag name, by doing something similar to Code Listing 7.15.

Code Listing 7.16 shows the resulting content when we apply the XBL binding from Code Listing 7.15 to the <box> element shown in Code Listing 7.12. As you can see, we are able to separate children of the bound element by their type.

```
<?xml version="1.0"?>
<window
  xmlns="http://www.mozilla.org/keymaster/gatekeeper/there.is.only.
    xul">
 <box id="includesbox">
  <xul:text label="I am anonymous content"/>
  <xul:box>
   <button id="button1" label="button1"/>
   <button id="button1" label="button2"/>
   <text label="I am explicit content!"/>
  </xul:box>
 </box>
</window>
```

Code Listing 7.14 Content displayed with the binding.

```
<bindings xmlns="http://www.mozilla.org/xbl"
xmlns:xul="http://www.mozilla.org/keymaster/gatekeeper/there.is.only.
  xul">
 <binding id="multichildrenbinding">
  <content>
   <xul:text label="I am anonymous content"/>
   <box>
    <!-- All <text> node children of the bound element will go here-->
    <children includes="text"/>
   </box>
   <toolbar>
    <!-- All <button> node children of the bound element will go
      here-->
    <children includes="button"/>
   </toolbar>
  </content>
 </binding>
</bindings>
```

Code Listing 7.15 Children insertion with multiple <children> nodes.

```
<?xml version="1.0"?>
<window
  xmlns="http://www.mozilla.org/keymaster/gatekeeper/there.is.only.
    xul">
 <box id="includesbox">
  <text label="I am anonymous content"/>
  <box>
   <text label="I am explicit content!"/>
  <box>
  <toolbar>
   <button id="button1" label="button1"/>
   <button id="button1" label="button2"/>
  </toolbar>
 </box>
</window>
```

Code Listing 7.16 Content displayed with multiple <children> example.

Attribute Inheritance with Anonymous Content

Using XBL, attributes on anonymous content can be inherited from attributes on the bound element. When the attribute is set or removed on the bound element, the corresponding attribute on the anonymous content also changes. This is often very helpful when you are creating a composite element consisting of smaller elements and where the developer may have access to only the bound element. To do this, you may use the inherits attribute on the anonymous content.

The value of the inherits attribute can be a comma-separated list of attribute names or attribute-attribute mapping pairs. Because anonymous content can inherit only from the bound element, you may need to use the inherits attribute to specify the mapping of the inherited attributes of the bound element to the designated attributes on the content element. In this case, the value "myattribute=inheritedattribute" could be in the list, signifying the appropriate mapping of the inherited attribute to the new attribute.

To demonstrate attribute inheritance in XBL, we will extend our first XBL opinion poll example from Code Listing 7.8, Code Listing 7.9, and Code Listing 7.10. Like our original example, we would like to have an opinion poll of two questions, but we want to make a subtle change. Instead of having the text of the question in the main XUL file, we will delegate that duty to the anonymous content in the XBL file. Instead of having the <toolbar> element be the bound element, we will include the <toolbar> in the anonymous content, and we will have a <box> be the bound element. We will give each bound <box> element a question attribute, leaving the implementation details about the presentation of the question to the anonymous content. Code Listing 7.17 shows the explicit XUL content.

```
<?xml version="1.0"?>
<?xml--stylesheet href="promptstyles.css" type="text/css"?>

<!-- This is a simple example of using XBL to hide the
    implementation details of different classes of
    XUL widgets, and having the anonymous content inherit
    from the bound element!
-->

<window
  xmlns="http://www.mozilla.org/keymaster/gatekeeper/there.is.only.
    xul"
  xmlns:html="http://www.w3.org/1999/xhtml"
  align="vertical">

  <html:center>
   <html:h1>
    Opinion Poll!
   </html:h1>
  </html:center>

  <box class="yesnobox"  align="vertical"
        question="Would you like to play a game?"/>
  <box class="opinionbox" align="vertical"
        question="Roadkill can be a healthy food supplement."/>

</window>
```

Code Listing 7.17 XUL file with explicit content.

Because each <box> element in our main XUL file has a question attribute, we would like to inherit from that attribute in our XBL content. The XBL file for this example is shown in Code Listing 7.18.

As you can see, the <xul:label> element in Code Listing 7.18 inherits its value attribute from the bound element's question attribute. If we did this right, each <box> should contain a <label> element showing the question and a toolbar showing the correct buttons. Now, we need to bind our elements to the correct binding, and this has been done with the CSS file shown in Code Listing 7.19.

Finally, Figure 7.3 shows the result of our example. The anonymously generated <label> element successfully inherited its value from the question attribute of the bound element.

Now that we have discussed generating anonymous content and attribute inheritance, the fun begins.

```
<?xml version="1.0"?>
<!-- This file is a demonstration of how
   anonymous content can inherit from
   the bound element.
 -->
<bindings xmlns="http://www.mozilla.org/xbl"
       xmlns:xul="http://www.mozilla.org/keymaster/gatekeeper/there.
         is.only.xul">

 <binding id="yesnoprompt">
  <content>
    <xul:label inherits="value=question"/>
    <xul:toolbar>
      <xul:button label="Click Here for Yes"/>
      <xul:button label="Click Here for No"/>
      <xul:button label="Huh? What are you talking about?"/>
     </xul:toolbar>
   </content>
  </binding>

  <binding id="agreeprompt">
   <content>
     <xul:label inherits="value=question"/>
     <xul:toolbar>
      <xul:button label="I agree with that opinion."/>
      <xul:button label="I disagree with that opinion."/>
      <xul:button label="I could care less!"/>
     </xul:toolbar>
  </content>
 </binding>
</bindings>
```

Code Listing 7.18 XBL file inheriting from bound elements.

```
/*
  promptstyles.css
 */

/* basic styles for XUL widgets */
box
{
  border : 2px solid black;
   padding: 2px;
}

button
{
   background-color: yellow;
}

/* Bindings for our classes of toolbars! */

box.yesnobox
{
  -moz-binding: url(promptbindings.xml#yesnoprompt);
}

box.opinionbox
{
  -moz-binding: url(promptbindings.xml#agreeprompt);
}
```

Code Listing 7.19 New CSS for inheritance example.

Adding Properties and Methods with XBL

In XBL, you can add properties and methods to a bound element. When you create composite widgets, most widget developers want to encapsulate the internals of the widget, only allowing users of the widget to know the widget's API. In this case, we can encapsulate properties and methods with XBL. Code Listing 7.20 shows XBL skeleton code for adding properties and methods to a binding. As anonymous content was placed in the <content> section, properties and methods are placed in the <implementation> section.

Properties, which are defined by the XBL <property> tag, have two subelements—<getter> elements and <setter> elements. When a script reads the bound element's property that is defined in the binding, the code in the <getter> section will execute. When a script changes the element's property defined in the XBL binding, the code in the <setter> section will execute. A developer may set the <property> element's readonly attribute to true if an outside application should not change the property.

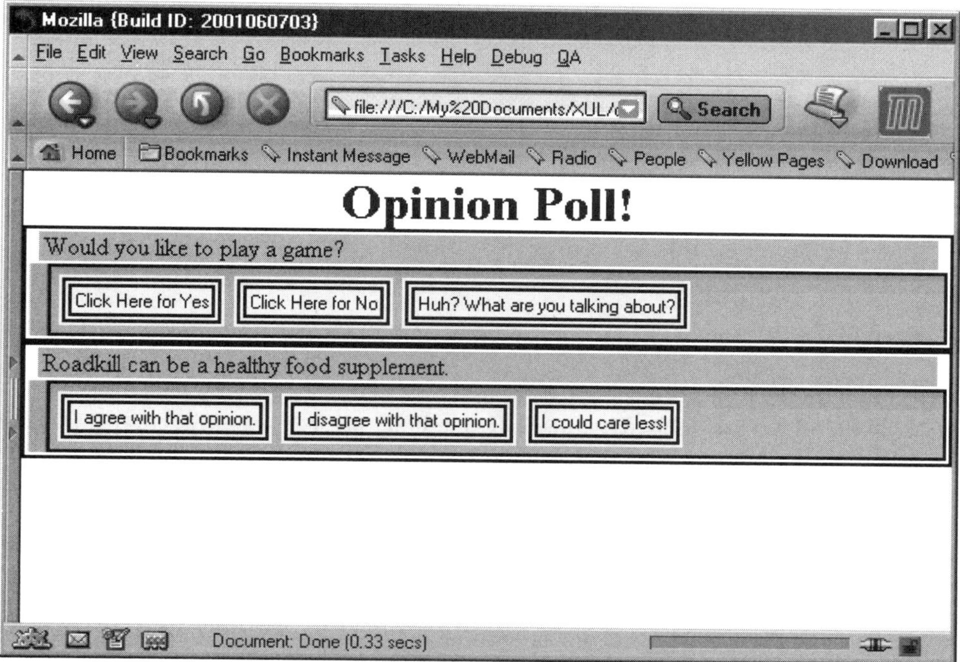

Figure 7.3 Result of inheritance example.

```
<?xml version="1.0"?>

<bindings xmlns="http://www.mozilla.org/xbl"
xmlns:xul="http://www.mozilla.org/keymaster/gatekeeper/there.is.only.
  xul">
 <binding id="binding1">
  <content>
   <!-- content goes here -->
  </content>

  <implementation>
   <method name="method1">
     <parameter name="param1"/>
     <body>
      <!-- JavaScript goes here! -->
     </body>
   </method>

   <property name="property1">
    <getter>
```

continues

Code Listing 7.20 XBL skeleton code for properties and methods.

```
      <!- JavaScript goes here! ->
     </getter>
     <setter>
      <!-- JavaScript goes here! -->
     </setter>
    </property>
   </implementation>
  </binding>
</bindings>
```

Code Listing 7.20 XBL skeleton code for properties and methods.

Methods, which are defined by the XBL <method> tag, represent functions that may be called on the bound element. As functions may have multiple parameters that are passed in, the <method> tag may have <parameter> subelements, representing the parameters that will be passed in. The body of the method is placed in the <body> tag and is a child of the <method> tag.

Note that all of the content in the XBL file must be well-formed XML. Although JavaScript resides in some of these tags (<body>, <getter>, <setter>) for methods and properties, the JavaScript must not break the well-formed structure of the XML. It is sometimes easy to forget this, and use greater-than (>) and less-than (<) signs when making comparisons. A simple solution is to put the script in a CDATA section within the script elements or to use "<" and ">" symbols to replace < and >.

To demonstrate properties and methods in XBL, we will create a grading application example. In our example, we would like a reusable composite widget that will contain the input data for all of the grades for a student in a class, and we would like this widget to have a getAverage() method, a curve property representing the curve that will be added to the final grade, and a grade property that will be the student's final grade. In our example, we will bind <box> element of class gradebox to a binding that contains that internal content, the getAverage() method, and the curve and grade properties. We will use JavaScript to access the bound object's properties and methods. Our design for the grading application is shown in Figure 7.4.

Figure 7.4 shows the graphical representation of our design. Looking at the design will help you visualize the big picture when looking at our application. In Code Listing 7.21, we create our composite widget with the id of gradebox. As you can see, each box consists of the following content:

- A <text> widget that inherits the bound element's name property and takes its value.
- Three <box> widgets that contain a <text> widget describing a grade, and a <textbox> widget for the user to type in the grade. These widgets will be for the midterm, term paper, and final.
- A box containing the children of the bound element.

In Code Listing 7.21, you can see that we have added the sections for the getAverage() method. In this method, we have one parameter: the curve that will be added to the final

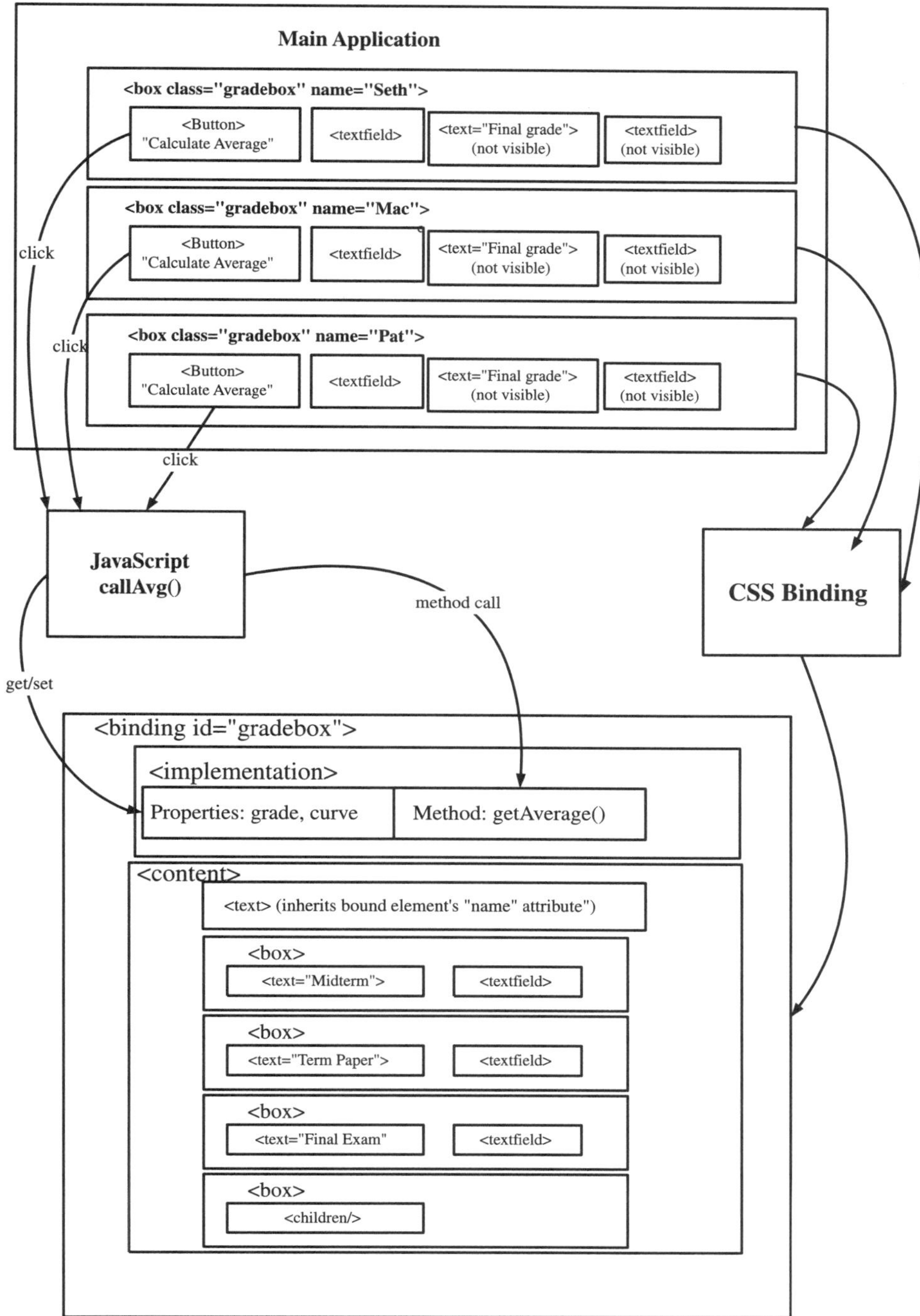

Figure 7.4 Design for our grading example.

```
<?xml version="1.0"?>

<bindings xmlns="http://www.mozilla.org/xbl"
       xmlns:xul="http://www.mozilla.org/keymaster/gatekeeper/there.
         is.only.xul"
       xmlns:html="http://www.w3.org/1999/xhtml">

 <binding id="gradebox">
  <content>
    <html:h3><xul:label inherits="value=name"/></html:h3>
    <xul:box>
     <xul:label value="Midterm:       "/>
     <xul:textbox id="mid" value="0"/>
    </xul:box>
    <xul:box>
     <xul:label value="Term Paper: "/>
     <xul:textbox id="term" value="0"/>
    </xul:box>
    <xul:box>
     <xul:label value="Final Exam:  "/>
     <xul:textbox id="final" value="0"/>
    </xul:box>
    <xul:box>
     <children/>
    </xul:box>
  </content>
  <implementation>
   <method name="getAverage">
     <parameter name="curve"/>
     <body>
      <!-- Remember - these can not be retrieved by your
           usual DOM methods. We want to access anonymous
           nodes!
      -->
      var mid = document.getAnonymousNodes(this)[1].lastChild.
        value;
      var term= document.getAnonymousNodes(this)[2].lastChild.
        value;
      var fin = document.getAnonymousNodes(this)[3].lastChild.
        value;
      var sum = eval(mid) + eval(term) + eval(fin);
      var avg = eval(sum/3);
      return (eval(avg) + eval(curve));
     </body>
 </method>
<property name="curve">
  <getter>
```

Code Listing 7.21 Bindings for grading application.

```
      var curve = this.getAttribute("curve");
      if (isNaN(curve))
         this.setAttribute("curve",0);

      return this.getAttribute("curve");
     </getter>
     <setter>
       var v=eval(val);
       if (!isNaN(v))
       {
          return this.setAttribute('curve',v);
       }
       else
       {
          return this.getAttribute('curve');
       }
     </setter>
    </property>
    <property name="grade">
     <getter>
       var avg = this.getAverage(this.curve);
       if (isNaN(avg))
       {
          return ("Not Computable");
         }
         if (avg &gt;= 60)
         {
          return ("PASS");
         }
         return ("FAIL");
       </getter>
      </property>
     </implementation>
    </binding>
  </bindings>
```

Code Listing 7.21 Bindings for grading application (Continued).

average of the student. As you can see from the body of the getAverage() method, we are using the DOM XBL Interface to call the getAnonymousNodes() function. Why is this? When this code is executed, anonymous content can't be accessed via the normal DOM interface. We do this instead to get the elements (our <textbox> elements) that we need to do our calculation.

The <setter> and <getter> sections of our curve property are fairly simple. In the <setter> function, we evaluate the passed-in value, which is always "val", and if it is a good value, we set the curve attribute to the value. When the <getter> is called, we check to see whether it is a real value. If it is not, we set it to 0 (zero) and return it. If the existing curve property is a real value, we return the value of the curve property.

The <grade> property sections are a bit more complex, and we have only a <getter> section. When an outside script reads the grade property, the <getter> section is called. First, it retrieves the curve property, and it passes the value of the curve to the getAverage() method. Then, it determines whether the average is a PASS or a FAIL and returns a "PASS" or a "FAIL" string. Note that the properties and methods included in the bindings can reference and call other properties and methods in the binding section.

Code Listing 7.22 shows our main application. In the XUL file, we have a place for the teacher to add the curve, and three boxes represent three students who are taking the class. Each box has explicit content, including a button that is used to calculate the average. Each box has two invisible elements—a <text> element and a <textbox> element that represent the student's final grade—which are invisible because their collapsed attributes are set to true. Each box responds to a click event by calling the local callAvg() method that is in a local JavaScript file, grades.js.

```
<?xml version="1.0"?>
<?xml-stylesheet href="gradestyles.css" type="text/css"?>
<window
  xmlns="http://www.mozilla.org/keymaster/gatekeeper/there.is.only.
    xul"
  xmlns:html="http://www.w3.org/1999/xhtml"
  align="vertical">

 <script src="grades.js"/>

 <html:center>
   <html:h1>
    Grades for CS 767: Intro to XBL
   </html:h1>
   <html:p/>
   <box>
    <html:b>
        <text value="Curve for this class:"/>
    </html:b>
        <textbox id="curvenum" value="0"/>
   </box>
 </html:center>

 <!-- Our bound elements -->
 <box id="seth"  align="vertical"
       name="Seth"
        class="gradebox">

        <button label="Calculate Average"
             onclick="callAvg(this.parentNode)"/>
```

Code Listing 7.22 XUL file–grading application.

```
        <textbox/>
        <label class="finalgrade" value="FINAL GRADE:"
               collapsed="true"/>
        <textbox collapsed="true" disabled="true"/>
  </box>
  <box id="mac" align="vertical"
        name="MacGregor"
        class="gradebox">

        <button label="Calculate Average"
              onclick="callAvg(this.parentNode)"/>
        <textbox/>
        <label class="finalgrade"
            value="FINAL GRADE:" collapsed="true"/>
        <textbox collapsed="true" disabled="true"/>
  </box>
  <box id="dez" align="vertical"
        name="Pat"
        class="gradebox">

        <button label="Calculate Average"
             onclick="callAvg(this.parentNode)"/>
        <textbox/>
        <label class="finalgrade"
            value="FINAL GRADE:" collapsed="true"/>
        <textbox collapsed="true" disabled="true"/>
  </box>
</window>
```

Code Listing 7.22 XUL file–grading application (Continued).

In our JavaScript file in Code Listing 7.23, we define a function, callAvg(). Each box calls this method when responding to its click event and passes itself in as a parameter. When this occurs, the following happens:

1. The function uses the DOM function getElementById() to retrieve the value of the curvenum textbox.
2. The function sets the box's curve property, which calls the code in the XBL <setter> section.
3. The function calculates the average for the student by calling the box's getAverage() method.
4. If the average is a real number, the function finds the textbox where the average grade calculation goes and sets the textbox's value to the average. It then sets the

```
/*
   grades.js - Used to demonstrate XBL method calling
               and property "getting" and "setting!"
*/
function callAvg(box)
{
  var curve = document.getElementById("curvenum").value;

  //calls the "setter" on the curve property
  box.curve = curve;

  var avg = box.getAverage(curve);

  if (!isNaN(avg))
  {
      //sets the textbox for average calculation
      box.firstChild.nextSibling.value = avg;

      var finalgradetf = box.lastChild;
      var finalgradetext = box.lastChild.previousSibling;
      finalgradetf.setAttribute("collapsed", "false");
      finalgradetext.setAttribute("collapsed", "false");

      //calls the "getter" on the grade property
      finalgradetf.setAttribute("value", box.grade);
  }
  else alert("Please enter correct values!");
}
```

Code Listing 7.23 JavaScript for grading application.

"final grade" <text> elements and <textbox> elements' collapsed attribute to false, making them visible.

5. Finally, the function sets the value attribute of the final grade text field to the box's grade property, essentially calling the XBL <getter> section for the grade property.

In Code Listing 7.24, we included the style sheet for our grading application, where we bind all <box> elements with classes of gradebox to our binding in Code Listing 7.21.

The resulting XUL grading application is shown in Figure 7.5. When the teacher filled in all of the grades for the semester, she clicked the Calculate Average button, which called the JavaScript method in Code Listing 7.23, calculating the user's final average, and determining the final grade of each user.

```
/*
 gradestyles.css
 */

button
{
 background-color: yellow;
 border: 1px solid black;
 padding: 3px;
}

text.finalgrade
{
 font-weight: bold;
 padding: 4px;

}
box.gradebox
{
 -moz-binding: url(avgbindings.xml#gradebox);
 border: 2px solid black;
 padding: 2px;
}
```

Code Listing 7.24 Style sheet for grading application.

Adding Event Handlers with XBL

After the last section on adding properties and methods with XBL, learning about event handlers should be easy. Sometimes, it may be helpful to pass events into our composite widgets to let our anonymous content handle the event. We can do this by using <handler> elements inside a binding. A handler contains script that is executed when the designated event is triggered on the bound element. The syntax for writing handlers is quite easy, and the skeleton code of an XBL file with the handler syntax is shown in Code Listing 7.25.

In Code Listing 7.25, the <handlers> container has one or more handlers for particular events. The required attribute in the <handler> element is the event attribute. The event attribute specifies the event to which our XBL code is listening. When we are writing XUL and HTML/JavaScript code, we're used to seeing event handlers such as onClick(), onBlur(), and onFocus(), and the events that these handlers are responding to are click, blur, and focus, respectively. Here is an example of writing a handler in XBL for an onclick eventd:

```
<handler event="click" action="youClickedMe()"/>
```

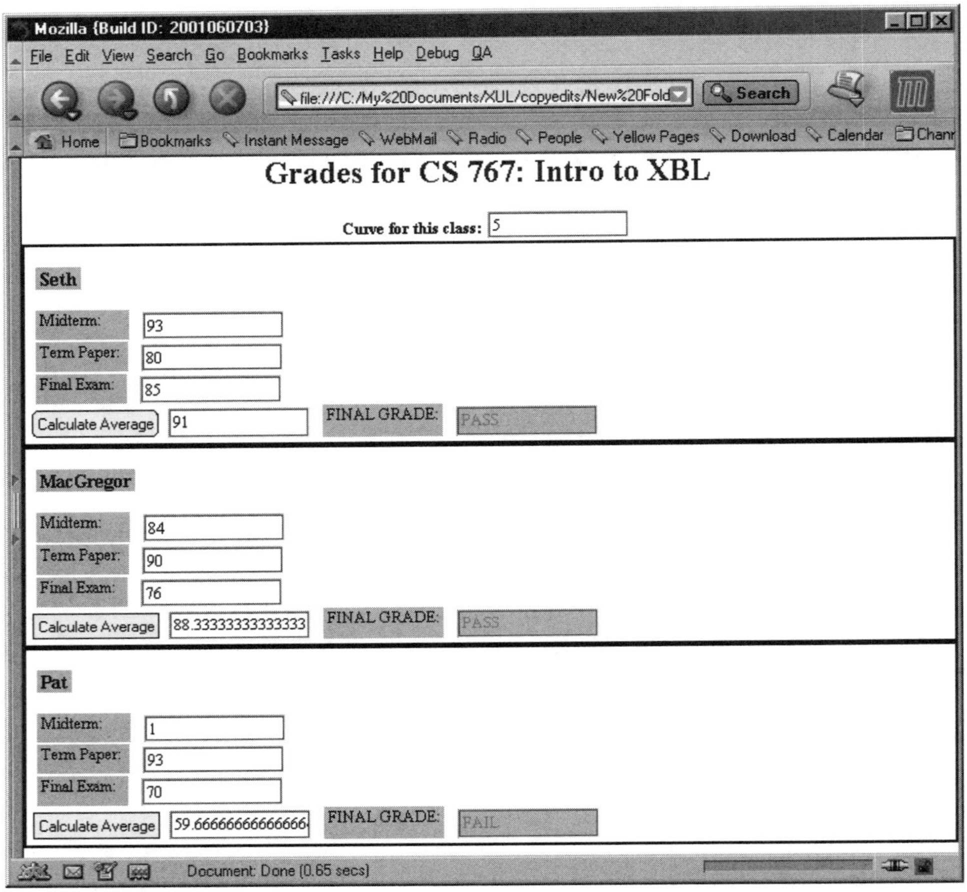

Figure 7.5 Screen shot of grading application.

By writing handlers in XBL, you can either put script in the action attribute, or you can put script in the body of the <handler> element itself. How could this be helpful? When you are abstracting implementation details by creating a composite widget, you may need to pass events on to some of your inner elements that should really handle those events. For example, in our grading application example from Code Listing 7.21 through Code Listing 7.24, we might want to give a helpful tip to the user the first time he clicks on the user's box on screen. We can capture the click event and respond to it if the user clicks anywhere in the box. Code Listing 7.26 augments our previous XBL to include a click handler, and it also includes a new property, helpfultip. Because it could probably be very annoying to give a helpful tip every time the user clicks in the box, we will just give the user a helpful tip the first time. The augmented code is shown at the end of Code Listing 7.26.

```
<?xml version="1.0"?>

<bindings xmlns="http://www.mozilla.org/xbl"
xmlns:xul="http://www.mozilla.org/keymaster/gatekeeper/there.is.only.
  xul">
  <binding id="element-name">
   <content>
    <!-- content goes here -->
   </content>
   <handlers>
     <handler id ="handler1"  <!-- not required, but recommended -->
         event="command" <!-- event name reference is required! -->
         action=""/>     <!-- JavaScript goes in this section! -->
                       <!-- Or, you can add script as the child
                          of the handler element. -->
       </handler>
    </handlers>
 </binding>
</bindings>
```

Code Listing 7.25 Skeleton code for adding event handlers.

```
<?xml version="1.0"?>

<bindings xmlns="http://www.mozilla.org/xbl"
       xmlns:xul="http://www.mozilla.org/keymaster/gatekeeper/there.
         is.only.xul"
       xmlns:html="http://www.w3.org/1999/xhtml">

  <binding id="gradebox">
   <content>
      <html:h3><xul:text inherits="label=name"/></html:h3>
      <xul:box>
       <xul:text label="Midterm:       "/>
       <xul:textbox id="mid" value="0"/>
      </xul:box>
      <xul:box>
       <xul:text label="Term Paper: "/>
       <xul:textbox id="term" value="0"/>
      </xul:box>
      <xul:box>
       <xul:text label="Final Exam:  "/>
       <xul:textbox id="final" value="0"/>
      </xul:box>
```

continues

Code Listing 7.26 Grading application with a “click” handler.

```
        <xul:box>
          <children/>
        </xul:box>
      </content>
      <implementation>
        <method name="getAverage">
          <parameter name="curve"/>
          <body>
            <!-- Remember - these can not be retrieved by your
              usual DOM methods. We want to access anonymous
              nodes!
            -->
            var mid = document.getAnonymousNodes(this)[1].lastChild.value;
            var term = document.getAnonymousNodes(this)[2].lastChild.value;
            var fin = document.getAnonymousNodes(this)[3].lastChild.value;
            var sum = eval(mid) + eval(term) + eval(fin);
            var avg = eval(sum/3);
            return (eval(avg) + eval(curve));
        </body>
          </method>
      <property name="curve">
        <getter>
          var curve = this.getAttribute("curve");
          if (isNaN(curve))
            this.setAttribute("curve",0);

          return this.getAttribute("curve");
        </getter>
        <setter>
          var v=eval(val);
          if (!isNaN(v))
          {
            return this.setAttribute('curve',v);
          }
          else
          {
            return this.getAttribute('curve');
          }
        </setter>
      </property>
      <property name="grade">
        <getter>
          var avg = this.getAverage(this.curve);
          if (isNaN(avg))
          {
            return ("Not Computable");
          }
          if (avg &gt;= 60)
```

Code Listing 7.26 Grading application with a "click" handler (Continued).

```
        {
          return ("PASS");
        }
        return ("FAIL");
      </getter>
    </property>
    <!-- This is a new property that defaults to
         true at initialization.
      -->
    <property name="helpfultip">
      <getter>
       var value = this.getAttribute("helpfultip");
       if (value == "")
       {
         return (true);
       }
       else
       {
         return (false);
       }
      </getter>
      <setter>
         return (this.setAttribute("helpfultip", val));
      </setter>
    </property>
  </implementation>
  <handlers>
    <handler event="click">

      if (this.helpfultip != false)
      {
       alert("Make certain that you fill out all grades for " +
         this.getAttribute("name") + " before you calculate!");
       this.helpfultip = false;
      }
    </handler>
  </handlers>
 </binding>
</bindings>
```

Code Listing 7.26 Grading application with a "click" handler (Continued).

As you can see from the <handler> section in Code Listing 7.26, we check the helpfultip property of the bound element, and if it is set to true, it will pop up an alert. The screen shot for this example is shown in Figure 7.6. Before the screen shot was taken, the user clicked in the box for Seth, and an alert popup message was sent to the screen. Note that with the XBL in Code Listing 7.26, one popup message will appear for each box, because each box is bound to the binding with the id “gradebox”.

Inheriting from Bindings and Elements

Now that we have discussed the generation of anonymous content, properties, and methods by using bindings, we will mention binding inheritance. In an earlier section, we discussed attribute inheritance in XBL in which we could inherit attributes from a

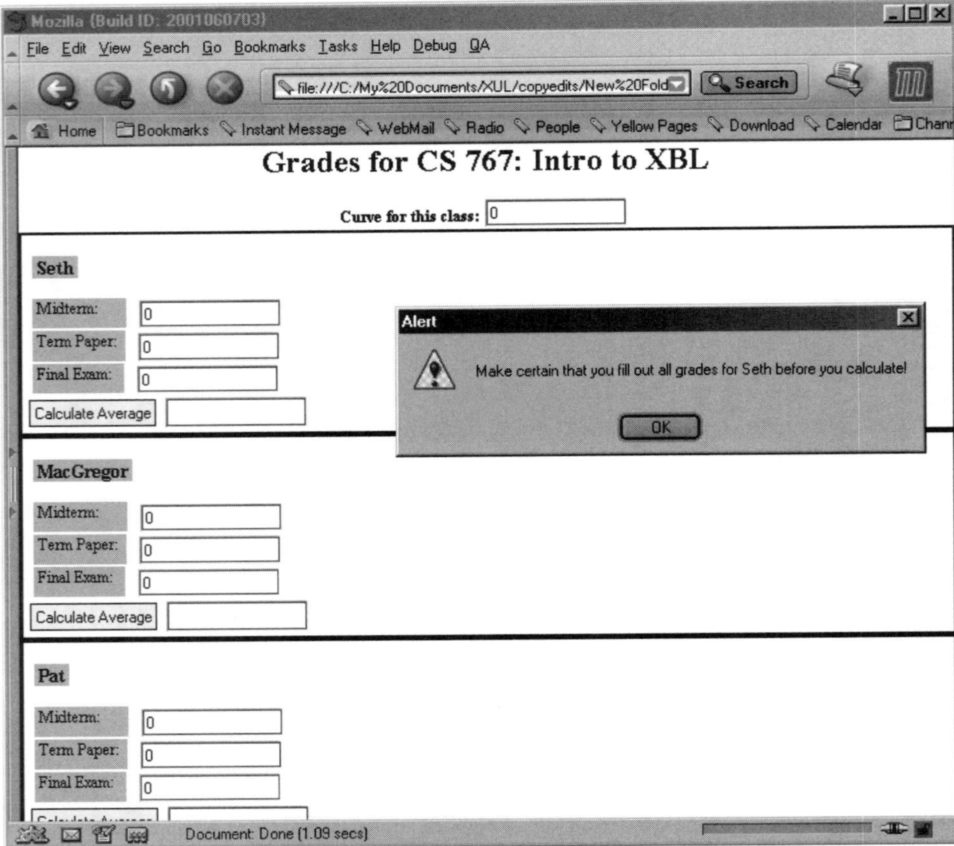

Figure 7.6 Screen shot of grading application with handler.

bound element. Another form of inheritance in XBL is binding inheritance. By using the extends attribute on the <binding> element, a binding may inherit contents, event handlers, and additional interfaces from another binding or element. We may use binding inheritance in two ways:

Inheritance from other bindings. For example: <binding id="binding1" extends="mybindings.xml#foo"/>

Inheritance from other elements. For example: <binding id="binding2" extends="xul:box"/>

The inclusion of binding inheritance allows you to create bindings that can be subclassed and extended to promote binding reuse.

Summary

By using XUL overlays and XBL with XUL, you can build reusable modular components. In this chapter, we went over the syntax of XUL overlays and XBL, we gave tutorials on how to use them, and gave several examples of how you can use them to share resources in a XUL software library. Throughout this chapter, we showed how the technologies of XUL overlays and XBL can provide reusability and extensibility in XUL-based software projects.

Up to this point of the book, we have focused on the details of mechanisms in XUL that can be used in practical applications. The next section of the book focuses on several practical applications—combining the technologies we have discussed and presenting them in real-world scenarios and case studies.

Notes

[1]Mozilla.org, *XML Binding Language—W3C Note*, http://www.w3.org/TR/xbl/,W3C Note, February, 2001.

[2]Mozilla.org, 2001.

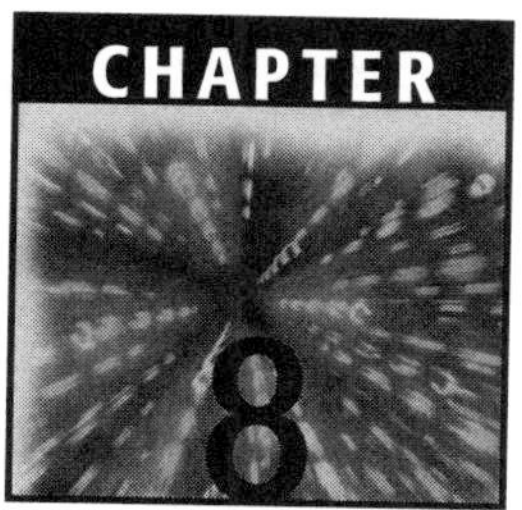

The jXUL Open Source Project

XML gives Java something to do.
Jon Bosak, *XML, Java, and the Future of the Web*

In this chapter we will examine a prototype of the jXUL project. The purpose of jXUL is to integrate XUL into the Java platform. We will examine the goals of the project and its initial design and then walkthrough an explanation of its major components. The walk-through will be accompanied by code samples and screen shots. The chapter will conclude with a discussion of the project's future direction and information on how you can get involved. For more information on how to become involved with the jXUL Open Source Project, please visit the official Web site at http://www.jxul.org.

Why jXUL?

The motivation for the jXUL open source project is to create a cross-platform execution engine for Mozilla's Application Object Model. This engine would free XUL applications from the browser and allow the use of XBL to be the standard for all user interfaces, both Web and for standalone applications. The concept of isolating code from the user interface description has been around a long time. In fact, the Macintosh has allowed the storage of user interface resource descriptions in a separate resource fork in data files since 1984. As an example of the power of jXUL, Figure 8.1 is the jXUL version of the XUL example application, the Business Asset Manager introduced in Chapter 4, "Building a Simple XUL Interface."

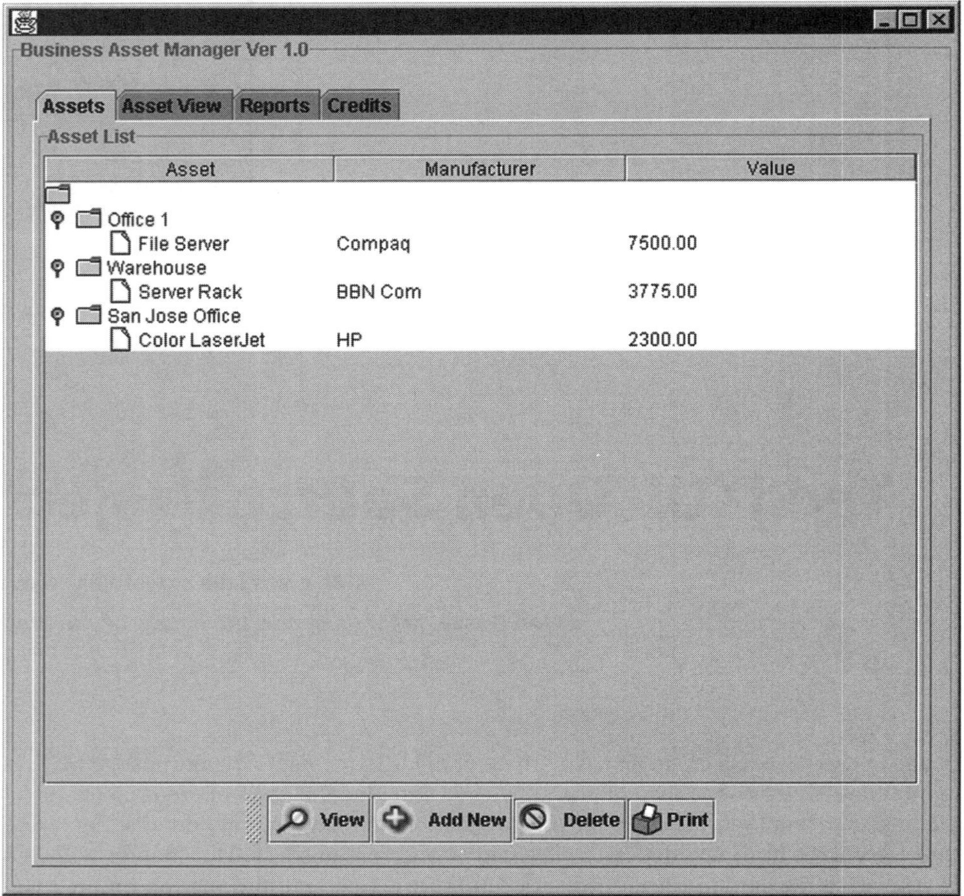

Figure 8.1 jXUL implementation of xulExample.xul.

The jXUL project gives you a good idea of the the power of the XUL programming language. Now let's examine how jXUL can execute XUL applications on the Java platform.

NOTE **For up-to-date information on the status of the jXUL project, please go to http://www.jxul.org.**

The jXUL Architecture

The jXUL architecture is split into a foundation, container, and application layer. Figure 8.1 depicts the layers in the jXUL architecture. The architecture is composed of vertical and horizontal layers. The separation allows for abstractions to be limited to small

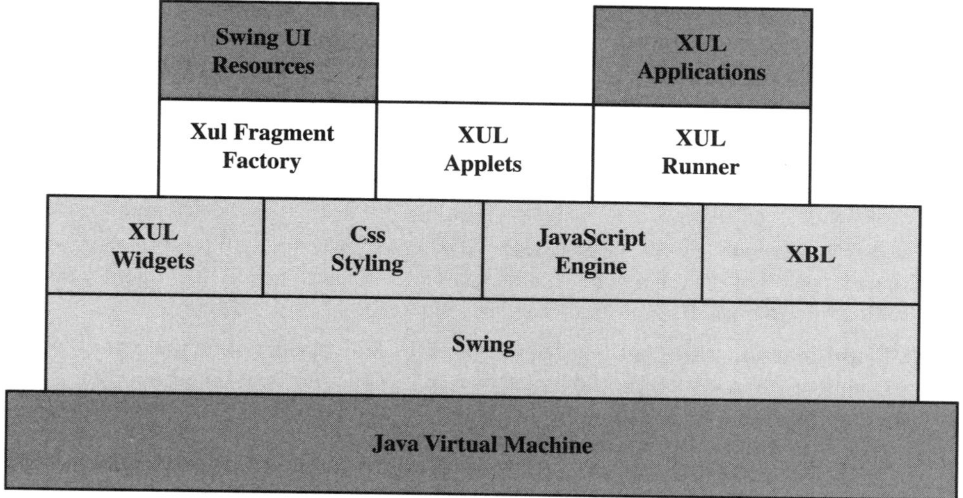

Figure 8.2 The jXUL architecture.

functional areas. Such small abstractions are more easily understood, mixed, matched and implemented.

A description of each layer follows:

XUL widgets. Each XUL element is represented with its own class that extends an existing Swing JComponent. These classes will be instantiated either from a DOM element or a text fragment from a XUL file.

CSS styling. A set of classes representing CSS, CSS styles, and the ability to apply these styles to XUL widgets.

JavaScript engine. Supports XUL applications by embedding the Rhino JavaScript interpreter. Secondly, a package (JavaScript) will be created to represent the translation of JavaScript built-in objects (such as documents and windows) into their Java GUI counterparts.

XBL (XML Binding Language). This part has not yet been designed. As an open source project, you can provide input into the design and assist in the coding.

XUL Runner. Modeled after the AppletRunner. This Java program will run complete XUL applications (allowing scripting in JavaScript). The goal is to allow a XUL application to be shipped as a standalone Java program. The XUL Runner will start out by parsing a XUL XML file and creating a DOM. The DOM will be traversed, and XUL widgets will be created. Every XUL widget (subclass of JComponent) will be associated to its corresponding DOM node in a peer map. If a CSS file exists, it will be parsed, and CSS Style objects and a CSS Stylesheet object will be created. That stylesheet will be applied to the XUL-DOM. Lastly, if a JavaScript script exists, it will be parsed by Rhino and linked to the XUL-DOM by way of proxy objects. Lastly, all JavaScript fragments that act as event handlers will be registered with their associated JComponents in the peer map.

XUL applets. The ability for an applet to receive a XUL document as a parameter or via an URL on its host and render the user interface. This functionality has not yet been implemented.

XUL Fragment Factory. Parsing of a text fragment that describes a single XUL widget will generate a instantiated XUL widget object. If the XUL fragment is a container, it will be allowed to have child elements. Appropriate event handlers will be passed into the factory method at instantiation.

Swing resources. The use of XUL as a Java Swing resource will require a simple way to connect the Java event-handling mechanisms to the XUL widgets. This will be done both programmatically and via a simple XML wrapper.

XUL applications. Another key requirement for XUL applications will not only to be able to run them on the Java platform but to be able to debug them. Being able to step through the XUL file, line by line, to properly debug it is a very ambitious goal. This will be extremely helpful to XUL hackers.

Now let's examine the current implementation of the components of the jXUL platform in detail.

jXUL Components

The current implementation centers around the XUL Runner application. In this section we will examine the components that make up the XUL Runner and how they function. The general concept of operation is that the XUL Runner runs one or more XUL applications. A XUL application reads in and executes a XUL file and any other files associated with it (like cascading stylesheets or JavaScript scripts). We will begin with the Main class of the XUL Runner, which is the Java program run from the command line (in the org.jxul.xulrunner package).

XUL Runner

The XUL Runner Main class is a simple class that acts as a launch point for XUL applications. The initial implementation of this class is a simple command line interface. Later plans include a GUI console, which will also be necessary to debug jXUL and XUL applications. The concept of execution for this class is to accept the name of a XUL file on the command line, parse the XUL file into a Document Object Model (DOM), then create a XUL application object, and pass the object to the DOM, and finally to start the XUL application in its own thread.

NOTE **The current implementation of the XUL Runner Main class uses the W3C DOM implementation; however, we are considering switching to the JDOM. See http://www.jdom.org for more details on JDOM.**

Code Listing 8.1 is the majority of source code for the Main class. The class uses the Java API for XML Parsing (JAXP) classes (DocumentBuilderFactory and DocumentBuilder) to get a document.

```
public class Main
{
    // ...
     public static void main(String args[])
     {
        // ...
        try
        {
            String curDir = System.getProperty("user.dir");

            String inputFile = args[0];
            File f = new File(inputFile);

            if (f.exists())
            {
                // ensure document is well-formed
                DocumentBuilderFactory factory =
                  DocumentBuilderFactory.newInstance();
                DocumentBuilder dbldr = factory.newDocumentBuilder();
               //note that we need to do something when there are
               //chrome: references in the DTD
                Document doc = dbldr.parse(new File(inputFile));

                // assemble the XulApplication
                XulApplication xulApp = new XulApplication(doc);

                // start it
                xulApp.start();
            }
            else
                System.out.println("File: " + args[0] +
                  " does not exist. Aborting.");
        } catch (Throwable t)
          {
            t.printStackTrace();
          }
    }
}
```

Code Listing 8.1 XUL Runner Main class.

Here is an example of how to run the XUL Runner Main class:

```
>java org.jxul.xulrunner.Main xulex1.xul
```

The file xulex1.xul exists in the demos directory of the jXUL distribution. Running it generates Figure 8.1.

XUL Application

A XUL application is a separate thread of execution that represents a single XUL application. It is possible that the XUL Runner may invoke multiple XUL applications. Although that may not be practical, the fact that a XUL application is a separate thread will be necessary if the XUL Runner is stepping through it under the control of a debugging thread. The conceptual model of a XUL application is the translation of a XUL tree into a window and a set of graphical components and then to optionally style those components, optionally attach JavaScript functions to those components, and lastly show the Window. Code Listing 8.2 presents the data members of the XUL Application class.

The purpose of each data member in Code Listing 8.2 is as follows:

Document xulDoc. This is the DOM document that contains the XUL XML elements.

Hashtable peerMap. A hashtable that maps each element in the DOM to its GUI peer. This is necessary so that JavaScript code or a stylesheet rule that wants to select a specific XUL element can act on its visual representation (the GUI peer).

XulDom xulDom. The XulDom class encapsulates the document and peerMap in a single object.

```
/**
 * A Xul Driven Application.
 */
public class XulApplication extends Thread
{
    //... debug variable and static code omitted
    Document xulDoc;

    /**
     * Mapping between Xul elements and their gui peers.
     * Necessary to map between the declarative description and
     * the implementation.  This will allow both processing of
     * stylesheets and targets for scripted actions.
     */
    Hashtable peerMap = new Hashtable();

    /**
     * Encapsulation of the doc and corresponding peers.
     */
    XulDom xulDom = new XulDom();

    StyleSheet styleSheet;

    Element root;
    XulWindow window;
    XulMenuBar menuBar;
    //Javascript engine
    XulJsEngine jsEngine = null;
```

Code Listing 8.2 The XUL Application class data members.

Stylesheet styleSheet. A reference to a CSS object that represents a sort of CSS DOM in which the CSS is represented solely by Java objects. This is covered in greater detail in a later section, "Cascading Style Sheet Implementation."

XulWindow window and XulMenuBar menubar. These are top-level widgets that are created first. The XulWindow is the top-level container for all other widgets.

XulJsEngine jsEngine. A singleton class that represents the JavaScript engine which executes JavaScript functions. This will be discussed in detail in the "Embedded JavaScript Engine" section later in this chapter.

Code Listing 8.3 presents the constructor for the XulApplication class.

The XulApplication class constructor receives the XUL document from the XUL Runner Main class. The constructor creates a XULDOM object, extracts the root element from the document, and ensures that the root element is a XUL window or XUL overlay (or it throws an exception). Code Listing 8.4 is the run() method of the XulApplication class. The run method is not executed directly; it is invoked when the thread starts by the Java virtual machine. Even though Code Listing 8.4 takes up two pages, it has been reduced to its bare minimum. The complete source code is available at http://www. jxul.org.

The run() method in the XUL application is the workhorse of the XUL Runner application. Here is the method's sequence of events:

- If a cascading stylesheet is present, process it.
- Create a XUL window that extends JFrame. The XUL window code is presented in detail in Code Listing 8.5 and Code Listing 8.6.
- Normalize the DOM using the DomUtil.normalizeDocument() method, which eliminates all blank text nodes (like normally ignored carriage returns between elements). This simplifies the processing of the DOM.
- Iterate through all the child elements. If a child element matches a known (and implemented) XUL widget, create the widget and add it to the XUL window. The XulSyntax class abstracts the names of the XUL widgets into constants so that syntax changes to the XUL language will affect only a single file.

```
public XulApplication(Document xulDoc) throws XulFormatException
    {
        this.xulDoc = xulDoc;
        xulDom.setXulDoc(xulDoc);
        xulDom.setPeerMap(peerMap);

        // root element should be a window
        root = xulDoc.getDocumentElement();
        if (!root.getTagName().equals(XulSyntax.ELEMENT_WINDOW) &&
           !root.getTagName().equals(XulSyntax.ELEMENT_OVERLAY))
            throw new XulFormatException("Root element must be a " +
           XulSyntax.ELEMENT_WINDOW + "or an " +
XulSyntax.ELEMENT_OVERLAY);
    }
```

Code Listing 8.3 The XulApplication class constructor.

```
public void run()
    {
        try
        {
            // TBD - check for xml-stylesheet processing instruction
            // if there - parse it.
            NodeList siblings = xulDoc.getChildNodes();
            int siblingCount = siblings.getLength();
            // pi?
            for (int i=0; i < siblingCount; i++)
            {
                org.w3c.dom.Node sibling = siblings.item(i);
                int nType = sibling.getNodeType();
                if (nType ==
                  org.w3c.dom.Node.PROCESSING_INSTRUCTION_NODE)
                {
                    // ... CSS Implementation discussed later
                }
            }

            /* render the Application
            - create the Xul Window */
            window = new XulWindow(root);

            // normalize the DOM tree
            DomUtil.normalizeDocument(root);

            /* now that we have a window,
            iterate through the child elements of the Window.
            The children will be widgets to add to the window. */
            if (root.hasChildNodes())
            {
                NodeList children = root.getChildNodes();

                int childCount = children.getLength();

                for (int i=0; i < childCount; i++)
                {
                    org.w3c.dom.Node child = children.item(i);

                    if (debug)
                        System.out.println("Child[" + i + "]" +
                        child.getNodeName() + "-" +
                        child.getNodeValue());
                    String childElementName = child.getNodeName();
              // add the widgets
```

Code Listing 8.4 The XulApplication class run() method.

```
            if
    (childElementName.equalsIgnoreCase(XulSyntax.ELEMENT_TREE))
            {
             XulTree tree = new XulTree((Element)child, peerMap);
             window.getContentPane().add(tree);
             peerMap.put(child, tree);
             }
            else
                 if
  (childElementName.equals(XulSyntax.ELEMENT_MENUBAR))
                 {
                     // create a XulMenuBar
                     menuBar = new XulMenuBar((Element)child,
                       peerMap);
                     // set the menu bar
                     window.setJMenuBar(menuBar);
                 }
                 else if
 (childElementName.equals(XulSyntax.ELEMENT_BOX))
                 {
                     // create a XulBox
                     XulBox box = new XulBox((Element)child,
peerMap);
                     // add it to the window
                     window.getContentPane().add(box);

                     // add to peerMap
                     peerMap.put(child, box);
                 }
// ... other widget code omitted for brevity

// ... JavaScript Implementation discussed later

          // if a styleSheet exists - apply it
          if (styleSheet != null)
              styleSheet.apply(xulDom);

          // have size?
          int w = window.getWidth();
          int h = window.getHeight();
          if (w <= 0 && h <= 0)
              window.pack();

          // show the window
          System.out.println("SHOWING THE WINDOW.");
          window.show();
```

Code Listing 8.4 The XulApplication class run() method (Continued).

```
            } catch (Exception e)
            {
              e.printStackTrace();
            }
        }
    }
```

Code Listing 8.4 The XulApplication class run() method (Continued).

- If a stylesheet exists, apply it.
- If a script exists, load it into the JavaScript engine.
- Set the window size if attributes existed in the XulWindow element; otherwise set the window size just large enough to hold all of its children.
- Show the window with the show() method.

The majority of code in this method is matching the child elements to the appropriate XUL widget, creating the widget and adding it to the XUL window. Let's examine the implementation of the XUL widgets.

XUL Widgets

A XUL widget is a subclass of a specific Java Swing component. The goal is to match up each XUL graphical element with its Java Swing counterpart. We will examine only the source code for a single widget because all the widget implementations follow the same pattern: create the GUI component, tailor it by examining the attached attributes in the XUL element, and finally, style it if any CSS styles are present.

NOTE The authors are considering changing the design to make the Java Swing component a peer and subclass of a generic XulElement. See http://www.jxul.org for the current state of this proposal.

Window

The window element is the root element of most XUL files (except overlays) and is implemented by subclassing JFrame. Code Listing 8.5 shows the data members of the XulWindow class.

The XulWindow class' data members fall into two categories: the XML element, which holds any attached attributes specified in the XUL file, and a data member for each legal attribute that may be present in the XUL file.

NOTE Most of the XUL widgets have not implemented all of the XUL attributes for each widget. Only the key attributes have been implemented at the time of this writing.

```
/**
 * A XUL Window.
 */
public class XulWindow extends JFrame
{
    // ... debug variable and static code omitted

    private Element windowElement;

    // window attributes
    String style;
    String title;
    String titlemodified;
    String titlemenuseparator;
    String id;
    String xmlns;
    String onload;
    String onunload;
    String windowtype;
    String align;
    protected int width = -1, height = -1;
    String persist;
    int x = -1, y = -1;
    String ondraggesture;

    public int getWidth() { return width; }
    public int getHeight() { return height; }
    public String getOnLoad() { return onload; }
```

Code Listing 8.5 Data members of the XulWindow class.

Code Listing 8.6 is the XulWindow constructor. It is important to understand what this constructor represents of all the widget constructors. The behavior of the constructor follows this pattern: check for the existence of each legal attribute; if the attribute exists, extract its value; and set its corresponding property (if one exists) in the Java Swing component.

A sample XUL window element is presented in Code Listing 8.7 and rendered in Figure 8.3.

Menu

The XUL menu widget enables you to create a popup menu and attach it to a menu bar. Code Listing 8.7 is a simple XUL menu inside a XUL window.

Figure 8.3 is the GUI generated when Code Listing 8.7 is run in the XULRunner.

```
public XulWindow(Element windowElement)
    {
        this.windowElement = windowElement;

        // extract the attributes (if any)
        Attr titleAttr =
          windowElement.getAttributeNode(XulSyntax.WINDOW_ATTR_TITLE);
        if (titleAttr != null)
        {
            title = titleAttr.getNodeValue();
            if (title != null && !StringUtil.isBlank(title))
                this.setTitle(title);
        }

        Attr titlemodifiedAttr =
          windowElement.getAttributeNode(XulSyntax.
          WINDOW_ATTR_TITLEMODIFIED);
        if (titlemodifiedAttr != null)
            titlemodified = titlemodifiedAttr.getNodeValue();
// ... many attributes omitted for brevity

        Attr xAttr =
          windowElement.getAttributeNode(XulSyntax.WINDOW_ATTR_X);
        if (xAttr != null)
        {
            String xStr = xAttr.getNodeValue();
            x = Integer.parseInt(xStr);
        }

        Attr yAttr =
          windowElement.getAttributeNode(XulSyntax.WINDOW_ATTR_Y);
        if (yAttr != null)
        {
            String yStr = yAttr.getNodeValue();
            y = Integer.parseInt(yStr);
        }

        if (x > 0 && y > 0)
            this.setLocation(x,y);
        Attr ondraggestureAttr =
          windowElement.getAttributeNode(XulSyntax.
          WINDOW_ATTR_ONDRAGGESTURE);
        if (ondraggestureAttr != null)
            ondraggesture = ondraggestureAttr.getNodeValue();
    }

    public void sizeToContent()
    {
        pack();
    }
}
```

Code Listing 8.6 The XulWindow constructor.

```
<?xml version="1.0" ?>
<?xml-stylesheet href="css1.css" type="text/css"?>
   <window
xmlns="http://www.mozilla.org/keymaster/gatekeeper/there.is.only.xul"
   align="vertical"
   title="Xul Test 2"
   width="400"
   height="200"
>
        <menubar>
             <menu value="AAA">
                  <menupopup>
                       <menuitem value="a01"/>
                       <menuitem value="a02"/>
                       <menuseparator/>
                       <menuitem value="b01"/>
                       <menuitem value="b02"/>
                       <menuseparator/>
                       <menuitem value="c01"/>
                       <menuitem value="c02"/>
                  </menupopup>
             </menu>
        </menubar>
   </window>
```

Code Listing 8.7 Sample XUL menu.

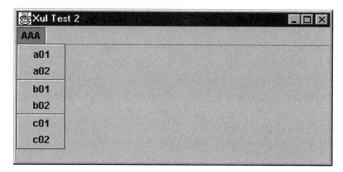

Figure 8.3 Popup menu (xul2.xul).

Button

A XUL button represents a clickable button. Code Listing 8.8 places several button inside a box, which is equivalent to a Java Panel, and then inside a window.

When Code Listing 8.8 is run in the XULRunner, The GUI shown in Figure 8.4 is generated.

```
<window
xmlns="http://www.mozilla.org/keymaster/gatekeeper/there.is.only.xul"
   align="vertical" >
        <box align="horizontal">
        <button value="R"  />
        <button value="L"  />
        <button value="B"  />
        <button value="T"  />
        </box>
        <box class="vertical" align="vertical">
              <button id="a" value="AAA"  />
              <button value="BBB"  />
              <button value="CCC"  />
        </box>
   </window>
```

Code Listing 8.8 A sample XUL window with buttons.

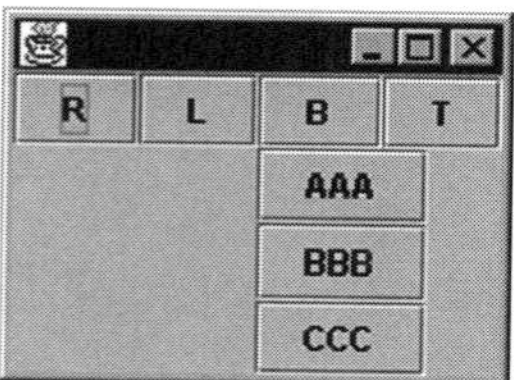

Figure 8.4 jXUL buttons.

Checkbox

A checkbox is a component that maintains one of two states (checked or unchecked). Code Listing 8.9 adds a XUL file to demonstrate some simple checkboxes inside a box, which vertically aligns them inside the window. The other interesting aspect about this file is its use of the style attribute. We will discuss "Cascading Style Sheet Implementation" later in this chapter.

When Code Listing 8.9 is run in the XUL Runner, the GUI in Figure 8.5 is generated. You should notice that the style background-color was applied to the box.

Image

This is very similar to the HTML image tag and enables you to easily add images to your GUI. Code Listing 8.10 demonstrates both the image element and a text element vertically aligned in a box.

When Code Listing 8.10 is run in the XUL Runner, the GUI displayed in Figure 8.6 is generated.

While other widgets are implemented, we will not show them all here. Here is a list of widgets currently implemented in jXUL: box, bulletinboard, button, checkbox, checkboxmenuitem, grid, hbox, keyset, label, image, menu, menubar, menuitem, radiobutton,

```
<?xml version="1.0" ?>
<?xml-stylesheet href="chrome://global/skin/" type="text/css"?>
<window id="checkboxes"
          xmlns:html="http://www.w3.org/1999/xhtml"
xmlns="http://www.mozilla.org/keymaster/gatekeeper/there.is.only.xul">
          <box style="background-color: lightblue;" orient="vertical">
                 <checkbox value="James Joyce" checked="true" />
            <checkbox value="Joseph Conrad" />
            <checkbox value="William Faulkner" />
      </box>
</window>
```

Code Listing 8.9 XUL checkboxes aligned vertically in a window.

Figure 8.5 jXUL checkboxes.

```
<window title="test image">
<box style="background-color: lightgrey;"
           orient="vertical"
           autostretch="never">
         <image src="apple.gif" />
         <text value="Icon" />
      </box>
</window>
```

Code Listing 8.10 An image and text description.

Figure 8.6 jXUL image.

radiogroup, radiomenuitem, stack, tab, tabbox, tabpanel, textbox, title, titledbox, toolbar, toolbox, tree, treecell, treehead, treechildren, treeitem, treerow, vbox, and window.

Cascading Style Sheet Implementation

Cascading Style Sheets are implemented in the XUL Runner by first parsing the stylesheet into an object representation and then applying the resulting Stylesheet object to the XULDOM. Remember that the XULDOM is an encapsulation of the DOM and the peerMap. Code Listing 8.11 demonstrates these two actions in the XUL application source code.

The CSS parser generates a Stylesheet object. A Stylesheet object contains a set of styles. A style is a selector and a set of CSS statements. A CSS statement is a CSS property name and value combination. The CSS parser creates this Stylesheet object by working with a CssLexer class that generates CssTokens. A CssToken is either a selector or a statement.

NOTE Although the parsing architecture described is simple, the authors are considering replacing it with the W3C Simple API for CSS (SAC), which is a CSS parser created by the W3C and available at http://www.w3.org/Style/CSS/SAC/.

After a CSS object is created, it can be applied to a XULDOM object. An example of this was seen in the checkbox example in Code Listing 8.9 and was displayed in Figure 8.5. The box used a style attribute that set the background color to light blue. Code Listing 8.12 is a more advanced example. It is a portion of a CSS file for the Pagman game.

When the pagman.xul file is executed in the XUL Runner application, it parses the CSS file and generates the screen in Figure 8.7.

Embedded JavaScript Engine

In order to execute JavaScript functions on the XUL document, the XUL Runner embeds the Rhino JavaScript interpreter. Rhino is a JavaScript intepreter written in pure Java and available at www.mozilla.org/rhino/. The Rhino interpreter is encapsu-

```
// get from File
CssParser parser = new CssParser(href);
styleSheet = parser.parse();
...
// if a styleSheet exists - apply it
if (styleSheet != null)
     styleSheet.apply(xulDom);
```

Code Listing 8.11 CSS implementation in the XulApplication class.

```
image.upper-left-corner {
   list-style-image: url(ul_corner.gif);
}
image.upper-right-corner {
   list-style-image: url(ur_corner.gif);
}
image.lower-left-corner {
   list-style-image: url(ll_corner.gif);
}
image.lower-right-corner {
   list-style-image: url(lr_corner.gif);
}
image.horizontal-wall {
   list-style-image: url(horiz_wall.gif);
}
image.vertical-wall {
   list-style-image: url(vert_wall.gif);
}
```

Code Listing 8.12 Part of pagman.css.

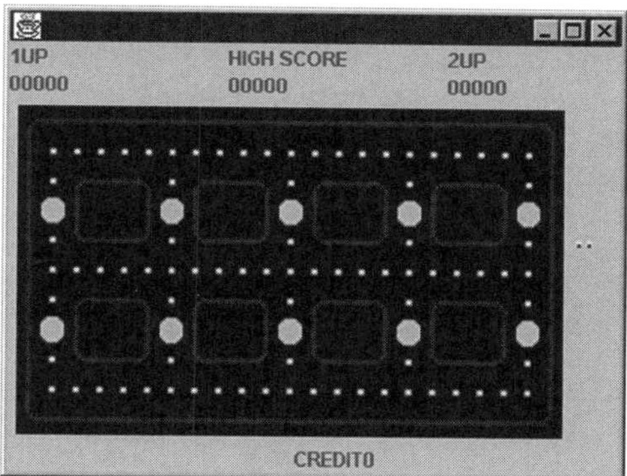

Figure 8.7 The Pagman game in XUL Runner.

lated in the XulJsEngine class. Code Listing 8.13 is the code in the XulApplication class that gets an instance of the JavaScript engine. If a script is present, it loads the script.

After the XulJsEngine has been initialized and a script loaded, the methods in the script can be invoked. For example, Code Listing 8.13 demonstrates the invocation of a windowOnLoad function if the onload attribute of window includes some JavaScript. Although we can invoke JavaScript functions, those functions are going to want to access the elements in the DOM and execute standard browser functions. That is where we must bridge the gap between the JavaScript environment and the XUL-DOM. To do that, we have a JavaScript package that includes the following classes:

```
String script = null;
File scriptfile = null;

jsEngine = jsEngine.getInstance();

if (child.hasChildNodes())
{
NodeList scriptChildren = child.getChildNodes();
     org.w3c.dom.Node first = scriptChildren.item(0);
     script = first.getNodeValue();
}
else
{
     Attr srcAttr = ((Element)child).getAttributeNode("src");
     if (srcAttr != null)
          script = srcAttr.getNodeValue();
          System.out.println("attribute src is " + script);
     scriptfile = new File(script);
}

if (script != null)
{
     if (!jsEngine.setXulDom(xulDom))
               System.out.println("Cannot get a reference to the JS doc
object.");

     // add the script to the context
     if (scriptfile != null && scriptfile.exists())
          jsEngine.loadScriptFile(scriptfile);
     else
          jsEngine.loadScript(script);
}

...

// if an onLoad script - run it
String windowOnLoad = window.getOnLoad();
if (windowOnLoad != null)
{
// run it
     jsEngine.executeFunction(windowOnLoad, "windowOnLoad");
}
```

Code Listing 8.13 Using the XulJsEngine in the XulApplication class.

XulJsDocument. This is the object that will represent the document object in the JavaScript environment (in other words, in any scripts we want to execute). As such, this object is the main interface between the XUL-DOM and the JavaScript interpreter. It has key methods such as getElementById().

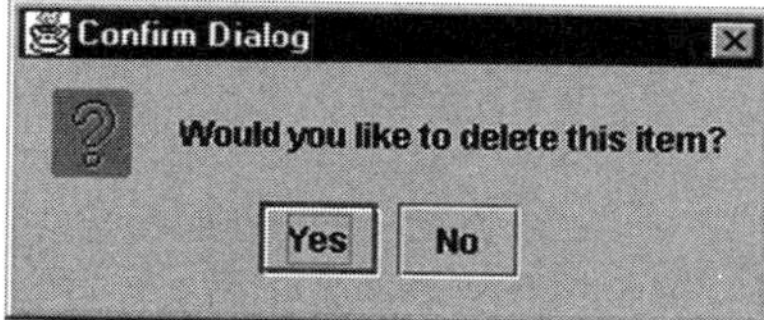

Figure 8.8 JavaScript triggered alert in the XUL Runner.

XulJsElement. This is the element that will be returned from getElementById() and represents an element in the XUL document that can be scripted in a JavaScript script.

XulJsWindow. This will represent the window object in the scripting environment.

XulJsFunctions. This class contains common JavaScript functions such as alert() and confirm().

In the XUL Runner application shown in Figure 8.1, clicking on the delete button invokes a JavaScript script, which in turn calls alert() and generates the window shown in Figure 8.8.

jXUL Packages

The jXUL project is currently separated into six packages. The function of each package is as follows:

css. The css package contains all the classes relating to the CSS implementation. This package will need to track the progress of the CSS standard. This package should also develop into a generic framework for styling Java GUI components (not just the jXUL components).

framework. This is the largest package in the system. It contains all the widget classes.

framework.treetable. A subpackage for all the supporting classes to the XulTree widget.

js. This is the JavaScript class that contains the bridge classes between the Rhino JavaScript engine and the XUL-DOM. Again, the end state of this package should be a generic framework for connecting Rhino to a Java DOM or JDOM.

util. This package contains a set of utility classes for string and DOM manipulation.

xulrunner. This package contains the bootstrap classes of the XUL Runner application, including Main and XulApplication.

There is no shortage of ideas for this platform, which is reflected in a slew of proposed packages like applet, kvm, plugin, framework.ejb, framework.jsp, and even xform. The development of these proposed packages will depend on this project's success in attracting other developers.

Getting Involved in the jXUL Project

The jXUL project (hosted at http://www.jxul.org) began as a small experiment developed by the book's authors, with a goal of turning it into a vibrant open source project. In order to transform this project into a viable OS project, we will expand the project in two ways: infrastructure and participants. By *infrastructure* we mean the hosting of the project and the tools to both develop the project and develop a community around the project.

The site contains minimal documentation and access to the source code. At the site, you can also sign up on the announce list server to receive update announcements. The plans for the site are to improve it in three ways:

- Improve the source code management by moving the source into a CVS repository.
- Improve community discussion by adding threaded discussion forums.
- Add a developer list for active developers.

As an open source project, we are actively seeking outside developers to assist us with this work. We believe this project has a tremendous amount of promise to fulfill its potential. Each package and major project needs a module owner. As a system, we also need to standardize on a build system (problem "ant" from jakarta.apache.org), improve the documentation, and improve the suite of demos.

Challenges for the jXUL Project

There are several significant challenges to running XUL applications out of their "native" browser environment , including:

HTML and DHTML rendering. XUL enables you to intersperse HTML elements with your XUL elements. Many HTML elements like bold, underline, headers, and emphasis require free-form rendering. Such rendering may be difficult or impossible to emulate via the placement of fixed components in a window and may require a dynamically painted display. Support of such full-blown XUL (if that is an objective of this project) may require embedding the Mozilla rendering engine (Gecko) in the XUL Runner via the Blackwood project (see www.mozilla.org/projects/blackwood/ for more information on Blackwood). This same issue surfaces with the implementation of complex CSS styles (like those commonly used in dynamic HTML).

Emulation of the browser object hierarchy. Many JavaScript objects are related either to an HTML document or to the functions of a browser (like a back button and history). For example, the window object contains a frames array that would be extremely difficult to implement. Most of these probably will not be implemented; however, where we draw the line will affect the number of XUL applications that can be run as standalone.

XUL debugging. The current XUL Runner prototype does not support debugging. Further design work needs to be done to determine how debugging hooks should be inserted into the architecture.

Other design issues. Each new use for the jXUL platform has potential design ramifications. For example, support for XUL applets may force eliminating the Rhino engine in favor of a LiveConnect bridge. Another example is using the jXUL platform as an XFORM renderer. More information on XFORM can be found at http://www.w3.org/MarkUp/Forms/.

Summary

This chapter introduced the jXUL open source project, which will integrate XUL into the Java platform. After presenting the Business Asset Manager example, we covered the jXUL architecture, the jXUL components including the jXUL widgets, and the current state of the project.

The jXUL architecture is divided into foundation, container, and application layers. The foundation layer includes the XUL widgets, CSS styling, JavaScript engine, and XBL. The container layer includes the XUL Runner and XUL Fragment Factory. The application layer includes swing resources and XUL applications.

The jXUL components are the pieces of the architecture currently implemented and primarily consist of the components comprising the XUL Runner. The XUL Runner Main class parses the XML document and passes the DOM to the XUL application. The XUL application loads any CSS or scripts present, instantiates a XUL window, and then iterates through the child nodes in the DOM. The child nodes in the DOM are matched to their corresponding graphical components; the component is instantiated; and then the component is added to the XUL window. The XUL widgets are subclasses of swing components that contain XUL attributes. We examined the window, menu, button, checkbox, and image widgets. We ended the section by examining the CSS and JavaScript implementations in the XUL Runner.

We summarized the current state of the project by describing the current Java packages, the current project status, and some challenges we have to overcome. There are seven Java packages: cs, framework, framework.treetable, js, util, and xulrunner. Our plan is to move from a small internal project to a broader, more open, and community-based project. Lastly, we discussed four challenges that could affect the design of the system: HTML rendering, emulation of the browser object hierarchy, XUL debugging, and other platform uses like XUL applets and xforms.

Case Study: Creating a Customizable Browser Portal

The Web of today, the vast unstructured mass of information, may in the future be transformed into something more manageable—and thus something far more useful.

Ora Lassila, "Introduction to RDF Metadata"

Many Web sites enable members to customize their pages. Through a Web interface, users can add their favorite stock quotes and program intelligent agents to look for interesting news items. These sites are sometimes called information portals, and the customization logic resides on the server. Many examples of these portals can be found today: My Yahoo! and My Netscape are just two examples. The server recognizes the user with a cookie, and the Web site displays the user's information when the Web page is visited. Users with multiple accounts need to visit one Web site at a time to see their customized information.

Using XUL, you can embed information from Web portals in the application of the browser itself. We can use XUL to create a facility for fast access to multiple information portals. In Chapter 6, "RDF and XUL Templates," we demonstrated that XUL content could be generated automatically from RDF data sources. We also have shown throughout this book that the architectures of the Netscape 6.x and Mozilla browsers are flexible enough to accommodate maximum customizability. The case study in this chapter presents one example of inserting an information portal in an application, using the facilities that already exist in the Netscape 6.x browser. This example applies the concepts presented throughout this book to present a step-by-step tutorial on creating a solution.

In this case study, we define the problem that we will address and outline our approach to the solution. This case study focuses on existing XUL code in the Web browser, and we focus on how that code will address the solution to our problem. The case study highlights virtually every XUL-related technology that we have discussed in this book—CSS, JavaScript, RDF, XUL templates, XUL overlays, and XBL—and shows you how all of these technologies work together to present a real-world solution.

Defining the Problem

Users on the Internet today have multiple personal portals that store their information. These information portals are provided by a number of different vendors and are usually separated by content specialization. This case study revolves around a fictitious company, XYZPORTAL.COM, an organization that mines and assimilates information for the public's consumption. This company houses many portals of news, data, and live feeds, and they have developed a Web front end to this information. Their portals have a Web interface where users can log in over the Web to check their information. Over the years, XYZPORTAL.COM's business has been successful, but lately, their users have been complaining. The organization serves many sophisticated users who belong to several of their portals, but the users also belong to many other portals. The users' central complaint is that they are tired of spending several hours of their day logging on to all of these portals to check and download information. Instead, they would like to have all of the information come to them and be available instantly, and they would like to be able to organize the data any way that they want.

Of course, you can solve this problem in many ways. How can XYZPORTAL.COM solve it in a way that requires little overhead and investment? They would like to develop a solution that fits their customers' needs and to present a solution that handles the presentation of our raw information—hopefully without rewriting all of their code.

Approaching the Solution

Thankfully, the CTO of XYZPORTAL.COM has heard about XUL, and she has sent this book to her senior engineers. From Chapter 6, "RDF and XUL Templates," the engineers learned that XUL could be dynamically generated from content from multiple data sources. They downloaded the most recent version of Netscape, and they are intrigued by the functionality of My Sidebar, which has several tabs containing information within the browser. The engineers at XYZPORTAL.COM think that they could change the browser to put their information sources in the My Sidebar tabs, but they would like to study the underlying XUL and JavaScript code in the browser to see how the sidebar functionality works.

This case study provides an in-depth overview of how Netscape's "My Sidebar" works. This case study shows you how XYZPORTAL.COM can solve users' problems by customizing the browser to provide in-browser portals. By focusing on this XUL code written for the Netscape 6.x browser, you will increase your knowledge as a designer and a developer for real-world applications.

Under the Hood: An In-Depth Look at Netscape's "My Sidebar"

Figure 9.1 shows the Netscape 6.x browser. Highlighted on the left is "My Sidebar," which has the tabs What's Related, Search, Buddy List, Stocks, and News. The Mozilla

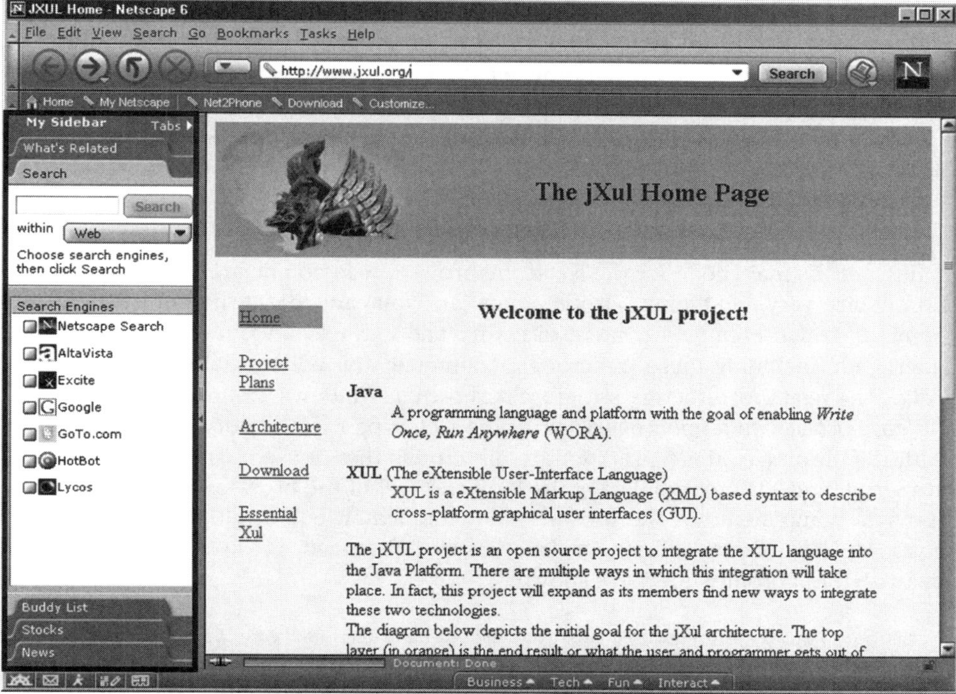

Figure 9.1 A look at "My Sidebar."

browser also has this functionality. This part of the browser is customizable. We can add tabs to the sidebar, and we can control the content in the tabs. As you click on each tab, the content of each tab is displayed. Some of the content displayed inside each tab is HTML content from Web pages, and some of the content is XUL content written by the engineers at Netscape. The Tabs area on the sidebar lets you customize the browser. When you click on the Tabs->Customize Sidebar button, a new dialog appears, enabling you to add or delete tabs. This section of the case study focuses on the code used to create Netscape's "My Sidebar". Inspecting the code of this browser component should give you lots of ideas on how to solve the dilemma of this case study, providing a solution for XYZPORTAL.COM.

How can we look at how this component of the browser was written? As we mentioned in Chapter 1, "What Is XUL?", the Netscape engine of the browser parses XUL, JavaScript, XBL, and CSS content. This content is packaged in multiple JAR files, which are packaged in the chrome directory in the Netscape browser. On Windows platforms, this directory is usually C:\Program Files\Netscape\Netscape 6\chrome. To look at the underlying code, you need to extract the information from the JAR archive files. The jar executable is part of the J2SE (Java 2 Standard Edition) development kit, and it is necessary for extracting files from the archive.

TIP JAR stands for Java Archive, and similar to TAR and ZIP, it is a format for compressing and packaging many files and directories into one file. For added

security, a JAR file can be digitally signed. The contents of a JAR file can be read at run-time, and it can be used for breaking up pieces of your code base into particular modules. For these purposes, the engineers at Netscape have used the JAR format to store most of the user interface content. You can look at this content by extracting it from these files as we describe in this chapter. For more information on the JAR executable and to download the J2SE software development kit that contains it, visit java.sun.com/.

Much of the main code for the Netscape browser is in comm.jar. By changing to the chrome directory and typing "jar xvf comm.jar," you can extract the information from comm.jar, which creates a content directory and extracts several directories of data underneath, including these directories: communicator, editor, global, navigator, and necko. The resulting directory structure is shown in Windows Explorer in Figure 9.2.

Figure 9.2 shows a good overview of the Netscape 6.x directory structure. Underneath the chrome*/content* directory are directories that house most of the XUL, CSS, JavaScript, and XBL for displaying the look and feel of the browser. These directories represent components of the browser—communicator, editor, global, navigator, and necko. All files under this directory structure are referenced via the chrome URL, beginning with the "chrome:" prefix as shown:

```
chrome://component-name/content/component-subdirectory/file.xul
```

For example, looking at the directory structure in Figure 9.2, if we wanted to reference a file named bookmark.xul in the bookmarks directory under the communicator component, we would reference it using this URL:

```
chrome://communicator/content/bookmarks/bookmark.xul
```

As you can see from Figure 9.2, the communicator module has many subdirectories, including code for bookmarks, directory, help, and history. On the same level as the chrome directory is the components directory, which includes JavaScript for exposed methods in the Netscape browser and DLLs. This components directory is an important one for this case study, and we will be revisiting it a little later.

The focus of much of this study is on the sidebar directory, contained in the communicator directory. We first look at the chrome://communicator/content/sidebar/ directory, which contains the XUL code for the "My Sidebar" panels.

Code in the Sidebar Directory

The sidebar directory contains the XUL, JavaScript, XML, and CSS necessary for the look and feel of the sidebar component. For this case study, we focus on some of these files in detail. We recommend that you look at all of these files to get a better understanding of how the sidebar component is designed:

customize.js. This JavaScript file contains code for customizing the My SideBar panel. It contains functions to find data sources and to do a lot of the work for

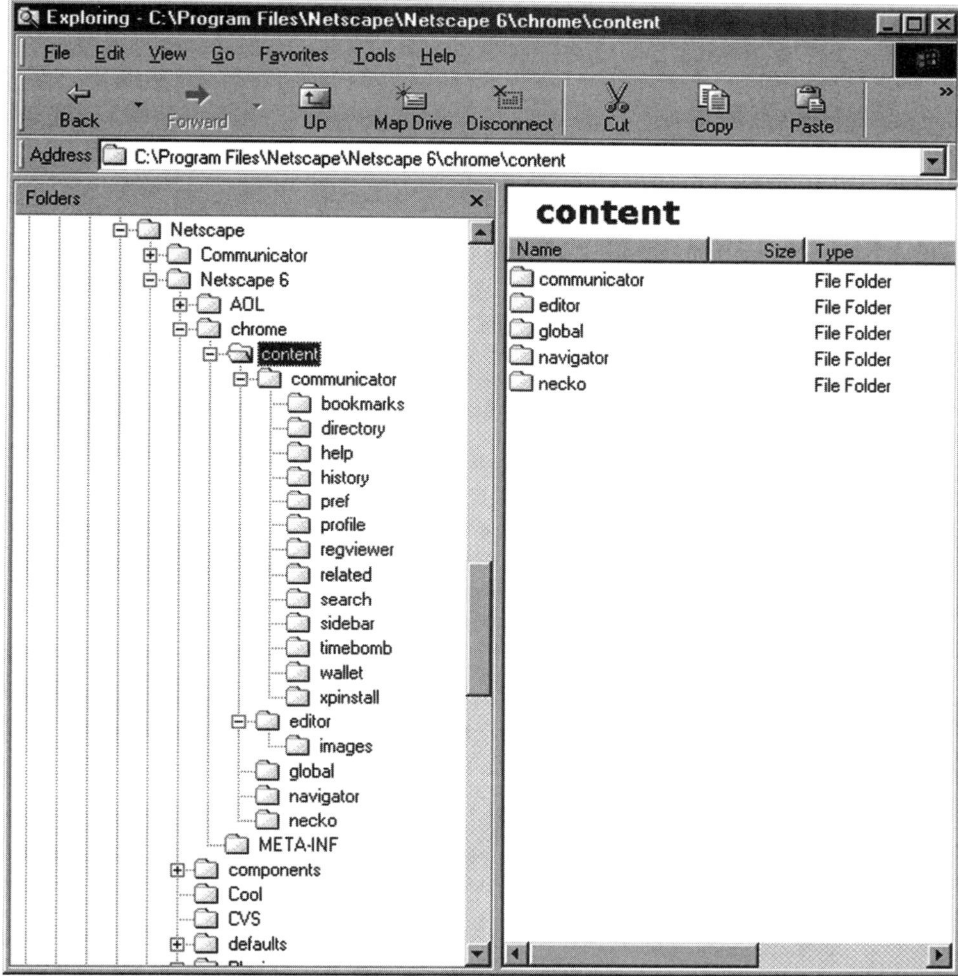

Figure 9.2 Result of extracting comm.jar.

creating the user's settings for My Sidebar. This file is loaded by the XUL file customize.xul.

customize.xul. This XUL file describes the "Customize Sidebar" dialog used in customizing the "My SideBar" Panel . This file is a description of the XUL components used to build the dialog and loads the JavaScript file customize.js when it is loaded. This file is initially loaded by the SidebarCustomize( ) function in sidebarOverlay.js.

customize-panel.js. This JavaScript file is used for refreshing the customize panel. Its Init( ) and RefreshPanel( ) functions are called by customize-panel.xul when the XUL file is loaded and unloaded, respectively.

customize-panel.xul. This XUL file is used for refreshing the contents of the GUI. It is called by the CustomizePanel( ) function in customize.js, which is called by clicking on the "Customize Tab" button described in customize.xul.

local-panels.rdf. This is the list of master RDF data sources used in the sidebar panel.

preview.js. This JavaScript file has code used to Preview the user's sidebar selection. Its only function, Init( ), is called by preview.xul and sets the contents of the preview frame described by preview.xul.

preview.xul. This XUL file describes the interface to build a Preview dialog of the user's sidebar selection. This simple file is a window and a frame of content that previews a sidebar tab when the user clicks on the Preview button in the customize sidebar dialog (in customize.xul). The Preview button calls the PreviewPanel( ) function in customize.js, which loads preview.xul.

sidebarBindings.xml. This XML file describes the XBL bindings of the sidebar.

sidebarOverlay.css. This main CSS file lists the properties of the sidebar components.

sidebarOverlay.js. This main JavaScript file controls the functionality of the sidebar. This file initializes the main user interface for the sidebar dialog by looking for the RDF data sources that describe all of the sidebar tabs. The SidebarCustomize( ) function in this file to bring up the customize dialog is initially called by the file sidebarOverlay.xul.

sidebarOverlay.xul. This main XUL overlay describes the main sidebar interface. It loads sidebarOverlay.js. This overlay file is loaded by the main Netscape browser XUL file in chrome://navigator/content/navigator.xul.

Throughout this book, we have looked at CSS, RDF, XUL templates, XUL overlays, JavaScript, and XBL separately. As we can see from the sidebar directory, "My Sidebar" uses all of these technologies together. Figure 9.3 shows a high-level view of the design of "My Sidebar."

Figure 9.3 shows the information flow of the files in the sidebar directory, and it shows how we can use XUL, CSS, XUL overlays, and XBL together in a real-world project. As you can see, Netscape uses overlays to reuse this sidebar code in two places: in the Netscape Navigator application and in its Web page editor application. Each application lays the sidebar component over a box in its main XUL file. The sidebarOverlay.xul file loads a CSS file, sidebarOverlay.css, which applies style to the overlay and also attaches XBL bindings to elements within the overlay file. The main overlay file uses XUL templates to dynamically generate content, and it loads a JavaScript file, sidebarOverlay.js.

The JavaScript functions in sidebarOverlay.js are the entry points for the instantiation of many more XUL files. Because the focal point of this design is the XUL overlay file, take a look at that file's source code in Code Listing 9.1.

As you can see from Code Listing 9.1, Netscape uses RDF data sources with XUL templates to load the data into the sidebar component. The <action> section of the first template creates <menuitem> elements from the RDF-generated content. The second

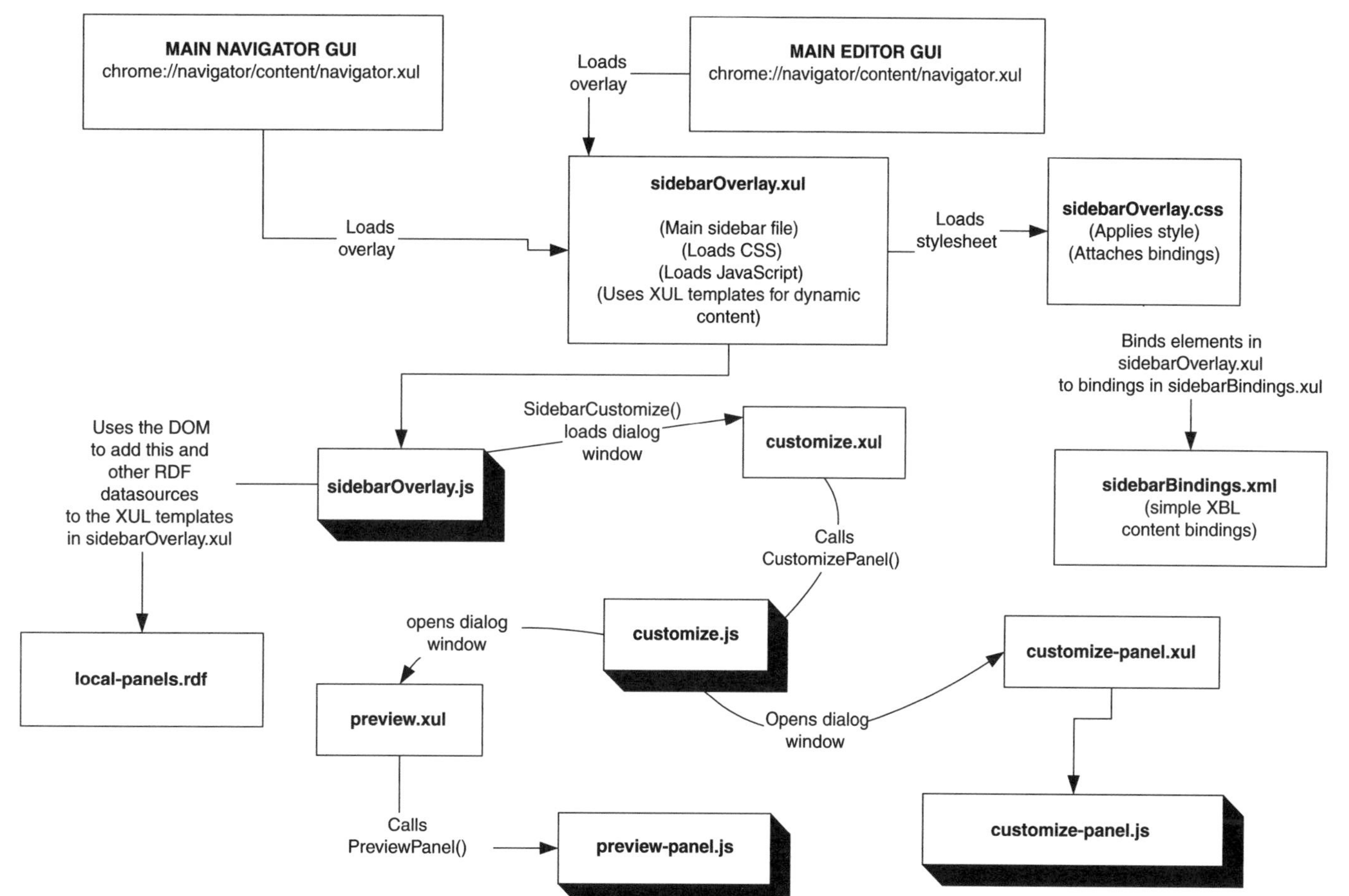

Figure 9.3 Design of "My Sidebar".

```
<?xml version="1.0"?>
<!--  The contents of this file are subject to the Netscape Public
  License Version 1.1 (the "NPL"); you may not use this file
  except in compliance with the NPL.  You may obtain a copy of
  the NPL at http://www.mozilla.org/NPL/  Software distributed
  under the NPL is distributed on an "AS
  IS" basis, WITHOUT WARRANTY OF ANY KIND, either express or
  implied. See the NPL for the specific language governing
  rights and limitations under the NPL.  The Initial Developer of
  this code under the NPL is Netscape Communications Corporation.
  Portions created by Netscape are  Copyright (C) 1999 Netscape
Communications Corporation.  All Rights Reserved.
  -->
<?xml-stylesheet
href="chrome://communicator/content/sidebar/sidebarOverlay.css"
type="text/css"?> <!DOCTYPE window SYSTEM
"chrome://communicator/locale/sidebar/sidebarOverlay.dtd">

<overlay id="sidebarOverlay"
  xmlns:html="http://www.w3.org/1999/xhtml"
xmlns=
"http://www.mozilla.org/keymaster/gatekeeper/there.is.only.xul">

<!-- Overlay the sidebar panels -->  <box id="sidebar-box"
orient="vertical"
       persist="hidden width collapsed">
    <splitter id="sidebar-panels-splitter" collapse="after"
      onmouseup="PersistHeight();" hidden="true">
      <spring flex="1"/>
      <grippy/>
      <spring flex="1"/>
    </splitter>

    <box id="sidebar-panels-splitter-box"
         align="vertical" flex="1"
         persist="hidden">
    <sidebarheader id="sidebar-title-box"
                   class="sidebarheader-main"
                   value="&sidebar.panels.label;"
                   persist="hidden" type="box"
                   collapse="after"
                   onmouseup="PersistHeight();">
                <menubutton id="sidebar-panel-picker"
                  menubuttontype="sidebar-panels"
                  class="button-toolbar-4" crop="right"
                  oncreate="SidebarBuildPickerPopup();"
```

Code Listing 9.1 sidebarOverlay.xul.

```
                    value="&sidebar.picker.label;" >

          <!-- This section of the code will build a menupopup
               that lists all possible sidebar content. The
               XUL template will build a list of menuitems.
            -->
          <menupopup id="sidebar-panel-picker-popup"
                     popupanchor="topright"
datasources="rdf:null"
                     ref="urn:sidebar:current-panel-list">
            <template>
              <rule>
                <conditions>
                  <content uri="?uri"/>
                  <triple subject="?uri"
                    predicate=
                    http://home.netscape.com/NC-rdf#panel-list
                    object="?panel-list"/>
                   <member container="?panel-list"
                         child="?panel"/>
                    <triple subject="?panel"
                    predicate=
                     "http://home.netscape.com/NC-rdf#title"
                     object="?title" />
                </conditions>
                <bindings>
                <binding subject="?panel"
                      predicate=
                      "http://home.netscape.com/NC-rdf#exclude"
                      object="?exclude"/>
               </bindings>

                <!-- For each panel found in the XUL template, this
                     action section will add a menuitem.
                  -->                <action>
<menuitem uri="?panel"
                   type="checkbox"
                   oncommand="SidebarTogglePanel(event.target);"
                    value="?title"
                    exclude="?exclude"/>                </action>
</rule>            </template>            <menuitem
value="&sidebar.customize.label;"
               oncommand="SidebarCustomize();" />
            <menuseparator />
          </menupopup>
        </menubutton>
```

continues

Code Listing 9.1 Continued.

```
</sidebarheader>

<!-- The XUL template beneath this box will create the
     actual sidebars that will reside in the "My Sidebar"
     area. The <action> section below will show the final
     content that is built.
  -->
<box id="sidebar-panels" align="vertical"
  datasources="rdf:null"
  ref="urn:sidebar:current-panel-list"
  persist='last-selected-panel height collapsed'
  flex="1*">
 <template id="sidebar-template">
<rule>
  <conditions>
    <content uri="?uri"/>
        <triple subject="?uri" object="?panel-list"
          predicate=
           "http://home.netscape.com/NC-rdf#panel-list" />
           <member container="?panel-list" child="?panel"/>
            <triple subject="?panel" object="?title"
          predicate=
           "http://home.netscape.com/NC-rdf#title" />
         <triple subject="?panel" object="?content"
          predicate=
            "http://home.netscape.com/NC-rdf#content" />
      </conditions>
      <bindings>
        <binding subject="?panel" object="?exclude"
          predicate=
           "http://home.netscape.com/NC-rdf#exclude" />
           </bindings>
      <!-- In this section of the code, the XUL template
           will build the content of the inside of the sidebar!
        -->
      <action>              <box uri="?panel"
           class="box-texttab texttab-sidebar"
           onclick="SidebarSelectPanel(this,false,false)"
           align="left"                 hidden="true"
           value="?title"
        exclude="?exclude" />
        <box uri="?panel"
             flex='1*'
             hidden="true" orient="vertical"
             loadstate="never loaded">
              <box flex='1' orient="vertical"
```

Code Listing 9.1 sidebarOverlay.xul (Continued).

```
                        class="iframe-panel loadarea">
                   <box orient="horizontal" flex="1"
                        autostretch="never">
                     <image class="image-panel-loading"/>
                       <text class="text-panel-loading"
                        value="&sidebar.loading.label;"/>
                     <button value="&sidebar.loading.stop.label;"
                       hidden="true"
onclick="SidebarStopPanelLoad(
this.parentNode.parentNode.parentNode.previousSibling);"/>
</box>
                   <spring flex="100%"/>
                 </box>
                 <iframe class="iframe-panel" flex='1*'
                        src="about:blank"
                        hidden="true" collapsed="true"
                   content="?content" />
                 <iframe class="iframe-panel" flex='1*'
                   src="about:blank"                  hidden="true"
collapsed="true"
                   content="?content" type="content" />
               </box>
             </action>
           </rule>
         </template>
         <box id="sidebar-iframe-no-panels"
              class="iframe-panel" orient="vertical" flex="1"
               hidden="true">
          <html>&sidebar.no-panels.state;</html>
              <html>&sidebar.no-panels.add;</html>

           <html>&sidebar.no-panels.hide;</html>
         </box>
       </box>
     </box>
   </box>

   <!-- Splitter on the right of sidebar -->
   <splitter id="sidebar-splitter" collapse="before"
             persist="state hidden"
             class="chromeclass-extrachrome sidebar-splitter"
             autostretch="never"
             orient="vertical"
             onmouseup="SidebarFinishClick();">
      <grippy class="sidebar-splitter-grippy"
              onclick="SidebarCleanUpExpandCollapse();"/>
```

continues

Code Listing 9.1 sidebarOverlay.xul (Continued).

```
    </splitter>

    <!-- View-->Sidebar toggle -->
    <menupopup id="menu_View_Popup">
      <menuitem id="sidebar-menu" type="checkbox"
        value="&sidebarCmd.label;"
        accesskey="&sidebarCmd.accesskey;"
        oncommand="SidebarShowHide();"
        position="2"/>
    </menupopup>

    <!-- Scripts go last, because they peek at state to tweak
         menus -->  <script language="JavaScript"     src=
       "chrome://communicator/content/sidebar/sidebarOverlay.js"/>
  </overlay>
```

Code Listing 9.1 Continued.

template's <action> section creates a series of boxes and an <iframe> element that contains content from the RDF data source. This action section is what will create the framed area in the sidebar that contains data. One thing that may look unusual about Code Listing 9.1 is that the *datasources* value referenced by the "sidebar-panel-picker-popup" <menupopup> element and the "sidebar-panels" box element is "rdf:null". If a XUL template's data source is null, how can we ever populate data into the template?

The last few lines of Code Listing 9.1 answer that question. The JavaScript file sidebarOverlay.js calls Netscape's locator service to find the proper resources, and the functions in sidebarOverlay.js use the DOM API to modify the "rdf:null" data sources element defined by the XUL file. In our next section, we take a look at how XUL and JavaScript work together to make My Sidebar work.

Sidebar XUL and JavaScript Communication

In the Netscape browser, XUL and JavaScript work together to load resources and add event-driven functionality. In the preceding code listing, we saw that the main XUL file loads sidebarOverlay.js. At the bottom of sidebarOverlay.js, we see two lines:

```
addEventListener("load", sidebar_overlay_init, false);
addEventListener("unload", sidebar_overlay_destruct, false);
```

Code Listing 9.2 shows the portions of sidebarOverlay.js, in which datasources are loaded on instantiation of the sidebar object. As you can see from the global variables section, an RDF service in the Netscape engine locates data sources. In the function sidebar_overlay_init( ), which is called on initial loading, the sidebar object loads initial datasources from Netscape's RDF service. The function then adds these data sources to

```
//Portions of sidebarOverlay.js
////////////////////////////////////////////////////////////////
// Global variables                                           //
////////////////////////////////////////////////////////////////

// Uncomment for debug output
const SB_DEBUG = false;

// The rdf service
const RDF_URI = '@mozilla.org/rdf/rdf-service;1';
var RDF = Components.classes[RDF_URI].getService();
RDF = RDF.QueryInterface(Components.interfaces.nsIRDFService);

const NC = "http://home.netscape.com/NC-rdf#";

// The directory services property to find panels.rdf
const PANELS_RDF_FILE = "UPnls";
const SIDEBAR_VERSION = "0.1";

// The default sidebar:
var sidebarObj = new Object;
sidebarObj.never_built = true;

// ... OTHER FUNCTIONS DELETED for this listing

function sidebar_overlay_init() {
  sidebarObj.panels = new sbPanelList('sidebar-panels');
  sidebarObj.datasource_uri = get_sidebar_datasource_uri();
  sidebarObj.resource = 'urn:sidebar:current-panel-list';

  sidebarObj.master_datasources = "";
  sidebarObj.master_datasources = get_remote_datasource_url();
  sidebarObj.master_datasources += "
        chrome://communicator/content/sidebar/local-panels.rdf";
  sidebarObj.master_resource = 'urn:sidebar:master-panel-list';
  sidebarObj.component =
        document.firstChild.getAttribute('windowtype');

  // Initialize the display
  var sidebar_element = document.getElementById('sidebar-box');
  var sidebar_menuitem =
                     document.getElementById('sidebar-menu');

if (sidebar_is_hidden())
{
    if (sidebar_menuitem)
```

continues

Code Listing 9.2 Loading initial RDF in sidebarOverlay.js.

```
    {
      sidebar_menuitem.setAttribute('checked', 'false');
    }
}
else {
    if (sidebar_menuitem)
    {
      sidebar_menuitem.setAttribute('checked', 'true');
    }

    if (sidebarObj.never_built)
    {
      sidebarObj.never_built = false;

      // Show the header for the panels area. Use a splitter if
      // there is stuff over the panels area.

      var sidebar_panels_splitter =
         document.getElementById('sidebar-panels-splitter');
      if (sidebar_element.firstChild != sidebar_panels_splitter)
      {
         sidebar_panels_splitter.removeAttribute('hidden');
      }

      // Add the user's current panel choices to the template
      // builder, which will aggregate it with the other
      // datasources that describe the individual panel's title,
      // customize URL, and content URL.

      var panels = document.getElementById('sidebar-panels');
      panels.database.AddDataSource(RDF.GetDataSource(
                                 sidebarObj.datasource_uri));
      panels.database.AddObserver(panel_observer);
      panels.setAttribute('ref', sidebarObj.resource);
    }
    if (sidebar_is_collapsed())
    {
      sidebarObj.collapsed = true;
    }
    else
    {
      sidebarObj.collapsed = false;
    }
    sidebar_open_default_panel(100, 0);
  }
}
```

Code Listing 9.2 Continued.

```
function get_sidebar_datasource_uri()
{
  try
  {
    var sidebar_file = sidebar_get_panels_file();
    var file_url =
     Components.classes["@mozilla.org/network/standard-
url;1"].createInstance(Components.interfaces.nsIFileURL);
    file_url.file = sidebar_file;
    return file_url.spec;
  }
  catch (ex)
  {
     // This should not happen
     debug("Error: Unable to load panels file.\n");
  }
   return null;
}
```

Code Listing 9.2 Loading initial RDF in sidebarOverlay.js (Continued).

the sidebar-panels XUL element that we referenced in the last section. This replaces the "rdf:null" value for the data sources that we saw in the XUL file in Code Listing 9.1. Similarly, the other XUL element that we had questions about, sidebar-panel-picker-popup, has data sources loaded in another JavaScript function, SidebarBuildPickerPopup( ), which is not listed here.

For the template code associated with the sidebar-panels box, the most important code to understand in Code Listing 9.2 is the following, which finds the element via the DOM API and sets the correct resources:

```
var panels = document.getElementById('sidebar-panels');
    panels.database.AddDataSource(RDF.GetDataSource(
                                 sidebarObj.datasource_uri));
    panels.database.AddObserver(panel_observer);
    panels.setAttribute('ref', sidebarObj.resource);
```

RDF for Sidebar Resources

In Code Listing 9.2, we saw one RDF file referenced as a master datasource in the sidebar_overlay_init( ) function. This datasource was "chrome://communicator/content/sidebar/local-panels.rdf," which, of course, resides in the main sidebar directory. Let's look at this RDF structure in Code Listing 9.3.

The format of the RDF file in Code Listing 9.3 is quite simple. Each resource in the urn:sidebar:panel-group:recommended group has two subelements: nc:title and nc:content. As you can see from the <template> sections in the overlay file in Code Listing 9.1, these attributes represent the name on each tab in the sidebar, as well as the internal content, respectively. This particular file shows the master data sources and is

```
<?xml version="1.0"?> <!-- -*- Mode: SGML -*- -->
<!DOCTYPE RDF SYSTEM "chrome://communicator/locale/sidebar/local-
panels.dtd" >
<rdf:RDF xmlns:rdf="http://www.w3.org/1999/02/22-rdf-syntax-ns#"
         xmlns:nc="http://home.netscape.com/NC-rdf#">

  <rdf:Description about="urn:sidebar:master-panel-list">
    <nc:panel-list>
      <rdf:Seq>
        <rdf:li>
          <rdf:Description
               about="urn:sidebar:panel-group:recommended"/>
        </rdf:li>
      </rdf:Seq>
    </nc:panel-list>
  </rdf:Description>

  <rdf:Description about="urn:sidebar:panel-group:recommended">
    <NC:title>&sidebar.panel-group.recommended;</NC:title>
    <nc:panel-list>
      <rdf:Seq>
        <rdf:li resource="urn:sidebar:panel:im-panel"/>
        <rdf:li resource="urn:sidebar:panel:whats-related"/>
        <rdf:li resource="urn:sidebar:panel:search"/>
        <rdf:li resource="urn:sidebar:panel:bookmarks"/>
      </rdf:Seq>
    </nc:panel-list>
  </rdf:Description>

  <rdf:Description about="urn:sidebar:panel:im-panel">
    <nc:title>&sidebar.im-panel.label;</nc:title>
    <nc:content>chrome://aim/content/SidebarPanel.xul</nc:content>
  </rdf:Description>

  <rdf:Description about="urn:sidebar:panel:whats-related">
    <nc:title>&sidebar.whats-related.label;</nc:title>
    <nc:content>chrome://communicator/content/related/related-
panel.xul</nc:content>
  </rdf:Description>

  <rdf:Description about="urn:sidebar:panel:search">
    <nc:title>&sidebar.search.label;</nc:title>
    <nc:content>chrome://communicator/content/search/search-
panel.xul</nc:content>
  </rdf:Description>

  <rdf:Description about="urn:sidebar:panel:bookmarks">
```

Code Listing 9.3 local-panels.rdf.

```
    <nc:title>&sidebar.bookmarks.label;</nc:title>
    <nc:content>chrome://communicator/content/bookmarks/bm-
panel.xul</nc:content>
  </rdf:Description>

</rdf:RDF>
```

Code Listing 9.3 local-panels.rdf (Continued).

referenced when customizing the sidebar. If you recall from Code Listing 9.1 and the design of the sidebar in Figure 9.1, the Customize Sidebar dialog appears when a <menuitem> is selected, calling the SidebarCustomize( ) JavaScript function in sidebarOverlay.js. The SidebarCustomize( ) function creates a new dialog with the contents of customize.xul.

Figure 9.4 is a screen shot of customizing the browser when you choose the Tabs-> Customize Sidebar . . . option on the sidebar menu. This dialog is described in the cus-

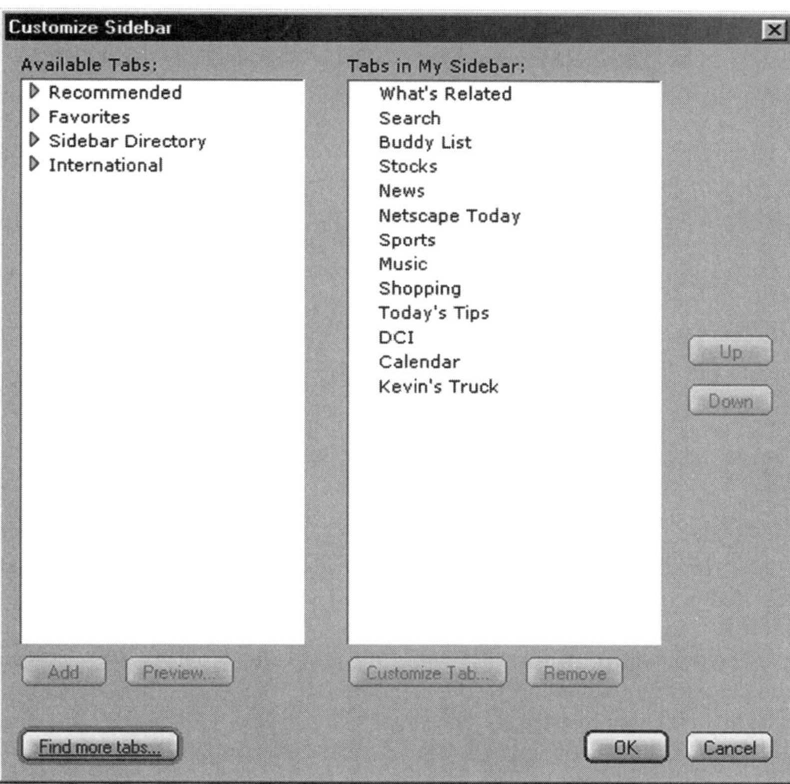

Figure 9.4 The Customize Sidebar dialog.

tomize.xul file and enables you to add information sources that are listed in the localpanels.rdf file shown in Code Listing 9.3. Find more tabs . . . also contains a link to this dialog. This link enables us to find other data sources on the Internet so that we can add them to My Sidebar.

In the customize.xul file, we found that the Find more tabs . . . button calls BrowseMorePanels( ) in the customize.js file. This function causes the browser to go to a particular Web site with links that deliver HTML pages with JavaScript content. These links perform operations on our local browser. Remember when we mentioned before that the components directory contained some JavaScript files that exposed public methods? Let's look at the components directory, so that we can find out how this relates to My Sidebar!

The Components Directory

The components directory, or the directory in Figure 9.2 shown as "C:\Program Files\Netscape\Netscape 6\components," is a directory full of DLLs and a few JavaScript files. One of these files is nsSidebar.js. In Figure 9.3, we showed you the dialog for customizing the browser. When the Find more Tabs button is clicked, it sends the browser to an URL that calls the addPanel( ) method in the sidebar object. This function resides in nsSidebar.js and is shown in Code Listing 9.4.

Any call to addPanel( ) can be made from a Web page on the Internet. When this JavaScript function is called, it adds a new component to the list of RDF data sources for the sidebar. Code Listing 9.5 shows how this function is called. When this call is made, the browser pops up a window asking the user whether he wants to add the resource. If the user clicks OK, a new tab will be added to the sidebar, with the content enclosed within that tab window. A screen shot of this is shown in Figure 9.5.

Now that we have studied how "My Sidebar" was created, let's try to solve the problem of XYZPORTAL.COM. They were interested in how they could present a customizable in-browser portal for their users.

Customizing My Sidebar for the Case Study

Lucky for us, the engineers at Netscape have done an excellent job designing "My Sidebar." They have put an infrastructure in place for users to be able to easily customize their browser. It would indeed be possible for XYZPORTAL.COM to create RDF files that describe their information, and it could also be possible for their senior engineers to change XUL code for their users to download and install in the browser. The code in chrome://communicator/content/sidebar would definitely be easy to customize. Engineers could change the code and repackage comm.jar with the JAR executable. Because of their look into "My Sidebar," the company is considering customizing the browser even further. The company is so impressed with how "My Sidebar" is designed, that they have decided to change their name to XULPORTAL.COM.

```
nsSidebar.prototype.addPanel=
function (aTitle, aContentURL, aCustomizeURL)
{
    debug("addPanel(" + aTitle + ", " + aContentURL + ", " +
          aCustomizeURL + ")");

    if (!this.window)
    {
        debug ("no window object set, bailing out.");
        throw Components.results.NS_ERROR_NOT_INITIALIZED;
    }

    sidebarURLSecurityCheck(aContentURL);

    // Create a "container" wrapper around the current panels to
    // manipulate the RDF:Seq more easily.
    var panel_list =
     this.datasource.GetTarget(this.rdf.GetResource(this.resource),
    this.rdf.GetResource(nsSidebar.prototype.nc+"panel-list"), true);
    if (panel_list) {

     panel_list.QueryInterface(Components.interfaces.nsIRDFResource);
    } else {
        // Datasource is busted. Start over.
        debug("Sidebar datasource is busted\n");
  }

    var container = Components.classes[CONTAINER_
CONTRACTID].createInstance
                                               (nsIRDFContainer);
    container.Init(this.datasource, panel_list);

    /* Create a resource for the new panel and add it to
       the list */
    var panel_resource =
            this.rdf.GetResource("urn:sidebar:3rdparty-panel:"
            + aContentURL);
    var panel_index = container.IndexOf(panel_resource);
    if (panel_index != -1)
    {
        var titleMessage, dialogMessage;
        try {
            var stringBundle = getStringBundle(
     "chrome://communicator/locale/sidebar/sidebar.properties");
            if (stringBundle) {
                titleMessage =

              stringBundle.GetStringFromName("dupePanelAlertTitle");
```

continues

Code Listing 9.4 addPanel( ) in nsSideBar.js.

```
                dialogMessage =
              stringBundle.GetStringFromName("dupePanelAlertMessage");
                dialogMessage = dialogMessage.replace(/%url%/,
                                aContentURL);
            }
        }
        catch (e) {
            titleMessage = "My Sidebar";
            dialogMessage = aContentURL + " already exists in My" +
                                      " Sidebar.";
        }

        var cDlgService = Components.classes["@mozilla.org/appshell/
commonDialogs;1"].getService();
        if (cDlgService)
            cDlgService =
  cDlgService.QueryInterface(Components.interfaces.nsICommonDialogs);
        cDlgService.Alert(this.window, titleMessage, dialogMessage);

        return;
    }

    var titleMessage, dialogMessage;
    try {
        var stringBundle = getStringBundle(
          "chrome://communicator/locale/sidebar/sidebar.properties");
        if (stringBundle) {
            titleMessage =

            stringBundle.GetStringFromName("addPanelConfirmTitle");
            dialogMessage =
            stringBundle.GetStringFromName("addPanelConfirmMessage");
            dialogMessage = dialogMessage.replace(/%title%/, aTitle);
            dialogMessage = dialogMessage.replace(/%url%/,
                            aContentURL);
            dialogMessage = dialogMessage.replace(/#/g, "\n");
        }
    }
    catch (e) {
        titleMessage = "Add Tab to My Sidebar";
        dialogMessage = "Add the Tab '" + aTitle + "' to My
                        Sidebar?\n\n" + "Source: " + aContentURL;
    }

    var cDlgService = Components.classes["@mozilla.org/appshell/
commonDialogs;1"].getService();
    if (cDlgService)
        cDlgService =
```

Code Listing 9.4 addPanel( ) in nsSideBar.js (Continued).

```
    cDlgService.QueryInterface(Components.interfaces.nsICommonDialogs);
     var rv = cDlgService.Confirm(this.window, titleMessage,
                                  dialogMessage);

     if (!rv)
         return;

     /* Now make some sidebar-ish assertions about it... */
     this.datasource.Assert(panel_resource,
                            this.rdf.GetResource(this.nc + "title"),
                            this.rdf.GetLiteral(aTitle),
                            true);
     this.datasource.Assert(panel_resource,
                            this.rdf.GetResource(this.nc + "content"),
                            this.rdf.GetLiteral(aContentURL),
                            true);
     if (aCustomizeURL)
         this.datasource.Assert(panel_resource,
                                this.rdf.GetResource(this.nc +
                                "customize"),
                                this.rdf.GetLiteral(aCustomizeURL),
                                true);

     container.AppendElement(panel_resource);

     // Use an assertion to pass a "refresh" event to all the
     // sidebars.
     // They use observers to watch for this assertion
     // (in sidebarOverlay.js).
     this.datasource.Assert(this.rdf.GetResource(this.resource),
                            this.rdf.GetResource(this.nc + "refresh"),
                            this.rdf.GetLiteral("true"),
                            true);
     this.datasource.Unassert(this.rdf.GetResource(this.resource),
                              this.rdf.GetResource(this.nc +
  "refresh"),
                              this.rdf.GetLiteral("true"));

     /* Write the modified panels out. */
     this.datasource.QueryInterface(nsIRDFRemoteDataSource).Flush();

 }
```

Code Listing 9.4 Continued.

After much debate, the senior engineers at the fictitious company have decided that the easiest and least expensive way to make fast changes to their Web site is to keep their current infrastructure and to make minor modifications to their dynamically generated HTML. If they change their information links to add a panel for each information

```
<SCRIPT LANGUAGE="JavaScript">
function testfunction()
{
      if ((typeof window.sidebar == "object")
       && (typeof window.sidebar.addPanel == "function"))
        {
            window.sidebar.addPanel ("Truck News",
                "http://www.geocities.com/trumantruck/",
                "http://www.geocities.com/trumantruck/");
            window.history.back();
        }
      else
      {
          alert("This page is enhanced for Netscape 6.");
      }

 }
</SCRIPT>
<body onLoad='testfunction()'>
```

Code Listing 9.5 Calling addPanel( ).

source, they will satisfy the needs of their customers. As a result, they may even win over more customers.

Code Listing 9.6 shows the HTML that the new and improved XULPORTAL.COM has created for their users. For the purposes of this example, assume that the user authenticates with the Web server via some access-control mechanism and is sent to this page. From here, all the user has to do is click on each link to add this to his "My Panel" in the Netscape browser. Figure 9.6 shows a screen capture of the page in action!

The HTML for the Web page was quite simple to modify. The engineers at XULPORTAL.COM changed their links to JavaScript function calls to their own addPanel( ) JavaScript function, which makes the call to the user's browser.

Summary

In this case study, we were able to see how an organization can quickly make browser customizations without changing any browser code or XUL markup. In doing so, we looked at how Netscape used a combination of XUL, CSS, RDF, XBL, and JavaScript to engineer "My Sidebar." This brings up a very interesting point—an application like Netscape can be designed with open APIs to provide customization. In this example, no XUL code had to be modified, because the JavaScript functions dynamically altered the content of the XUL file.

Because XUL was used to build the Netscape browser, you can see how all of the related technologies of XUL can be used together. This case study focused on the

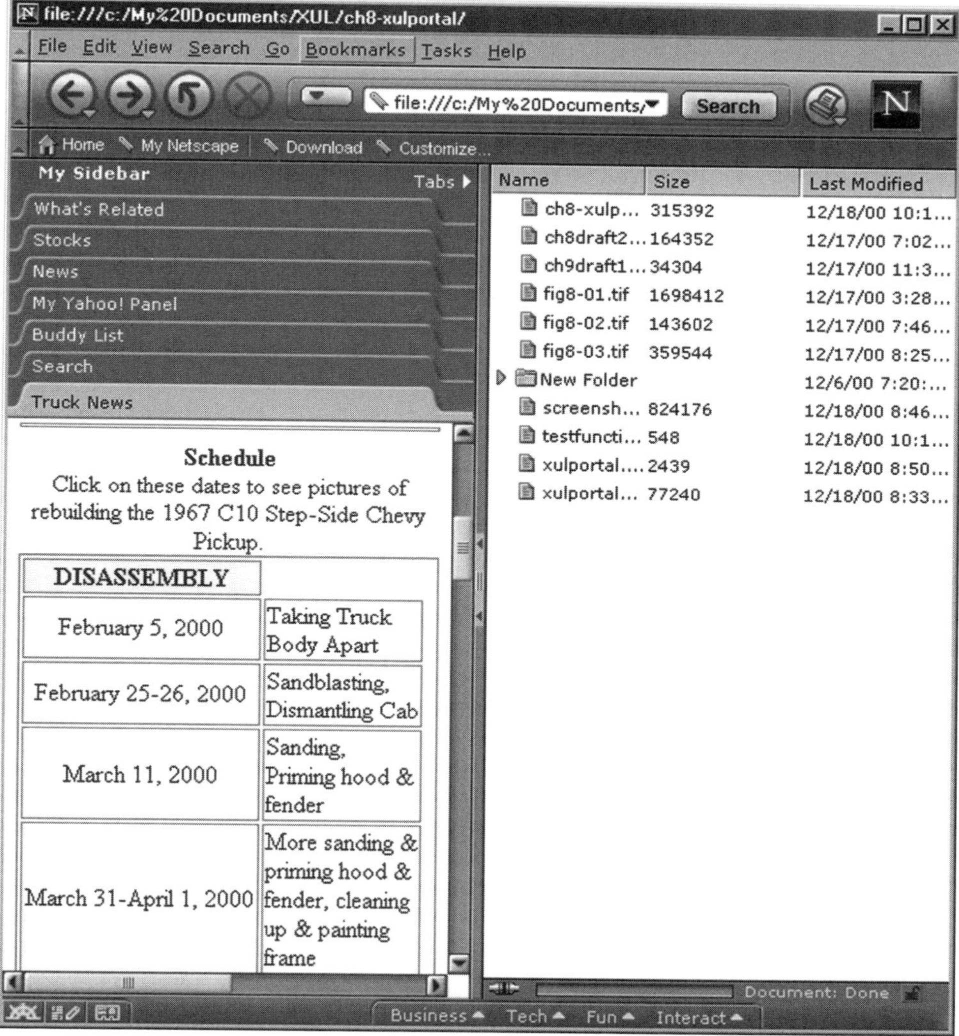

Figure 9.5 Effect of calling addPanel( )

design of one component of the Netscape browser in order to solve a real-world problem. The authors recommend that you navigate the XUL code of the latest version of the browser to see how you can leverage existing solutions.

As this chapter is a case study revolving around the design and implementation of Netscape's sidebar, the next chapter is a case study of creating an e-commerce Web site using XUL. Like this case study, the technologies presented throughout this book will be used together to create a XUL application for immediate use.

```
<HTML>
 <HEAD>

  <SCRIPT LANGUAGE="JavaScript">
  function addPanel(title , url)
  {
    if ((typeof window.sidebar == "object") &&
        (typeof window.sidebar.addPanel == "function"))
    {
      window.sidebar.addPanel (title, url, url);
    }
    else
    {
      alert("This page is enhanced for use with Netscape 6.
             Click OK to download it!");

      window.location.href=
             "http://home.netscape.com/download/index.html"
    }
  }
  </SCRIPT>
  <TITLE>XULPORTAL.COM's News Collection</TITLE>
 </HEAD>
 <BODY>
  <CENTER>
  <IMG SRC="xulportalcom.jpg">
  <H1>Welcome, Joey Bush!</H1>
  The following news sources are currently set up for your
  subscription at XULPortal.com!
  Our data dog is busy FETCHING data for you 24 hours a day. To
  activate the data into your "My SideBar" panel in your
Netscape/Mozilla browser,
  click on any of the links below!

  <HR>
   <H2>Medical News Sources</H2>
   <TABLE BORDER>
    <TR><TD><A HREF="javascript:addPanel('Parkinsons
Research','http://xulportal.com/park/')">
                Parkinsons Research </A>
        </TD>
        <TD><A HREF="javascript:addPanel('Neurology News',
'http://xulportal.com/neuro')">
                Neurological Discussions</A>
        </TD>
```

Code Listing 9.6 Generated HTML for our site.

```
        <TD><A HREF="javascript:addPanel('Cancer Research', 'http://
xulportal.com/cancer/')">
            Latest Cancer Research Links</A>
        </TD>
     </TR>
     </TABLE>
     <TABLE BORDER>
      <TR><TD>
        <A HREF="javascript:addPanel('Live Audio from AMA', 'http://
xulportal.com/feed/ama/')">
            Live Feed from American Medical Association Conference</A>
          </TD></TR>
     </TABLE>
     <H2>Legal News Sources</H2>
     <TABLE BORDER>
     <TR><TD><A HREF="javascript:addPanel('Current Legal Briefs',
'http://xulportal.com/leg/')">
                  Today's Legal Briefs</A>
        </TD>
        <TD><A HREF="javascript:addPanel('Criminal Law', 'http://
xulportal.com/crimlaw')">
                  Criminal Law Discussions</A>
        </TD>
        <TD><A HREF="javascript:addPanel('Henrico Court - Live Feed',
'http://xulportal.com/henrico/')">
            Live Feed from Henrico County Court</A>
        </TD>
     </TR>
    </TABLE>
     <TABLE BORDER>
      <TR><TD>
        <A HREF="javascript:addPanel('Search Lexus/Nexus', 'http://
xulportal.com/lexus/')">
            Click here to embed Lexus/Nexus Searches in Your
Browser!</A>
          </TD></TR>
     </TABLE>
 </BODY>
</HTML>
```

Code Listing 9.6 Generated HTML for our site.

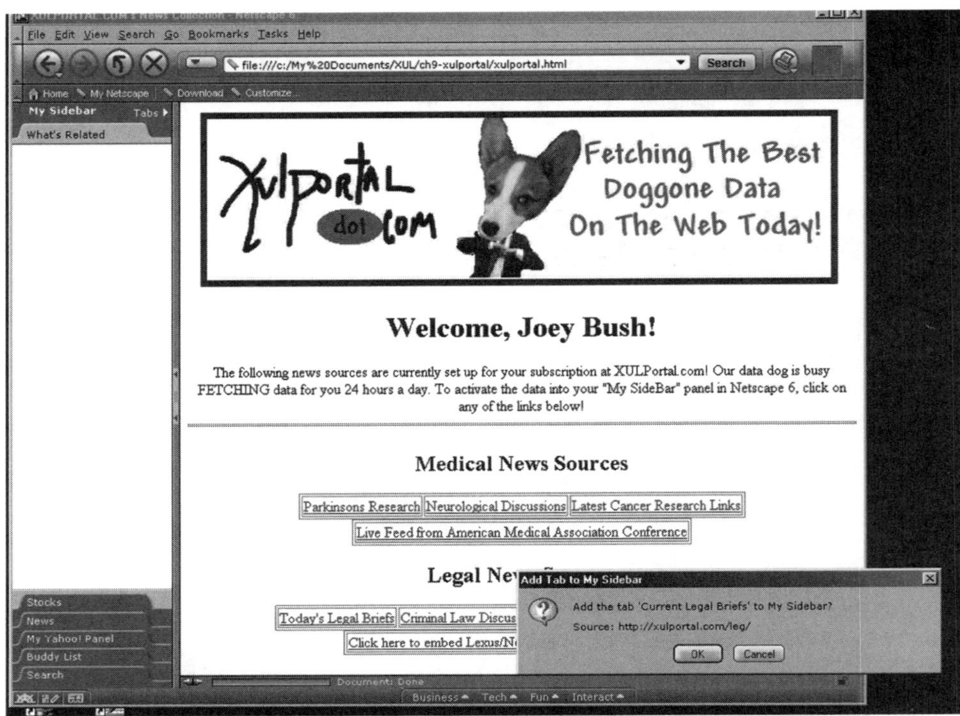

Figure 9.6 The resulting Web site.

Case Study: Building an E-Commerce User Interface with XUL

Designing a software system is 80 percent design, 20 percent coding, and 0 percent sweat equity. No sweat equity because if you had spent the whole 80 percent properly designing your system, there should be almost no effort involved except punching keys.

Jeremy Güggenbühler, 1999

Now that you are grounded in the fundamental operations of using the technologies leveraged in XUL, you are ready to combine these technologies to create a single user interface. In this chapter, we discuss the practical application of four important concepts. The first is the layout of individual XUL user interface components. The second is the manipulation of interface elements through the use of event handling via JavaScript and the Document Object Model Application Programming Interface (DOM API). The third is the creation and connection of multiple dynamic data sources with XUL templates through the use of Resource Description Framework (RDF) data sources. The final concept is the reusability aspect of XUL through the use of overlays.

For us to simply present these concepts in an abstract fashion would not be conducive to your long-term use. Therefore, we will present these concepts in the context of a real-world application. Although it is a real-world application, we have to ground it in the fact that it will not accept orders on a real-time system. This case study is created as a tutorial on how to develop such a system with XUL. Our application is an e-commerce site called BeaconTrade.Com. BeaconTrade.Com is a Web-based user interface created by us for a fictional business, BeaconTrade Outfitters.

Defining the Problem

BeaconTrade Outfitters is a local fishing and sporting gear store. The owner, John, wants to create a Web-based interface to ply his wares, but he doesn't want to create some cumbersome system that he himself cannot maintain. He has done some research, talked to his buddies—even his 13-year-old technophile nephew—and has come up with some great ideas.

He wants the latest and greatest technologies to be incorporated into his site design. He knows that it will have to be easy for him to learn, because he is not the technophile that his 13-year-old nephew is, and he will have to maintain this system. He sells fishing and sporting gear, not information technology services. So, he will design a system that he and others, should his business grow, can learn and maintain with minimal effort.

John has seen other sites that are able to personalize their user interface for each customer. He would like to add this feature, but he's not sure how to accomplish that.

BeaconTrade Outfitters, although a small Mom and Pop shop, has customers in several countries. Primarily, he exports to only five other countries from the United States. He will need to accommodate that aspect into his design.

BeaconTrade Outfitters already gets daily information from suppliers. John has two outside suppliers for this information. His supplier for the products he sells publishes a real-time report of available stock items. He also has a supplier for currency exchange rates, which is published on a daily basis. John knows that these items will be published in RDF. So he needs to have the ability to take RDF data and incorporate that easily into his interface design.

BeaconTrade already has an in-store database for his customers' orders. This database can be easily published through middleware application software to RDF. He already uses Cold Fusion to publish Web-based reports for invoice control and to order histories. So, he wants to incorporate views that he has already created.

He wants to build a component-based architecture so that he can just add the aforementioned data sources as pluggable databases.

Not a fan of continually clicking through multiple pages to get to the information he needs, John wants a single user interface. Not sure how he is going to do this, John stumbles across a new user interface language called the eXtensible User interface Language. He buys a great book, *Essential XUL Programming*, and heads back to the store. He knows that all his customers are using the Netscape Navigator product, so using XUL will not be a problem. He is excited about the aspect of this great new language and sets out to formalize all his requirements.

Analyzing the Requirements

Now that he has gathered the requirements through various means, John is ready to turn them into a formalized set. To achieve his goals, he has set the following requirements:

XML. XML allows interoperability between his suppliers and his application. It also forms the basis for which he may extend his application without having to learn a new language. XUL enables him to maintain his application in a common English-like language. He chose XUL because it also provides him this extensibility and a sensible approach to user interface development.

Single user interface. XUL allows the development of a single point of entry to his entire product catalog. No continual clicking through many pages of a large on-line catalog. He can organize user interface elements very easily through the use of trees or menus.

Component-based architecture. He needs the ability to plug and play different data providers. With that in mind, he has to design a user interface that will be modularized, separating his data source from his presentation.

Catalog provider and currency rates provider. His suppliers give him real-time XML-based data sources formatted in RDF. Rather than combining the data into the interface, XUL provides an abstraction for pluggable data sources. He can use XUL to accomplish this through the use of elements cycling through RDF data sources. Although he can basically use RDF in almost any XML-based application, XUL is the easiest in which to develop a user interface with an RDF data source.

Order history. He already has a Microsoft Access database in which he stores customer information including their order history. He intends to keep this and does not want to replace this system. He will transform this data using Cold Fusion to pull it from the Microsoft Access database to generate an RDF data source.

Personalization features. He wants the user interface to change based upon the customer's logon ID. This requires the use of JavaScript manipulating document elements through the use of the DOM API to personalize those elements elected customizable. Those customizable elements include the shopping basket and order history. In the future, he may want to make additional area customizable. With XUL, he will be able to this with little or no effort.

Foreign exchange rate conversion. His customers in foreign countries require his site to be able to convert U.S. dollar prices into foreign prices. He wants them to be able to set the exchange rate in which they would like to see the prices.

Shopping basket. The shopping basket needs to show customers their order and the quantity that they have ordered. When a customer is finished shopping, she will click the check out button, and the order will be sent back to the store's database.

John decides that a Unified Modeling Language (UML) Use Case diagram would help him to design a better product. He creates a Use Case diagram, as shown in Figure 10.1, which enables him to see all of the possible operations that a user can do.

John arrives at the general consensus that XUL will solve all his interface creation problems. The capabilities to add data sources and overlays interchangeably and to access elements through the DOM give XUL its strongest selling points. XUL allows him to quickly piece together a dynamically built, open standards-based user interface totally accessible through the Web.

Designing the User Interface

Now that he has designed the UML Use Case diagram, he can begin designing the Component Based Architecture for Beacontrade.com.

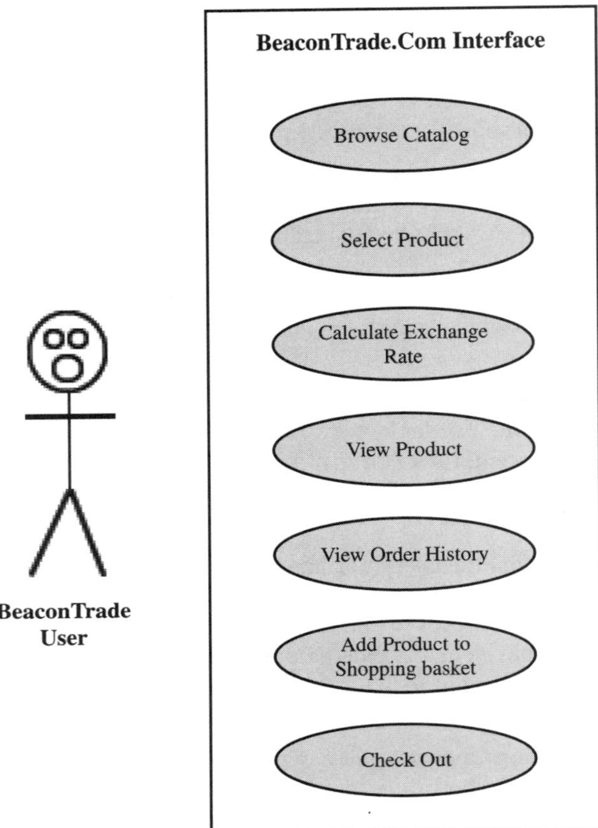

Figure 10.1 UML Use Case diagram.

Designing the Component Architecture

The interface will be built on a component-based architecture as shown in Figure 10.2. This architecture allows John to modularly fit smaller pieces of code into his larger XUL user interface. From a maintenance standpoint, this is better because it is easier to debug. It is also easier to retrofit the components into a new interface. For example, if John wanted to create an interface for customers who buy in bulk, he could easily create just another main interface. He then could modify certain price elements of the catalog provider to give the customer bulk prices.

In Figure 10.2, his components consist of two external data providers for CatalogProvider and Currency Rates. Another component, an internal RDF data source orderHistory, will be created from a transformation of a Microsoft Access database to RDF via Cold Fusion. John still wants to make this more modularized. He decides that he would like to use overlays to further his interface's extensibility. Overlays allow him to overlay another XUL element or file into another XUL element or interface component.

Designing the UI Layout

One thing that he does is a hand sketch of the components that will be laid out on screen. This sketch gives him a feel for any kind of design issues he may have before he starts coding a larger interface. This sketch is demonstrated in Figure 10.3. It also affords him the opportunity to develop common sizing standards for his user interface elements and to determine whether those elements will be absolute or relative positioned.

Designing the Event Handlers in JavaScript

John starts the design process of the JavaScript event-handling packages. These packaged functions will help the user to navigate the user interface, to select products, to calculate foreign currencies, and to order the products.

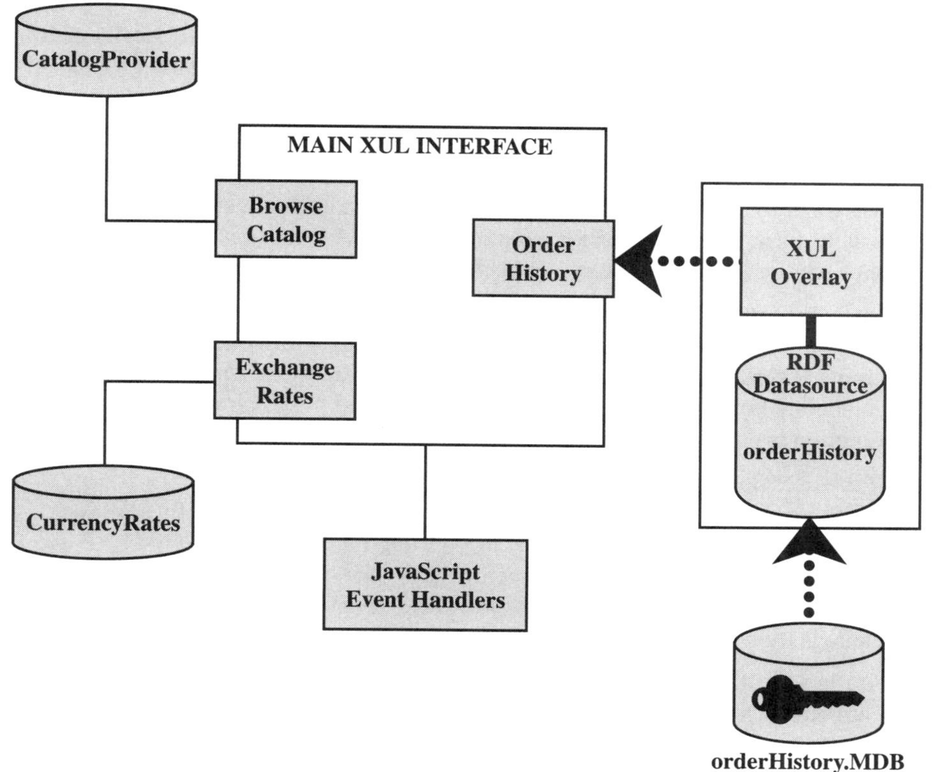

Figure 10.2 Component-based architecture.

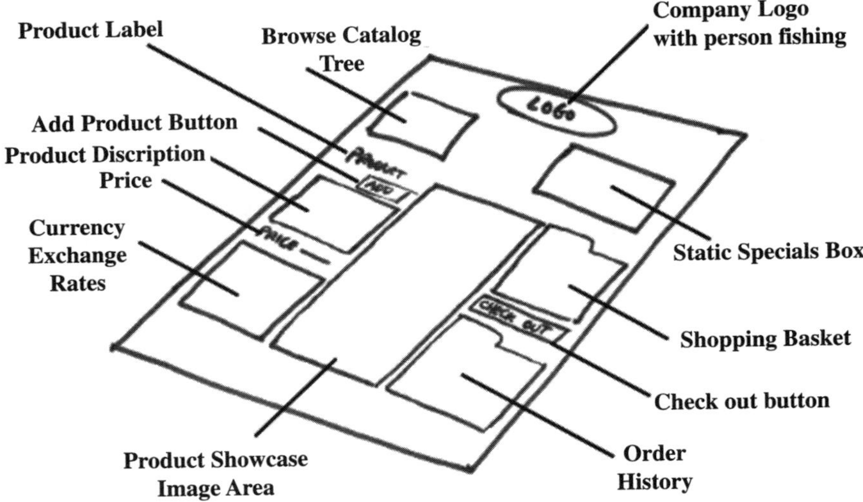

Figure 10.3 Hand sketch of UI layout.

Personalization package. To personalize his user interface, John needs to define the areas of the interface that are customizable. These areas include the shopping basket, order history, and a hidden HTML input type for storing the user's name. He has designed two JavaScript functions called setUserID() and personalize(). The setUserID() function is simply designed to gather the user's name through a JavaScript prompt. The function then assigns that user's name, through the DOM, to the orderID value attribute.

The second function, personalize(), gathers the orderID value attribute and assigns it to a JavaScript variable, name. It then adds the name to two variables called sbask (shopping basket) and ordHist (order history). It then reassigns, through the DOM, the labels for the shopping basket and order history.

Price calculations package. To calculate different prices, the user will first select an item from the Browse Catalog tree. The price of the product is put into an empty HTML hidden input type container element, priceDisplay. The user may select any item from the Browse Catalog tree, and the price will change. This function is calculateCurrency().

If the user decides to select a foreign currency from the Currency Exchange Rates tree, the price will be recalculated based upon the currently selected exchange rate. It pulls the product price from the currently selected Browse Catalog tree item and the exchange rate from the currently selected Currency Exchange Rates tree item. These two values are multiplied, and the resulting value is then displayed in the priceDisplay element.

At the same time, visual clues tell the user which currency he or she has collected. These include the country flag icon and the currency denomination. The country flag icon will change based upon the currently selected exchange rate. The currency denomination will also change based upon the currently selected exchange rate; however it will be stored in an HTML input type container element, currencyNote. The default value for this will always be United States Dollars, USD. The four other foreign currencies he will have to accommodate will be Germany, DM; ITALY, LIRA; JAPAN, YEN; and the United Kingdom, POUND. These functions will be called setForeign(), convertPrice(), and calculateForeign().

John knows that the products of the exchange rate conversion will inevitably result in large decimalized numbers. To pretty up these numbers, he will have to create a function to mask the numbers to 2 decimal places. He will call this function maskNumber().

Shopping. John will be creating a shopping cart feature into his site. When a user clicks on the Add Product button, that product will be added to the current order. The shopping cart will keep track of these items until the user is ready to place the order. To place the order, the user will click the Checkout button, and the order will be sent back to the order database on John's server. He does this with a simple form submission feature. He will create two functions, addProductToBasket() and checkOut().

NOTE **Because this system is designed as a tutorial, the order will just be placed in a textarea container and will be *virtually* placed onto the server. No actual form submission to a server will occur.**

Now that John has created a thorough design for his interface—designing the component architecture, laying out his individual user interface elements, and describing the event handling in JavaScript—he is ready to move on to creating the data source models for his component architecture.

Building the User Interface

To build the user interface, he first has to create the data sources by modeling the Catalog Provider, Currency Rates, and Order History data sources. So he sets off to model the CatalogProvider data source.

Modeling the CatalogProvider Data Source

John's manufacturer provides him with an XML-based catalog of items formatted in RDF. Refer to Table 10.1 and Code Listing 10.1. He will be getting the product id, product name, product manufacturer, price, the image name of the product, and a brief description of the product. This is enough information to create a very nice browsing feature for his site. For each product, he knows there is a unique key called id.

Notice in Code Listing 10.1, that his RDF data source is an ordered sequence of data elements. This means that when an XUL element cycles through the RDF data source it

Table 10.1 CatalogProvider data.

DATA ELEMENTS IN CATALOGPROVIDER.RDF
productid()
prodName()
prodManufacturer()
price()
productPage()
prodDesc()

```
<?xml version="1.0" encoding="UTF-8"?><rdf:RDF
xmlns:rdf="http://www.w3.org/1999/02/22-rdf-syntax-ns#"
xmlns:NC="http://home.netscape.com/NC-rdf#">
  <rdf:Seq ID="root">
    <rdf:li>      <rdf:Description id="flyrod1" NC:name="flyrod">
<NC:prodName>Bamboo Fly Rod</NC:prodName>
        <NC:productid>flyRod</NC:productid>
        <NC:prodManufacturer>Beacon Trade
          Outfitters</NC:prodManufacturer>
        <NC:price>1809.99</NC:price>
        <NC:productPage>flyrod.jpg</NC:productPage>
        <NC:prodDesc>Grab this classic fly rod and you will be fishing
          in no time!  Lightweight and easy to handle
          rod.</NC:prodDesc>
      </rdf:Description>
    </rdf:li>

    <rdf:li>      <rdf:Description id="waders1" NC:name="waders">
<NC:prodName>McKinley Highback Waders</NC:prodName>
        <NC:productid>highbackwaders</NC:productid>
        <NC:prodManufacturer>Aurora Borealis</NC:prodManufacturer>
        <NC:price>245.99</NC:price>
        <NC:productPage>highbackwaders.jpg</NC:productPage>
        <NC:prodDesc>These highback waders are guaranteed not to make
          you sweat!  Well maybe if you run the Boston Marathon in
          them.  Nylon and breathable will make your fishing
          experience one you can remember in memories, not in your
          clothes!</NC:prodDesc>
      </rdf:Description>
    </rdf:li>
```

Code Listing 10.1 CatalogProvider.rdf.

```
    <rdf:li>
      <rdf:Description id="shoes1" NC:name="shoes">
<NC:prodName>North River Wading Shoes</NC:prodName>
<NC:productid>shoes</NC:productid>
<NC:prodManufacturer>AlbertaGear</NC:prodManufacturer>
<NC:price>169.45</NC:price>
        <NC:productPage>wadingshoes.jpg</NC:productPage>
        <NC:prodDesc>These North River Wading Shoes will keep you warm
          without making you sweat and tested to temperatures just 1
          degree above absolute zero.</NC:prodDesc>
      </rdf:Description>
    </rdf:li>
    <rdf:li>      <rdf:Description id="vest1" NC:name="vest">
<NC:prodName>Snake River Fishing Vest</NC:prodName>
<NC:productid>vest</NC:productid>
        <NC:prodManufacturer>Beacon Trade
          Outfitters</NC:prodManufacturer>
        <NC:price>42.55</NC:price>
        <NC:productPage>fishingvest.jpg</NC:productPage>
        <NC:prodDesc>This styling Coldwater Fishing Vest is guaranteed
          to get you dates faster than any sports car.  Comes with 49
          pockets and breathable, mesh lining.</NC:prodDesc>
      </rdf:Description>
    </rdf:li>
  </rdf:Seq>
</rdf:RDF>
```

Code Listing 10.1 CatalogProvider.rdf (Continued).

will grab only that data in that order. RDF essentially creates a graph of arcs and nodes that can be cached in the browser. This presents a more powerful approach in XML development, as you may keep that data source cached in memory. This is totally unlike XSLT, as XML data is transformed and then thrown away.

Modeling the CurrencyRates Data Source

John's bank provides, on a daily basis, all the exchange rates for foreign currency conversion. This file is also given to him as items formatted in RDF. Refer to Table 10.2 and Code Listing 10.2. He will be able to extract the following information from the currencyRates.rdf data source: id, currencyRate, country, denomination, date, and time. This is more than enough information for him. The only data he really needs are the currencyRate and denomination. They can be represented as the following: DM 2.144607. Which essentially means a dollar will buy 2.144607 times more Deutsche Marks. This RDF data source is also an ordered sequence.

Table 10.2 CurrencyRates Data Model

DATA ELEMENTS IN CURRENCYRATES.RDF
id()
currencyRate()
country()
denomination()
date()
time()

```
<?xml version="1.0" encoding="UTF-8"?>
<rdf:RDF xmlns:rdf="http://www.w3.org/1999/02/22-rdf-syntax-ns#"
 xmlns:NC="http://home.netscape.com/NC-rdf#">
   <rdf:Seq id="root">
      <rdf:li>
         <rdf:Description id="DM" NC:name="DM">
            <NC:currencyRate>2.144607</NC:currencyRate>
            <NC:country>GE</NC:country>
            <NC:denomination>DM</NC:denomination>
            <NC:date>6-26-2001</NC:date>
            <NC:time>1500</NC:time>
         </rdf:Description>
      </rdf:li>
      <rdf:li>
         <rdf:Description id="LIRA" NC:name="LIRA">
            <NC:currencyRate>2123.448</NC:currencyRate>
            <NC:country>IT</NC:country>
            <NC:denomination>LIRA</NC:denomination>
            <NC:date>6-26-2001</NC:date>
            <NC:time>1500</NC:time>
         </rdf:Description>
      </rdf:li>
      <rdf:li>
         <rdf:Description id="YEN" NC:name="YEN">
            <NC:currencyRate>115.6080</NC:currencyRate>
            <NC:country>JP</NC:country>
            <NC:denomination>YEN</NC:denomination>
            <NC:date>6-26-2001</NC:date>
            <NC:time>1500</NC:time>
         </rdf:Description>
      </rdf:li>
```

Code Listing 10.2 CurrencyRates.rdf.

```
        <rdf:li>
           <rdf:Description id="POUND" NC:name="POUND">
              <NC:currencyRate>0.689436</NC:currencyRate>
              <NC:country>UK</NC:country>
              <NC:denomination>POUND</NC:denomination>
              <NC:date>6-26-2001</NC:date>
              <NC:time>1500</NC:time>
           </rdf:Description>
        </rdf:li>
        <rdf:li>
           <rdf:Description id="USD" NC:name="USD">
              <NC:currencyRate>1</NC:currencyRate>
              <NC:country>US</NC:country>
              <NC:denomination>USD</NC:denomination>
              <NC:date>6/26/2001</NC:date>
              <NC:time>1500</NC:time>
           </rdf:Description>
        </rdf:li>
     </rdf:Seq>
  </rdf:RDF>
```

Code Listing 10.2 CurrencyRates.rdf (Continued).

Modeling the OrderHistory Data Source

John already has an order history database in Microsoft Access as seen in Figure 10.4. He doesn't want to get rid of it. So what he did was create an Allaire Cold Fusion page that generates the RDF data source. He did this by posing a query to the specified database table, orderHistory, and then outputting the fields into the correct position of the RDF source. Code Listing 10.3 is the Cold Fusion marked-up RDF file that will dynamically build the RDF data source in Code Listing 10.4.

NOTE **How do you configure RDF to be dynamically generated from Cold Fusion? The answer is very simple. In your Cold Fusion-enabled Web server, you have to add a new MIME content type and association for RDF. On Win32 platforms, this can be done in the following way: In your Web server's MIME-type registry 1) add .rdf as a content type that is associated with wwwserver/wsapi and 2) add .rdf as a file extension association that points to \CFUSION\Bin\WSCF.dll. If you have doubts about this, just check the association and content type for the .cfm file extension. Copy and paste its values from the Web server's mime-type registry.**

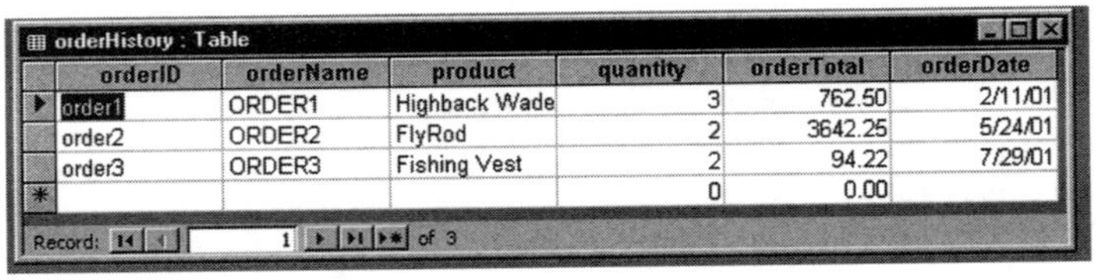

orderHistory : Table

	orderID	orderName	product	quantity	orderTotal	orderDate
▶	order1	ORDER1	Highback Wade	3	762.50	2/11/01
	order2	ORDER2	FlyRod	2	3642.25	5/24/01
	order3	ORDER3	Fishing Vest	2	94.22	7/29/01
*				0	0.00	

Record: 1 of 3

Figure 10.4 OrderHistory table.

```
<CFQUERY datasource="ODBCdatabase" name="orders">
     SELECT * FROM orderHistory
</CFQUERY><?xml version="1.0" encoding="UTF-8"?>
<rdf:RDF xmlns:rdf="http://www.w3.org/1999/02/22-rdf-syntax-ns#"
xmlns:NC="http://home.netscape.com/NC-rdf#">

   <rdf:Seq id="orders">

      <CFOUTPUT QUERY="orders">
         <rdf:li>
            <rdf:Description id="#orderID#" NC:name="#orderName#">
               <NC:product>#product#</NC:product>
               <NC:quantity>#quantity#</NC:quantity>
               <NC:orderTotal>$#orderTotal#</NC:orderTotal>
               <NC:orderDate>#orderDate#</NC:orderDate>
            </rdf:Description>
         </rdf:li>
      </CFOUTPUT>
   </rdf:Seq>
</rdf:RDF>
```

Code Listing 10.3 OrderHistory.rdf

```
<?xml version="1.0" encoding="UTF-8"?>
<rdf:RDF xmlns:rdf="http://www.w3.org/1999/02/22-rdf-syntax-ns#"
xmlns:NC="http://home.netscape.com/NC-rdf#">

  <rdf:Seq id="orders">

    <rdf:li>
      <rdf:Description id="order1" NC:name="ORDER1">
        <NC:product>Highback Waders</NC:product>
        <NC:quantity>3</NC:quantity>
        <NC:orderTotal>$762.50</NC:orderTotal>
        <NC:orderDate>11 Feb</NC:orderDate>
      </rdf:Description>
    </rdf:li>
```

Code Listing 10.4 OrderHistory.rdf (after Cold Fusion transformation).

```
    <rdf:li>
      <rdf:Description id="order2" NC:name="ORDER2">
        <NC:product>FlyRod</NC:product>
        <NC:quantity>2</NC:quantity>
        <NC:orderTotal>$3642.25</NC:orderTotal>
        <NC:orderDate>24 May</NC:orderDate>
      </rdf:Description>
    </rdf:li>

    <rdf:li>
      <rdf:Description id="order3" NC:name="ORDER3">
        <NC:product>Fishing Vest</NC:product>
        <NC:quantity>2</NC:quantity>
        <NC:orderTotal>$94.22</NC:orderTotal>
        <NC:orderDate>29 July</NC:orderDate>
      </rdf:Description>
    </rdf:li>

  </rdf:Seq>
</rdf:RDF>
```

Code Listing 10.4 OrderHistory.rdf (after Cold Fusion transformation)(Continued).

Creating and Populating the User Interface

Now it is time for John to start creating his individual user interface elements. Three elements—Browse Catalog tree, Currency Exchange Rates tree, and the Order History tree—all take advantage of the component-based architecture. The first two elements are connected to RDF data sources via XUL templates. The order history element is connected to an XUL overlay that just happens to have a XUL template to connect to RDF data sources.

Creating the Window

First John creates the window root element. This element contains all the namespace information that he will need to properly attribute elements. He does this with the following code:

```
<window align="left" orient="vertical"
  xmlns:html="http://www.w3.org/TR/REC-html40"
  xmlns="http://www.mozilla.org/keymaster/
         gatekeeper/there.is.only.xul"
  xmlns:rdf="http://www.w3.org/1999/02/22-rdf-syntax-ns#"
  xmlns:NC="http://home.netscape.com/NC-rdf#"
  title="Welcome to Beacontrade.com"
```

```
class="dialog"
onload="setUserID()"
style="background-color: #64849f">
```

Notice that because he is using RDF data sources he has to define the namespace for RDF, which is *xmlns:rdf*. He also wants the user to input his/her userID for the personalization feature of the interface. So, he assigns a JavaScript function setUserID() to the onload attribute.

NOTE Notice the onload attribute in the window element; this is not the same as onLoad in HTML. Because attributes in XML must be lowercase, onload in this case also follows the same rules. You could possibly run into parsing problems or your script not being executed.

Creating the Logo

John has to create his logo. He's a bit of an artist, so cranking up Adobe PhotoShop is not a problem. He creates his logo (Figure 10.5), saves it to a file, and then adds the following code to his index.xul document. This align="left" attribute in hbox will left-justify all child elements underneath hbox .

```
<hbox align="center">
   <image src="logo.gif"/>
</hbox>
```

Personalization Field

John decides to put in his personalization container element, userID, right after the logo, which is as good a place as any. So he adds the following code and assigns the element to contain a null value:

```
<html:input type="hidden" id="userID" name="orderIDContainer"
value="null"/>
```

Browse Catalog Tree

The next step he takes is to create the Browse Catalog feature. First he creates the label for "Browse our Catalog". This is represented in the following code:

```
<label value="Browse our Catalog" style="color: white; font-weight:
bold"/>
```

Figure 10.5 BeaconTrade.com logo.

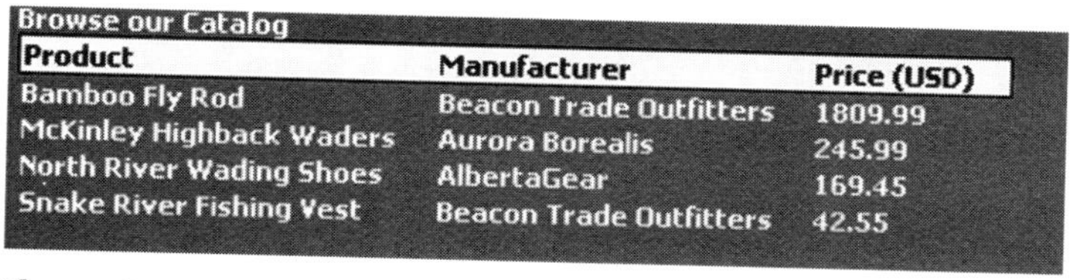

Browse our Catalog		
Product	**Manufacturer**	**Price (USD)**
Bamboo Fly Rod	Beacon Trade Outfitters	1809.99
McKinley Highback Waders	Aurora Borealis	245.99
North River Wading Shoes	AlbertaGear	169.45
Snake River Fishing Vest	Beacon Trade Outfitters	42.55

Figure 10.6 Browse Catalog tree.

John knows that he can create dynamically built trees. See Figure 10.6. After reading Chapter 6, "RDF and XUL Templates," he knows that these data elements can be connected via RDF and XUL templates. The first thing he does is create his tree element and then connect it to the RDF file via the *datasources* attribute. He then uses the *ref* attribute to connect the handle for the datasource to the root element of the catalogProvider.rdf RDF graph. In this example, it is *root*.

After he has this handle for his tree element, he can start cycling through this RDF graph. In the first treeitem element, he creates a reference to the *id* node. This node is an individual record. Any child elements underneath this treeitem element can be populated with nodes from the RDF data source graph.

To do this, John needs to assign only a child element's attribute. In one treecell element, he creates the following dynamically built label attribute. He references the RDF namespace along with the child node (prodName) in the RDF graph.

```
label="rdf:http://home.netscape.com/NC-rdf#prodName"
```

In this example he populates the product column with the preceding value. This is repeated for other elements including the manufacturer and price. He wants to add other elements into each record, but he doesn't want them to be visible to the user. These elements include productPage, prodDesc, and productID. So, he assigns them to hidden HTML input types. He then can access these elements through the DOM as child elements of the currently selected tree item. Please see Code Listing 10.5.

This is a more simplified version of creating an RDF/XUL template built UI element and is intended to give you an overall perspective of how RDF works.

```
<!-- Browse Catalog Box -->
<vbox style="font-weight:bold" flex="2" height="250">
   <text value="Browse our Catalog" style="color: white;
     font-weight: bold"/>
   <tree id="productList" height="80" datasources="datasources.rdf"
     ref="datasources.rdf#root" style="color:white; font-
     weight:bold;background-color: transparent">

      <treecolgroup>
        <treecol flex="1"/>
        <treecol flex="1"/>
```

continues

Code Listing 10.5 Browse Catalog tree.

```
      <treecol flex="1"/>
    </treecolgroup>

    <treehead style="color: #000000; background-color: #FFFFCC;
      border: 1px solid black">
       <treerow>
          <treecell label="Product"/>
          <treecell label="Manufacturer"/>
          <treecell id="treeCellPrice" label="Price (USD)"/>
       </treerow>
    </treehead>

    <template>
       <treechildren>
          <treeitem uri="..." id="rdf:http://home.netscape.com
            /NC-rdf#ID">
             <treerow idref="rdf:http://home.netscape.com
               /NC-rdf#ID" onclick="viewItem()">
                <treecell name="prodName"
                  label="rdf:http://home.netscape.com
                  /NC-rdf#prodName"/>
                <treecell name="prodManufacturer"
                  label="rdf:http://home.netscape.com
                  /NC-rdf#prodManufacturer"/>
                <treecell name="price"
                  label="rdf:http://home.netscape.com
                  /NC-rdf#price"/>
                <html:input type="hidden" name="page"
                  value="rdf:http://home.netscape.com
                  /NC-rdf#productPage"/>
                <html:input type="hidden" name="prodDescription"
                  value="rdf:http://home.netscape.com
                  /NC-rdf#prodDesc"/>
                <html:input type="hidden" name="productID"
                  value="rdf:http://home.netscape.com
                  /NC-rdf#productID"/>
             </treerow>
          </treeitem>
       </treechildren>
    </template>
  </tree>
</vbox>
```

Code Listing 10.5 Browse Catalog tree (Continued).

Create Specials Box

John wants to create a static specials box. Again in Adobe PhotoShop, he creates an image that he will occasionally use for specials. This week it just happens to be fleece classic hunting coats. So, he adds the following code to create his specials box as demonstrated in Figure 10.7:

```
<!-- Specials Box -->
<hbox flex="1" align="center" style="background-color:
  transparent">
    <image src="huntingjackets.gif"/>
</hbox>
```

Create the Product Description Area

The product description area is the area of the user interface that will change the most when a user selects an item. These items include the product label, add product button, and the product description (Figure 10.8).

Create the Product Label

He creates the product label that is more of a container element for the future product name than an empty label element. This element will change when user selects an item in the Browse Catalog tree. The product name from the currently selected *Browse Catalog* tree item will be assigned to the product label value. This is done in the following code:

```
<label id="prodDescriptionTitle" value="" style="color: white;
  font-weight: bold; font-size: 15px"/>
```

Figure 10.7 Specials box.

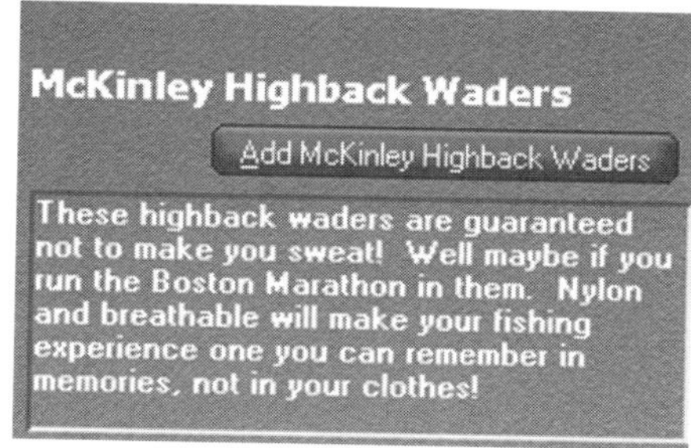

Figure 10.8 Product description area.

Create the Add Product Button

He creates the Add Product button, which is similar to the product label, in that it is a container element for the product name (Figure 10.9). Because he wants it to align right of the product label, he will have to create a parent element hbox to hold his button. He then assigns the hbox's align attribute a value of "right". He also creates a call to the JavaScript function addProductToBasket(). He creates the container with the following code:

```
<hbox align="right">
   <button id="addButton" label="Add Product"
     oncommand="addProductToBasket()" accesskey="a"/>
</hbox>
```

Create the Product Description Area

He creates an HTML text area that acts as the container for the product description. He makes this text area a virtually wrappable, read-only element. He creates this with the following code:

```
<html:textarea id="prodDescriptionText" rows="6" cols="25"
  style="color: white; background-color: transparent;
  font-size: 12px; font-weight:bold" autostretch="never"
  readonly="true" wrap="virtual">
   This is the description of your product.
</html:textarea>
```

Create the Price Labels and Hidden Data Element for Denomination

The price label and the hidden data element for currency denomination, currencyNote, are elements that will also change. The price label will visibly change, while the currencyNote element's value will change in the background. He adds Code Listing 10.6 to create these items. These items are viewable in Figure 10.9.

```
<!-- Price Display Area -->
<hbox style="color: white; background-color:
  transparent; font-size: 12px; font-weight:bold">

   <label id="priceText" value="Price :"/>
   <label id="priceDisplay" value="" style="color: white;
     background-color: transparent; font-size: 12px; font-
     weight:bold"/>
</hbox>
```

Code Listing 10.6 Price display area.

Price :USD 245.99

Figure 10.9 Price display area.

Create the Currency Rate Tree

He creates his second data source driven element, the Currency Rate tree. This element, as shown in Figure 10.10, has three areas: the flag icon, the Currency Exchange Rates label, and the currency rates. It is represented in Code Listing 10.7.

```
<tree id="currencyRateTable" datasources="currencyRates.rdf"
  ref="currencyRates.rdf#root" style="color:white; font-
  weight:bold;background-color: transparent">
   <treehead style="color: #000000; background-color:
     #FFFFFF; border: 1px solid black">

      <treecolgroup>
         <treecol width="100"/>
         <treecol width="50"/>
      </treecolgroup>

      <treerow>
         <treecell>
            <image id="flag" src="USD.gif"/>
            <text value="   Currency Exchange Rates"
              style="color: black"/>
         </treecell>

         <treecell value=""/>
      </treerow>
   </treehead>

   <template>
      <treechildren>
         <treeitem uri="..." id="rdf:http://home.netscape.com
           /NC-rdf#name">
            <treerow idref="rdf:http://home.netscape.com
              /NC-rdf#name" onclick="setForeign()">
               <treecell name="country"
                 label="rdf:http://home.netscape.com
                 /NC-rdf#country"/>
               <treecell name="rate"
                 label="rdf:http://home.netscape.com
                 /NC-rdf#currencyRate"/>
                <html:input type="hidden" id="denomination"
```

continues

Code Listing 10.7 Currency Rate tree.

```
                        value="rdf:http://home.netscape.com
                        /NC-rdf#denomination"/>
                </treerow>
            </treeitem>
        </treechildren>
    </template>
</tree>
```

Code Listing 10.7 Currency Rate tree (Continued).

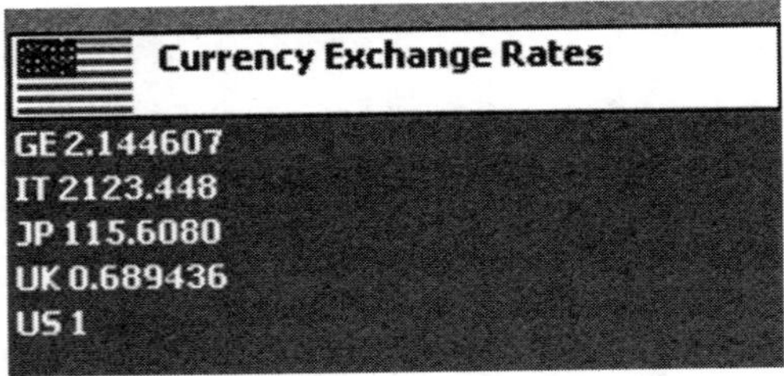

Figure 10.10 Currency Rate tree.

Creating the Product Display Area

The product display area, as demonstrated in Figure 10.11, is essentially just a box with an image contained within it. It changes when the viewItem() function is called. It is represented by the following code:

```
<vbox align="center" valign="center" height="350" width="250">  <image
id="prodDisplay" src="startscreen.jpg"/></vbox>
```

Create the Shopping Basket

The shopping basket, as demonstrated in Figure 10.12, is an HTML text area on top of a one-tab tabpanel. The tab on the tabpanel will be customized with the user's name after the personalize() function is called. This is done after the setUserID() has been called and after the first item is selected from the Browse Catalog feature.

The shopping basket is represented in Code Listing 10.8.

Create the Checkout Button

Creating the checkout button for John is eerily similar to creating HTML form buttons. See Figure 10.13. This button, which will activate the checkOut() function, is represented by the following code:

```
<button id="checkOut" value="Check out" oncommand="checkOut()"/>
```

Figure 10.11 Product display area.

```
<!-- Shopping Basket -->
<vbox flex="1" height="75">
   <tabbox>
      <tabs>
         <tab id="basket" selected="true"
           label="Shopping Basket"/>
         <spring flex="1"/>
      </tabs>

      <tabpanel orient="vertical" autostretch="always"
        flex="1" style="background-color: transparent">
         <vbox style="background-color: transparent">
            <html:textarea id="shoppingBasket" name="shopBask"
              rows="5" cols="25" style="color: white; background-
              color: transparent; font-size: 12px; font-weight:bold"
              autostretch="never" readonly="true" wrap="virtual">
               --empty--
            </html:textarea>
         </vbox>
      </tabpanel>
   </tabbox>
   <button id="checkOut" label="Check out" oncommand="checkOut()"/>
</vbox>
```

Code Listing 10.8 Shopping basket.

Figure 10.12 Shopping basket.

Figure 10.13 Checkout button.

Create the orderHistory Tree

Creating the orderHistory tree will be the apex of creating John's e-commerce interface. See Figure 10.14. He can create this orderHistoryTree in at least four ways. One would be for him to create a static tree in the main interface. The second would be to create a static tree in an overlay file. The third would be to create a dynamic tree in an overlay file from a static RDF data source. Finally, John could create a dynamic tree in an overlay file from a RDF data source generated from a database. Because John already had the database, he chose the fourth option.

To create his overlay, all he has to do is create a new XUL file. Instead of the root element being a window, it is an overlay. In this overlay, he has created it so that it pulls information from his RDF data source. That RDF data source, orderHistory.rdf, was dynamically generated by a Cold Fusion application that John created in Code Listing 10.3. This is demonstrated in Code Listing 10.9. This overlay is then called in the main interface with the following code.

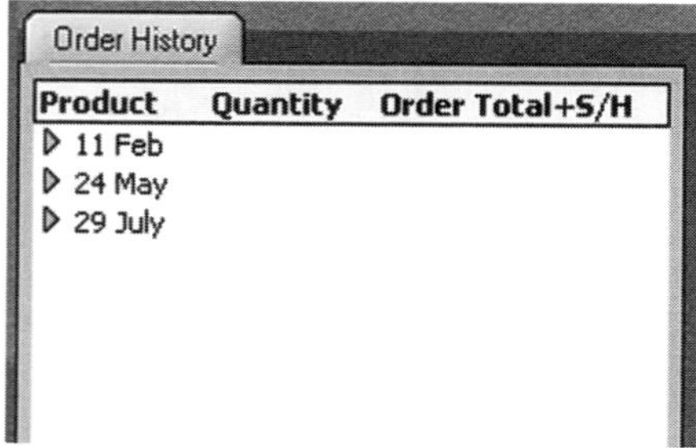

Figure 10.14 OrderHistory tree.

```
<tree id="orderHistoryTree" style="background-color: transparent;
font-color:black"/>
<?xml version="1.0" encoding="UTF-8"?>
<overlay id="orderHistoryOverlay"
xmlns="http://www.mozilla.org/keymaster/gatekeeper/there.is.only.xul"
xmlns:rdf="http://www.w3.org/1999/02/22-rdf-syntax-ns#"
xmlns:NC="http://home.netscape.com/NC-rdf#">

   <tree id="orderHistoryTree" flex="1"  height="80"
     datasources="orderHistory.rdf" ref="orderHistory.rdf#orders"
     style="background-color: white">

      <treecolgroup>
         <treecol flex="1"/>
         <treecol flex="1"/>
         <treecol flex="1"/>
      </treecolgroup>

      <treehead style="background-color: #FFFFCC; border:
        1px solid black; font-color:black">
         <treerow>
            <treecell label="Product" style="font-weight:bold;
              font-color:black"/>
            <treecell label="Quantity" style="font-weight:bold;
              font-color:black"/>
            <treecell label="Order Total+S/H" style="font-weight:
              bold; font-color:black"/>
         </treerow>
      </treehead>

      <template>
         <treechildren flex="100%" style="background-color:
           transparent; font-color:black">
            <treeitem container="true" open="false"  uri="..."
              id="rdf:http://home.netscape.com/NC-rdf#root">
              <treerow>
                 <treecell class="treecell-indent"
                   label="rdf:http://home.netscape.com
                   /NC-rdf#orderDate"/>
              </treerow>

              <treechildren>
                 <treeitem>
                    <treerow>
                       <treecell class="treecell-indent"
```

continues

Code Listing 10.9 overlayFile2.xul.

```
                            label="rdf:http://home.netscape.com
                            /NC-rdf#product"/>
                          <treecell label="rdf:http://home.netscape.com
                            /NC-rdf#quantity"/>
                          <treecell label="rdf:http://home.netscape.com
                            /NC-rdf#orderTotal"/>

                       </treerow>
                    </treeitem>
                 </treechildren>

               </treeitem>
            </treechildren>
         </template>
      </tree>
   </overlay>
```

Code Listing 10.9 overlayFile2.xul (Continued).

Creating the Event Handlers with JavaScript

For *personalization*, John creates two functions, setUserID() and personalize(). The function setUserID() is called when the interface has finished loading and prompts the user for a username. For all intensive purposes, this is not a real username in some database. It is any name the user would like to type in.

The function personalize will get the user's ID from the userID element. The userID is then used to personalize parts of the user interface such as the Shopping Basket label and Order History label.

```
function setUserID()
{
   var name = prompt("First you need to sign in
                          with your username:");
   document.getElementById('userID').
     setAttribute("value",name);
}
function personalize()
{
   name = document.getElementById('userID').
     getAttribute("value");

   // Personalization Code
   sbask = name + "'s Shopping Basket";
   ordHist = name + "'s Order History";
   document.getElementById('basket').
     setAttribute("label",sbask);
```

```
    document.getElementById('orderHistory').
      setAttribute("label",ordHist);
}
```

Price calculations are functions that John creates to allow him to convert prices to and from foreign currencies and to set variables within the document:

The function calculateCurrency() is called after the function viewItem() is called. The function is passed the currently selected currency note. The function gets the currently selected product from the productList tree. It then retrieves the price from the currently selected product and then assigns it to the variable price. It then assigns to the currencyNote field in the interface, the currently selected currency. That currency may be one of the following five currencies: USD, POUND, LIRA, YEN, or DM.

The function will call other nested functions such as convertPrice() and maskNumber to calculate the currency conversion and mask the number to two decimal places. It will then take that formatted price and assign it to the priceDisplay field in the user interface.

```
function calculateCurrency(elm)
{
   var tree=document.getElementById('productList');
   var items=tree.selectedItems;
   price = items[0].firstChild.childNodes.item(2).
     getAttribute('label');

   document.getElementById('currencyNote').
     setAttribute("value",elm);

   var cur = document.getElementById('currencyNote').
     getAttribute('value');

   convertedPrice = convertPrice(price,elm);
   convertedPrice = maskNumber(convertedPrice);
   priceToDisplay = elm + " " +convertedPrice;

   document.getElementById('priceDisplay').
     setAttribute("value",priceToDisplay);
}
```

The function setForeign() is called when a user selects a currency conversion from the currencyRate table. It then retrieves the country, currency rate, and denomination fields from the interface. It then changes the flag's image source location. This is to reflect the change in currency and to give the user a visual cue. It then sets the currencyNote field the value of the denomination, which will be one of the following five currencies: USD, POUND, LIRA, YEN, or DM.

```
function setForeign()
{
   var tree=document.getElementById('currencyRateTable');
```

```
    var items=tree.selectedItems;
    country = items[0].firstChild.childNodes.
      item(0).getAttribute('value');

    rate = items[0].firstChild.childNodes.
      item(1).getAttribute('label');

    denomination = items[0].firstChild.childNodes.
      item(2).getAttribute('value');

    imageName = denomination + ".gif";
    document.getElementById('flag').
      setAttribute("src",imageName);

    document.getElementById("currencyNote").
      setAttribute("value",denomination);
    viewItem();
}
```

The function calculateForeign() gets the currently selected exchange rate and then calculates the price.

```
function calculateForeign(price)
{
    var tree=document.getElementById('currencyRateTable');
    var items=tree.selectedItems;

    exchangeRate = items[0].firstChild.childNodes.
      item(1).getAttribute('label');
    return(price * exchangeRate);
}
```

The function convertPrice() is called by the calculateCurrency() function and is used to make a distinction between whether to convert the price or not.

```
function convertPrice(USDPrice,denomination)
{
    if(denomination != "USD")
        return(calculateForeign(USDPrice));
    else
        return price;
}
```

The function maskNumber() is called by the calculateCurrency() function after the price is converted. The converted price will be the raw floating point number. The maskNumber() function re-calculates the price to two decimal places.

```
function maskNumber(price)
{
```

```
    var str = "" + Math.round(eval(price) * Math.pow(10,2));

    while(str.length <= 2)
    {
      str = "0" + str;
    }
    var decpoint = str.length - 2;
    return str.substring(0,decpoint) + "." +
       str.substring(decpoint,str.length);
}
```

Once he has the conversion and pricing event handlers built, he goes on to create the shopping cart.

Creating the Shopping Cart

The following functions will create the shopping cart and ordering feature of John's site.

Step A gets the currently selected product from the productList tree. From that selection, it assigns the text description, product name, image location, description, and product identification number to the JavaScript variables *txt*, *title*, *image*, *desc*, and *productID*.

Step B checks to see if the shopping basket is empty or not. If it is empty, it will then add the selected product to the shopping basket.

```
function addProductToBasket()
{
   // Step A
   var tree=document.getElementById('productList');
   var items=tree.selectedItems;

   if (items.length==0)
   {
      alert("No items are selected.");
   }else
   {
      txt="You have selected:\n\n";
      for (t=0;t<items.length;t++)
      {
         txt+=items[t].firstChild.childNodes.item(1).
           getAttribute('value')+'\n';
         title = items[t].firstChild.childNodes.item(0).
           getAttribute('value');
         image  = items[t].firstChild.childNodes.item(3).
           getAttribute('value');
         desc = items[t].firstChild.childNodes.item(4).
           getAttribute('value');
         productID = items[t].firstChild.childNodes.item(5).
           getAttribute('value');
      }
   }
```

```
    // Step B
    currentShoppingBasket = document.getElementById('shoppingBasket').
      getAttribute('value');
    if(currentShoppingBasket == "--empty--")
    {
       currentShoppingBasket = productID + "---Qty 1";
    }else
    {
       currentShoppingBasket = currentShoppingBasket + "\n" + productID +
"---Qty 1";
    }
    // Step C
    document.getElementById('shoppingBasket').
      setAttribute("value",currentShoppingBasket);
}
function checkOut()
{
    var emptyStuff = "--empty--";

    document.getElementById('shoppingBasket').
      setAttribute("value",emptyStuff);

    alert("Thank you "+document.getElementById('orderID').
      getAttribute('value')+" ... \nYour order is on its way");
}
```

Now that he has all his event handlers, it's time to test his data-driven XUL user interface.

Navigating the Finished Product

He is finished (Figure 10.15)! John is now ready to launch his XUL-emblazoned site. He decides to take his interface for a test drive. To do this, he loads his main interface file, index.xul (shown in the next section) into Netscape Navigator.

To his surprise, it works superbly! When prompted, he fills out his username (which can be any name at this point) and then selects a product from the Browse Catalog tree. The product label, add product button, product description, price, and image changed based on his selection. This was done through the DOM API and JavaScript, manipulating XUL and HTML elements on the fly.

He also created a component-based architecture that allowed him to create pluggable data sources to his interface. With this component-based architecture, he was able to create a connection through XUL overlays and XUL templates to a legacy database.

He also created a user interface that allows his customers a single point of entry to his product catalog. No muss, no fuss. This XUL interface with its component-based architecture also affords him ease of maintenance.

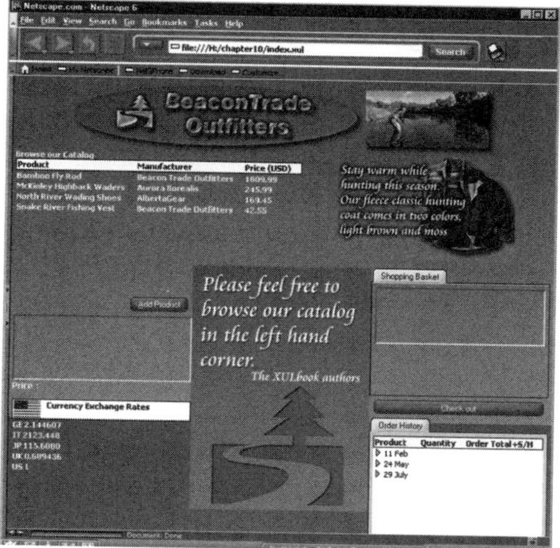

Figure 10.15 The finished e-commerce XUL interface.

Main XUL Interface File

```
<?xml version="1.0"?
<?xml-stylesheet href="chrome://navigator/skin/" type="text/css" ?>
<?xul-overlay href="overlayFile2.xul"?>

<window align="left" orient="vertical"
xmlns:html="http://www.w3.org/TR/REC-html40"
xmlns="http://www.mozilla.org/keymaster/gatekeeper/there.is.only.xul"
xmlns:rdf="http://www.w3.org/1999/02/22-rdf-syntax-ns#"
xmlns:NC="http://home.netscape.com/NC-rdf#" title="Welcome to
Beacontrade.com" class="dialog" onload="setUserID()"
style="background-color: #64849f">

   <script language="javascript" src="eventhandlers.js"/>
      <!-- Main Header section -->
         <hbox align="center">
            <image src="logo.gif"/>
            <html:input type="hidden" id="userID"
              name="orderIDContainer" value="null"/>
         </hbox>

      <!-- Main browse section -->
         <hbox flex="4">

         <!-- Browse Catalog Box -->
         <vbox style="font-weight:bold" flex="2" height="250">
            <text value="Browse our Catalog" style="color: white;
```

```
    font-weight: bold"/>
  <tree id="productList" height="80"
    datasources="datasources.rdf" ref="datasources.rdf#root"
    style="color:white; font-weight:bold;background-color:
    transparent">

     <treecolgroup>
        <treecol flex="1"/>
        <treecol flex="1"/>
        <treecol flex="1"/>
     </treecolgroup>

     <treehead style="color: #000000; background-color:
       #FFFFCC; border: 1px solid black">
        <treerow>
           <treecell label="Product"/>
           <treecell label="Manufacturer"/>
           <treecell id="treeCellPrice" label="Price
             (USD)"/>
        </treerow>
     </treehead>

     <template>
        <treechildren>
           <treeitem uri="..."
             id="rdf:http://home.netscape.com/NC-rdf#ID">
              <treerow
                idref="rdf:http://home.netscape.com/NC-
                rdf#ID" onclick="viewItem()">
                 <treecell name="prodName"

                   label="rdf:http://home.netscape.com/NC-
                   rdf#prodName"/>
                 <treecell name="prodManufacturer"

                   label="rdf:http://home.netscape.com/NC-
                   rdf#prodManufacturer"/>
                 <treecell name="price"

                   label="rdf:http://home.netscape.com/NC-
                   rdf#price"/>
                 <html:input type="hidden" name="page"

                   value="rdf:http://home.netscape.com/NC-
                   rdf#productPage"/>
                 <html:input type="hidden"
                   name="prodDescription"

                   value="rdf:http://home.netscape.com/NC-
                   rdf#prodDesc"/>
                 <html:input type="hidden" name="productID"
```

```
                    value="rdf:http://home.netscape.com/NC-
                    rdf#productID"/>
                </treerow>
              </treeitem>
            </treechildren>
          </template>
        </tree>
      </vbox>

      <!-- Specials Box -->
      <hbox flex="1" align="center" style="background-color:
        transparent">
         <image src="huntingjackets.gif"/>
      </hbox>
    </hbox>

    <hbox flex="1" height="25">
      <label value=""/>
    </hbox>

    <!-- Shopping Area -->
    <hbox flex="4">

      <!-- Product Display Area -->
      <vbox height="450" width="250" halign="center">
        <html:p/>
        <label id="prodDescriptionTitle" value="" style="color:
          white; font-weight: bold; font-size: 15px"/>

        <hbox align="right">
          <button id="addButton" label="Add Product"
            oncommand="addProductToBasket()" accesskey="a"/>
        </hbox>

        <html:textarea id="prodDescriptionText" rows="6" cols="25"
          style="color: white; background-color: transparent;
          font-size: 12px; font-weight:bold" autostretch="never"
          readonly="true" wrap="virtual">
           This is the description of your product.
        </html:textarea>

        <!-- Price Display Area -->
          <hbox style="color: white; background-color:
            transparent; font-size: 12px; font-weight:bold">
             <label id="priceText" value="Price :"/>
             <label id="priceDisplay" value="" style="color:
               white; background-color: transparent; font-size:
               12px; font-weight:bold"/>
          </hbox>
          <hbox>
            <label value=""/>
```

```
    <html:input type="hidden" id="currencyNote"
      name="currency" value="USD"/>
</hbox>

<vbox>
    <tree id="currencyRateTable"
      datasources="currencyRates.rdf"
      ref="currencyRates.rdf#root" style="color:white;
      font-weight:bold;background-color: transparent">

       <treehead style="color: #000000; background-
         color: #FFFFFF; border: 1px solid black">

           <treecolgroup>
              <treecol width="100"/>
              <treecol width="50"/>
           </treecolgroup>

           <treerow>
              <treecell>
                 <image id="flag" src="USD.gif"/>
                 <text value="   Currency Exchange Rates"
                   style="color: black"/>
              </treecell>

              <treecell value=""/>
           </treerow>
       </treehead>

       <template>
           <treechildren>
              <treeitem uri="..."
                id="rdf:http://home.netscape.com/NC-
                rdf#name">
                 <treerow

                   idref="rdf:http://home.netscape.com
                   /NC-rdf#name" onclick="setForeign()">
                    <treecell name="country"

                      label="rdf:http://home.netscape.com
                      /NC-rdf#country"/>
                    <treecell name="rate"

                      label="rdf:http://home.netscape.com
                      /NC-rdf#currencyRate"/>
                    <html:input type="hidden"
                      id="denomination"

                      value="rdf:http://home.netscape.com
                      /NC-rdf#denomination"/>
```

```
                </treerow>
              </treeitem>
            </treechildren>
          </template>
        </tree>
      </vbox>
    </vbox>

    <vbox align="center" valign="center" height="350"
      width="250">
       <image id="prodDisplay" src="startscreen.jpg"/>
    </vbox>
    <!-- Ordering Area -->
    <vbox flex="1">

       <!-- Shopping Basket -->
       <vbox flex="1" height="75">

          <tabbox>
             <tabs>
                <tab id="basket" selected="true"
                  label="Shopping Basket"/>
                <spring flex="1"/>
             </tabs>

             <tabpanel orient="vertical" autostretch="always"
               flex="1" style="background-color: transparent">
                <vbox style="background-color: transparent">
                   <html:textarea id="shoppingBasket"
                     name="shopBask" rows="5" cols="25"
                     style="color: white; background-color:
                     transparent; font-size: 12px; font-
                     weight:bold" autostretch="never"
                     readonly="true" wrap="virtual">
                      --empty--
                   </html:textarea>
                </vbox>
             </tabpanel>
          </tabbox>

          <button id="checkOut" label="Check out"
            oncommand="checkOut()"/>
       </vbox>

       <!-- Order History -->
       <vbox flex="1">

          <tabbox>
             <tabs>
                <tab id="orderHistory" selected="true"
                  label="Order History"/>
```

```
                        <spring flex="1"/>
                     </tabs>

                    <tabpanel orient="vertical" autostretch="always"
                       flex="1">

                        <vbox>
                           <tree id="orderHistoryTree"
                             style="background-color: transparent;
                             font-color:black"/>
                        </vbox>
                     </tabpanel>
                  </tabbox>
               </vbox>
            </vbox>
         </hbox>
</window>
```

JavaScript Event Handling File

```
function viewItem()
{
   var tree=document.getElementById('productList');
   var items=tree.selectedItems;

   if (items.length==0)
   {
      alert("No items are selected.");
   } else
   {
      txt="You have selected:\n\n";
      for (t=0;t<items.length;t++)
      {
         txt+=items[t].firstChild.childNodes.item(1).
           getAttribute('value')+'\n';
         title = items[t].firstChild.childNodes.item(0).
           getAttribute('label');
         image  = items[t].firstChild.childNodes.item(3).
           getAttribute('value');
         desc = items[t].firstChild.childNodes.item(4).
           getAttribute('value');
      }
   }
   var orderID = document.getElementById('orderID').
     getAttribute("value");

   if(orderID == "null")
   {
      setUserID();
```

```
    }else{
        document.getElementById('prodDisplay').
          setAttribute("src",image);
        document.getElementById('prodDescriptionTitle').
          setAttribute("value",title);
        var cur = document.getElementById('currencyNote').
          getAttribute('value');
        calculateCurrency(cur);
        addButton = "Add "+title;
        personalize();
        document.getElementById('addButton').
          setAttribute("label",addButton);
        document.getElementById('prodDescriptionText').
          setAttribute("value",desc);
    }
}
function calculateCurrency(elm)
{
    var tree=document.getElementById('productList');
    var items=tree.selectedItems;
    price = items[0].firstChild.childNodes.item(2).
      getAttribute('label');
    document.getElementById('currencyNote').
      setAttribute("value",elm);
    var cur = document.getElementById('currencyNote').
      getAttribute('value');
    convertedPrice = convertPrice(price,elm);
    convertedPrice = maskNumber(convertedPrice);
    priceToDisplay = elm + " " +convertedPrice;
    document.getElementById('priceDisplay').
      setAttribute("value",priceToDisplay);
}
function setForeign()
{
    var tree=document.getElementById('currencyRateTable');
    var items=tree.selectedItems;
    country = items[0].firstChild.childNodes.item(0).
      getAttribute('value');
    rate = items[0].firstChild.childNodes.item(1).
      getAttribute('label');
    denomination = items[0].firstChild.childNodes.item(2).
      getAttribute('value');

    imageName = denomination + ".gif";
    document.getElementById('flag').
      setAttribute("src",imageName);
    document.getElementById("currencyNote").
      setAttribute("value",denomination);
    viewItem();
}
function calculateForeign(price)
{
```

```
    var tree=document.getElementById('currencyRateTable');
    var items=tree.selectedItems;
    exchangeRate = items[0].firstChild.childNodes.item(1).
      getAttribute('label');
    return(price * exchangeRate);
}
function convertPrice(USDPrice,denomination)
{
    if(denomination != "USD")
      return(calculateForeign(USDPrice));
    else
      return price;
}
function maskNumber(price)
{
    var str = "" + Math.round(eval(price) * Math.pow(10,2));
    while(str.length <= 2)
    {
       str = "0" + str;
    }
    var decpoint = str.length - 2;
    return str.substring(0,decpoint) + "." +
      str.substring(decpoint,str.length);
}
function setUserID()
{
    var name = prompt("First you need to sign in with your username:");
    document.getElementById('orderID').
      setAttribute("value",name);
}
function personalize()
{
    name = document.getElementById('orderID').
      getAttribute("value");
    // Personalization Code
    sbask = name + "'s Shopping Basket";
    ordHist = name + "'s Order History";
    document.getElementById('basket').
      setAttribute("label",sbask);
    document.getElementById('orderHistory').
      setAttribute("label",ordHist);
}
function addProductToBasket()
{
    var tree=document.getElementById('productList');
    var items=tree.selectedItems;
    if (items.length==0)
    {
       alert("No items are selected.");
    }else
```

```
    {
        txt="You have selected:\n\n";
        for (t=0;t<items.length;t++)
        {
            txt+=items[t].firstChild.childNodes.item(1).
              getAttribute('value')+'\n';
            title = items[t].firstChild.childNodes.item(0).
              getAttribute('value');
            image  = items[t].firstChild.childNodes.item(3).
              getAttribute('value');
            desc = items[t].firstChild.childNodes.item(4).
              getAttribute('value');
            productID = items[t].firstChild.childNodes.item(5).
              getAttribute('value');
        }
    }
    currentShoppingBasket = document.getElementById('shoppingBasket').
      getAttribute('value');
    if(currentShoppingBasket == "--empty--")
    {
        currentShoppingBasket = productID + "---Qty 1";
    }else
     {
        currentShoppingBasket = currentShoppingBasket + "\n" +
          productID + "---Qty 1";
     }
    document.getElementById('shoppingBasket').
      setAttribute("value",currentShoppingBasket);
}
function checkOut()
{
    var emptyStuff = "--empty--";
    document.getElementById('shoppingBasket').
      setAttribute("value",emptyStuff);
    alert("Thank you "+document.getElementById('orderID').
      getAttribute('value')+" ... \nYour order is on its way");
}
```

Overlay Files

OverlayFile.xul

```
<?xml version="1.0" encoding="UTF-8"?>

<overlay id="orderHistoryOverlay"
```

```
xmlns="http://www.mozilla.org/keymaster/gatekeeper/there.is.only.xul">
   <tree id="orderHistoryTree" flex="1">

      <treecolgroup>
         <treecol flex="1"/>
         <treecol flex="1"/>
         <treecol flex="1"/>
      </treecolgroup>
      <treehead style="background-color: #FFFFCC;
        border: 1px solid black; font-color:black">
         <treerow>
            <treecell label="Product"/>
            <treecell label="Quantity"/>
            <treecell label="Order Total+S/H"/>
         </treerow>
      </treehead>

      <treechildren flex="100%">
         <treeitem container="true" open="false">

            <treerow>
               <treecell class="treecell-indent" label="11 Feb"/>
            </treerow>

            <treechildren>
               <treeitem>
                  <treerow>
                     <treecell class="treecell-indent"
                       label="Highback Wader"/>
                     <treecell label="3"/>
                     <treecell label="$762.50"/>
                  </treerow>
               </treeitem>
            </treechildren>
         </treeitem>

         <treeitem container="true" open="false">
            <treerow>
               <treecell class="treecell-indent" label="24 May"/>
            </treerow>

            <treechildren>
               <treeitem>
                  <treerow>
                     <treecell class="treecell-indent"
                       label="Fly Rod"/>
                     <treecell label="2"/>
                     <treecell label="$3642.25"/>
                  </treerow>
               </treeitem>
            </treechildren>
```

```
          </treeitem>

          <treeitem container="true" open="false">

             <treerow>
                <treecell class="treecell-indent" label="29 July"/>
             </treerow>

             <treechildren>
                <treeitem>
                   <treerow>
                      <treecell class="treecell-indent"
                        label="Fishing Vest"/>
                      <treecell label="2"/>
                      <treecell label="$94.22"/>
                   </treerow>
                </treeitem>
             </treechildren>
          </treeitem>
       </treechildren>
    </tree>
 </overlay>
```

OrderHistory.rdf

```
<?xml version="1.0" encoding="UTF-8"?>
<rdf:RDF xmlns:rdf="http://www.w3.org/1999/02/22-rdf-syntax-ns#"
xmlns:NC="http://home.netscape.com/NC-rdf#">

  <rdf:Seq ID="orders">

    <rdf:li>
      <rdf:Description ID="order1" NC:name="ORDER1">
        <NC:product>Highback Waders</NC:product>
        <NC:quantity>3</NC:quantity>
        <NC:orderTotal>$762.50</NC:orderTotal>
        <NC:orderDate>11 Feb</NC:orderDate>
      </rdf:Description>
    </rdf:li>

    <rdf:li>
      <rdf:Description ID="order2" NC:name="ORDER2">
        <NC:product>FlyRod</NC:product>
        <NC:quantity>2</NC:quantity>
        <NC:orderTotal>$3642.25</NC:orderTotal>
        <NC:orderDate>24 May</NC:orderDate>
      </rdf:Description>
    </rdf:li>
```

```
      <rdf:li>
        <rdf:Description ID="order3" NC:name="ORDER3">
          <NC:product>Fishing Vest</NC:product>
          <NC:quantity>2</NC:quantity>
          <NC:orderTotal>$94.22</NC:orderTotal>
          <NC:orderDate>29 July</NC:orderDate>
        </rdf:Description>
      </rdf:li>

    </rdf:Seq>
  </rdf:RDF>
```

Summary

This chapter hopefully has given you some ideas of your own to develop a larger user interface using XUL elements. Whether its populating user interface elements with dynamic RDF data sources or promoting reusability in your interface through the use of overlays, XUL is the perfect language specification for creating user interfaces.

XUL can create these user interfaces in a time unrivaled by any other programming language's windowing API. We can say this because the user interface for Beacon-Trade.com was created in only two days, with minimal implementation issues. All code for this project is listed in this chapter. The appendices will provide you with an element reference to XUL and a theme reference to creating Netscape themes.

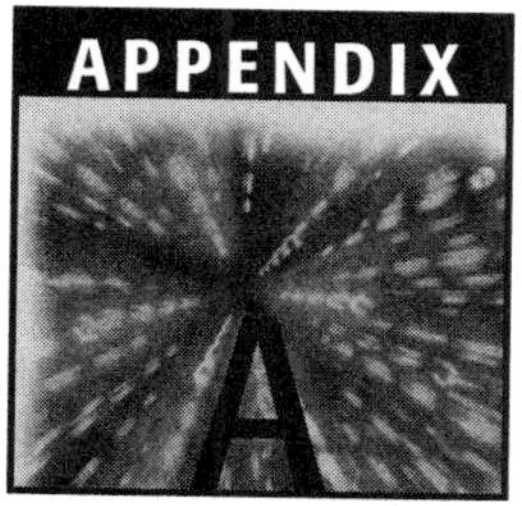

XUL Programmer's Reference

This appendix is a reference of XUL elements, their attributes, and how they are used in XUL programming. This appendix has six major sections:

"XUL Elements." This section lists each XUL element and briefly describes its properties.

"XUL Core Attributes, Methods, and Properties." This section lists attributes, JavaScript methods, and JavaScript properties that are common to each XUL element.

"Basic Attributes." This section lists and defines certain attributes that are common to many XUL elements.

"Event Handler Attributes." This section discusses these attributes of XUL elements that trigger JavaScript events.

"Visual Examples." This section provides visual examples of the basic types of visual elements and their use.

All elements are printed in brackets as they exist in XUL documents—for example, <elementName>. Attributes and JavaScript properties are listed in *italics*, and all JavaScript methods are listed in regular font with an open parenthesis, the parameters that are called, followed by the closed parenthesis—for example, methodName(param1, param2, param3) .

XUL Elements

The element reference may provide the following sections in a tabular format:

Contained by. If the element is usually a child of a certain element, this item will be listed in the table. If the "contained by" section is not listed, you are to assume that it could be contained by any element.

Contains. If the element usually contains specific children related to its functionality, this will be listed in the table. If the "contains" section is not listed for an element, you are to assume that it may contain any element.

Attributes. If the element contains attributes in addition to the XUL core attributes, these will be listed. If there is an important attribute that relates to the element, this will be denoted in the text before the table.

Properties/Methods Used by JavaScript. If the element has properties that are referenced by JavaScript, or if the element has methods (function calls) that can be called with JavaScript, they will be listed in this section. If this section is not listed, assume that no special properties or methods (other than the XUL Core Methods and Properties) for that element will be referenced by JavaScript.

See Also. If the element is related to other XUL elements, they will be listed in this section.

Relevant Chapters/Examples. This references chapters or examples throughout this book.

<action>

Used with XUL templates, this tag provides generated content based on rule matches. Based on variable bindings produced by the rule matches, this section generates the dynamically generated XUL content.

Contained by	<rule>
Relevant Chapters/Examples	Chapter 6, "RDF and XUL Templates"
See Also	<rule>, <template>

<arrowscrollbox>

This is a box element that provides arrows to allow the user to scroll through its contents. When the user places his mouse over the arrows, the box will scroll.

Attributes	*align, autostretch, collapsed, crop, debug, flex, height, left, orient, top, valign, width*
See Also	<autorepeatbutton>, <scrollbox>

<autorepeatbutton>

This is an element used to provide the scrollbuttons in the <arrowscrollbox> element.

Attributes	*autostretch, flex, height, src, width*
See Also	<scrollbox>

<binding>

Optionally used in XUL templates for dynamically generating XUL content, this element is used to provide variable bindings to a node. Very similar to the <triple> tag, it is used to match an attribute of a node to a new variable that can be used in the <action> section of a rule using the subject-predicate-object syntax. Because this element is a logical, nonvisible element, it does not contain the XUL core attributes. It does, however, contain the XUL core properties and methods.

Contained by	<bindings>
Attributes	*subject, predicate, object*

Relevant Chapters/Examples	Chapter 6, "RDF and XUL Templates"
See Also	<rule>, <template>, <bindings>, <triple>

<bindings>

Optionally used in XUL templates for dynamically generating XUL content, this element lists multiple variable bindings. This element contains one or more <binding> elements and is a sibling of the <conditions> element. This element is a logical element and does not contain the XUL core attributes or properties and methods.

Contained by	<rule>
Relevant Chapters/Examples	Chapter 6, "RDF and XUL Templates"
See Also	<rule>, <template>, <bindings>, <conditions>

<box>

This is a container element that can have any number of child elements. Unless otherwise changed by the *align* attribute, this element defaults to a horizontal alignment.

Attributes	*align, autostretch, collapsed, crop, debug, flex, height, left, orient, top, valign, width*
See Also	hbox, vbox

<broadcaster>

Contained by the <broadcasterset> element, this element is used to broadcast events to send attribute changes to XUL elements that are observing the broadcaster. The <observer> elements reference the broadcaster its *id* attribute. Often, elements observe a broadcaster's *oncommand* or *label* attribute. However, a broadcaster can include any attribute that could be observed by other elements.

Contained by	<broadcasterset>
Attributes	*id, (any attribute—sometimes label or oncommand)*
Relevant Chapters/Examples	"Broadcasters, Observers, and Commands" in the "Visual Examples" section of this appendix.
See Also	<broadcasterset>, <observes>

<broadcasterset>

Contains one or more broadcasters. This element is a nonvisible, logical element and does not contain the XUL core attributes or properties and methods.

Contains	<broadcaster>
Relevant Chapters/Examples	"Broadcasters, Observers, and Commands" in the "Visual Examples" section of this appendix.
See Also	<broadcaster>,<observes>

<browser>

This element presents a read-only view of a Web document referenced by an URL in the source attribute.

Contained by	N/A
Attributes	*autostretch, flex, height, left, src, top, width*
Properties Used by JavaScript	*browserShell*, the object that has browser functionality
See Also	<iframe>

<bulletinboard>

This element is a container element that allows its children to be positioned with absolute positioning. Elements contained by this element need to have left and top attributes set to specify their positioning.

Contained by	N/A
Attributes	*debug, flex, height, left, top, width*

<button>

This button can be pressed by the user. JavaScript events are attached to this XUL element. The *src* attribute contains the URL of the image that will appear on the button. The *label* attribute sets the label of the button. The *tooltip* and *tooltiptext* attributes are used for popups that occur when the user places her mouse over the button. The *tooltip* attribute defines the *id* of a XUL <popup> element when the developer wants to define customized popups. The *tooltiptext* attribute lists the text that will "pop up" on a mouseover event.

Contained by	N/A
Attributes	*accesskey, crop, default, disabled, flex, left, height, orient, src, top, tooltip, tooltiptext, label, width*
Properties Used by JavaScript	The following properties reference attributes of the button and are accessible and changable by JavaScript: *accesskey, crop, disabled, imgalign, src, label*
See Also	<autorepeatbutton>, <scrollbox>

<checkbox>

This is an element that is a box that can be checked on and off by the user. The *checked* attribute being set to "true" or "false" sets the state of this XUL element, and the *label* attribute sets the label of the checkbox.

Attributes	*accesskey, checked, crop, default, disabled, flex, left, height, orient, src, top, label, width*
Properties Used By JavaScript	The following properties reference attributes of this element and are accessible and changeable by JavaScript: checked, accesskey, crop, disabled, imgalign, src, label
See Also	<autorepeatbutton>, <scrollbox>

<colorpicker>

This XUL element provides a grid of colors from which the user can choose. The *color* attributes contains the value of the current selected color. The *palettename* attribute is an optional attribute with possible values of "standard", "grey", and "web", and it specifies what type of palette to load into the element.

Contained by	N/A
Attributes	*align, autostretch, color, crop, debug, flex, height, left, orient, palettename, top, valign, width*
Properties Used by JavaScript	The following properties reference attributes of this element and are accessible and changeable by JavaScript: *color*
Relevant Chapters/Examples	"Broadcasters, Observers, and Commands" in the "Visual Examples" section of the appendix.

<column>

This XUL element is a column contained by the <columns> element. Every child of this element will be placed in a cell of the column's grid.

Contained by	<columns>
Attributes	*align, autostretch, collapsed, crop, debug, flex, height, left, orient, top, valign, width*
Relevant Chapters/Examples	"Stacks, Decks, and Grids" in the "Visual Examples" section of this appendix.
See Also	<columns>, <grid>

<columns>

This XUL element defines the columns of a grid. A child of the <grid> element, it contains one to many <column> elements.

Contained by	<grid>
Contains	<column>
Attributes	*Align, autostretch, collapsed, crop, debug, flex, height, left, orient, top, valign, width*
Relevant Chapters/Examples	"Stacks, Decks, and Grids" in the "Visual Examples" section of this appendix.
See Also	<column>, <grid>

<command>

Used to modularize procedural functionality, the <command> element can be invoked by JavaScript by executing the XUL core doCommand(id) method, which executes a command based on the *id* of the <command> element. Because of this, each <command> element should have a unique identifier *id* attribute, as well as an *oncommand* event handler attribute, that references the functionality which should be executed when the command is invoked.

Contained by	<commandset>
Attributes	*id, oncommand*
Relevant Chapters/Examples	"Broadcasters, Observers, and Commands" in the "Visual Examples" section of this appendix.
See Also	<commands>, <commandset>, doCommand() core JavaScript function

<commands>

A container for a <commandset>, this simple container has no special attributes.

Contains	<commandset>
See Also	<command>, <commandset>, doCommand() core JavaScript function

<commandset>

A container for multiple <command> elements, it is used to group <command> elements into functional sets. The *id* attribute is used to uniquely identify the commandset. It may specify a command update handler to update its set of commands by using the attributes commandupdater, events, and *oncommandupdate*. When *commandupdater* is set to true, it means that this element will update its commands with a handler set by its *oncommandupdate* attribute. The *events* attribute specifies a comma-separated list of events to respond to when someone calls window.updateCommands() with one of these events. A <commandset>'s command update handler can do anything needed to update the commands.

Contains	A set of <command> elements
Attributes	*id, commandupdater, events, oncommandupdate*
Relevant Chapters/Examples	"Broadcasters, Observers, and Commands" in the "Visual Examples" section of this appendix.
See Also	<command>, <commands>, doCommand() core JavaScript function

<conditions>

Used with XUL templates, this tag is used to provide conditions for a rule. Contained in this element can be <content>, <member>, and <triple> elements, which create variable bindings from RDF data sources. When these conditions apply, the rule's <action> section generates dynamic content based on the variable bindings. This element is a logical element and does not contain the XUL core attributes or properties and methods.

Contained by	<rule>
Contains	<triple>, <member>, <content>
Relevant Chapters/Examples	Chapter 6, "RDF and XUL Templates"
See Also	<rule>, <template>, <content>,<member>, <triple>

<content>

Used to bind a variable to a content node in a XUL template, this element is required to be in the rule's <condition> section. This tag must contain the *uri* attribute, which matches each RDF data source for which the rule is to be applied. The value of the *uri* attribute can begin with a question mark (?) denoting a variable that will be bound to the data source applied by the XUL template. Because this element is a logical, nonvisible element, it does not contain the XUL core attributes. It does, however, contain the XUL core properties and methods.

Contained by	<conditions>
Attributes	*uri*

Properties Used by JavaScript	The following properties reference attributes of this element and are accessible and changeable by JavaScript: *uri*
Relevant Chapters/Examples	Chapter 6, "RDF and XUL Templates"
See Also	<rule>, <template>, <conditions>,<member>, <triple>

<deck>

This XUL element displays only one of its children at a time. The deck's *index* attribute lists which child element is to be displayed. The first child is referenced as the"0th element in the index.

Contained by	N/A
Attributes	*align, autostretch, collapsed, crop, debug, flex, height, index, left, orient, top, valign, width*
Relevant Chapters/Examples	"Stacks, Decks, and Grids" in the "Visual Examples" section of this appendix.

<editor>

This element presents a writeable view of the Web document specified in the *src* attribute.

Attributes	*autostretch, flex, height, left, src, top, width*
Properties Used by JavaScript	*editorShell*—similar to the browserShell property in the <browser> element.
See Also	<iframe>, <browser>

<grid>

The grid is an element that contains <rows> and <columns> elements.

Contains	<rows>, <columns>
Attributes	*align, autostretch, collapsed, crop, debug, flex, height, left, orient, top, valign, width*
Relevant Chapters/Examples	"Stacks, Decks, and Grids" in the "Visual Examples" section of this appendix.
See Also	<rows>, <columns>

<grippy>

This element appears on a splitter element or within a toolbox element. When someone clicks on the <grippy> element, it collapses or maximizes the components within its container.

Contained by	<toolbox>, <splitter>
Attributes	*accesskey, crop, default, disabled, flex, left, height, orient, src, top, width*
See Also	<splitter>, <toolbox>

<groupbox>

A <groupbox> element is a titled border around a box. If the first child of the element is a <label> element, it will set the border around itself as the value of the <label> element.

Contains	<label>
Attributes	*align, autostretch, crop, debug, flex, height, left, orient, top, valign, value, width*
See Also	Title

<hbox>

This is a container element that can contain any number of child elements. It is equivalent to the <box> element, defaulting to horizontal orientation.

Attributes	*align, autostretch, collapsed, crop, debug, flex, height, left, orient, top, valign, width*
See Also	<box>, <vbox>

<iframe>

Equivalent to the <browser> element, this element provides a view of a Web document, using the src attribute to specify the URL.

Attributes	*Autostretch, flex, height, left, src, top, width*
See Also	<browser>, <editor>

<image>

Equivalent to the HTML <img> element, this XUL element displays an image, using the *src* attribute to point to the URL of the image.

Contained by	N/A
Attributes	*flex, height, src, width*

<key>

This XUL element defines a keyboard shortcut, which can trigger event handlers. For visible printable characters, the *charcode* attribute sets the character that must be pressed. Otherwise, for nonprintable characters, the *keycode* attribute sets the keycode that must be pressed. The *modifiers* attribute is a comma-delimited list of modifier keys that should be used in tandem with the *charcode* or *keycode* attribute, and the possible list of the *modifier* attribute includes shift, alt, meta, control, and accel. When the *cancel* attribute is set to true, the events will be cancelled. Event attributes that are usually associated with keys are *onkeyup*, *onkeydown*, *onkeypress*, and *oncommand*.

Keycodes are preceded by the letters "VK_", and most of these are shown here:

VK_1, VK_2, VK_3. Numbers on the keyboard

VK_A, VK_B, VK_C. Letters on the keyboard.

VK_HOME, VK_END. The Home and End keys

VK_LEFT, VK_RIGHT. The Left Arrow and Right Arrow keys

VK_PAGE_UP, VK_PAGE_DOWN. The Page Up and Page Down keys

VK_INSERT, VK_DELETE, VK_ESCAPE. The Insert, Delete, and Esc keys

VK_F1, VK_F2, et al. The function keys

VK_NUMPAD0, VKNUMPAD1, VK_NUMPAD2. The keys on the number pad

VK_ENTER, VK_ALT, VK_CONTROL, VK_PRINTSCREEN. Other special keys

Contained by	<keyset>
Attributes	*Cancel, charcode, disabled, keycode, modifiers*
Relevant Chapters/Examples	*Broadcasters, Observers, and Commands in the "Visual Examples" section of this appendix.*
See Also	<keyset>

<keyset>

This is an invisible container element for <key> elements.

Contains	Multiple <key> elements
Attributes	*id, xulkey*
Relevant Chapters/Examples	*Broadcasters*, *Observers*, and *Commands* in the "Visual Examples" section of this appendix.
See Also	<key>

<label>

Unlike the <block> element, the <label> element is a text element label that does not wrap. It can be used as a label for another element by using the *for* attribute. If the text does not fit, it will be cropped according to the crop attribute.

Attributes	*crop, flex, for, height, left, orient, top, label, width*
See Also	<html>

<member>

Used with XUL templates to bind a variable to a node that matches children or containers of an element, the <member> element is contained in the rule's <condition> section. The child attribute matches the child of the current element, and the container attribute matches the container of the current element. The values of these two attributes are variable references, which begin with a question mark (?) denoting a variable that will be bound to the value of the child or container of the referenced node. Because this element is a logical, nonvisible element, it does not contain the XUL core attributes. It does, however, contain the XUL core properties and methods.

Contained by	<conditions>
Attributes	*child, container*
Relevant Chapters/Examples	Chapter 6, "RDF and XUL Templates"
Properties Used by JavaScript	The following properties reference attributes of this element and are accessible and changeable by JavaScript: *child, container*
See Also	<rule>, <template>, <content>,<member>, <triple>

<menu>

This element is contained by the <menubar> element. When the user clicks on this element, its child <menupopup> element is displayed. Its *data* attribute can contain information important to the XUL application and can be accessible by JavaScript.

Contained by	<menubar>
Contains	<menupopup>
Attributes	*accesskey, crop, data, disabled, flex, left, height, orient, src, top, label, width*
Properties Used by JavaScript	The following properties reference attributes of this element and are accessible and changeable by JavaScript: *data*
See Also	<menubar>, <menubutton>, <menuitem>, <menulist>, <menupopup>

<menubar>

This element is the main menu bar that contains menu elements.

Contains	<menu>
Attributes	*Align, autostretch, collapsed, crop, debug, flex, height, left, orient, top, valign, width*
See Also	<menu>, <menubutton>, <menuitem>, <menulist>, <menupopup>

<menubutton>

This element displays a button that, when clicked, displays a drop-down menu. Like the <menulist> element, a <menubutton> does not have to appear in the <menubar> hierarchy. It could be placed in any container. It contains a <menupopup> element that is the drop-down menu. Like <menu> and <menulist>, this element may include a *data* attribute that could contain information relative to the XUL application, and it can be referenced and manipulated as a JavaScript property. When the button is clicked, a function in the optional *oncommand* event attribute can be called.

Contains	<menupopup>
Attributes	*accesskey, crop, data, disabled, flex, left, orient, src, top, label, width*
Properties Used by JavaScript	The following properties reference attributes of this element and are accessible and changeable by JavaScript: *data*
See Also	<menu>, <menubar>, <menuitem>, <menulist>, <menupopup>

<menuitem>

The <menuitem> element is a single choice in a <menupopup> element. The *label* attribute contains the text that appears on the menuitem, and the *src* attribute may contain an URL of an image that appears on the menuitem. The *acceltext* attribute may contain the shortcut key used to select the menuitem, and the attributes *accesskey* and *modifiers* can also be used to represent key shortcuts, similar to the attributes in the <key> element. Like <menubutton> and <menulist>, this element may include a *data* attribute that could contain information relative to the XUL application, and it can be referenced and manipulated as a JavaScript property. When the <menuitem> element is clicked, a function in the optional *oncommand* event attribute can be called.

Contained by	<menupopup>
Attributes	*acceltext, accesskey, crop, data, disabled, flex, height, key, left, modifiers, oncommand, orient, src, top, label, width*
Properties Used by JavaScript	The following properties reference attributes of this element and are accessible and changeable by JavaScript: *Data*
See Also	<menu>, <menubar>, <menubutton>, <menulist>, <menupopup>

<menulist>

This element is a drop-down list of selectable items. When an item is selected, that selected choice is displayed in the list. Like the <menubutton> element, a <menulist> does not have to appear in the <menubar> hierarchy; it could be placed in any container. It contains a <menupopup> element that is the drop-down menu. The element's *label* attribute sets the label that will appear on the menulist. If the element's *editable* property is set to true, the user can type on the menulist to change its label. Like <menu> and <menubutton>, it may include a *data* attribute that could contain information relative to the XUL application, and it can be referenced and manipulated as a JavaScript property. In addition, two properties that can be referenced by JavaScript are *selectedItem and selectedIndex*, which return the value of the currently selected item and index of the item in the list, respectively.

Contains	<menupopup>
Attributes	*accesskey, crop, data, editable, label*
Properties Used by JavaScript	*data, selectedItem, selectedIndex*
See Also	<menu>, <menubar>,<menubutton>, <menupopup>

<menupopup>

This is a XUL element container that contains <menuitem> elements and will pop up these elements in a popup window. The <menupopup> has the *activeChild* property that can be used by JavaScript to reference or change the currently active <menuitem> element that it contains. The closePopup() JavaScript method is used to close the popup menu. The openPopup() method is used to display the popup menu relative to another element, specified by its parameters. Like the <popup> element, a <menupopup> element may have *oncreate* and *ondestroy* event attributes. A function set to the *oncreate* attribute will be called immediately before the information is popped up. A function set to the *ondestroy* attribute will be called immediately after the element disappears.

Contained by	<menu>, <menulist>, <menubutton>
Contains	<menuitem>
Attributes	*align, autostretch, crop, debug, flex, height, left, oncreate, ondestroy, orient, top, valign, width*
Properties Used by JavaScript	*activeChild*

Methods Used by JavaScript	closePopup(), openPopup (element, x, y, popupType, anchor, align)
See Also	<menu>, <menubutton>, <menuitem>, <menulist>,<menubar>, <popup>

<menuseparator>

This element is a thin line used to separate menu items. If the *label* attribute is set, a label will appear on the <menuseparator> element.

Contained by	<menupopup>
Attributes	*crop, flex, height, label, left, orient, top,width*
See Also	<menu>, <menubar>, <menubutton>, <menupopup>

<outliner>

Similar to the <tree> element, the <outliner> element displays data in tabular form. Unlike the <tree> element, however, populating an <outliner> with a large amount of data is incredibly fast. The <outliner> element also has added features, like sorting a column by clicking on the column name. Unlike the <tree> element, the <outliner> is entirely populated by a script.

Contains	<outlinercol>, <outlinerbody>
Attributes	*align, autostretch, collapsed, crop, debug, flex, height, left, orient, top, valign, width*
Properties Used by JavaScript	*currentIndex, selectionHead, selectionTail*
See Also	<outlinercol>, <outlinerbody>, <tree>

<outlinerbody>

The single element where the content of the <outliner> element is placed, this element occurs once within an <outliner> element. Users can select multiple rows of an outliner element, and when a row is selected by the user, the *onselect* event is sent to this element. The *onselect* attribute is usually set to a JavaScript function that handles the selection.

Contains	<outlinercol>, <outlinerbody>
Attributes	*align, autostretch, collapsed, crop, debug, flex, height, left, onselect, orient, valign, width*
See Also	<outlinercol>, <outliner>

<outlinercol>

The <outlinercol> element describes a column in the <outliner> widget. The *label* attribute for this element sets the label in the column. The *primary* attribute for the <outlinercol> can be set to true if it contains nested rows. Setting the *cycler* attribute to true or false denotes whether it can be turned "on" or "off."

Contains	?
Attributes	*align, autostretch, cycler, collapsed, crop, debug, flex, height, label, orient, primary, valign, width*
See Also	<outlinerbody>, <outliner>, <outlinercol>

<observes>

This element listens to <broadcaster> elements. The <observes> element also can listen to an attribute of an element, and when it is notified, it responds to the event with its *onbroadcast* attribute. The *element* attribute references the *id* of the element to which it is listening, and the *attribute* attribute references the attribute of the element to which it is listening. The *onbroadcast* attribute represents a JavaScript function which is called when the observer is responding to an event.

Attributes	*attribute, element, onbroadcast*
Relevant Chapters/Examples	"Broadcaster/Observer Example" in the "Visual Examples" section of this appendix.
See Also	<menu>, <menubutton>, <menuitem>, <menulist>,<menubar>

<overlay>

The overlay element is the root node of its own XUL file and is used for component reuse in XUL. The <overlay> element may contain a number of XUL elements. In a main XUL file that references an overlay file, an element with the same ID as an element in the <overlay> will be overlayed by the elements contained by the referenced overlay element. As this is a special element, it does not inherit any of the XUL Core attributes, methods, or properties.

Contains	Any XUL element
Attributes	*class, id*
Relevant Chapters/Examples	Chapter 7, "XUL Overlays and XBL," and Chapter 9, "Case Study: A Customizable Portal"

<popup>

A <popup> element is a container that pops up its child elements in a popup window and is commonly used for tooltips. When a XUL element sets its *tooltip* attribute to a <popup> element's ID, that <popup> element will be used as the tooltip. A child of the <popupset> element, it is never visible unless it is called by the JavaScript openPopup() method or when it is set up as a tooltip by another element. The <popup> element is similar to the <menupopup> element in the sense that it has the same attributes, methods, and properties. The openPopup() method is used to display the popup menu relative to another element, specified by its parameters. The closePopup() JavaScript method is used to close the popup menu. The *activeChild* property that can be used by JavaScript to reference or change the currently active item that the popup contains.

Like the <menupopup> element, a <popup> element may have *oncreate* and *ondestroy* event attributes. A function set to the *oncreate* attribute will be called immediately before the information is popped up. A function set to the *ondestroy* attribute will be called immediately after the element disappears.

Contained by	<popupset>
Attributes	*align, autostretch, crop, debug, flex, height, left, oncreate, ondestroy, orient, top, valign, width*
Properties Used by JavaScript	*activeChild*
Methods Used by JavaScript	closePopup(), openPopup (element, x, y, popupType, anchor, align)
See Also	<popupset>

<popupset>

The popupset element is an invisible container of popup elements. As this is an invisible container element, it does not inherit any of the XUL core attributes, methods, or properties.

Contains	<popup>
See Also	<popup>

<progressmeter>

The <progressmeter> element displays the status or progress of an operation. As the operation continues, the progressmeter's value increases. The element's *progresstext* attribute is the text that is displayed above the progressmeter. The *value* attribute can take values from 1 to 100, representing the percentage of completion of a task. The element's *mode* attribute can be set to "determined" if the value of the meter is determined by the element's *value* attribute. The *mode* attribute is set to "undetermined" if it is an indeterminate progress meter. The *mode*, *value*, and *progresstext* attributes can also be referenced or changed as JavaScript properties. The <progressmeter> optionally can contain an <observes> element in order to observe the progress of another element.

Contains	<observes>
Attributes	*align, autostretch, collapsed, crop, debug, flex, height, left, mode, orient, progresstext, top, valign, value, width*
Properties Used by JavaScript	*mode, progresstext, value*

<radio>

A <radio> element, sometimes referred to as a radio box, is an item that can be turned on or off. Radio elements are usually grouped together in a <radiogroup>, where only one radio element can be turned on at a time. The *group* attribute represents the group to which a <radio> element belongs. When the <radio> element is not contained by the <radiogroup> element, the *group* attribute is quite important, because only one item in a group can be turned on at a time. The *src* and the *label* attributes are optional attributes that list the image URL and the title of the radio item that will appear beside it, respectively. Like many other XUL elements, it may include a *data* attribute that could contain information relative to the XUL application, and it can be referenced and manipulated as a JavaScript property. In addition, the *accesskey, crop, disabled, group, imgalign, src,* and *label* attributes can also be referenced and changed as JavaScript properties. A <radio> element can also optionally have an *oncommand* event attribute.

Contained by	<radiogroup>
Attributes	*accesskey, crop, data, disabled, flex, group, height, left, orient, src, top, label, width*
Properties Used by JavaScript	The following properties reference attributes of this element and are accessible and changeable by JavaScript: *accesskey, crop, data, disabled, group, src, label*
See Also	<radiogroup>

<radiogroup>

A <radiogroup> is an element that acts as a group of <radio> buttons, and only one of these radio elements can be selected, or on, at a time. The <radiogroup> element can contain a <label> element and multiple <radio> elements. If the first child of <radiogroup> is a title element, it will be used as the titled border around the contained <radio> elements. The element contains one JavaScript property, *selectedItem*, which is the selected radio button in the group. The element's method, *checkAdjacentElement()* unselects the currently selected radio button, and either selects the next adjacent <radio> element or the previous adjacent <radio> element, depending on whether the "next" parameter has a true or false value. A <radiogroup> element can also have an *oncommand* event attribute.

Contains	<label>, <radio>
Attributes	*align, autostretch, crop, debug, flex, height, left, orient, top, valign, width*
Properties Used by JavaScript	*SelectedItem*
Methods Used by JavaScript	checkAdjacentElement (next)
See Also	<radio>

<resizer>

This element is used for window resizing but is seldom used.

Contained by	<Window>
Attributes	*align, autostretch, crop, debug, dir, flex, height, left, orient, top, valign, width*

<row>

The row element is a container of XUL elements that represents a visual row contained by the <rows> element. Within a <rows> element, the row with the most children determines the number of columns in each row of the grid.

Contained by	<rows>
Attributes	*align, autostretch, collapsed, crop, debug, flex, height, left, orient, top, width*
Relevant Chapters/Examples	*Stacks, Decks, and Grids* in the "Visual Examples" section of this appendix.
See Also	<rows>, <grid>, <columns>, <column>

<rows>

The rows element creates the rows of a grid.

Contained by	<grid>
Contains	<row>
Attributes	*align, autostretch, collapsed, crop, debug, flex, height, left, orient, top, valign, width*
Relevant Chapters/Examples	*Stacks, Decks, and Grids* in the "Visual Examples" section of this appendix.
See Also	<row>, <grid>, <columns>, <column>

<rule>

The <rule> element is used to define a logical rule in a XUL template. It must contain a <conditions> element as its first child and an <action> element as its last child, and they represent the conditions that must be met and the action that will be performed to dynamically generate content, respectively. Optionally, the <rule> element may contain a <bindings> element after the <conditions> section for optional variable bindings. When the <condition> section of a rule is matched, XUL content is dynamically generated in the <action> section. The optional *iscontainer* attribute is set to true or false when the rule's match is dependent on the node being marked as a container. If it is not specified, the rule will match whether or not the node is a container. The optional *isempty* attribute is set to true or false when the rule's match depends on the node having or not having children, respectively.

Contained by	<template>
Contains	<conditions>, <bindings> (optional), <action>
Attributes	*iscontainer, isempty*
Relevant Chapters/Examples	Chapter 6, "RDF and XUL Templates"
See Also	<template>, <conditions>,<member>, <content>,<triple>,<actions>, <bindings>, <binding>

<script>

Exactly the same as the <script> tag used with HTML, this element declares a JavaScript script used by the XUL window. The *src* attributes specifies the URL or filename of the script, or it can contain the actual script content.

Contained by	<window>
Attributes	*src*
Relevant Chapter(s)/Examples	Chapter 4, "XUL Interfaces," (main example),Chapter 7, "XBL and Overlays," and Chapter 9, "Case Study: A Customizable Portal"

<scrollbar>

The <scrollbar> element is used when the container contains elements than are larger than itself. The scrollbar element is placed in the container to allow the user to scroll within the window. The scrollbar's *curpos* attribute represents the current position of the thumb of the scrollbar and defaults to 0 but ranges from 0 to the scrollbar's *maxpos* attribute. The *pageincrement* attribute is the amount that the value of *curpos* changes when the area after the thumb of the scrollbar is clicked.

Contains	<slider>, <scrollbarbutton>
Attributes	*align, autostretch, collapsed, crop, curpos, debug, flex, height, increment, left, maxpos, orient, pageincrement, top, valign, width*
See Also	<scrollbarbutton>, <slider>, <thumb>

<scrollbarbutton>

The <scrollbarbutton> element is the button at the end of the scrollbar that is used to control the position of the scrollbar thumb.

Contained by	<scrollbar>
Attributes	*accesskey, crop, disabled, flex, height, left, orient, src, top, type, value, width*
See Also	<scrollbar>, <slider>, <thumb>

<scrollbox>

The scrollbox element is a box container with scrollbars inside it. It is used when the elements inside of it are too big to be shown without scrolling.

Attributes	*align, autostretch, collapsed, crop, debug, flex, height, left, orient, top, valign, width*
See Also	<box>, <hbox>, <vbox>, <scrollbar>

<separator>

Very similar to the <spring> element, the <separator> element is used to separate parts of a container, taking up space without displaying anything.

Contained by	Any Container element
Attributes	*crop, flex, height, left, orient, top, value, width*
See Also	<spring>,<toolbarseparator>

<slider>

The slider element is used in implementing a scrollbar and is the scrollbar without the scrollbar-button elements.

Contained by	<scrollbar>
Attributes	*align, autostretch, collapsed, crop, curpos, debug, flex, height, increment, left, maxpos, orient, pageincrement, top, valign, width*
See Also	<scrollbar>, <scrollbarbutton>, <thumb>

<splitter>

The splitter element is an element that appears before or after an associated element. When the splitter is dragged, the sibling elements are resized. When the grippy part on the splitter is clicked, one sibling element is collapsed. It can be contained by any visible container and does not have any children.

Attributes	*align, autostretch, collapse, debug, flex, height, left, orient, resizeafter, resizebefore, top, valign, width*
See Also	<grippy>

<spring>

The <spring> element is used to separate parts of a container, taking up space without displaying anything. It is equivalent to the <separator> element.

Contained by	Any Container element
Attributes	*crop, flex, height, left, orient, top, value, width*
See Also	<separator>

<stack>

The <stack> element places its children on top of each other and displays them all at once. The children elements are placed in stack order, with the first child being placed on the bottom.

Attributes	*align, autostretch, collapsed, crop, debug, flex, height, left, orient, top, valign, width*
Relevant Chapters/Examples	"Stacks, Decks, and Grids" in the "Visual Examples" section of this appendix.

<statusbar>

This is a box with status text inside of it. It may contain a number of <statusbarpanel> elements.

Contains	<statusbarpanel>
Attributes	*align, autostretch, collapsed, crop, debug, flex, height, left, orient, top, valign, width*
Properties Used by JavaScript	*src,value*
See Also	<statusbarpanel>

<statusbarpanel>

This element is a special status button contained in a <statusbar> element. Many <statusbarpanel> elements can be contained in a <statusbar>. For example, in the Netscape 6.x browser, a status bar at the bottom of the browser contains a <statusbarpanel> button that means work offline/online, a <statusbarpanel> that shows status (for example, "Document Done"), and a <statusbarpanel> that shows the security of the current session (locked/unlocked) button. The optional *src* attribute of the <statusbarpanel> element can reference the URL of an image that appears on the element. The optional *value* attribute contains text that will appear in the <statusbarpanel> element. The attributes *accesskey, crop, disabled, imgalign, src,* and *value* can all be referenced and changed as JavaScript properties.

Contained by	<statusbar>
Attributes	*accesskey, crop, flex, height, orient, src, value, width*
Properties Used by JavaScript	*accesskey, crop, disabled, src, value*
See Also	<statusbar>

<stringbundle>

This element can be used to load resources from property files. The *src* attribute specifies the URL of the property file. For a given property name, a user can call getString(propertyname) on this object to return the value of a certain property.

Contained by	<stringbundleset>
Attributes	*src*
Methods Used by JavaScript	getString(keyname)
See Also	<stringbundleset>

<stringbundleset>

This element is simply a container for <stringbundle> elements, and is used to group many <stringbundle> elements together.

Contains	<stringbundle>

<tab>

A <tab> element is a single tab inside of a tabbed panel (a <tabbox> element), and it represents the upper, clickable, labeled portion of the tabbed panel. When the user clicks on the tab, the associated content of this tab, which is in enclosed in its sibling element, <tabpanel>, is brought to the front of the tabbed panel. The *selected* attribute is a Boolean attribute that shows whether the current tab is selected and showing in the foreground. The *label* attribute is the label that is showing on the tab. The *selected* and *label* attributes are also properties that can be referenced and changed by JavaScript. In addition, the <tab> element has a JavaScript *tabs* property that represents the parent <tabs> element of the tab.

Contained by	<tabs>
Attributes	*align, autostretch, collapsed, crop, debug, flex, height, left, orient, selected, top, valign, label, width*
Properties Used By JavaScript	*selected, tabs, label*
Relevant Chapters/Examples	Chapter 4, "XUL Interfaces," main example
See Also	<tabbox>, <tabs>, <tabpanels>

<tabbox>

The <tabbox> element is the main element used to display tabbed panels. This element should contain two children. The first element is a <tabs> that contains the tabs listing the titles of each tab, and the second child should be the <tabpanels> that contains the contents of each tab. Like the <tabs> element, it contains the JavaScript property *selectedTab*, which allows the developer to reference or change the currently selected <tab> element.

Contains	<tabs>, <tabpanels>
Attributes	*align, autostretch, crop, debug, flex, height, left, orient, top, valign, width*
Properties Used by JavaScript	*selectedTab*
Relevant Chapters/Examples	Chapter 4, "XUL Interfaces," main example
See Also	<tabs>, <tab>, <tabpanels>

<tabpanel>

The <tabpanel> element is a child of the <tabpanels> element, and serves as a container for other XUL elements.

Contained by	<tabpanels>
Contains	XUL elements for each tab
Attributes	*align, autostretch, collapsed, crop, debug, flex, height, left, orient, top, valign, width*

Relevant Chapters/Examples	Chapter 4, "XUL Interfaces," main example
See Also	<tabs>, <tab>,<tabpanels>, <tabbox>

<tabpanels>

The <tabpanels> element should be the second child of <tabbox>, and it contains the contents of each selected tab. Each child that <tabpanels> contains is the content of each tab. For example, if the third child of <tabpanels> is a <box> element that contains buttons, this will correspond to the third <tab> element in its sibling element, <tabs>. When the third <tab> is clicked, the contents of the third child of <tabpanels> will be displayed. The *index* attribute of tabpanel is the index (starting with 0 representing the first child) into the children of <tabpanels> that is currently being displayed. The *index* attribute is also a JavaScript property that can be used to reference or change the page currently being displayed.

Contained by	<tabbox>
Contains	<tabpanel> elements
Attributes	*align, autostretch, collapsed, crop, debug, flex, height, index, left, orient, top, valign, width*
Relevant Chapters/Examples	Chapter 4, "XUL Interfaces,"main example
Properties/Methods Used by JavaScript	*index*
Relevant Chapters/Examples	"Layout Example" in the "Visual Examples" section of this appendix.
See Also	<tabs>, <tab>, <tabbox>

<tabs>

The first child element of <tabbox>, the <tabs> element contains a list of tab elements. It contains the JavaScript property *selectedTab*, which allows the developer to reference or change the currently selected <tab> element. The JavaScript method *advanceSelectedTab()* either selects the next or previous selected tab, depending on the argument being "1" or "−1".

Contained by	<tabbox>
Contains	<tab> elements
Attributes	*align, autostretch, collapsed, crop, debug, flex, height, left, orient, top, valign, width*
Properties Used by JavaScript	*selectedTab*
Properties/Methods Used by JavaScript	advanceSelectedTab(next)
Relevant Chapters/Examples	Chapter 4, "XUL Interfaces," main example
See Also	<tabbox>, <tab>, <tabpanels>

<template>

The template element is used to declare a template for the dynamic construction of elements from RDF data sources. This element is contained by any XUL elements referencing a data source with the *datasource* attribute that corresponds to a list of RDF data sources. Because this element is a logical, nonvisible element, it does not contain the XUL core attributes, JavaScript properties, or methods.

Contained by	Any XUL element referencing a *datasource* attribute
Contains	<rule>
Relevant Chapter(s)	Chapter 6, "RDF and XUL Templates"
See Also	<rule>, <conditions>, <member>, <content>, <triple>, <actions>, <bindings>, <binding>

<textbox>

The <textbox> element is a field in which the user can enter text, and it has many options. By default, a <textbox> contains one line, but the Boolean *multiline* attribute can be used to display multiple rows of text. The *maxlength* attribute is the maximum possible length (number of characters) of this field of text. The Boolean *readononly* attribute of <textbox> dictates whether or not the user can change the text. The *type* attribute of <textbox> can be set to "password" if you want to hide (with stars) what the user types. The *label* attribute is an attribute that is the text that will be presented in the text field.

The Boolean *autocomplete* and the *searchSessionType* attributes are interesting attributes that let the browser try to finish the text in the textbox; when *autocomplete* is true, the application looks at the *searchSessionType* attribute to determine how to guess the completion of the textbox. The *searchSessionType* attribute can either be urlbar or addrbook, pertaining to the user's URL history or names in his address book.

The <textbox> element has JavaScript properties that can be referenced or modified. The *selectionStart* property is an integer index value which is entered into the beginning position of the selected text, with 0 being the first character of the textbox. The *selectionEnd* property is the integer index value which is entered into the beginning position of the end of the selected text. The *textLength* property is the length of the value of the text entered in the textbox and can be referenced only and not modified by JavaScript. The JavaScript select() method in <textbox> selects all of the text in the textbox. The JavaScript setSelectionRange() method selects a portion of the text in the textbox, depending on its parameter range of "beginpos" and "endpos", which represents the integer values of where to start and end the selection, respectively.

Attributes	*accesskey, autocomplete, disabled, left, maxlength, multiline, readonly, search SessionType, size, top, type, value*
Properties Used by JavaScript	*selectionEnd, selectionStart, textLength*
Methods Used by JavaScript	select(), setSelectionRange (beginpos, endpos)

<thumb>

The thumb element is used to implement the scrollbar and slider elements. It is the rectangular object used to move the contents of the container within the scrollbar.

Contained by	<scrollbar>
Attributes	*align, autostretch, collapsed, crop, debug, disabled, flex, height, left, orient, top, valign, width*
See Also	<scrollbar>, <slider>, <scrollbarbutton>

<label>

The <label> element is used to provide a caption in a <groupbox> or a <radiogroup> element. Often, the <label> element contains a <label> element that contains the text of the title. Otherwise, its attribute *value* contains the text of the title. The <label> element can contain any XUL element, because a developer might want images or other elements in the title.

Contained by	<radiogroup>, <groupbox>
Contains	Any element, but usually a <label> element defining the title text.
Attributes	*crop, flex, height, left, orient, top, value, width*
See Also	<groupbox>, <radiogroup>

<toolbar>

A <toolbar> can contain any element, but it usually contains <button> elements and defaults to horizontal orientation. It can also contain a <toolbarseparator> to put space between buttons. In the case of using drag-and-drop with toolbars, the *dragdroparea* attribute may identify, via ID, a child element within the toolbar, which listens for the drag-and-drop events, such as draggesture, dragdrop, dragover, and dragexit. When a <toolbar> may want to respond to these events directly, the <toolbar> may use the *ondraggesture, ondragdrop, ondragover,* and *ondragexit* attributes.

Contained by	<toolbox> or any other container element
Contains	Usually contains <button>,<toolbarseparator>
Attributes	*align, autostretch, collapsed, crop, debug, dragdroparea, flex, height, left, orient, top, valign, width*
See Also	<toolbox>, <button>, <toolbarseparator>

<toolbarseparator>

The <toolbarseparator> element is used to separate buttons in a toolbar, taking up space without displaying anything. It is equivalent to the separator element but is used only within toolbars.

Contained by	<toolbar>
Attributes	*crop, flex, height, left, orient, top, label, width*
See Also	<spring>,<separator>,<toolbar>

<toolbox>

A <toolbox> is an optional container for toolbars. If a <toolbar> is placed inside a toolbox, a <grippy> element is displayed on its left or upper edge. The user may click the <grippy> to collapse the toolbar. The <toolbox> element can contain many <toolbar> elements, and it has two JavaScript methods. The collapseToolbar() method collapses the toolbar passed in as a parameter that is contained by the <toolbox> element. The expandToolbar() method expands the toolbar passed in as a parameter that is contained by the <toolbox> element.

Contains	One to many <toolbar> elements
Attributes	*align, autostretch, collapsed, crop, debug, flex, height, left, orient, top, valign, width*
Methods Used by JavaScript	collapseToolbar(toolbar), expandToolbar(toolbar)
See Also	Toolbar, grippy

<tree>

One of the most often used elements in XUL, the <tree> element is the main tree widget that can contain hierarchical, tree-based rows of elements, making it sometimes look like a combination of a table and a tree. This widget can contain any number of rows and columns. The tree's *multiple* attribute can be set to true or false, denoting whether it allows multiple items to be selected within it. The <tree> element must contain two children: a <treehead> element that defines the names of the columns and a <treechildren> element that defines the children (or tree items) of the tree. It may also contain a <treecolgroup> element that contains information about the columns of the tree. Tree content is very often generated from RDF data sources in XUL templates.

The <tree> element has two JavaScript properties: *selectedIndex* and *selectedItems*. The *selectedIndex* property is the integer index of the selected item in the tree, with 0 being the first element in the tree. The *selectedItems* property is an array of all of the selected items, which are <treeitems>, in the tree. Both properties can be referenced and changed by JavaScript.

The <tree> element has JavaScript methods that pertain to visibility, and the visibility concept is quite important. A visible element is one that is viewable by the user. For example, if there is a tree in a scrollable container, there may be rows and treeitems that are not visible because they have been scrolled off the visible area. The ensureElementIsVisible() method passes in an element contained by the tree, and if the tree is in a scrollable container, the scrollbar scrolls so that the element is visible. The ensureElementIndexIsVisible() method is quite similar but passes in the index of the element in the tree. The getIndexOfFirstVisibleRow() method returns the index of the first row in the tree that is visible to the user. The getNumberOfVisibleRows() method returns the number of rows that are currently visible in the tree.

The <tree> element has many JavaScript methods pertaining to finding and selecting items in the tree. The addItemToSelection() method passes in a <treeitem> element that is included in the tree and includes that item in the current selection. The select Item() method selects the <treeitem> element that is the parameter and deselects all other items. The clearItemSelection() method clears all selected items in the tree. The toggleItemSelection() method passes in a <treeitem> element and either selects or deselects that item contained within the tree. The removeItemFromSelection() method passes in a <treeitem> element, and it deselects this item from the tree. The getIndexOfItem() passes in a <treeitem> element as a parameter, and the index of that item in the tree is returned, with the 0th item being the first item in the tree. The getItemAtIndex() method passes in an index integer value and returns the treeitem that is at that position in the tree. The getNextItem() method passes in a <treeitem> element (item) and an integer (delta) and returns the item that is delta items after the treeitem passed. (For example, tree.getNextItem(item, 3) returns the item 3 places after the passed-in item.) The getPreviousItem() method finds the previous item in the same way. The getRowCount() method returns the number of rows in the tree. Very similar to the ensureElementIsVisible(), the scrollToIndex() passes in an integer value of the index of the item to be scrolled to but always forces a scroll event on the scrollbar.

Contains	<treecolgroup> <treehead><treechildren>
Attributes	*align, autostretch, collapsed, crop, debug, flex, height, left, multiple, orient, top, valign, width*
Properties Used by JavaScript	*selectedIndex, selectedItems*
Methods Used by JavaScript	Getting & Setting Treeitem visibility: ensureElementIsVisible (element), ensureIndexIsVisible (index), getIndexOfFirstVisibleRow(), getNumberOfVisibleRows (), Finding & Selecting Tree Information: addItemToSelection (item), clearItemSelection(), getIndexOfItem(item), getItemAtIndex (index), getNextItem (item, delta), getPreviousItem (item, delta), getRowCount (), removeItemFromSelection (item), scrollToIndex (index), select Item (item), toggleItemSelection (item)

Relevant Chapters/Examples	"Tree Examples" in the "Visual Examples" section of this appendix, and Chapter 4, "XUL Interfaces" (main example)
See Also	<treecell>, <treechildren>, <treecol>, <treecolgroup>, <treehead>, <treeitem>, <treerow>

<treecell>

A <treecell> element is a container element within a <treerow>. Although it usually contains text, it can contain any element. If it does not contain an element, it uses the *label* attribute to set the text of the <treecell>.

Contained by	<treerow>
Attributes	*align, autostretch, collapsed, crop, debug, flex, height, left, orient, top, valign, label, width*
Relevant Chapters/Examples	"Tree Examples" in the "Visual Examples" section of this appendix.
See Also	<tree>, <treechildren>, <treecol>, <treecolgroup>, <treehead>, <treeitem>, <treerow>

<treechildren>

A treechildren element is a tree element that defines multiple treeitem elements. It has no attributes and is just a simple container.

Contained by	<tree>
Contains	<treeitem> elements
Relevant Chapters/Examples	"Tree Examples" in the "Visual Examples" section of this appendix.
See Also	<tree>, <treecell>, <treecol>, <treecolgroup>, <treehead>, <treeitem>, <treerow>

<treecol>

A <treecol> element is contained by the <treecolgroup> element and contains sizing and other information about a specific column of the tree that will be referenced in the <treehead> element. This is an optional element in a tree widget.

Contained by	<treecolgroup>
Attributes	*align, autostretch, collapsed, crop, debug, flex, height, left, orient, top, valign, width*
Relevant Chapters/Examples	"Tree Examples" in the "Visual Examples" section of this appendix.
See Also	<tree>, <treecell>, <treechildren>, <treecolgroup>, <treehead>, <treeitem>, <treerow>

<treecolgroup>

An optional simple container contained by the <tree> element, it contains a collection of <treecol> elements, which contain information about the columns of the tree.

Contained by	<treecolgroup>
Relevant Chapters/Examples	"Tree Examples" in the "Visual Examples" section of this appendix.
See Also	<tree>, <treecell>, <treechildren>, <treecolgroup>, <treehead>, <treeitem>, <treerow>

<treehead>

A treehead defines the header row (or column names) of the tree. It contains <treecell> elements

Contained by	<tree>
Contains	<treecell> elements
Attributes	*align, autostretch, collapsed, crop, debug, flex, height, left, orient, top, valign, width*
Relevant Chapters/Examples	"Tree Examples" in the "Visual Examples" section of this appendix.
See Also	<tree>, <treecell>, <treecol>, <treecolgroup>, <treechildren>, <treeitem>,<treerow>

<treeitem>

A <treeitem> element contains <treerow> elements, and each <treeitem> element can be clicked to select the row of the tree. The <treeitem> element has three methods that can be called by JavaScript: open(), close(), and toggleOpenState(). The open() method expands the <treeitem> so that the contained <treerow> elements are visible, and the close() method collapses the <treeitem> so that the contained <treerow> elements are not visible. The toggleOpenState() method either collapses or expands the item, depending on its current state.

Contained by	<treechildren>
Contains	<treerow> elements
Attributes	*align, autostretch, collapsed, container, crop, debug, flex, height, left, open, orient, selected, top, valign,width*
Methods Used by JavaScript	*open(), close(), toggleOpenState()*
Relevant Chapters/Examples	"Tree Examples" in the "Visual Examples" section of this appendix.
See Also	<tree>, <treecell>, <treecol>, <treecolgroup>, <treechildren>, <treehead>, <treerow>

<treerow>

A treerow element is contained within a treeitem element and represents single rows of the tree.

Contained by	<treeitem>
Contains	<treecell> elements
Attributes	*align, autostretch, collapsed, crop, debug, flex, height, left, orient, top, valign, width*
Relevant Chapters/Examples	"Tree Examples" in the "Visual Examples" section of this appendix.
See Also	<tree>, <treecell>, <treecol>, <treecolgroup>, <treechildren>, <treehead>, <treeitem>

<triple>

Used with XUL templates to bind a variable to a node that matches the subject-predicate-object relationship in an RDF data source, this element is contained in the rule's <condition> section. The values of these attributes are variable references, which begin with a question mark (?) denoting variables that will be bound to the subject-predicate-object relationship. Because this element is a logical, nonvisible element, it does not contain the XUL core attributes. It does, however, contain the XUL core properties and methods.

Contained by	<conditions>
Attributes	*subject, predicate, object*
Relevant Chapters/Examples	Chapter 6, "RDF and XUL Templates"
See Also	<rule>, <template>, <content>,<member>, <triple>

<vbox>

<vbox> is a container element that can contain any number of child elements. It is equivalent to the box element, except for the fact that it defaults to vertical orientation.

Attributes	*align, autostretch, collapsed, crop, debug, flex, height, left, orient, top, valign, width*
See Also	<box>, <vbox>

<window>

The <window> element is the root node of the XUL document. Common attributes that are used in the <window> element are the *onload* and *onunload* event attributes described in the "Event Attributes for XUL" section of this appendix.

Contains	Any XUL element
Attributes	*align, autostretch, collapsed, crop, debug, flex, height, left, onload, onunload, orient, persist, title, top, valign, width*

XUL Core Attributes, Properties, and Methods

The following attributes, JavaScript properties, and JavaScript methods are core attributes inherent in every XUL element, unless otherwise stated in the "XUL Elements" section of this appendix.

XUL Core Attributes

Although the following attributes are the core and can be used by the XUL elements, many of these are only relevant when used in certain circumstances (XUL templates, XUL overlays, etc.). This section lists each attribute and describes the circumstances in which they are used. Corresponding to the syntax of this appendix, attributes are printed in *italics*.

allownegativeassertions. (true or false) This attribute is only relevant on a XUL element with a *datasources* attribute. When multiple data sources are used, one data source may override an assertion that another makes. Setting this attribute to true allows the override. (See Chapter 6, "RDF and XUL Templates").

chromeclass. This attribute is used to label an element belonging to a certain class of objects and specifies what type of chrome is being loaded.

class. This attribute represents the style class of the element.

coalesceduplicatearcs. (true or false) This element is relevant only on a XUL element with a *datasources* attribute. If the value of this attribute is true, no duplicate references will be denoted by the RDF graph in the following XUL template, in the case that there are several arcs pointing to the same node in the RDF graph. If the value of this attribute is false, the subsequent XUL template will allow duplicate references. (See Chapter 6, "RDF and XUL Templates.")

context. This attribute is set to the value of the ID of a popup element that should appear when the user right-clicks on the XUL element.

datasources. Used to reference an external data source in XUL templates for dynamic XUL generation, this attribute is a set of data sources separated by spaces. The values for this attribute can be URLs of multiple RDF files or internal references to the applications, such as rdf:bookmarks. The application combines all data sources into what is called a composite data source referenced by the *database* property of the same element. Sometimes, when looking at the Netscape XUL code, you will see "rdf:null" as a value of the *datasource* attribute, because a script dynamically adds data sources to the object with the *database* property. (See Chapter 6, "RDF and XUL Templates.")

grippytooltiptext. For composite widgets that may contain <grippy> elements, such as <toolbar> elements, <menubar> elements, and <box> elements, this text appears when the user places his mouse over the grippy.

id. This attribute uniquely identifies a XUL element, and it is used when finding elements with the DOM API (for example, getElementById()).

insertafter. This attribute only applies to elements that are children of <overlay> elements. This attribute specifies the unique identifier *(id)* of the element that the current element should appear after. If there is no such *id*, this attribute is ignored. This attribute overrides the *position* attribute if it matches an element.

insertbefore. This attribute only applies to elements that are children of <overlay> elements. This attribute specifies the unique identifier *(id)* of the element that the current element should appear before. If there is no such *id*, this attribute is ignored. This attribute overrides the *position* attribute if it matches an element.

observes. This attribute is set to the *id* of a <broadcaster> element that is being observed by the element.

persist. This attribute lists the attributes of the XUL element that will be stored persistently. When the application is restarted, the values of these attributes will be remembered. Attributes of the element are stored in this element, separated by spaces.

popup. This attribute is set to the *id* of a <popup> element that should pop up when a user clicks on it.

popupalign. This attribute is relevant only when there is a *popup* attribute that specifies a <popup> element. It specifies the position at which corner of the popup appears at the location set by the *popupanchor* attribute. The acceptable values are "bottomleft," "bottomright," "topleft," and "topright."

popupanchor. This attribute is relevant only when there is a *popup* attribute that specifies a <popup> element. It specifies the position at which corner of the current element the popup appears. If not specified, this defaults to "none," where the popup element pops up at the current mouse position, and acceptable values are "none," "bottomleft," "bottomright," "topleft," and "topright."

position. This attribute applies only to elements that are children of <overlay> elements. This attribute specifies the position (beginning with 1 for the 1st element) where the element is placed. If the *insertbefore or insertafter* attribute successfully matches an element, the *position* attribute is ignored.

ref. This attribute is relevant only on a XUL element with a *datasources* attribute when generating content based on XUL templates. This attribute specifies the URI of the root node in a RDF data source. (See Chapter 6, "RDF and XUL Templates.")

style. CSS style rules can be placed directly in the *style* attribute to any XUL element. (See Chapter 3, "Using Cascading Style Sheets.")

tooltip. This attribute is set to the *id* of the <popup> element that should pop up when the user hovers his/her mouse over the element.

uri. This attribute is only relevant on a XUL element that is being dynamically generated in the <action> section of a XUL <template> element. It is used with XUL templates to give dynamically generated content unique IDs that map to RDF data sources. (See Chapter 6, "RDF and XUL Templates.")

XUL Core JavaScript Properties

The next two sections list JavaScript properties that are accessible by XUL elements. These properties are placed into two sections: DOM (Document Object Model) properties that are available for use with any XML-based object in JavaScript and Non-DOM properties that correspond directly to XUL elements.

DOM JavaScript Properties

attributes. This property is an array of DOM "Attr" objects.

childNodes. This property is an array of the children of the current element.

firstChild. This property is the first child of the element.

lastChild. This property is the last child of the element.

nextSibling. This property is the next sibling, or the element that occurs immediately after the current element.

nodeName. This property is the tag name of the element. For example, a <menu> element's nodeName is menu.

nodeType. For all XUL elements, the value is 1, which means that it is an element.

nodeValue. This property is the value of the node, if it has a value.

ownerDocument. This property is the document in which the element is contained.

parentNode. This property is the parent (or container) element.

previousSibling. This property refers to the element immediately before the current element.

tagName. Equivalent to the *nodeName* attribute, this is the tag name of the element.

Non-DOM JavaScript Properties

boxObject. This property is relevant only when the XUL element is derived from the <box> element. Most containers in XUL are derived from boxes. The *boxObject* property contains four attributes that can be referenced or changed: *x*, *y*, *width*, and *height*.

builder. This property is a JavaScript object, and it is relevant to XUL elements that are within a <template> element for dynamically generated content. When you might want to rebuild content when the data sources have changed, you may call the rebuild() method on the builder object.

className. This property is relevant to every XUL element, and it is used to get and set the *class* attribute.

controllers. This property is an object that contains controller objects that can be set up in JavaScript to perform commands. A controller object allows you to associate more functions with XUL elements in JavaScript, but a controller can be used by many XUL elements by using the appendController() method on the *controllers* property and passing in a new controller object.

database. This property is a JavaScript object that represents a composite data source created when a XUL element references one or more data sources with the *datasources* attribute. The *database* property has several methods: AddDataSource(datasource), RemoveDataSource(datasource), AddObserver(observer), and RemoveObserver(observer). When JavaScript is used to find the current data sources and change the current *datasources* attribute for an element, this property is used. A good example of this is shown in Code Listing 9.2 in Chapter 9, "A Customizable Portal."

id. This property allows a JavaScript script to set or get the *id* attribute of a XUL element.

resource. This property is usually used with RDF and XUL templates when associating XUL elements with URIs of RDF resources and can be passed into Netscape's RDF engine by calling the RDF.GetResource(element.resource) method.

style. This property allows a JavaScript script to set or get the *style* attribute of a XUL element.

XUL Core JavaScript Methods

The next two sections list JavaScript methods that can be used to access XUL elements. These methods are placed into two sections: DOM (Document Object Model) methods that are available for use with any XML-based object in JavaScript and Non-DOM methods that correspond directly to XUL elements.

DOM JavaScript Methods

appendChild(node). This JavaScript method appends a new node (the parameter) to the end of an element's children. This JavaScript method could be used to add buttons to a toolbar or menuitems to a menu. It returns the appended child.

cloneNode (deep). This JavaScript method performs a copy of the current node and returns it. If the "deep" parameter is set to true, the method returns the current node and all of its descendants. Otherwise, it returns the node by itself.

getAttribute(name). This JavaScript method returns the XUL element's attribute value specified by the "name" parameter.

getAttributeNS(namespace, name). This method returns the element's attribute value that matches the given name and namespace.

getAttributeNode(name). Based on the "name" parameter of the attribute, this JavaScript method returns the element's *Attr* object, which can be used to manipulate the attribute.

getAttributeNodeNS(namespace, name). This JavaScript method returns the element's *Attr* object that can be used to manipulate the attribute, based on the attributes' "name" and "namespace" that are passed in.

getElementsByTagName(name). This JavaScript method returns an array of child elements of the current element that match the tag name that is passed in.

getElementsByTagNameNS(namespace,name). This JavaScript method returns an array of child elements of the current element that match the tag name and namespace that is passed in.

hasAttribute(name). This JavaScript method returns the Boolean value "true" or "false," based on whether or not the element has the attribute specified by the "name" parameter that is passed in.

hasAttributeNS(namespace,name). This JavaScript method returns the Boolean value "true" or "false," based on whether or not the element has the attribute specified by the attributes' "name" and "namespace" parameters that are passed in to the method.

hasChildNodes ( ). This method returns "true" if the node contains any child elements.

insertBefore (newchild, currentchild). This method inserts the "newchild" node right before the "currentchild" node that is a current child of the XUL element. It returns the new child node.

removeAttribute (name). If the element has an attribute matching "name," this JavaScript method removes it.

removeAttributeNS (namespace, name). If the element has an attribute with matching "name" in the given namespace "namespace," this JavaScript method removes it.

removeChild (child). This method removes the child passed in as a parameter and returns the child.

replaceChild (newchild, oldchild). This JavaScript method replaces a child element of the current XUL element. Specified by the parameters, the "oldchild" element is replaced by a new "newchild" element, and the old removed child is returned.

setAttribute (name,value). This JavaScript method changes the value of the attribute specified by "name" to the value "value."

setAttributeNS (namespace, name, value). This JavaScript method changes the value of the attribute specified by "name" and "namespace" to the value "value."

Non-DOM JavaScript Methods

addBroadcasterListener(attribute, element). By using this JavaScript method, an element can observe an attribute on a <broadcaster> element. Equivalent to setting the *observes* and *attribute* attributes on an element, this element listens to the element's attribute, and when this attribute is changed, the event is fired, and the attribute is notified. The "attribute" parameter is the attribute that it is listening to, and the "element" parameter is the <broadcaster> element to which the element is listening.

addEventListener(type, listener, capture). This JavaScript method adds a new event listener for the event specified on an element. The "type" parameter is the event type. (For example, the types for "onclick" and "oncommand" are "click" and "command," respectively). The "listener" parameter is the name of a function that will handle the event. The "capture" parameter is a Boolean parameter ("true" or "false"), denoting whether or not the event should capture.

blur(). This JavaScript method removes focus from the element.

click(). This JavaScript method executes a click on the XUL element, essentially calling the onClick() event handler for the element.

doCommand(id). This method executes a <command> element that has the *id* of the value passed into the JavaScript method.

focus(). This JavaScript method gives focus to the element.

getElementsByAttribute(attribute, value). This JavaScript method is a convenience function that returns an array of all of the elements in the document with the given attribute with the given value.

removeBroadcastListener(attribute, element). The opposite of the addBroadcastListener() JavaScript function, this JavaScript method removes the broadcast listener from an element.

removeEventListener(type, listener, capture). The opposite of the addEventListener JavaScript function, this JavaScript method removes the event listener from an element.

Basic XUL Attributes

Although not common to every XUL element, the following attributes are used by many XUL elements. In the "XUL Elements" section of this appendix, these would be listed in the "Attributes" section if they apply to the element.

align. Usually an attribute of container elements, *align* determines the alignment of the children of the container. Possible values for the *align* attribute are "left," "center," and "right".

accesskey. Usually an attribute for various types of <button> and <menuitem> elements, this attribute can be set to a letter that is used as a shortcut key. The letter is usually one of the characters in the element's text label and usually appears underlined. When the user presses ALT and the access key is defined by the *accesskey* attribute, the element will be activated.

autostretch. Used in many XUL elements, this attribute determines whether the item stretches to fill its space.

collapsed. An attribute that is used for many XUL elements, when set to "true" the *collapsed* attribute will make the element not visible.

crop. Usually an attribute corresponding to container elements with labels and text, the *crop* attribute gives direction on how to cut off areas that do not fit in a space. The possible values of this attribute are "left," "right," "center," and "none" to specify where the cropping (usually text cutting) should occur.

data. Many XUL elements include a *data* attribute that can be set to contain information relative to the XUL application. This causes no XUL-specific functionality, but it is usually referenced and manipulated as a JavaScript property.

debug. An attribute that can be set to a Boolean property, this attribute can be set to "true" to draw extra borders around the element and all of its descendants. For different types of container elements, horizontally aligned containers are drawn with blue borders, and vertically aligned containers are drawn with red borders. Borders above flexible elements (see *flex* attribute) will be wavy. This is done for debugging purposes, so that the XUL developer can work out alignment issues.

disabled. This Boolean attribute, which can be set to "true" or "false," is used to "grey out" <menu>, <menuitem>, and <button> elements to make them disabled.

flex. An attribute used by many XUL elements, the *flex* attribute indicates the flexibility of an item. Items that are very flexible grow and shrink to fit their space. The value of the *flex* attribute is usually a percentage (*flex*="100%"). An element with a large flexibility grows more than an element with lower flexibility. The layout manager determines the ratio of flexibility before the elements are drawn.

height. This attribute sets the value of the height of the element in pixels.

left. For some XUL elements, this specifies the position of the left edge of the element.

orient. The *orient* attribute is used by many XUL elements to specify whether the children of an element are oriented vertically or horizontally. The possible values for this attribute are "vertical" and "horizontal."

top. For some XUL elements, this specifies the position of the top edge of the element

valign. For many XUL elements, this attribute specifies the vertical alignment of the children of an element. The possible values are "top," "bottom," "middle," and "baseline" to specify whether the children are aligned by their top edges, their bottom edges, centered vertically, or by their text baseline, respectively.

width. This attribute sets the value of the width of the element in pixels.

Event Attributes for XUL

The following attributes set up optional event attributes for most visible XUL elements. In this section, we will reference these attributes as event handlers and attributes interchangeably, and we will reference the values of these attributes as "event handlers." For example, we will say that the following <button> element contains an *onclick* attribute, or we could also say that we are setting its *onclick* event handler to "clickFunction()." At the same time, we will say that the onclick event occurs when the user clicks on the button:

```
<button id="test_element" onclick="clickFunction()"/>
```

The value of each of these attributes is set to a JavaScript function call. For each of the event handler attributes in this section, we give a brief description, and wherever possible, we reference an example in sections of this book.

onblur. The opposite of an *onfocus* event attribute, the *onblur* event is called when the focus has left an element.

onbroadcast. This attribute is relevant when the element is an observer of a <broadcaster> element by containing the <observes> element or by using the *observes* attribute. The *onbroadcast* event is called when the listened attributes of the <broadcaster> are changed. An example of the usage of this attribute is shown in the "Broadcasters, Observers, and Commands" example, under the "Visual Examples" section of this appendix.

onchange. Usually related to an <observer> element, this event is triggered when an element's attributes (or the attribute that an observer is listening to) is changed.

onclick. This attribute is used for any clickable elements such as <button>. When the button is pressed with the mouse, the *onclick* event handler will be called.

onclose. This attribute is used for the <window> element and is used to gather information about the window before it is closed or to override the close() method. When the window.close() method is called, the event handler (JavaScript function) referenced by this attribute will be called. If the JavaScript function that is referenced by this attribute returns "true," the window will close normally. If the JavaScript function returns false, the window will not close.

oncommand. This attribute is used to set an action event handler for various elements, such as <button>, <menuitem>, and <command> elements. The *oncommand* event handler is called when an action is performed on the item (usually a click). It can be used as an alternative to the *onclick* attribute. An example of the usage of this attribute is shown in the "Broadcasters, Observers, Commands, and Keys" example, under the "Visual Examples" section of this appendix.

oncommandupdate. Used for the <commandset> element when the *commandupdater* attribute is true, this event is called when one of the <command> elements contained by the <commandset> is updated. A command is updated when its controller changes its *disabled* attribute to "true" or "false."

oncreate. An event called immediately before a <popup> or <menupopup> element is popped up, this attribute can be called to change the contents of the popup before it appears.

ondblclick. Like the *onclick* attribute, this can be set to call a function when a user double-clicks on an element.

ondestroy. An event called immediately after a <popup> or <menupopup> element is closed, this attribute can be set to call a function to process information after the popup.

ondragdrop. An event that is called at the end of a drag-and-drop event (the drop) when the user releases his mouse. The function set to this attribute should handle the result of the drag-and-drop operation.

ondragenter. This event is called in a drag-and-drop event when the user's mouse first enters an element. The function set to this attribute can handle the beginning of the drag-and-drop information.

ondragexit. This event is called after an *ondragdrop* event and when the user's mouse leaves an element in the drag-and-drop event. The function set to this attribute should be used carefully (because it can be called multiple times).

ondraggesture. This event is called at the beginning of a drag-and-drop event (the drag).

ondragover. This event is called during a drag-and-drop event when an item is being dragged over an element. When this attribute is set to a JavaScript event handler, the event handler is usually used to allow or deny the element being dragged to be dropped into the element.

onfocus. This event is called when a XUL element receives focus, and it is the opposite of an *onblur* event. When an element has focus, it can receive key events. Although the usage of this event attribute is not used in the example,
we call the window.focus() method to allow key commands in the "Broadcasters, Observers, Commands, and Keys" example, under the "Visual Examples" section of this appendix.

oninput. Used for <textbox> elements, this event is called when a key is pressed into a <textbox>. For <textbox> elements, this is exactly the same as the *onkeypress* event. This can be used for "smart" <textbox> functionality, where the programmer might want to try to finish the item in the <textbox> for the user.

onkeydown. When an element has focus and the user presses a key, this event is called when the key is down but not yet released.

onkeypress. When an element has focus, and the user presses a key, this event is called. This is similar to the *oninput* event for the <textbox> element.

onkeyup. When an element has focus, and the user presses a and releases a key, this event is called.

onload. Associated with the <window> element, this event is called after the XUL document has been completely loaded.

onmousedown. When the user clicks his mouse on an element, this event is called when the mouse is down and is not released.

onmousemove. When the user moves his mouse over an element, this event is called.

onmouseout. When the user's mouse does not appear over an element, this event is called.

onmouseover. When the user's mouse appears (or hovers) over an element, this event is called.

onmouseup. When the user clicks his mouse on an element, this event is called after the mouse click has been released.

onoverflow. Pertaining to container elements like the <box> element, this event is called when there is not enough given space to display its contents. By setting a JavaScript event handler to this attribute, you can handle this dilemma by resizing the window or by asking the user to resize the window until the *onoverflowchanged* or *onunderflow* event occurs, which means that the item has enough space to display it.

onoverflowchanged. When a container's "overflow" state has changed, this means that it either now has enough space to display its contents, or it means that it now does not have enough space to display its contents. When this state is changed, this event is called.

onselect. Usually associated with <tree> elements, this element is called when an item in the tree is selected.

onunderflow. When a container's "overflow" state has changed to the point where it has enough space to display its contents, this event is called.

onunload. Pertaining to the <window> element, this event is called after the window has been closed.

Visual Examples of XUL Elements

This section lists a few examples that demonstrate some XUL elements and concepts that may not have been emphasized in the rest of this book. The examples listed in this section demonstrate a few important concepts:

Stacks, Decks, and Grids. This example shows these types of layout elements.

Tree Examples. Although there were many examples of trees in this book, this example shows the versatility of the XUL tree elements.

Broadcasters, Observers, Commands, and Keys. This example demonstrates the power of using broadcasters and observers.

Stacks, Decks, and Grids

Code Listing A.1 shows an example XUL file of how the <stack>, <deck>, and <grid> elements are used. Figure A.1 shows a screen capture of the result. The example is a <grid> element that contains both a <stack> and a <deck> element, which contains buttons.

Figure A.1 shows that the <stack> elements are placed directly on top of each other, causing the first row of the example to look like the text string, "Hello, World!" Because the *index* attribute of the <deck> element is "2," we see the "Card C" button being displayed in the second row. If the user clicks on the button in the deck, it will call the toNextCard() JavaScript function, which will cycle through the elements in the deck.

Tree Examples

The following two examples of using trees show how versatile XUL tree elements can be. Our first example, in Code Listing A.2 and shown in Figure A.2 shows how <tree> elements can look like a simple table. Our second example, shown in Code Listing A.3 and Figure A.3 shows how our tree can look like a combination of a tree and a table.

Figure A.2 shows the result of the tree listing from Code Listing A.1.

In Code Listing A.3, we add two folders, Relatives and Business Associates, demonstrating the user interface shown in Figure A.3.

```
<?xml version="1.0"?>
<!-- Stacks, Decks, and Grids Example
 -->
<window id="main-window" xmlns:html="http://www.w3.org/1999/xhtml"

xmlns="http://www.mozilla.org/keymaster/gatekeeper/there.is.only.xul">
   <html:script language="JavaScript">
     function toNextCard()
     {
          var deck = document.getElementById("deckexample");
          var index = deck.getAttribute("index");
          index++;
          if (index > 2)
               index = 0;
          deck.setAttribute("index",index);
     }
   </html:script>
   <grid flex="1" >
      <!-- We will only have one column in our grid, and it will
           have 100%, flexibility -->
      <columns>
         <column flex="1"/>
      </columns>

      <rows>
        <row flex="1"
             style="background-color:lightblue; border: 1px solid
black">
           <!--Stacks pile everything on top of each other!-->
           <stack>
             <button label="Hello" />
             <button label="       ," />
             <button label="              World!"/>
           </stack>
        </row>
        <row flex="1" style="border: 3px solid black">
           <!-- For the deck, the index attribute is important! -->
           <deck id="deckexample" index='2' flex="1">
             <button label="Card A" style="background-color:yellow;"
                     onclick="toNextCard()"/>
             <button label="Card B" style="background-color:orange;"
                     onclick="toNextCard()"/>
             <button label="Card C" style="background-
color:lightgreen;"
                     onclick="toNextCard()"/>
           </deck>
        </row>
      </rows>
   </grid>

</window>
```

Code Listing A.1 Stack, deck, and grid example.

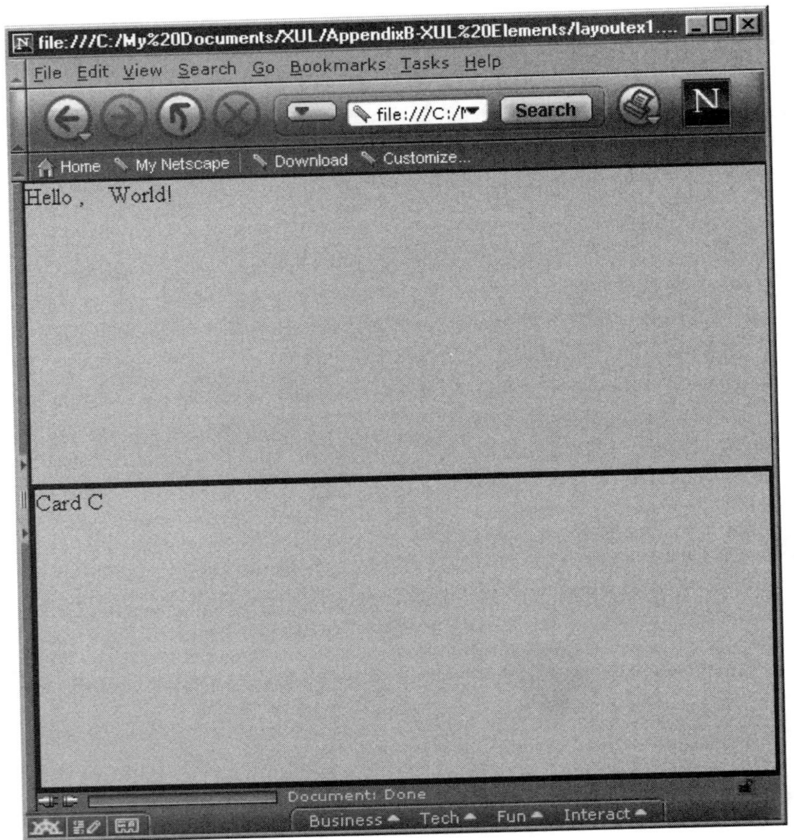

Figure A.1 Stack, deck, and grid example.

```
<?xml version="1.0"?>
<!-- This is a good example of how the XUL "tree" element
     can look like a table. It will be an "address book"
     box with a purple background, containing a tree that
     has three columns and four rows.
 -->
<window id="main-window" xmlns:html="http://www.w3.org/1999/xhtml"
       xmlns="http://www.mozilla.org/keymaster/gatekeeper/
there.is.only.xul">
 <box style="background-color: #FFCCFF; border: 1px solid blue"
flex="1">
   <tree flex="1" >
      <!--the treecolgroup part makes the tree columns align properly!
 -->
```

Code Listing A.2 An addressbook table.

```
        <treecolgroup>
          <treecol flex="1"/>
          <treecol flex="1"/>
          <treecol flex="1"/>
        </treecolgroup>
        <treehead style="background-color: #FFFFCC; border: 1px solid
         black">
          <treerow>
            <treecell label="Name"/>
            <treecell label="Address"/>
            <treecell label="Phone Number"/>
          </treerow>
        </treehead>
        <treechildren >
          <treeitem >
            <treerow >
              <treecell label="Sean Cullinan"/>
              <treecell label="4545 Strawberry Place"/>
              <treecell label="555-1342"/>
            </treerow>
          </treeitem>
          <treeitem>
            <treerow>
              <treecell label="Allen Finch"/>
              <treecell label="123 Mockingbird Lane"/>
              <treecell label="555-1112"/>
            </treerow>
          </treeitem>
          <treeitem>
            <treerow>
              <treecell label="Pat Ledesma"/>
              <treecell label="423 Rockingham Dr"/>
              <treecell label="555-2341"/>
            </treerow>
          </treeitem>
          <treeitem>
            <treerow>
              <treecell label="Kenny Stockman"/>
              <treecell label="32 Hornist Ave"/>
              <treecell label="555-3452"/>
            </treerow>
          </treeitem>
        </treechildren>
    </tree>
  </box>
</window>
```

Code Listing A.2 An addressbook table (Continued).

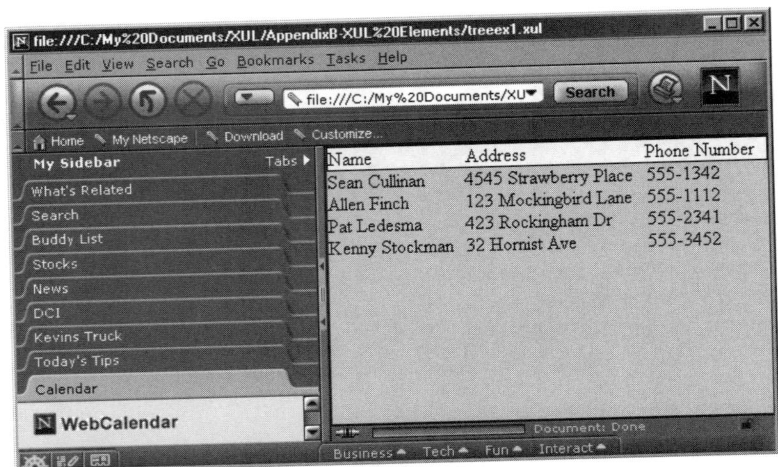

Figure A.2. Screen capture of addressBook.

```
<?xml version="1.0"?>
<!-- This is a good example of how the XUL "tree" element
     can have columns with multiple expandable elements
 -->

<window id="main-window" xmlns:html="http://www.w3.org/1999/xhtml"
        xmlns="http://www.mozilla.org/keymaster/gatekeeper/
        there.is.only.xul">

 <box style="background-color: #FFCCFF; border: 1px solid blue"
flex="1">
        <tree open="true" container="true" flex="1">
           <treecolgroup>
           <treecol flex="1"/>
           <treecol flex="1"/>
           <treecol flex="1"/>
           </treecolgroup>
           <treehead
              style="background-color: #FFFFCC; border: 1px solid
               black">
             <treerow>
                 <treecell label="Name"/>
                 <treecell label="Address"/>
                 <treecell label="Phone Number"/>
             </treerow>
           </treehead>
          <treechildren id="panelChildren" flex="1">
            <treeitem container="true" open="true"
                      id="relFolder" position="3">
```

Code Listing A.3 An addressbook with multiple folders.

```
            <treerow>
              <treecell class="treecell-indent" label="Relatives"/>
            </treerow>
            <treechildren id="Relatives" flex="1">
              <treeitem>
                <treerow>
                  <treecell class="treecell-indent" label="Gran"/>
            <treecell   label="1234 Main St"/>
                  <treecell  label="555-4321"/>
                </treerow>
              </treeitem>
              <treeitem>
                <treerow>
                  <treecell class="treecell-indent" label="Abah"/>
            <treecell   label="321 Fairview Lane"/>
                  <treecell  label="555-5231"/>
                </treerow>
              </treeitem>              </treechildren>
          </treeitem> <!-- end of relatives -->
          <!-- business -->
          <treeitem container="true" open="true" id="busFolder"
           position="3">
            <treerow>
              <treecell class="treecell-indent"
                label="Business Associates"/>
            </treerow>
            <treechildren id="Business" flex="1">
              <treeitem>
                <treerow>
                  <treecell class="treecell-indent"
                  label="Dave Bishop"/>
            <treecell   label="1234 XML Drive"/>
                  <treecell  label="555-2134"/>
                </treerow>
              </treeitem>
              <treeitem>
                <treerow>
                  <treecell class="treecell-indent" label="Joe
                    Pecore"/>
                 <treecell   label="2123 XSLT Lane"/>
                  <treecell  label="555-2345"/>
                </treerow>
              </treeitem>
            </treechildren>
          </treeitem> <!-- end of business associates -->
        </treechildren>
      </tree>
    </box>
</window>
```

Code Listing A.3 An addressbook with multiple folders (Continued).

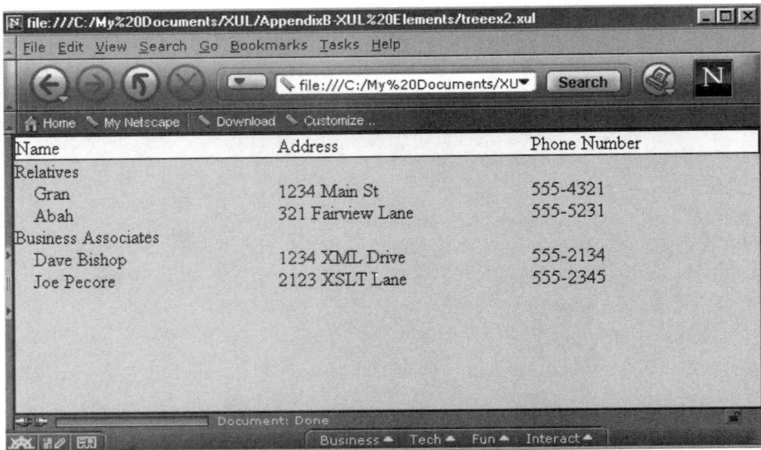

Figure A.3 AddressBook folder example.

Broadcasters, Observers, and Commands

In this example, we will demonstrate the power of using broadcasters, observers, and commands. When many elements in application call the same function or depend on the same information, it is sometimes helpful to centralize functionality. XUL enables developers to do this by having elements observe <broadcaster> and <command> elements.

A <command> element usually represents an executable JavaScript function and is used when many elements (such as <key>s, <button>s, and <menuitem>s) call the function. Any element can call the function of the <command> element by using the *observes* attribute and referencing the ID of the <command> element.

Although <broadcaster> elements can do the same thing as <command> elements, the <broadcaster> element is mainly used when many elements want to share one attribute. Sometimes, elements need to listen to only one attribute (usually the disabled attribute) from a broadcaster. When a change to the <broadcaster>'s attribute occurs, this fires an event that will change the observer element's attribute. An element can observe a <broadcaster> or a <command> by setting its *observes* and *attribute* attributes to the broadcaster ID and the attribute it wants to listen to, or it can contain an <observes> element. Of course, elements may observe many broadcasters or commands.

The following example shows that we can centralize functionality with <command> and <broadcaster> elements and shows how we can use <observers> or the *observes* attribute to connect these elements to common functionality. In our example, we have buttons, menus, and menuitems that share common functionality. To demonstrate the functionality of broadcasters and observers, we have presented different ways of observing commands and broadcasters in the example. Code Listing A.4 shows the XUL file that demonstrates the elements; Code Listing A.5 shows the JavaScript for this example; and Code Listing A.6 shows the CSS for this example. Figure A.4 shows the result.

Our example is simple. The functionality commands of this program are "open," "cut," "copy," and "paste." In our example, we have menuitems, keys, and buttons that will perform this functionality. In Code Listing A.4, we have a set of <broadcasters> in a <broadcasterset>, and we have one <command> element in a <commandset> that perform this functionality. At the same time, we have included a <colorpicker> element, and we have four buttons in our example observing a <broadcaster> that changes its *colorname* attribute every time the user clicks on a different color in the <colorpicker>. When someone clicks on the <colorpicker> element, the selectColor() function from the JavaScript file in Code Listing A.5 is called.

The four buttons at the bottom of the user interface of this application will be listening to this broadcaster, and when it gets an *onbroadcast* event, it will call the changeColor() JavaScript function. When someone clicks on the <colorpicker> element, the selectColor() function from Code Listing A.5 is called. In the selectColor() JavaScript function, we set the attribute of the colorcaster broadcaster to the color that was selected. When this happens, the broadcaster sends its events to every element observing it.

A screen shot of this example is shown in Figure A.4.

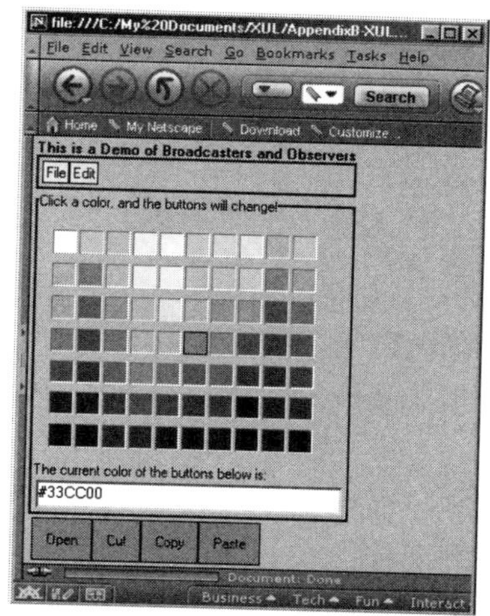

Figure A.4 Screen capture of the broadcaster/observer example.

```
<?xml version="1.0"?>
 <?xml-stylesheet href="appendixdefaults.css" type="text/css"?>
 <!-- This is an example of how broadcasters, observers,
      and commands work!
   -->
<window class="dialog"
    xmlns:html="http://www.w3.org/1999/xhtml"
    xmlns="http://www.mozilla.org/keymaster/gatekeeper/
there.is.only.xul"
    orient="horizontal"
    >
  <!-- This contains our JavaScript functions -->
  <script src="broadcaster.js"/>
  <!-- These are our broadcasters -->
  <broadcasterset>
        <broadcaster  id="colorcaster"/>
        <broadcaster  id="cmd_open" oncommand="sayFunction('Open')"/>
        <broadcaster  id="cmd_cut"  oncommand="sayFunction('Cut')"/>
        <broadcaster  id="cmd_copy" oncommand="sayFunction('Copy')"/>
```

continues

Code Listing A.4 XUL file for broadcaster/observer example.

```
    </broadcasterset>
    <!-- These are our commands -->
    <commandset>
          <command id="cmd_paste" oncommand="sayFunction('Paste')"/>
    </commandset>
    <!-- These are our keyboard shortcuts! -->
    <keyset>
           <key id="deleteKey" keycode="VK_DELETE" observes="cmd_cut" />
           <key id="insertKey" keycode="VK_INSERT" continues
  observes="cmd_paste"/>
    </keyset>
    <!-- This vertically-oriented box will contain everything -->
    <box orient="vertical" valign="middle" flex="0">
       <label value="This is a Demo of Broadcasters and Observers"
             style="font-weight: bold"/>
       <!-- Our demo menu -->
       <menubar>
        <menu id="File" label="File">
         <menupopup>
           <menuitem id="fileopen" label="Open" observes="cmd_open"/>
         </menupopup>
        </menu>
        <menu id="Edit" label="Edit">
           <menupopup>
              <menuitem id="editcut" label="Cut" observes="cmd_cut"/>
              <menuitem id="editcopy" label="Copy" observes="cmd_copy"/>
              <menuitem id="editpaste" label="Paste"
 observes="cmd_paste"/>
           </menupopup>
        </menu>
       </menubar>
       <!-- This is a titlebox around the colors -->
       <groupbox orient="vertical" valign="middle" flex="0">
          <label value="Click a color, and the buttons will change!"/>
       <!-- Our colorpicker widget -->
         <colorpicker id="ColorPicker"
                      palettename="standard"
                      persist="palettename"
                      onclick="selectColor(this)"/>
         <label value="The current color of the buttons below is:"/>
         <textbox id="colorfield" value="#FFFFFF"/>
       </groupbox>
     <!-- Our box of buttons! -->
       <box>
        <button id="button1"
              label="Open">
```

Code Listing A.4 XUL file for broadcaster/observer example (Continued).

```
        <observes element="colorcaster"
                  attribute="colorname"
                  onbroadcast="changeColor(this)"/>
        <observes element="cmd_open"
attribute="oncommand"/>
       </button>
       <button id="button2" label="Cut">
        <observes element="colorcaster"
                  attribute="colorname"
                  onbroadcast="changeColor(this)"/>
        <observes element="cmd_cut"
                  attribute="oncommand"/>
       </button>
       <button id="button3" label="Copy"
             observes="cmd_copy">
         <observes element="colorcaster"
                   attribute="colorname"
                   onbroadcast="changeColor(this)"/>
       </button>
      <button id="button4" label="Paste"
             observes="cmd_paste">
         <observes element="colorcaster"
                   attribute="colorname"
                   onbroadcast="changeColor(this)"/>
      </button>
    </box>
  </box>
</window>
```

Code Listing A.4 Continued.

```
//broadcaster.js
 function sayFunction(str)
 {
      alert("This is a placeholder for the '" + str + "' function.");
      window.focus();
 }
 function selectColor(colorpicker)
 {
       var colorname=colorpicker.color;
        var colorcaster = document.getElementById("colorcaster");
        if (colorcaster)
            colorcaster.setAttribute("colorname", colorname);
 }
```

continues

Code Listing A.5 JavaScript file for broadcaster/observer example.

```
function changeColor(observer)
{
        var colorcaster = document.getElementById("colorcaster");
        var colorname=colorcaster.getAttribute("colorname")
        var button = observer.parentNode;
        var cfield = document.getElementById("colorfield");
       if (colorname)
       {
        button.setAttribute("style", "background-color: " + colorname);
        //now let's change the textbox!
        cfield.setAttribute("value", colorname);
       }
}
```

Code Listing A.5 JavaScript file for broadcaster/observer example (Continued).

```
/* appendixdefaults.css */
window
 {
      background-color     : lightgrey;
      color                : black;
      padding              : 0px;
      font-family          : sans-serif;
      font                 : dialog;
      user-focus           : ignore;
      font-family          : sans-serif;
      font                 : dialog;
  }
box
  {
    padding: 3px;
  }
menubar
  {
    border : 2px solid black;
  }
menu
  {
background-color: yellow;
    border            : 1px solid black;
    padding           : 2px;
  }
menuitem
  {
```

Code Listing A.6 CSS for broadcaster/observer example.

```
    background-color: yellow;
    border           : 1px solid black;
    padding          : 3px;
  }
button   {
    background-color : white;
    color            : black;
    border           : 1px solid black;
    padding          : 5px;
  }
textbox
  {
     height : 30px;
  }

groupbox
  {
    color: black;
    border : 2px solid black;
  }
/* XUL <colorpicker> pieces */
.colorpickertile
  {
    width                    : 20px;
    height                   : 20px;
    margin                   : 1px;
    border-left              : 1px solid threedshadow;
    border-top               : 1px solid threedshadow;
    border-right             : 1px solid threedhighlight;
    border-bottom            : 1px solid threedhighlight;
  }
 colorpicker
 {
   padding: 5px;
 }
.colorpickertile:hover
  {
    border                   : 1px solid #FFFFFF;
  }
.colorpickertile[selected="true"]
  {
    border                   : 1px solid #000000;
  }
```

Code Listing A.6 Continued.

Netscape Theme Reference

This appendix is a reference for building Netscape Themes. It is included to provide a thorough overview of how Netscape Themes are structured. There are two sections, the skin and interface reference.

Skin Reference. This section lists all files according to skin directory. Images are also listed with their respective CSS from which they are called. The skin reference is sorted by images and a list of each skin's CSS.

Interface Reference. This reference is for the Netscape Navigator browser. It is provided at only the top-level skin because the Netscape Navigator main browser interface contains multiple skins, and as such can be hard to decipher.

Skin Reference

The skin reference groups images according to the structure within its Theme. For this skin reference, we used the XULisCool Theme that we created in Chapter 5, "Creating Netscape Themes." This Theme is based off of Netscape's Modern-Mozillium Theme and may contain images still unmodified by the authors. The authors, therefore, acknowledge all copyrights to that of Netscape Communications.

This reference is grouped by skin name. Each skin is arranged by an image table and then a list of cascading style sheets, for example, Communicator skin. The image table contains the image, its filename, and its location within the cascading style sheets of the Themes. Some images may be called from multiple skins of the Theme and are so noted by listing the relative filename of the calling CSS.

After each image table is a list of CSS contained within each skin. If there are any XML binding files, they are so noted, following the cascading style sheets.

The skins referenced in order are:

- AIM skin
- Communicator skin
- Communicator's Bookmarks skin
- Communicator's Directory skin
- Communicator's Help skin
- Communicator's Profile skin
- Communicator's Regviewer skin
- Communicator's Related skin
- Communicator's Search skin
- Communicator's Sidebar skin
- Communicator's XPInstall skin
- Editor skin
- Messenger skin
- Messenger's Addressbook skin
- Messenger's Messengercompose skin
- Navigator skin

AIM Skin–/aim/skin/

The following files make up the AOL Instant Messenger (AIM) skin. The table shows the image, its filename, and where it is used in the AIM stylesheets.

Images

IMAGE	LOCATION	AIM STYLESHEET WHERE IT IS IMPLEMENTED
	Add_buddy_small.gif	SPSetupOrgOverlay.css
	Add_group_small.gif	SPSetupOrgOverlay.css

IMAGE	LOCATION	AIM STYLESHEET WHERE IT IS IMPLEMENTED
	Addbuddy.gif	Aim.css, app.css, findAFriend1_ 2.css, IM.css, IMAddBuddy.css
	Addgroup.gif	App.css
	Aim-enter.gif	
	Aim-exit.gif	
	Aimworld.gif	
	Away.gif	AimHdrViewOverlay.css, AimTaskMenu.css, App.css, SPBuddyOrgOverlay.css
	BiActive.gif	AimHdrViewOverlay.css, chatPanel.css, SPBuddyOrgOverlay.css
	BiAdmin.gif	
	BiAway.gif	AimHdrViewOverlay.css, SPBuddyOrgOverlay.css
	BiGoingOffline.gif	AimHdrViewOverlay.css, SPBuddyOrgOverlay.css
	BiGoingOnline.gif	AimHdrViewOverlay.css, SPBuddyOrgOverlay.css
	BiIdle.gif	AimHdrViewOverlay.css, SPBuddyOrgOverlay.css
	BiIgnore.gif	ChatPanel.css
	BiNotInList.gif	

IMAGE	LOCATION	AIM STYLESHEET WHERE IT IS IMPLEMENTED
	BiOffline.gif	
	BtnSignOn.gif	SPSignOnOrgOverlay
	Chat_small.gif	SPBuddyOrgOverlay.css
	Delete.gif	App.css, SidebarPanel.css, SPSetupOrgOverlay.css
	Delete_small.gif	SPSetupOrgOverlay.css
	Delete_small_ disabled.gif	SPSetupOrgOverlay.css
	Findbuddy.gif	App.css, findAFriendWizard.css
	Folder-closed.gif	SPSetupOrgOverlay.css
	Folder-open.gif	SPSetupOrgOverlay.css
	Gochat.gif	
	Ignoresmall.gif	ChatPanel.css
	Im.gif	FindAFriend1_2.css
	Im_small.gif	ChatPanel.css, SPBuddyOrgOverlay. css
	Im-addbuddy.gif	App.css, IM.css

IMAGE	LOCATION	AIM STYLESHEET WHERE IT IS IMPLEMENTED
	Im-addbuddy-clicked.gif	App.css, IM.css
	Im-addbuddy-disabled.gif	App.css, IM.css
	Im-addbuddy-hover.gif	App.css, IM.css
	Im-addresses.gif	
	Im-addresses-clicked.gif	
	Im-addresses-disabled.gif	
	Im-addresses-hover.gif	
	Im-addtogroup.gif	App.css
	Im-addtogroup-clicked.gif	App.css
	Im-addtogroup-disabled.gif	App.css
	Im-addtogroup-hover.gif	App.css
	Im-away.gif	AimTaskMenu.css, App.css
	Im-away-clicked.gif	AimTaskMenu.css, App.css
	Im-away-disabled.gif	AimTaskMenu.css, App.css

IMAGE	LOCATION	AIM STYLESHEET WHERE IT IS IMPLEMENTED
	Im-away-hover.gif	AimTaskMenu.css, App.css
	Im-block.gif	Chat.css, IM.css
	Im-block-clicked.gif	Chat.css, IM.css
	Im-block-disabled.gif	Chat.css, IM.css
	Im-block-hover.gif	Chat.css, IM.css
	Im-chat.gif	App.css
	Im-chat-clicked.gif	App.css
	Im-chat-disabled.gif	App.css
	Im-chat-hover.gif	App.css
	Im-decline.gif	
	Im-decline-clicked.gif	
	Im-decline-disabled.gif	
	Im-decline-hover.gif	
	Im-findbuddy.gif	App.css

IMAGE	LOCATION	AIM STYLESHEET WHERE IT IS IMPLEMENTED
	Im-findbuddy-clicked.gif	App.css
	Im-findbuddy-disabled.gif	App.css
	Im-findbuddy-hover.gif	App.css
	Im-gochat.gif	
	Im-gochat-clicked.gif	
	Im-gochat-disabled.gif	
	Im-gochat-hover.gif	
	Im-help.gif	App.css
	Im-help-clicked.gif	App.css
	Im-help-disabled.gif	App.css
	Im-help-hover.gif	App.css
	Im-ignore.gif	
	Im-ignore-clicked.gif	
	Im-ignore-disabled.gif	

IMAGE	LOCATION	AIM STYLESHEET WHERE IT IS IMPLEMENTED
	Im-ignore-hover.gif	
	Im-info.gif	Chat.css
	Im-info-clicked.gif	Chat.css
	Im-info-disabled.gif	Chat.css
	Im-info-hover.gif	Chat.css
	Im-invite.gif	Chat.css
	Im-invite-clicked.gif	Chat.css
	Im-invite-disabled.gif	Chat.css
	Im-invite-hover.gif	Chat.css
	Im-netbusiness.gif	App-shrimp.css
	Im-netbusiness-clicked.gif	App-shrimp.css
	Im-netbusiness-disabled.gif	App-shrimp.css
	Im-netbusiness-hover.gif	App-shrimp.css
	Im-save.gif	Chat.css

IMAGE	LOCATION	AIM STYLESHEET WHERE IT IS IMPLEMENTED
	Im-save-clicked.gif	Chat.css
	Im-save-disabled.gif	Chat.css
	Im-save-hover.gif	Chat.css
	Im-send.gif	App.css
	Im-send-clicked.gif	App.css
	Im-send-disabled.gif	App.css
	Im-send-hover.gif	App.css
	Im-sendim.gif	
	Im-sendim-clicked.gif	
	Im-sendim-disabled.gif	
	Im-sendim-hover.gif	
	Im-setup.gif	App.css
	Im-setup-clicked.gif	App.css
	Im-setup-disabled.gif	App.css

IMAGE	LOCATION	AIM STYLESHEET WHERE IT IS IMPLEMENTED
	Im-setup-hover.gif	App.css
	Im-speaker.gif	
	Im-speaker-clicked.gif	
	Im-speaker-disabled.gif	
	Im-speaker-hover.gif	
	Im-warn.gif	IM.css
	Im-warn-clicked.gif	IM.css
	Im-warn-disabled.gif	IM.css
	Im-warn-hover.gif	IM.css
	Info_small.gif	ChatPanel.css, SPBuddyOrgOverlay.css
	Invite.gif	Chat.css
	Print.gif	Chat.css
	Roominfo.gif	
	Savechat.gif	

IMAGE	LOCATION	AIM STYLESHEET WHERE IT IS IMPLEMENTED
	Send.gif	App.css, Chat.css, IM.css
	Speaker.gif	Pref-IM_notification.css
	Taskbar-aim-away.gif	AimTaskMenu.css
	Taskbar-aim-away-clicked.gif	AimTaskMenu.css
	Taskbar-aim-offline.gif	AimTaskMenu.css
	Taskbar-aim-offline-clicked.gif	AimTaskMenu.css
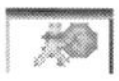	Taskbar-aim-online.gif	AimTaskMenu.css
	Taskbar-aim-online-clicked.gif	AimTaskMenu.css

AOL Instant Messenger Skin Cascading Style Sheets

- AddAwayMessage.css
- aim.css
- AimABTab.css
- AimGlobalOverlay.css
- aimHdrViewOverlay.css
- AimTaskMenu.css
- App-delta.css
- App-shrimp.css
- App.css
- AppPanel.css
- Chat-delta.css

- Chat-shrimp.css
- Chat.css
- chatInviteBuddy.css
- chatPanel.css
- findAFriend1_2.css
- findAFriendWizard.css
- IM-delta.css
- IM-shrimp.css
- IM.css
- IMAddBuddy.css
- IMComposeOrgOverlay.css
- IMKnockKnockOverlay.css
- migrationWizard.css
- migWiz0_0_0.css
- migWiz0_0_1.css
- migWiz1_0_0.css
- migWiz1_1_0.css
- migWiz2_0_0.css
- migWiz2_1_0.css
- migWiz2_1_1.css
- migWiz3_0_0.css
- migWiz4_0_0.css
- pref-IM.css
- pref-IM_away.css
- pref-IM_buddylist.css
- pref-IM_connection.css
- pref-IM_instantmessage.css
- pref-IM_instantmsg-delta.css
- pref-IM_instantmsg-shrimp.css
- pref-IM_notification.css
- pref-IM_privacy.css
- pwiz_panels.css
- SidebarPanel.css
- SPAwayOrgOverlay.css

- SPBuddyOrgOverlay.css
- SPConnectingOrgOverlay.css
- SPRegisterOrgOverlay.css
- SPSetupOrgOverlay.css
- SPSignOnOrgOverlay.css
- Warnings.css

Communicator Skin–/communicator/skin/

Images

IMAGE	LOCATION	AIM STYLESHEET WHERE IT IS IMPLEMENTED
	Broken.gif	SecurityOverlay.css
	Content-large.gif	Communicator.css
	Content-small.gif	Communicator.css
	Document.gif	Findresults.css, icons.css, search.css
	Document-error.gif	/navigator/skin/navigator.css
	Lock.gif	SecurityOverlay.css
	Offline.gif	Communicator.css
	Online.gif	Communicator.css
	Ptc-grippy-bg.gif	Toolbar.css

IMAGE	LOCATION	AIM STYLESHEET WHERE IT IS IMPLEMENTED
	Ptc-grippy-bg-active.gif	Toolbar.css
	Pt-grippy-bg.gif	/navigator/skin/navigator.css
	Pt-grippy-bg-active.gif	/navigator/skin/navigator.css
	Pt-grippy-btm.gif	/navigator/skin/navigator.css
	Pt-grippy-btm-active.gif	/navigator/skin/navigator.css
	Pt-grippy-top.gif	/navigator/skin/navigator.css
	Pt-grippy-top-active.gif	/navigator/skin/navigator.css
	Pt-separator.gif	Toolbar.css
	Tb-menubutton-dm.gif	Menubutton.css
	Tb-menubutton-dm-clicked.gif	Menubutton.css
	Tb-menubutton-dm-disabled.gif	Menubutton.css
	Tb-menubutton-dm-hover.gif	Menubutton.css
	Throbber-groove-bottom.gif	Brand.css

IMAGE	LOCATION	AIM STYLESHEET WHERE IT IS IMPLEMENTED
	Throbber-groove-left.gif	Brand.css
	Throbber-groove-right.gif	Brand.css
	Throbber-groove-top.gif	Brand.css
	Unlock.gif	SecurityOverlay.css

Communicator Skin Cascading Style Sheets

- Box.css
- Brand.css
- Button.css
- Communicator.css
- DialogOverlay.css
- Formatting.css
- Menubutton.css
- PrefPanels.css
- SecurityOverlay.css
- Splitter.css
- TasksOverlay.css
- Toolbar.css

Bookmarks Skin–/communicator/skin/bookmarks/

Images

IMAGE	LOCATION	AIM STYLESHEET WHERE IT IS IMPLEMENTED
	Bookmark-folder-closed.gif	Bookmarks.css

IMAGE	LOCATION	AIM STYLESHEET WHERE IT IS IMPLEMENTED
	Bookmark-folder-open.gif	Bookmarks.css
	Bookmark-item.gif	Bookmarks.css
	Bookmark-item-hover.gif	Bookmarks.css
	Home.gif	Bookmarks.css
	Personal-folder-closed.gif	Bookmarks.css
	Personal-folder-open.gif	Bookmarks.css

Bookmarks Skin Cascading Style Sheets

- bookmarks.css

Directory Skin– /communicator/skin/directory/

Images

IMAGE	LOCATION	AIM STYLESHEET WHERE IT IS IMPLEMENTED
	File-folder-closed.gif	Directory.css
	File-folder-open.gif	Directory.css
	File-icon.gif	Directory.css

Directory Skin Cascading Style Sheets

- directory.css

Help Skin–/communicator/skin/help/

No Image Maps

Help Skin Cascading Style Sheets

- help.css

Profile Skin–/communicator/skin/profile/

Images

IMAGE	LOCATION	AIM STYLESHEET WHERE IT IS IMPLEMENTED
	Activation.gif	
	Migrate.gif	Profile.css
	Profileicon-large.gif	Profile.css

Profile Skin Cascading Style Sheets

- NewProfile1_2.css
- Profile.css
- ProfileManager.css

Regviewer Skin–/communicator/skin/regviewer/

No Image Maps

Regviewer Skin Cascading Style Sheets

- Regviewer.css

Related Skin–/communicator/skin/related/

Images

IMAGE	LOCATION	AIM STYLESHEET WHERE IT IS IMPLEMENTED
	Sitemap.gif	Related.css

Related Skin Cascading Style Sheets

- Related.css

Search Skin–/communicator/skin/search/

Images

IMAGE	LOCATION	AIM STYLESHEET WHERE IT IS IMPLEMENTED
	Category.gif	
	Result.gif	

Search Skin Cascading Style Sheets

- Results.css
- Icons.css
- Internet.css
- Internetresults.css
- Search.css
- Search-editor.css

Sidebar Skin– /communicator/skin/sidebar/

Images

IMAGE	LOCATION	AIM STYLESHEET WHERE IT IS IMPLEMENTED
	Sbgrippy-left.gif	
	Sbgrippy-left-hover.gif	
	Sbgrippy-right.gif	
	Sbgrippy-right-hover.gif	
	Sbpicker-arrow.gif	Sidebar.css

IMAGE	LOCATION	AIM STYLESHEET WHERE IT IS IMPLEMENTED
	Sbsplitter-bg.gif	
	Sbtab-dark.gif	Sidebar.css
	Sbtab-darkondark-left.gif	Sidebar.css
	Sbtab-darkondark-right.gif	Sidebar.css
	Sbtab-darkonlight-left.gif	Sidebar.css
	Sbtab-darkonlight-right.gif	Sidebar.css
	Sbtab-light.gif	Sidebar.css
	Sbtab-lightondark-left.gif	Sidebar.css
	Sbtab-lightondark-right.gif	Sidebar.css

Sidebar Skin Cascading Style Sheets

- Customize.css
- Preview.css
- Sidebar.css

Sidebar Skin XML Binding Files

- SidebarSpliiterBindings.xml

XPInstall Skin– /communicator/skin/xpinstall/

No Image Maps

XPInstall Skin Cascading Style Sheets

- Xpinstall.css

Editor Skin–/editor/skin/

The editor skin follows a different directory structure. Its image files are located in the editor/skin/images/ subdirectory. Its cascading style sheets are contained in the /editor/skin/ subdirectory.

Images

IMAGE	LOCATION	AIM STYLESHEET WHERE IT IS IMPLEMENTED
	Images/Align.gif	EditorToolbars.css
	Images/Align_active.gif	EditorToolbars.css
	Images/Align_disabled.gif	EditorToolbars.css
	Images/Align_hover.gif	EditorToolbars.css
	Images/Anchor.gif	EditorToolbars.css
	Images/Anchor_clicked.gif	EditorToolbars.css
	Images/Anchor_disabled.gif	EditorToolbars.css
	Images/Anchor_hover.gif	EditorToolbars.css
B	Images/Bold.gif	EditorToolbars.css
B	Images/Bold_active.gif	EditorToolbars.css

IMAGE	LOCATION	AIM STYLESHEET WHERE IT IS IMPLEMENTED
	Images/Bold_disabled.gif	EditorToolbars.css
	Images/Bold_hover.gif	EditorToolbars.css
	Images/Bullets.gif	EditorToolbars.css
	Images/Bullets_active.gif	EditorToolbars.css
	Images/Bullets_disabled.gif	EditorToolbars.css
	Images/Bullets_hover.gif	EditorToolbars.css
	Images/Center.gif	EditorToolbars.css
	Images/Center_active.gif	EditorToolbars.css
	Images/Center_disabled.gif	EditorToolbars.css
	Images/Center_hover.gif	EditorToolbars.css
	Images/Dec-font-size.gif	EditorToolbars.css
	Images/Dec-font-size_active.gif	EditorToolbars.css
	Images/Dec-font-size_disabled.gif	EditorToolbars.css
	Images/Dec-font-size_hover.gif	EditorToolbars.css

IMAGE	LOCATION	AIM STYLESHEET WHERE IT IS IMPLEMENTED
<HTML>	Images/Editmode-html.gif	EditorToolbars.css
	Images/Editmode-normal.gif	EditorToolbars.css
	Images/Editmode-preview.gif	EditorToolbars.css
TD	Images/Editmode-tags.gif	EditorToolbars.css
	Images/Find.gif	EditorToolbars.css
	Images/Hline.gif	EditorToolbars.css
	Images/Hline-clicked.gif	EditorToolbars.css
	Images/Hline-disabled.gif	EditorToolbars.css
	Images/Hline-hover.gif	EditorToolbars.css
	Images/Hline-white.gif	EditorToolbars.css
	Images/Image.gif	EditorToolbars.css
	Images/Image-clicked.gif	EditorToolbars.css
	Images/Image-hover.gif	EditorToolbars.css
	Images/Image-white.gif	EditorToolbars.css

IMAGE	LOCATION	AIM STYLESHEET WHERE IT IS IMPLEMENTED
	Images/Img-align-bottom.gif	EditorDialog.css
	Images/Img-align-left.gif	EditorDialog.css
	Images/Img-align-middle.gif	EditorDialog.css
	Images/Img-align-right.gif	EditorDialog.css
	Images/Img-align-top.gif	EditorDialog.css
	Images/Inc-font-size.gif	EditorToolbars.css
	Images/Inc-font-size_active.gif	EditorToolbars.css
	Images/Inc-font-size_disabled.gif	EditorToolbars.css
	Images/Inc-font-size_hover.gif	EditorToolbars.css
	Images/Indent.gif	EditorToolbars.css
	Images/Indent_active.gif	EditorToolbars.css
	Images/Indent_disabled.gif	EditorToolbars.css
	Images/Indent_hover.gif	EditorToolbars.css
	Images/Italic.gif	EditorToolbars.css

IMAGE	LOCATION	AIM STYLESHEET WHERE IT IS IMPLEMENTED
	Images/Italic_active.gif	EditorToolbars.css
	Images/Italic_disabled.gif	EditorToolbars.css
	Images/Italic_hover.gif	EditorToolbars.css
	Images/Justify.gif	EditorToolbars.css
	Images/Justify_active.gif	EditorToolbars.css
	Images/Justify_disabled.gif	EditorToolbars.css
	Images/Justify_hover.gif	EditorToolbars.css
	Images/Left.gif	EditDialog.css, EditorToolbars.css
	Images/Left_active.gif	EditDialog.css, EditorToolbars.css
	Images/Left_disabled.gif	EditDialog.css, EditorToolbars.css
	Images/Left_hover.gif	EditDialog.css, EditorToolbars.css
	Images/Link.gif	EditorToolbars.css
	Images/Link-clicked.gif	EditorToolbars.css
	Images/Link-disabled.gif	EditorToolbars.css

IMAGE	LOCATION	AIM STYLESHEET WHERE IT IS IMPLEMENTED
	Images/Link-hover.gif	EditorToolbars.css
	Images/Link-white.gif	EditorToolbars.css
	Images/Map_checker.gif	EdImageMapPage.css
	Images/Map_circleTool.gif	EdImageMapPage.css
	Images/Map_contrast.gif	EdImageMap.css
	Images/Map_copy.gif	EdImageMap.css
	Images/Map_cut.gif	EdImageMap.css
	Images/Map_paste.gif	EdImageMap.css
	Images/Map_pointerTool.gif	EdImageMap.css
	Images/Map_polygonTool.gif	EdImageMap.css
	Images/Map_rectangleTool.gif	EdImageMap.css
	Images/Map_zoomIn.gif	EdImageMap.css
	Images/Map_zoomOut.gif	EdImageMap.css
	Images/NewFile.gif	EditorToolbars.css

IMAGE	LOCATION	AIM STYLESHEET WHERE IT IS IMPLEMENTED
	Images/NewFile-clicked.gif	EditorToolbars.css
	Images/NewFile-disabled.gif	EditorToolbars.css
	Images/NewFile-hover.gif	EditorToolbars.css
	Images/Numbers.gif	EditorToolbars.css
	Images/Numbers_active.gif	EditorToolbars.css
	Images/Numbers_disabled.gif	EditorToolbars.css
	Images/Numbers_hover.gif	EditorToolbars.css
	Images/Object-popup.gif	EditorToolbars.css
	Images/Object-popup_active.gif	EditorToolbars.css
	Images/Object-popup_disabled.gif	EditorToolbars.css
	Images/Object-popup_hover.gif	EditorToolbars.css
	Images/Openfile.gif	EditorToolbars.css
	Images/Openfile-clicked.gif	EditorToolbars.css
	Images/Openfile-disabled.gif	EditorToolbars.css

IMAGE	LOCATION	AIM STYLESHEET WHERE IT IS IMPLEMENTED
	Images/Openfile-hover.gif	EditorToolbars.css
	Images/Outdent.gif	EditorToolbars.css
	Images/Outdent_active.gif	EditorToolbars.css
	Images/Outdent_disabled.gif	EditorToolbars.css
	Images/Outdent_hover.gif	EditorToolbars.css
	Images/Preview.gif	EditorDialog.css, EditorToolbars.css
	Images/Preview-clicked.gif	EditorDialog.css, EditorToolbars.css
	Images/Preview-disabled.gif	EditorDialog.css, EditorToolbars.css
	Images/Preview-hover.gif	EditorDialog.css, EditorToolbars.css
	Images/Print.gif	EditorToolbars.css
	Images/Publish.gif	EditorToolbars.css
	Images/Right.gif	EditorDialog.css, EditorToolbars.css
	Images/Right_active.gif	EditorDialog.css, EditorToolbars.css
	Images/Right_disabled.gif	EditorDialog.css, EditorToolbars.css

IMAGE	LOCATION	AIM STYLESHEET WHERE IT IS IMPLEMENTED
	Images/Right_hover.gif	EditorDialog.css, EditorToolbars.css
	Images/Savefile.gif	EditorToolbars.css
	Images/Savefile-clicked.gif	EditorToolbars.css
	Images/Savefile-disabled.gif	EditorToolbars.css
	Images/Savefile-hover.gif	EditorToolbars.css
	Images/Savemod.gif	EditorToolbars.css
	Images/Span.gif	
	Images/Spell.gif	EditorToolbars.css
	Images/Spell-clicked.gif	EditorToolbars.css
	Images/Spell-disabled.gif	EditorToolbars.css
	Images/Spell-hover.gif	EditorToolbars.css
	Images/Table.gif	EditorToolbars.css
	Images/Table-clicked.gif	EditorToolbars.css
	Images/Table-disabled.gif	EditorToolbars.css

IMAGE	LOCATION	AIM STYLESHEET WHERE IT IS IMPLEMENTED
	Images/Table-hover.gif	EditorToolbars.css
	Images/Table-white.gif	EditorToolbars.css
	Images/Underline.gif	EditorToolbars.css
	Images/Underline_active.gif	EditorToolbars.css
	Images/Underline_disabled.gif	EditorToolbars.css
	Images/Underline_hover.gif	EditorToolbars.css

Editor Skin Cascading Style Sheets

- EdImageMap.css
- EdImageMapPage.css
- Editor.css
- EditorDialog.css
- EditorToolbars.css

Global Skin–/global/skin/

Images

IMAGE	LOCATION	AIM STYLESHEET WHERE IT IS IMPLEMENTED
	alert-icon.gif	Console.css, global.css
	animthrob.gif	/aim/skin/chat.css, /aim/skin/IM.css, /communicator/skin/brand.css

IMAGE	LOCATION	AIM STYLESHEET WHERE IT IS IMPLEMENTED
	animthrob_single.gif	/aim/skin/chat.css, /communicator/skin/brand.css
	arrow-down.gif	/communicator/skin/communicator.css, /communicator/skin/search/search-editor.css, /communicator/skin/sidebar/customize.css, /editor/skin/EditorDialog.css, /navigator/skin/navigator.css, button.css, formatting.css, menubutton.css
	arrow-left.gif	/communicator/skin/communicator.css, /communicator/skin/search/search-editor.css, /communicator/skin/sidebar/ customize.css, /editor/skin/EditorDialog.css, /navigator/skin/navigator.css, button.css, formatting.css, menubutton.css
	arrow-right.gif	/communicator/skin/communicator.css, /communicator/skin/search/search-editor.css, /communicator/skin/sidebar/customize.css, /editor/skin/EditorDialog.css, /navigator/skin/navigator.css, button.css, formatting. css, menubutton.css
	arrow-up.gif	/communicator/skin/communicator.css, /communicator/skin/search/search-editor.css, /communicator/skin/sidebar/customize.css, /editor/skin/EditorDialog.css, /navigator/skin/navigator.css, button.css, formatting.css, menubutton.css
	autorepeat-down.gif	Menu.css
	autorepeat-up.gif	Menu.css

IMAGE	LOCATION	AIM STYLESHEET WHERE IT IS IMPLEMENTED
	blank.gif	Filepicker.css
	button-active-left-btm.gif	Button.css
	button-active-left-mid.gif	Button.css
	button-active-left-top.gif	Button.css
	button-active-mid-btm.gif	Button.css
	button-active-mid-mid.gif	Button.css
	button-active-mid-top.gif	Button.css
	button-active-right-btm.gif	Button.css
	button-active-right-mid.gif	Button.css
	button-active-right-top.gif	Button.css
	button-def-active-left-btm	Button.css
	button-def-active-left-mid.gif	Button.css
	button-def-active-left-top	Button.css
	button-def-active-mid-btm.gif	Button.css

IMAGE	LOCATION	AIM STYLESHEET WHERE IT IS IMPLEMENTED
	button-def-active-mid-mid.gif	Button.css
	button-def-active-mid-top.gif	Button.css
	button-def-active-right-btm.gif	Button.css
	button-def-active-right-mid.gif	Button.css
	button-def-active-right-top.gif	Button.css
	button-def-left-btm.gif	Button.css
	button-def-left-mid.gif	Button.css
	button-def-left-top.gif	Button.css
	button-def-mid-btm.gif	Button.css
	button-def-mid-mid.gif	Button.css
	button-def-mid-top.gif	Button.css
	button-def-right-btm.gif	Button.css
	button-def-right-mid.gif	Button.css
	button-def-right-top.gif	Button.css

IMAGE	LOCATION	AIM STYLESHEET WHERE IT IS IMPLEMENTED
	button-dis-left-btm.gif	Button.css
	button-dis-left-mid.gif	Button.css
	button-dis-left-top.gif	Button.css
	button-dis-mid-btm.gif	Button.css
	button-dis-mid-mid.gif	Button.css
	button-dis-mid-top.gif	Button.css
	button-dis-right-btm.gif	Button.css
	button-dis-right-mid.gif	Button.css
	button-dis-right-top.gif	Button.css
	button-left-btm.gif	Button.css
	button-left-mid.gif	Button.css
	button-left-top.gif	Button.css
	button-mid-btm.gif	Button.css
	button-mid-mid.gif	Button.css

IMAGE	LOCATION	AIM STYLESHEET WHERE IT IS IMPLEMENTED
	button-mid-top.gif	Button.css
	button-right-btm.gif	Button.css
	button-right-mid.gif	Button.css
	button-right-top.gif	Button.css
	check-cb-check-disabled.gif	Checkbox.css
	check-cb-check-pressed.gif	Checkbox.css
	check-cb-check.gif	Checkbox.css
	check-cb-disabled.gif	Checkbox.css
	check-cb-pressed.gif	Checkbox.css
	check-cb.gif	Checkbox.css
	check-check-disabled.gif	Checkbox.css
	check-check.gif	Checkbox.css
	check-radio-check-disabled	Checkbox.css
	check-radio-check-pressed.	Checkbox.css

IMAGE	LOCATION	AIM STYLESHEET WHERE IT IS IMPLEMENTED
	check-radio-check.gif	Checkbox.css
	check-radio-disabled.gif	Checkbox.css
	check-radio-focused.gif	Checkbox.css
	check-radio-pressed.gif	Checkbox.css
	check-radio.gif	Checkbox.css
	closedtwisty.gif	/aim/skin/SPBuddyOrgOverlay.css, /communicator/skin/button.css, tree.css
	columnselect.gif	Tree.css
	dir-closed.gif	Filepicker.css
	dir-open.gif	Filepicker.css
	error-icon.gif	Console.css, global.css
	grippy-horizontal-active.gif	Splitter.css
	grippy-horizontal-after.gif	Splitter.css
	grippy-horizontal-before.gif	Splitter.css
	grippy-vertical-active.gif	Splitter.css

IMAGE	LOCATION	AIM STYLESHEET WHERE IT IS IMPLEMENTED
	grippy-vertical-after.gif	Splitter.css
	grippy-vertical-before.gif	Splitter.css
	loading.gif	/communicator/skin/bookmarks/bookmarks.css, /communicator/skin/directory/directory.css, /communicator/skin/related/related.css, /communicator/skin/search/findresults.css, /communicator/skin/search/icons.css, /communicator/skin/search/search.css, /communicator/skin/sidebar/sidebar.css
	mb-grippy-bg-active.gif	Menu.css
	mb-grippy-bg.gif	Menu.css
	mb-grippy-btm-active.gif	Menu.css
	mb-grippy-btm.gif	Menu.css
	mb-grippy-top-active.gif	Menu.css
	mb-grippy-top.gif	Menu.css
	mb-single-arrow.gif	Menu.css
	mbg.gif	Menu.css

IMAGE	LOCATION	AIM STYLESHEET WHERE IT IS IMPLEMENTED
	menu-arrow-disabled.gif	Menu.css
	menu-arrow-hover.gif	Menu.css
	menu-arrow.gif	Menu.css
	menu-check-disabled.gif	Menu.css
	menu-check-hover.gif	Menu.css
	menu-check.gif	Menu.css
	menu-radio-disabled.gif	Menu.css
	menu-radio-hover.gif	Menu.css
	menu-radio.gif	Menu.css
	menubar-bg.gif	Menu.css
	menuhover-yellow.gif	Menu.css
	menulist-active-arrow.gif	Menulist.css
	menulist-active-left-btm.gif	Menulist.css
	menulist-active-left-mid.gif	Menulist.css

IMAGE	LOCATION	AIM STYLESHEET WHERE IT IS IMPLEMENTED
	menulist-active-left-top.gif	Menulist.css
	menulist-active-mid-btm.gif	Menulist.css
	menulist-active-mid-mid.gif	Menulist.css
	menulist-active-mid-top.gif	Menulist.css
	menulist-active-right-btm.gif	Menulist.css
	menulist-active-right-mid.gif	Menulist.css
	menulist-active-right-top.gif	Menulist.css
	menulist-arrow.gif	Menulist.css
	menulist-dis-arrow.gif	Menulist.css
	menulist-dis-left-btm.gif	Menulist.css
	menulist-dis-left-mid.gif	Menulist.css
	menulist-dis-left-top.gif	Menulist.css
	menulist-dis-mid-btm.gif	Menulist.css
	menulist-dis-mid-mid.gif	Menulist.css
	menulist-dis-mid-top.gif	Menulist.css

IMAGE	LOCATION	AIM STYLESHEET WHERE IT IS IMPLEMENTED
	menulist-dis-right-btm.gif	Menulist.css
	menulist-dis-right-mid.gif	Menulist.css
	menulist-dis-right-top.gif	Menulist.css
	menulist-left-btm.gif	Menulist.css
	menulist-left-mid.gif	Menulist.css
	menulist-left-top.gif	Menulist.css
	menulist-mid-btm.gif	Menulist.css
	menulist-mid-mid.gif	Menulist.css
	menulist-mid-top.gif	Menulist.css
	menulist-right-btm.gif	Menulist.css
	menulist-right-mid.gif	Menulist.css
	menulist-right-top.gif	Menulist.css
	menupopupbg.gif	
	message-icon.gif	Global.css

IMAGE	LOCATION	AIM STYLESHEET WHERE IT IS IMPLEMENTED
	navbar-bg-leftcap.gif	Toolbar.css
	navbar-bg-rightcap.gif	Toolbar.css
	navbar-bg.gif	Toolbar.css
	opentwisty.gif	/aim/skin/SPBuddyOrgOverlay.css, /communicator/skin/button.css, tree.css
	preview.gif	/editor/skin/EditorToolbars.css
	print-clicked.gif	/aim/skin/chat.css, /communicator/skin/help/help.css, /editor/skin/EditorToolbars.css, /messenger/skin/messenger.css, /navigator/skin/navigator.css
	print-disabled.gif	/aim/skin/chat.css, /communicator/skin/help/help.css, /editor/skin/EditorToolbars.css, /messenger/skin/messenger.css, /navigator/skin/navigator.css
	print-hover.gif	/aim/skin/chat.css, /communicator/skin/help/help.css, /editor/skin/EditorToolbars.css, /messenger/skin/messenger.css, /navigator/skin/navigator.css
	print.gif	/aim/skin/chat.css, /communicator/skin/help/help.css, /editor/skin/EditorToolbars.css, /messenger/skin/messenger.css, /navigator/skin/navigator.css

IMAGE	LOCATION	AIM STYLESHEET WHERE IT IS IMPLEMENTED
	progress-bg.gif	Global.css
	progress-filler.gif	Global.css
	progressmeter-busy.gif	Global.css
	question-icon.gif	Global.css, /messenger/skin/messengercompose/messengercompose.css
	scroll-down-clicked.gif	Scrollbars.css
	scroll-down-disabled.gif	Scrollbars.css
	scroll-down.gif	Scrollbars.css
	scroll-left-clicked.gif	Scrollbars.css
	scroll-left-disabled.gif	Scrollbars.css
	scroll-left.gif	Scrollbars.css
	scroll-right-clicked.gif	Scrollbars.css
	scroll-right-disabled.gif	Scrollbars.css
	scroll-right.gif	Scrollbars.css
	scroll-thumb-horiz-disabled.gif	Scrollbars.css

IMAGE	LOCATION	AIM STYLESHEET WHERE IT IS IMPLEMENTED
	scroll-thumb-horiz-hover.gif	Scrollbars.css
	scroll-thumb-horiz.gif	Scrollbars.css
	scroll-thumb-horz-cl-expand.gi	Scrollbars.css
	scroll-thumb-horz-cl-grippy.gif	Scrollbars.css
	scroll-thumb-horz-cl-left.gif	Scrollbars.css
	scroll-thumb-horz-cl-right,gif	Scrollbars.css
	scroll-thumb-horz-expand.gif	Scrollbars.css
	scroll-thumb-horz-grippy.gif	Scrollbars.css
	scroll-thumb-horz-left.gif	Scrollbars.css
	scroll-thumb-horz-right.gif	Scrollbars.css
	scroll-thumb-vert-bottom.gif	Scrollbars.css
	scroll-thumb-vert-cl-bottom.gif	Scrollbars.css
	scroll-thumb-vert-cl-expand.gif	Scrollbars.css
	scroll-thumb-vert-cl-grippy.gif	Scrollbars.css

IMAGE	LOCATION	AIM STYLESHEET WHERE IT IS IMPLEMENTED
	scroll-thumb-vert-cl-top.gif	Scrollbars.css
	scroll-thumb-vert-disabled.gif	Scrollbars.css
	scroll-thumb-vert-expand.gif	Scrollbars.css
	scroll-thumb-vert-grippy.gif	Scrollbars.css
	scroll-thumb-vert-hover.gif	Scrollbars.css
	scroll-thumb-vert-top.gif	Scrollbars.css
	scroll-thumb-vert.gif	Scrollbars.css
	scroll-track-horz-middle.gif	Scrollbars.css
	scroll-track-vert-middle.gif	Scrollbars.css
	scroll-up-clicked.gif	Scrollbars.css
	scroll-up-disabled.gif	Scrollbars.css
	scroll-up.gif	Scrollbars.css
	search.gif	/messenger/skin/addressbook/addressbook.css
	simple-arrow-down-disabled.gif	/communicator/skin/communicator.css, /communicator/skin/search/search-editor.css, /communicator/skin/sidebar/customize.css

IMAGE	LOCATION	AIM STYLESHEET WHERE IT IS IMPLEMENTED
	simple-arrow-down.gif	/communicator/skin/communicator.css, /communicator/skin/search/search-editor.css, /communicator/skin/sidebar/customize.css
	simple-arrow-left-disabled.gif	/communicator/skin/ communicator.css, /communicator/skin/search/search-editor.css, /communicator/skin/sidebar/customize.css
	simple-arrow-left.gif	/communicator/skin/communicator.css, /communicator/skin/search/search-editor.css, /communicator/skin/sidebar/customize.css
	simple-arrow-right-disabled.gif	/communicator/skin/communicator.css, /communicator/skin/search/search-editor.css, /communicator/skin/sidebar/customize.css
	simple-arrow-right.gif	/communicator/skin/communicator.css, /communicator/skin/search/search-editor.css, /communicator/skin/sidebar/customize.css
	simple-arrow-up-disabled.gif	/communicator/skin/communicator.css, /communicator/skin/search/search-editor.css, /communicator/skin/sidebar/customize.css
	simple-arrow-up.gif	/communicator/skin/communicator.css, /communicator/skin/search/search-editor.css, /communicator/skin/sidebar/customize.css
	sortAscending.gif	Tree.css
	sortDescending.gif	Tree.css
	stop-clicked.gif	/messenger/skin/messenger.css, /messenger/skin/addressbook/addressbook.css, /messenger/

IMAGE	LOCATION	AIM STYLESHEET WHERE IT IS IMPLEMENTED
		skin/messengercompose/ messengercompose.css, /navigator/ skin/navigator.css
	stop-disabled.gif	/messenger/skin/messenger.css, /messenger/skin/addressbook/ addressbook.css, /messenger/ skin/messengercompose/ messengercompose.css, /navigator/ skin/navigator.css
	stop-hover.gif	/messenger/skin/messenger.css, /messenger/skin/addressbook/ addressbook.css, /messenger/ skin/messengercompose/ messengercompose.css, /navigator/ skin/navigator.css
	stop.gif	/messenger/skin/messenger.css, /messenger/skin/addressbook/ addressbook.css, /messenger/ skin/messengercompose/ messengercompose.css, /navigator/ skin/navigator.css
	tab-bot-border-leftcap.gif	Tabcontrol.css
	tab-bot-border-rightcap.gif	Tabcontrol.css
	tab-bot-border.gif	Tabcontrol.css
	tab-bot-clicked-left.gif	Tabcontrol.css
	tab-bot-clicked-middle.gif	Tabcontrol.css
	tab-bot-clicked-right.gif	Tabcontrol.css

IMAGE	LOCATION	AIM STYLESHEET WHERE IT IS IMPLEMENTED
	tab-bot-select-left.gif	Tabcontrol.css
	tab-bot-select-middle.gif	Tabcontrol.css
	tab-bot-select-right.gif	Tabcontrol.css
	tab-bot-unselect-left.gif	Tabcontrol.css
	tab-bot-unselect-middle.gif	Tabcontrol.css
	tab-bot-unselect-right.gif	Tabcontrol.css
	tab-clicked-left.gif	Tabcontrol.css
	tab-clicked-middle.gif	Tabcontrol.css
	tab-clicked-right.gif	Tabcontrol.css
	tab-select-left.gif	Tabcontrol.css
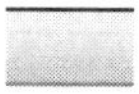	tab-select-middle.gif	Tabcontrol.css
	tab-select-right.gif	Tabcontrol.css
	tab-top-border-leftcap.gif	Tabcontrol.css
	tab-top-border-rightcap.gif	Tabcontrol.css

IMAGE	LOCATION	AIM STYLESHEET WHERE IT IS IMPLEMENTED
	tab-top-border.gif	Tabcontrol.css
	tab-unselect-left.gif	Tabcontrol.css
	tab-unselect-middle.gif	Tabcontrol.css
	tab-unselect-right.gif	Tabcontrol.css
	taskbar-addressbook-clicked.gif	/communicator/skin/tasksOverlay.css
	taskbar-addressbook.gif	/communicator/skin/tasksOverlay.css
	taskbar-aim-away.gif	/communicator/skin/tasksOverlay.css
	taskbar-aim-offline.gif	/communicator/skin/tasksOverlay.css
	taskbar-aim-online.gif	/communicator/skin/tasksOverlay.css
	taskbar-bg-left.gif	/communicator/skin/tasksOverlay.css
	taskbar-bg-right.gif	/communicator/skin/tasksOverlay.css
	taskbar-bg.gif	/communicator/skin/tasksOverlay.css
	taskbar-calendar.gif	/communicator/skin/tasksOverlay.css
	taskbar-composer-clicked.gif	/communicator/skin/tasksOverlay.css

IMAGE	LOCATION	AIM STYLESHEET WHERE IT IS IMPLEMENTED
	taskbar-composer.gif	/communicator/skin/tasksOverlay.css
	taskbar-groove-left.gif	/communicator/skin/tasksOverlay.css
	taskbar-groove-middle.gif	/communicator/skin/tasksOverlay.css
	taskbar-groove-right.gif	/communicator/skin/tasksOverlay.css
	taskbar-mail-clicked.gif	/communicator/skin/tasksOverlay.css
	taskbar-mail.gif	/communicator/skin/tasksOverlay.css
	taskbar-mailnew-clicked.gif	/communicator/skin/tasksOverlay.css
	taskbar-mailnew.gif	/communicator/skin/tasksOverlay.css
	taskbar-navigator-clicked.gif	/communicator/skin/tasksOverlay.css
	taskbar-navigator.gif	/communicator/skin/tasksOverlay.css
	taskbar-popup-arrow.gif	/communicator/skin/tasksOverlay.css
	tb-grippy-bg-active.gif	Toolbar.css
	tb-grippy-bg.gif	Toolbar.css
	tb-grippy-btm-active.gif	Toolbar.css

IMAGE	LOCATION	AIM STYLESHEET WHERE IT IS IMPLEMENTED
	tb-grippy-btm.gif	Toolbar.css
	tb-grippy-collapsed-active.gif	Toolbar.css
	tb-grippy-collapsed.gif	Toolbar.css
	tb-grippy-top-active.gif	Toolbar.css
	tb-grippy-top.gif	Toolbar.css

Global Skin Cascading Style Sheets

- Box.css
- Button.css
- CalendarOverlay.css
- Checkbox.css
- Colorpicker.css
- CommonDialog.css
- Console.css
- FilePicker.css
- Formatting.css
- Global.css
- Menu.css
- Menubutton.css
- Menulist.css
- Radio.css
- Scrollbars.css
- Splitter.css
- Tabcontrol.css
- Textfield.css
- Toolbar.css

- Tree.css
- WizardOverlay.css

Messenger Skin–/messenger/skin/

Images

IMAGE	LOCATION	AIM STYLESHEET WHERE IT IS IMPLEMENTED
	addtoab.gif	MsgHdrViewOverlay.css
	attach.gif	MsgHdrViewOverlay.css, threadPane.css, /messenger/skin/messengercompose/messengercompose.css
	check.gif	/global/skin/checkbox.css, /global/skin/menu.css, /global/skin/menulist.css, /global/skin/radio.css, subscribe.css
	dot.gif	Subscribe.css
	file-clicked.gif	/editor/skin/EditorToolbars.css, messenger.css
	file-disabled.gif	/editor/skin/EditorToolbars.css, messenger.css
	file-hover.gif	/editor/skin/EditorToolbars.css, messenger.css
	file.gif	/editor/skin/EditorToolbars.css, messenger.css
	flagcol.gif	
	flaggedmail.gif	ThreadPane.css

IMAGE	LOCATION	AIM STYLESHEET WHERE IT IS IMPLEMENTED
	folder-closed.gif	FolderPane.css, messenger.css
	folder-draft-open.gif	FolderPane.css, messenger.css
	folder-draft-share-open.gif	FolderPane.css, messenger.css
	folder-draft-share.gif	FolderPane.css, messenger.css
	folder-draft.gif	FolderPane.css, messenger.css
	folder-filed-open.gif	FolderPane.css, messenger.css
	folder-filed.gif	FolderPane.css, messenger.css
	folder-hasmail.gif	FolderPane.css, messenger.css
	folder-inbox-new.gif	FolderPane.css, messenger.css
	folder-inbox-open.gif	FolderPane.css, messenger.css
	folder-inbox-share-open.gif	FolderPane.css, messenger.css
	folder-inbox-share.gif	FolderPane.css, messenger.css
	folder-inbox.gif	FolderPane.css, messenger.css
	folder-mailserver.gif	FolderPane.css, messenger.css

IMAGE	LOCATION	AIM STYLESHEET WHERE IT IS IMPLEMENTED
	folder-new-open.gif	FolderPane.css, messenger.css
	folder-new.gif	FolderPane.css, messenger.css
	folder-newsgroup-new.gif	FolderPane.css, messenger.css
	folder-newsgroup.gif	FolderPane.css, messenger.css
	folder-open.gif	FolderPane.css, messenger.css
	folder-outbox-open.gif	FolderPane.css, messenger.css
	folder-outbox.gif	FolderPane.css, messenger.css
	folder-sent-open.gif	FolderPane.css, messenger.css
	folder-sent-share-open.gif	FolderPane.css, messenger.css
	folder-sent-share.gif	FolderPane.css, messenger.css
	folder-sent.gif	FolderPane.css, messenger.css
	folder-server-open.gif	FolderPane.css, messenger.css
	folder-server.gif	FolderPane.css, messenger.css
	folder-share-open.gif	FolderPane.css, messenger.css

IMAGE	LOCATION	AIM STYLESHEET WHERE IT IS IMPLEMENTED
	folder-share.gif	FolderPane.css, messenger.css
	folder-template-open.gif	FolderPane.css, messenger.css
	folder-template-share-open.gif	FolderPane.css, messenger.css
	folder-template-share.gif	FolderPane.css, messenger.css
	folder-template.gif	FolderPane.css, messenger.css
	folder-trash-open.gif	FolderPane.css, messenger.css
	folder-trash-share-open.gif	FolderPane.css, messenger.css
	folder-trash-share.gif	FolderPane.css, messenger.css
	folder-trash.gif	FolderPane.css, messenger.css
	forward-clicked.gif	messenger.css
	forward-disabled.gif	messenger.css
	forward-hover.gif	messenger.css
	forward.gif	messenger.css
	frown.gif	

IMAGE	LOCATION	AIM STYLESHEET WHERE IT IS IMPLEMENTED
	getmsg-clicked.gif	messenger.css
	getmsg-disabled.gif	messenger.css
	getmsg-hover.gif	messenger.css
	getmsg.gif	messenger.css
	inbox.gif	FolderPane.css, messenger.css
	less.gif	MsgHdrViewOverlay.css
	local-mailhost.gif	
	mailfolder.gif	
	message-mail-attach.gif	ThreadPane.css
	message-mail-imapdelete.gif	ThreadPane.css
	message-mail-new.gif	ThreadPane.css
	message-mail.gif	ThreadPane.css
	message-news-new.gif	ThreadPane.css
	message-news.gif	ThreadPane.css

IMAGE	LOCATION	AIM STYLESHEET WHERE IT IS IMPLEMENTED
	more.gif	MsgHdrViewOverlay.css
	newmsg-clicked.gif	Messenger.css
	newmsg-disabled.gif	Messenger.css
	newmsg-hover.gif	Messenger.css
	newmsg.gif	Messenger.css
	newshost.gif	
	next-clicked.gif	Messenger.css
	next-disabled.gif	Messenger.css
	next-hover.gif	Messenger.css
	next.gif	Messenger.css
	open-mailfolder.gif	
	outbox.gif	
	readcol.gif	ThreadPane.css
	readmail.gif	Messenger.css, threadPane.css

IMAGE	LOCATION	AIM STYLESHEET WHERE IT IS IMPLEMENTED
	reply-clicked.gif	Messenger.css
	reply-disabled.gif	Messenger.css
	reply-hover.gif	Messenger.css
	reply.gif	Messenger.css
	replyall-clicked.gif	Messenger.css
	replyall-disabled.gif	Messenger.css
	replyall-hover.gif	Messenger.css
	replyall.gif	Messenger.css
	server-local-new.gif	FolderPane.css, messenger.css
	server-local.gif	FolderPane.css, messenger.css
	server-mail-new.gif	FolderPane.css, messenger.css
	server-mail.gif	FolderPane.css, messenger.css
	server-news-lock.gif	FolderPane.css, messenger.css
	server-news-new.gif	FolderPane.css, messenger.css

IMAGE	LOCATION	AIM STYLESHEET WHERE IT IS IMPLEMENTED
	server-news.gif	FolderPane.css, messenger.css
	server-remote-lock.gif	FolderPane.css, messenger.css
	server-remote.gif	FolderPane.css, messenger.css
	sick.gif	
	smile.gif	
	thread-closed.gif	ThreadPane.css
	thread-new-closed.gif	ThreadPane.css
	thread-new-open.gif	ThreadPane.css
	thread-open.gif	ThreadPane.css
	threadcol.gif	ThreadPane.css
	trash-clicked.gif	Messenger.css, /messenger/skin/addressbook/addressbook.css
	trash-disabled.gif	Messenger.css, /messenger/skin/addressbook/addressbook.css
	trash-hover.gif	Messenger.css, /messenger/skin/addressbook/addressbook.css
	trash.gif	Messenger.css, /messenger/skin/addressbook/addressbook.css
	unreadmail.gif	Messenger.css, threadPane.css

IMAGE	LOCATION	AIM STYLESHEET WHERE IT IS IMPLEMENTED
	unthreadcol.gif	ThreadPane.css
	winclassic.gif	Pref-mailnews.css
	wink.gif	
	winwide.gif	Pref-mailnews.css

Messenger Skin Cascading Style Sheets

- AccountManager.css
- FieldMapImport.css
- FolderPane.css
- ImportDialog.css
- MailHeader.css
- Messenger.css
- MsgHdrViewOverlay.css
- Pref-mailnews.css
- Subscribe.css
- ThreadPane.css
- Wizard.css

Addressbook Skin– /messenger/skin/addressbook/

Images

IMAGE	LOCATION	AIM STYLESHEET WHERE IT IS IMPLEMENTED
	Abnewmsg.gif	
	Absynch.gif	ABSynch.css

IMAGE	LOCATION	AIM STYLESHEET WHERE IT IS IMPLEMENTED
	Absynch-clicked.gif	ABSynch.css
	Absynch-disabled.gif	ABSynch.css
	Absynch-hover.gif	ABSynch.css
	Directory.gif	
	Directory-open.gif	
	Edit.gif	Addressbook.css
	Edit-clicked.gif	Addressbook.css
	Edit-disabled.gif	Addressbook.css
	Edit-hover.gif	Addressbook.css
	List.gif	Addressbook.css
	Myaddrbk.gif	Addressbook.css
	Newcard.gif	Addressbook.css
	Newcard-clicked.gif	Addressbook.css
	Newcard-disabled.gif	Addressbook.css

IMAGE	LOCATION	AIM STYLESHEET WHERE IT IS IMPLEMENTED
	Newcard-hover.gif	Addressbook.css
	Newlist.gif	Addressbook.css
	Newlist-clicked.gif	Addressbook.css
	Newlist-disabled.gif	Addressbook.css
	Newlist-hover.gif	Addressbook.css
	Newmsgab.gif	Addressbook.css
	Newmsgab-clicked.gif	Addressbook.css
	Newmsgab-disabled.gif	Addressbook.css
	Newmsgab-hover.gif	Addressbook.css
	Person.gif	Addressbook.css, /messenger/skin/ messengercompose/ messengercompose.css
	Property.gif	

AddressBook Skin Cascading Style Sheets

- ABSynch.css
- Addressbook.css

Messengercompose Skin– /messenger/skin/messengercompose/

Images

IMAGE	LOCATION	AIM STYLESHEET WHERE IT IS IMPLEMENTED
	Address.gif	Messengercompose.css
	Address-clicked.gif	Messengercompose.css
	Address-disabled.gif	Messengercompose.css
	Address-hover.gif	Messengercompose.css
	Attach.gif	/messenger/skin/ msgHdrViewOverlay.css, /messenger/skin/threadPane.css, messengercompose.css
	Attach-clicked.gif	/messenger/skin/ msgHdrViewOverlay.css, /messenger/skin/threadPane.css, messengercompose.css
	Attach-disabled.gif	/messenger/skin/ msgHdrViewOverlay.css, /messenger/skin/threadPane.css, messengercompose.css
	Attach-hover.gif	/messenger/skin/ msgHdrViewOverlay.css, /messenger/skin/threadPane.css, messengercompose.css
	Quote.gif	Messengercompose.css
	Quote-clicked.gif	Messengercompose.css
	Quote-disabled.gif	Messengercompose.css

IMAGE	LOCATION	AIM STYLESHEET WHERE IT IS IMPLEMENTED
	Quote-hover.gif	Messengercompose.css
	Save.gif	Messengercompose.css
	Save-clicked.gif	Messengercompose.css
	Save-disabled.gif	Messengercompose.css
	Save-hover.gif	Messengercompose.css
	Send.gif	Messengercompose.css
	Send-clicked.gif	Messengercompose.css
	Send-disabled.gif	Messengercompose.css
	Send-hover.gif	Messengercompose.css
	SendConvAltering.gif	
	SendConvNo.gif	
	SendConvYes.gif	
	Spelling.gif	Messengercompose.css
	Spelling-clicked.gif	Messengercompose.css

IMAGE	LOCATION	AIM STYLESHEET WHERE IT IS IMPLEMENTED
	Spelling-disabled.gif	Messengercompose.css
	Spelling-hover.gif	Messengercompose.css
×	Stop.gif	/messenger/skin/messenger.css, /messenger/skin/addressbook/ addressbook.css, messengercompose.css

MessengerCompose Skin Cascading Style Sheets

- Messengercompose.css

Navigator Skin–/navigator/skin/

Images

IMAGE	LOCATION	AIM STYLESHEET WHERE IT IS IMPLEMENTED
	Back.gif	/communicator/skin/help/help.css, navigator.css
	Back-clicked.gif	/communicator/skin/help/help.css, navigator.css
	Back-disabled.gif	/communicator/skin/help/help.css, navigator.css
	Back-hover.gif	/communicator/skin/help/help.css, navigator.css
	Forward.gif	/communicator/skin/help/help.css, navigator.css
	Forward-clicked.gif	/communicator/skin/help/help.css, navigator.css

IMAGE	LOCATION	AIM STYLESHEET WHERE IT IS IMPLEMENTED
	Forward-disabled.gif	/communicator/skin/help/help.css, navigator.css
	Forward-hover.gif	/communicator/skin/help/help.css, navigator.css
	Navbar-inner-groove-left.gif	Navigator.css
	Navbar-inner-groove-middle.gif	Navigator.css
	Navbar-inner-groove-right.gif	Navigator.css
	Reload.gif	Navigator.css
	Reload-clicked.gif	Navigator.css
	Reload-disabled.gif	Navigator.css
	Reload-hover.gif	Navigator.css
	Stop.gif	Navigator.css
	Stop-clicked.gif	Navigator.css
	Stop-disabled.gif	Navigator.css
	Stop-hover.gif	Navigator.css
	Ubhist-keyword-popup.gif	Navigator.css

IMAGE	LOCATION	AIM STYLESHEET WHERE IT IS IMPLEMENTED
	Ubhist-keyword-popup-active.gif	Navigator.css
	Urlbar-left.gif	Navigator.css
	Urlbar-middle.gif	Navigator.css
	Urlbar-right.gif	Navigator.css

Navigator Skin Cascading Style Sheets

- Navigator.css

User Interface Reference

Netscape Navigator Browser

The user interface elements in Figure B.1 are referenced by the cascading style sheet that calls them.

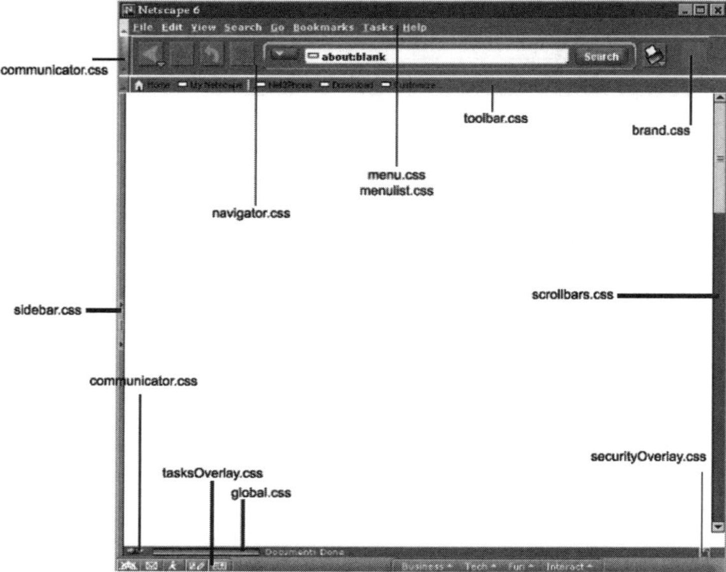

Figure B.1 User interface elements.

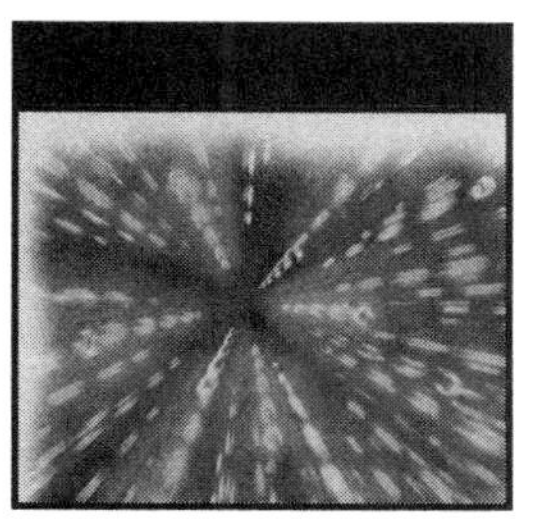

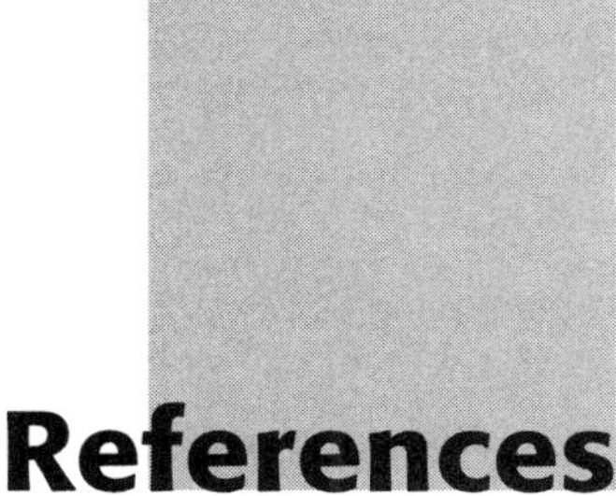

References

Churchill, Hyatt, Waterson, "XUL <template> reference," Mozilla.org, http://www.mozilla.org/doc/xul-template-reference.html, 2000.

Davis, Jack, and Susan Merritt, *The Web Design Wow! Book*, Peachpit, 1998.

Deakin, Neil, "XUL Element Reference," http://www.xulplanet.com/tutorials/xultu/elemref/mxdref.html, XulPlanet.com, 2001.

Deakin, Neil, "XUL Tutorial—Anonymous Content," http://www.xulplanet.com/tutorials/xultu/xblcontent.html, 2001.

Deakin, Neil, "XUL Tutorial," http://www.xulplanet.com/tutorials/xultu/, 2001.

Dickens, Charles, *A Tale of Two Cities*, 1859.

Dickens, Charles, *David Copperfield*, 1850.

Hyatt, David, "Writing Efficient CSS," Mozilla.org, http://www.mozilla.org/xpfe/goodcss.html, 2000.

Lassila, Ora, "Introduction to RDF Metadata," W3C Note 1997-11-13, http://www.w3.org/TR/NOTE-rdf-simple-intro.

Lie, Håkon, and Bert, Bos. *Cascading Style Sheets—Designing for the Web*, Harlow, England: Addison-Wesley, 1999.

Mozilla.org, "XPToolkit Project," http://www.mozilla.org/xpfe/.

Mozilla.org, "XUL Programmer's Reference Manual," http://www.mozilla.org/xpfe/xulref/, 2001.

Mozilla.org, "XML Binding Language," W3C Note, http://www.w3.org/TR/xbl/, W3C Note, February, 2001.

Raymond, Eric, "The Cathedral and the Bazaar," http://www.tuxedo.org/~esr/writings/cathedral-bazaar/cathedral-bazaar/, 2000.

Smith, Kevin, "Rebuilding the Truman," http://www.geocities.com/trumantruck/, 2001.

W3C Metadata Activity, "Resource Description Framework (RDF) Model and Syntax Specification," W3C Recommendation, http://www.w3.org/TR/REC-rdf-syntax/, February 22, 1999.

W3C Metadata Activity, "Resource Description Framework,"http://www.w3.org/RDF/, 2000.

W3C Working Group on Cascading Style Sheets and Properties, Cascading Style Sheets, level 2 CSS2 Specification, W3C Recommendation, http://www.w3.org/TR/REC-CSS2/, 1998.

W3C Working Group on Extensible Stylesheet Language, Version 1.0, W3C Recommendation, http://www.w3.org/TR/xsl/, 2000.

Waterson, Chris, "XUL Template Primer—Multiple Rules," Mozilla.org, http://www.mozilla.org/docs/xul/xulnotes/template-multi.html, 2000.

Waterson, Chris, "XUL Template Primer," Mozilla.org, http://www.mozilla.org/docs/xul/xulnotes/template-primer.html, 1999.

Index

A

absolute positioning, 62, **64**, 85
accesskey attribute, 91
<action> element, 145, **146**, 149, 156, **156**, 157-158, **158**, 160, 236, 242
activation splash screen theme, 114-115, **114**
active pseudo class, 59*t*
Add Product button, E-commerce UI, 274
addBinding method in, 178*t*
addProductToBasket(), 263, 274
adjacent nodes/selectors, 56
Adobe ImageStyler/PhotoShop/ GoLive, 108
AIM skin, 109, 113
alert dialog in JavaScript, 96, **97**, **98**
align attribute, 71, 84, 86, 91
align text property, 71
all sets or groups, 40-41
alternative container in RDF, 137
ampersand symbol, 33
animation, 115-116, **116**
annotations, 42
anonymous content, 44, 139, 140-142, 176, 179, **180**, 183, 186-191, **186**
ANY element, 28
any selectors, 58
AOL Instant Messenger (AIM), 109, 113
APIs, 9
applets in jXUL Open Source Project, 45, 212, 229
application class, jXUL, 212, 214-218, **214**, **215**, **216-218**
application layer, jXUL, 210-212, **211**
Application Object Model (AOM), 133, 143, 209
archival and extraction tools, 108
Asset List panel in UI, **87**, 88, **88-89**
Asset View panel in UI, 92-94, **92-93**
attribute attribute, XBL, 186
attribute selectors, 54-56
attributes, 23-24, 27, 29-30, 31*t*, 33, 39, 40, 83
  inheritance of, 206
  in overlay files, 170-171, 171*t*
  selectors for, 54-56

B

Back button, 124, 125*t*
backgrounds, 121
bag container in RDF, 136
Bazaar style programming, 4
BBEdit, 108
behavioral bindings, 6, 8
Behavioral Extensions to CSS (BECSS), 174
binary, 37*t*
binding (*See also* XML Binding Language), 7-8, **8**, 109-110, 167-168, 174-207, 167, 174
  rules for, 187
  themes and, 116, **119**, 126
  unique identifiers and, 176
  in XUL templates, 148-149, 158-160, **161-162**, **163**
<binding> and <bindings> elements, 148-149, 159-160, 176, 182, 183, 207
Blackwood project, 228
blinking text, 71
block display, 61
<body> element, XBL, 183, 185, 194
bookmarks, 123-124, 137-138, **137**, 149-152, **151**, **152**

boolean, 38*t*
border property, 64-70, **67**, **69**, 121
boxes, 9, 222
branding the browser for themes, 115-116, **116**, **117-118**
Browse Catalog tree, E-commerce UI, 270-271, **271-272**
BrowseMorePanels(), 248
building an interface, 81-106
 alert dialog in JavaScript for, 96, **97**, **98**
 Asset List panel for, **87**, 88, **88-89**
 Asset View panel for, 92-94, **92-93**
 buttons in, 90-91
 complete code for, 98, **99-104**
 Credits panel for, 96, **97**
 Document Type Definition (DTD) in, 83
 event handlers using JavaScript in,96-98, **97**, **98**, 105, **105-106**
 <iframe> element in, 96
 <label> element in, 92, 93
 <menu> elements in, 92-94
 namespace for, 84
 <radiogroup> and <radio> elements in, 92, 94
 Reports panel in, 94-96, **95**
 <spring> element in, 87
 subcomponents in, 84-85
 tabs and tab panels in, 82-83, 85-88, **85**, **86**, 92, 94-96, **95**
 text editor selection for, 82
 <textbox> element in, 92, 93
 titledbox component in, 84, **84**, **85**, 87
 toolbar/toolbox for, 90-91, **91**, 94
 views in, 92-93
 window element as main component in, 83-84, 87
 XML declaration in, 83
built-in types, 44
bulletinboard, 9, 222
busy or hover state, in animation, 115
button element, 10, **11**, 15, **16**, 17, 23, 90-91, 124-126, **124**, 168, 184, 222
 JavaScript associated with, 98
 in jXUL Open Source Project, 221, **222**
 naming conventions for, 124, 125*t*
byte, 37*t*

C

C++, 2
calculateCurrency(), 262, 281
calculateForeign(), 263, 282
Cascaded Style Sheet (CSS), 4, 6, 49-79, **78**
 Behavioral Extensions to CSS (BECSS) and, 174
 in Customizable Browser Portal, 231
 designer vs. user style sheets in, 75
 global.css file for, 77, **78**
 important tag in, 75
 inheritance in, 75
 jXUL Open Source Project and, 211, 215, 224, **224**, **225**
 in My Sidebar Customization, 236
 rules for, 51, 74-77
 selectors and declarations in, 51, 53-58, 55*t*
 syntax of, 53-54, 77
 themes using, 107, 108, 110-111, 116, 123
 in XBL, 176-177, 179, **180**
case sensitivity, 83, 98
CatalogProvider data source, E-commerce UI, 263-265, 264*t*, **264-265**
CDATA, 30, 31*t*, 37*t*, 194
century, 38*t*
character sets, 21-22
charcode attribute, XBL, 184
checkbox element, 23, 222, **223**
Checkout button, E-commerce UI, 276, **278**
checkOut(), 263, 276
child elements, 11, 28-29, 40, 44, 56-57, 88, 183, 187-188, **188**, **189**, 271
child selectors, 56-57
choice groups, 40-41
choice or logical OR operator, 28-29
chrome, 83, 108, 234
class attribute, 91
Cold Fusion Markup Language (CFML), 96, 267
colorpicker component of XUL, 2, **2**
colors in themes, 116, 119-123, 125
comm.jar file contents, 234, **235**
comments, 25
communicator component in My Sidebar Customization, 234
communicator skin, 9, 113
compact display, 61-62
complex types, 36, 39, 40-42
complexContent, 42
components directory in My Sidebar Customization, 234
<conditions> element, 145, **146**, 148-149, 160
connected set (*See* all sets)
container attribute, 145
container elements in RDF, 136-138
container layer, jXUL, 210-212, **211**
content models, 23, 33, 40
content panels, 9
content particles, 29, 41
<content> element, 145-147, 147*t*, 149-152, 176, 179, **180**, 183, 186, 192
contexual selectors, 56-58
contract identifiers, XUL templates, 144, 144*t*
convertPrice(), 281, 282
CORBA Interface Definition Language (IDL), 44
Credits panel in UI, 96, **97**, 96
cross-platform customizations of XUL, 2, 4
Cross-Platform Front End (XPFE), 3-4
css package, jXUL, 227
Currency Rate tree in E-commerce UI, 275, **275-276**
currency translation, 262-263, 281-282
CurrencyRates data source for E-commerce UI, 265, 266*t*, **266-267**
Customizable Browser Portal (*See also* My Sidebar customization), 231-256
 cascaded style sheets (CSS) in, 231
 design approach to, 232
 JavaScript in, 231
 My Sidebar customization in (*See* My Sidebar customization)
 overlays in, 231
 Resource Definition Framework (RDF) in, 231
 XML Binding Language (XBL) in, 231
 XUL templates in, 231
customize.js file in My Sidebar Customization, 234-235
CustomizePanel(), 236

D

data hiding, 7
data types, 30, 36, 44, 96
data, 38*t*
datasources attribute, 144, 144*t*, 242, 271
datasources, in RDF, 135-136, 140, **141**, 143-144
debugging XUL, 229
decimal, 37*t*
decks, 9
declarations, 5, 21-22, 25, 51, 53-58
decoration text property, 71
default namespace, 36
default value of attributes, 30, 40
descendent nodes, 56
descendent selectors, 57-58
designer vs. user style sheets in CSS, 75
dialogs, 9, 11
directory structure of Netscape 6.x, 234, **235**
display property, 61-62
Document, 44
Document Object Model (DOM), 8, 18, 44-48, **45**, **46**, **47**, 86, 91, 143
  in E-commerce UI, 257
  in jXUL Open Source Project, 211, 212, 214, 224
  in My Sidebar Customization, 245
  in themes, 111-112, **111**
  in XBL, 177-182, 178*t*, 197
document sample in XUL, **5**, 15, **16**
Document Type (DOCTYPE) declaration, 32, 26-27, 36
document type declaration, 22
Document Type Definition (DTD), 14, 17, 22, 26, 27-36, **33-36**, 83
double quotes to delimit strings, 83
Double, 38*t*
drop-down menus, 126
dropmarkers, 126
dynamic content, 11, 18, 111, 143
dynamic HTML (DHTML)
  in My Sidebar Customization, 251-253, **254-255**, **256**
  in jXUL Open Source Project, 228

E

ECMAScript, 44, 45
E-commerce User Interface, 257-296, **260**, **285**
  Add Product button for, 274
  Browse Catalog tree for, 270-271, **271-272**
  CatalogProvider data source for, 263-265, 264*t*, **264-265**
  Checkout button for, 276, **278**
  component architecture of, 260-261, **261**
  currency translation in, 265, 266*t*, 266-267, 275, **275-276**, 281-282
  design approach to, 259
  Document Model Object (DOM) in, 257
  JavaScript event handlers in, 257, 261-263, 280-283, **290-293**
  logo for, 270, **270**
  main XUL interface file code for, **285-290**
  navigation through, 284
  OrderHistory handling for, 267, 268*t*, **268**, **269**, 278, **278**, **279-280**, 295-296
  OverlayFile.xul for, **293-295**, 293
  personalization package for, 262, 270, 280
  price calculation package for, 262-263, 281
  Price Labels for, 275, **275**
  problem definition and requirements for, 257-259
  Product Description Area for, 273, **273**, 274
  Product Display Area in, 276, **277**
  Product Label for, 273
  Resource Description Framework (RDF) in, 257
  shopping basket application in, 262, 263, 276, **277**, **278**, 283-284
  Specials Box for, 272-273, **273**
  user interface layout for, 261, **262**
  window root element of, 269-270
  XUL templates in, 257
editor component of My Sidebar Customization, 234
editor skin, 9, 113
element attribute, XBL, 185
element-only content model, 28
elements, 22-23, 27-29, 33, 36-40, 44, 83
  declaration of, 27-29
  in overlay files, 170-171, 171*t*
  properties of, 60-74
  in RDF, 135-138, 138*t*
  simple types as, 36-40, 37-39*t*
  in XBL, 182
empty elements, 23, 28, 41-42
encapsulation, 7, 174, 214
encoding declaration, 21-22
end tag, 22, 23, 27
entities, 30-33, **32**
ENTITIES/ENTITY, 31*t*, 39*t*
enumerate type, 30, 31*t*, 44
event handlers (*See* JavaScript and event handlers)
eventhandlers.js, 105, **105-106**
events, 83
explicit content, XBL, 176, 186
extensibility of XUL, 167
Extensible Markup Language (XML), 1, 4-6, 19-49, 133
Extensible Stylesheet Language (XSL), 49
external entities, 30, 32
external subset (DOCTYPE), 27, 33

F

first-child pseudo class, 59*t*
fixed attributes, 40
FIXED keyword, 30
fixed positioning, 62
flex attribute, 84, 86, 87, 96
Float, 37*t*
focus pseudo class, 59*t*
font properties, 72-74, **75**, **76**
Forward button, 124, 125*t*
foundation layer, jXUL, 210-212, **211**
fragment factory, jXUL, 212
framework package, jXUL, 227
framework.treetable package, jXUL, 227

G

Gecko rendering engine, 4, 228
getAnonymousNodes method in, 178*t*, 197
<getter> element, 183-185, 192, 194, 197, 198, 200
GIF files, 108
global component of My Sidebar Customization, 234
global skin, 9, 113
global.css file, 77, **78**
Grading Application example of XBL, 194-200, **195-201**, **202**
graphs, in RDF, 138-142, **139**, **140**, **142**, **143**
grid, 222
grouping elements, 28-29, 40

H

<handler> and <handlers> elements, XBL, 176, 184

hasChildNode, 45
hash tables, 214
hbox, 222
height attribute, 122
Home icon, 124
horizontal layout values, 90
hover pseudo class, 59*t*
hover state, in animation, 115
href attribute for binding, 169-170, **170**
hypertext markup language (HTML), 7, **7**, 11, 19, **20**, 22, 46, **46**, 49-51, **51**, **52**, 84, 228

I

id attribute, XBL, 184
ID and IDS, 30, 31*t*, 39*t*
identifier in RDF, 139, 140-142
IDREF and IDREFS, 30, 31*t*, 39*t*
IE, 45
<iframe> element, 96, 242
image element, 222, **223**, 224, 222
image or paint programs, 108
imgalign attribute, 91
<implementation> element, XBL, 176, 184-185, 192
IMPLIED keyword, 30
important tag in CSS, 75
indent text property, 71
inheritance, 75
    of attributes, 189-191, **190**, **191**, **193**, 206
    of binding, 206-207
    of properties, 61
    of skins, 113, **113**
Init(), 235, 236
inline display, 61
insertafter/insertbefore attribute, 170-171, 171*t*
insertion point, XBL, 187-188, **188**, **189**
installation script (JavaScript) for theme, 127-128, **131**
Int, 37*t*
integer, 37*t*
interface building (*See* building an interface)
Interface Definition Language (IDL), 44
internal parsed entities, 30
internal subset (DOCTYPE), 27, 33
internationalization in XUL, 14, 17
ISO character sets, 22

J

Java (*See also* jXUL Open Source Project), 2, 4, 44, 209
Java API for XML Parsing (JAXP) classes, jXUL, 212
Java archive (JAR) files, 83
    in My Sidebar Customization, 233-234, 233
    in themes, 112, 113-114, 126, **130**
JavaScript and event handlers, 4, 8-9, **8**, 15, **16**, 17, 44, 46, 47, 91, 96-98, **97**, **98**, 105, **105-106**
    binding and, 176, 177-182
    buttons associated with, 98
    in Customizable Browser Portal, 231
    in E-commerce UI, 257, 261-263, 280-283, **290-293**
    in jXUL Open Source Project, 211, 215, 224-227, **225**, **226**, **227**
    in My Sidebar Customization, 236, 242-245, **243-245**
    personalization package using, 262, 280
    price calculation package using, 262-263
    shopping basket application using, 262, 263, 276, **277**, **278**, 283-284
    in themes installation script, 111-112, **111**, 127-128, **131**
    in XBL 183, 184, 194, 199-200, **200**, 201-206, **203-205**, **206**
JPG files, 108
js package, jXUL, 227
justification, 86
jXUL Open Source Project, 2, 4, 209-229
    applets in, XUL, 212
    application in, XUL, 212, 214-218, **214**, **215**, **216-218**, 229
    application layer of, 210-212, **211**
    Application Object Model (AOM) and, 209
    architecture, 210-212, **211**
    button element in, 221, **222**
    cascading style sheet (CSS) and, 211, 215, 224, **224**, **225**
    challenges to, 228
    checkbox element in, 222, **223**
    container layer of, 210-212, **211**
    debugging XUL in, 229
    Document Object Model (DOM) in, 211, 212, 214, 224
    emulation of browser object hierarchy through, 228
    foundation layer of, 210-212, **211**
    fragment factory in, 212
    getting involved in, 228
    hypertext markup language (HTML) and DHTML in, 228
    image element in, 222, **223**, 224
    Java API for XML Parsing (JAXP) classes and, 212
    JavaScript in, 211, 215, 224-227, **225**, **226**, **227**
    menu element in, 219, **221**
    packages of, 227
    Rhino parser for, 211, 224-227, 229
    run() method in, 215, **216-218**
    Swing resources and, 212, 218
    Web sites of interest to, 210, 228
    window element of, 218-219, **219**, **220**
    XML Binding Language (XBL) in, 211
    XUL Runner in, 211, 212-213, **213**, 224-227, **225**
    XUL widgets (JComponents) in, 211, 218-224
    xulExample.xul and, 209, **210**

K

keycode attribute, XBL, 184
keys, 42
keyset, 222
keystroke events, 91

L

<label> element, 9, 22, 85, 92, 93, 181, 222
lang pseudo class, 59*t*
language, 39*t*
lax value for processContents attribute, 42
letter spacing property, 71
line height property, 71
link pseudo class, 59*t*
LINK tag, 51, **52**
list type, 39-40
list-item display, 61
lists, 88
LiveConnect, 229
loadBindingDocument method in, 178*t*
loading an XUL file, 17
local filenames, XUL templates, 144, 144*t*
localization in XUL, 14, **15**, 18
logo, E-commerce UI, 270, **270**
Long, 37*t*

M

manifest.rdf file, 108, 126, **129**, **130**
margin property, 64-70, **67**, **68**, 121
markup languages, 19, 21
maskNumber(), 281, 282
member attribute, 145
<member> element, 145-147, 147*t*, 149-152
menubar, 22, **22**, 23, 222
menuButton class, 110
<menupopup> and <menuitem> elements in, 93-94, 120, 173-174, 222
menus and menu element, 9, 11, 17, 22, **22**, 23, 92, 93, 116, 118-124, **119**, 168, 222
  background colors for, 119-123
  disabled menuitem formatting in, 120
  drop-down menus in, 126
  in jXUL Open Source Project, 219, **221**
  overlays, demonstrating reusability of, 172-174, **172-173**, **174**, **175**
  popup, 120-122
  skinning, 116, 118-124, **119**
  text colors/fonts for, 119-123
  tooltip in, 122-123
messenger skin, 9, 113
metadata, 9, 21, 108
method of objects, 46-47
<method> element, XBL, 185, 194
methods added to bound elements using XBL, 192-200, **193-194**
minOccurs/maxOccurs, 41
mixed attribute, 42
mixed elements, 28
Modern Mozillium Theme, 110-112
modifiers attribute, XBL, 184
month, 38*t*
mouse click events, 91
Mozilla browser/mozilla.org, 2-4, 6, 9, 13, 16, 45, 77, 143, 162-163, 174, 228
multiple attributes, selectors for, 55
multiple rules in XUL templates, 152-158, **153-154**, **156**, **157**, **158**
My Sidebar customization, 232-256, **233**, **237**
  <action> element in, 236, 242
  add/delete tabs to, 233
  addPanel() in, 248, **249-251**, **252**, **253**
  binding in, 236
  cascaded style sheets (CSS) in, 236
  chrome URL and, 234
  comm.jar file contents in, 234, **235**
  communicator component of, 234
  components directory in, 234, 248
  Customize Sidebar dialog for, 247-248, **247**
  customize.js file in, 234-235
  customize.xul file in, 235
  customize-panel.js file in, 235
  customize-panel.xul in, 236
  datasources as null value in, 242
  directory structure of Netscape 6.x in, 234, **235**
  Document Object Model (DOM) and, 245
  dynamic HTML and, 251-253, **254-255**, **256**
  editor component of, 234
  Gecko component of, 234
  global component of, 234
  <iframe> element in, 242
  Java archive (JAR) files of, 233-234
  JavaScript in, 236, 242-245, **243-245**
  local-panels.rdf file in, 236, 245-248, **246-247**
  navigator component of, 234
  nsSidebar.js, 248, **249-251**
  overlays in, 236
  preview.js in, 236
  preview.xul file, 236
  Resource Definition File (RDF) and, 236-237, 245-248, **246-247**
  sidebarBindings.xml file in, 236
  sidebarOverlay.css file in, 236
  sidebarOverlay.js in, 236, 242-245, **243-245**
  sidebarOverlay.xul in, 236, **238-242**
  XML Binding Language (XBL), 236
  XUL templates in, 236-237

N

name attribute, 93, 185
Name, 39*t*
named element groups, 41
names of attributes, 24, 29-30, 54, 83
names of elements, 22, 28
namespace, 5, 15, 24-25, **25**, 36, 84, 135
navigation bar skinning, 124-126, **124**
navigator component of My Sidebar Customization, 234
navigator skin, 9, 113
NCName, 39*t*
NDATA, 32
negativeInteger, 37*t*
nesting element tags, 9
Netscape browser (*See also* themes), 4, 6, 9, 13, 15, 16, 45, 76-77, 84, 96, 107-131, 143, 162-163
  My Sidebar customization, 232-256, **233**, **237**
Netscape Communicator, 3
Netscape Composer files, 110
Netscape Messenger files, 110
NMTOKEN and NMTOKENS, 30, 31*t*, 39*t*
node and arc diagrams, in RDF, 138-142, **139**, **140**, **142**, **143**
nodeName, 45
nodes, 44, 45, 56, **57**, 138-142, **139**, **140**, **142**, **143**, 271
nodeType, 45
nonNegativeInteger/nonPositiveInteger, 37*t*
NOTATION, 30, 31*t*, 32, 39*t*
nullable fields, 42

O

object in RDF, 134, 135
onclick events, 91, 201-206, **203-204**
oncommand method, 91, 98
one-based position number of element, 171, 171*t*
onget/onset attribute, XBL, 185
Opera, 45
Opinion Poll example using XBL, 178-182, **178**, **179**, **180**, **181**
optional operator (question mark), 29
optional-and-repeatable operator (asterisk), 29
OR operator, 28-29
OrderHistory component for E-commerce UI, 267, 268*t*, **268**, **269**, 278, **278**, **279-280**, 295-296
orient attribute, 84, 94
origins and development of XUL, 3-4
<overlay> element, 168
OverlayFile.xul for E-commerce UI, **293-295**
overlays, 11-13, **14**, 17, 167-207, **168**, **169**, **170**, 215, 218
  in Customizable Browser Portal, 231
  in E-commerce UI, **293-296**
  elements and attributes in, 170-171, 171*t*

example of, 172-174, **172-173**, **174**, **175**
identifying content for, 168-169
insertafter/insertbefore attribute in, 170-171, 171*t*
in My Sidebar Customization, 236
one-based position number of element in, 171, 171*t*
<overlay> element of, 168
position attribute in, 171, 171*t*
priority of elements in, 171
referencing the overlay, href attribute, 169-170, **170**
reusability of XUL and, 167, 168
XML Binding Language (XBL) and, 167-168, 174-207

P

packaging a theme, 126
padding property, 64-70, **67**, **70**
<parameter> element, 185, 194
parameter entities, 32-33
parsed character data (*See* PCDATA)
parsing of XUL interface, 17, **17**
pattern matching in XUL templates, 146-147, **147**, 149-152
PCDATA, 28
percent symbol, 33
personalization package for UI, JavaScript, 262, 280
personalize(), 262, 276, 280
phase attribute, XBL, 184
PKZIP, 108
plugins, 45
popup menus, 120-122
portals (*See* Customizable Browser Portal)
position attribute, 171, 171*t*
position property, 62-64, **62**, **63**, **64**
positiveInteger, 37*t*
predicate in RDF, 134, 135
Preferences, to change themes, 107, 111
prefix for namespaces, 24
presence keywords, 30
price calculation package for UI, JavaScript, 262-263
Price Labels for E-commerce UI, 275, **275**
primitive types, 36, 39
print button, 98, 125-126, **127**
priority of elements in overlays, 171
processContents attribute, 42
processing instructions (PI), 21, 25-26
Product Description Area for E-commerce UI, 273, **273**, 274
Product Display Area in E-commerce UI, 276, **277**
Product Label for E-commerce UI, 273
progress meters, 9
prolog of schema, 36
properties added to bound elements using XBL, 192-200, **193-194**
properties object in RDF, 134, 136
property attribute, 46-47, 60-74, 186
<property> element, 185-186, 192
pseudo attributes, 26
pseudo classes/pseudo elements, 58-59, 59*t*, **60**, 61*t*
public identifiers, 27

Q-R

QName, 39*t*

<radiogroup> and <radio> elements, 92, 94, 222, 224
Raymond, Eric, 4
readonly attribute, 185
recurringDate/Day/Duration 38*t*,
ref attribute, 145, 271
referencing overlays, href attribute, 169-170, **170**
RefreshPanel(), 235
relative positioning, 62, 84, 85
Reload button, 124, 125*t*
removeBinding method in, 178*t*
removeChild, 45
repeated elements/repeatability operators, 29, 41
Reports panel in UI, 94-96, **95**
REQUIRED keyword, 30
required-and-repeatable operator (plus sign), 29
Resource Description Framework (RDF), 9, 11, 17, 133-165, **134**
anonymous resources in, 139, 140-142
bookmark file in, 137-138, **137**
Cold Fusion dynamic generation of, 267
container elements in, 136-138
in Customizable Browser Portal, 231
datasources in, 135-136, 140, **141**, 143-144
in E-commerce UI, 257
elements in, 135-138, 138*t*
graphs or node and arc diagrams in, 138-142, **139**, **140**, **142**, **143**
identifiers in, 139, 140-142
in My Sidebar Customization, 236-237, 245-248, **246-247**
namespaces in, 135
singular rules in, 149
syntax of, 134-143, **134**, **136**
tags in, 135-136, 138*t*
XUL templates and (*See also* XUL templates), 142-143
resources object in RDF, 134
reusability of XUL, 11-13, 167, 168
Rhino parser, 211, 224-227, 229
root element, 5, 22, 23, 26, 44, 83-84, 86, 96
<rule> element, 145, **146**, 148
run() method, jXUL, 215, **216-218**
run-in display, 61
Runner, 211-213, **213**, 224-227, **225**

S

schema, 27, 36-44, **42-44**
scope of namespace, 24-25
<script> element, 183
script tag, 15
scrollbars, 17
selectors, 51, 53-58, 55*t*
semicolon as separator, 53
sequence container in RDF, 137
sequence operator, 28-29
sequential set or sequence group, 40-41
serialization syntax in RDF, 135
setForeign(), 281
<setter> element, 185, 186, 192, 194, 197, 199
setUserID(), 262, 276, 280
shopping basket application, E-commerce UI, 262, 263, 276, **277**, **278**, 283-284
short, 37*t*
sibling nodes/selectors, 56
sidebar skin, 113
SidebarCustomize(), 235, 247
sidebarOverlay.xul in My Sidebar customization, 236, **238-242**
simple types, 39, 36-40, 37-39*t*, 44
simpleContent, 42
singular rules, XUL templates, 149
"skinning" a browser, 6-7, 9, **10**, 14
skins, 107, 110, 113, 116, 118-124, **119**
skip value for processContents attribute, 42
SmartUpdate utility, 126, 128
Specials Box for E-commerce UI, 272-273, **273**
splash screen, 114-115, **114**
<spring> element, 9, 87

src attribute, 96
stack, 9, 224
standalone document declaration, 21, 22
Standard Generalized Markup Language (SGML), 27
standardizing an object, 44-45
standards and technologies of XUL, 4-9, **5**
start tag, 22, 23, 27
statement object in RDF, 134
static positioning, 62, **65**, **66**
Stop button, 124, 125*t*
strict value for processContents attribute, 42
strikeouts, 71
string, 37*t*, 83
style attribute, 76
styles and stylesheets, 6-7. 15, 17, 25-26, 49
subelements, 23
subject in RDF, 134, 135
substitution groups, 42
Swing resources, jXUL, 212, 218
syntax of XML, 21-27, 36
SYSTEM keyword, 32, 27

T

tabs and tab panels, 17, 62, 82-83, 85-88, **85**, **86**, 92, 94-96, **95**, 224
tags, 19, 22, 23, 27, 83, 84, 135-136, 138*t*
<template> element, 145, 149
templates for themes, downloading, 108-112
templates, XUL (*See* XUL templates)
test elements (<content>, <triple> and <member>), 145-147, 147*t*
text, 23, 28
text display properties, 71-72, **71**, **72**, **73**
text editors, 82, 108
<textbox> element, 92, 93, 224
TextPad, 108
themes, 13-14, 18, 83, 107-131
- activation splash screen in, 114-115, **114**
- animation in, 115-116, **116**
- AOL Instant Messenger (AIM) files in, 109
- archival and extraction tools for, 108
- backgrounds, 121
- binding in, 109-110, 116, **119**, 126
- bookmark folder in, 123-124
- borders in, 121
- branding the browser for, 115-116, **116**, **117-118**
- buttons in, 124-126, **124**, 125*t*
- Cascading Style Sheet (CSS) in, 107, 108, 110-111, 116, 123
- changing themes using Preferences, 107, 111
- colors in, 116, 119-123, 125
- deliver and install, 127-129, **128**, **129**
- developing, 112-113
- directory for development of, 112-114
- Document Object Model (DOM) in, 111-112, **111**
- downloadable theme sites for, 107, 108
- drop-down menus in, 126
- filenames for, 128
- height attributes in, 122
- Home icon in, 124
- image or paint program for, 108
- inheritance of skins in, 113, **113**
- installation script in JavaScript for, 127-128, **131**
- JavaScript and Java archive (JAR) files in, 111-112, 113-114, 126, **130**
- manifest.rdf file for, 108, 126, **129**, **130**
- margins in, 121
- Modern Mozillium Theme example of, 110-112
- modularity of, 112, **112**
- navigating a new theme in, 110-112
- navigation bar skinning, 124-126, **124**
- Netscape files in, 109-110
- packaging of, 126
- print button in, 125-126, **127**
- registration of, 128
- skinning the menu in, 116, 118-124, **119**
- skins in, 107, 110, 113
- SmartUpdate utility for, 126, 128
- structure of, 109-110, **109**
- template download for, 108-112
- text editor for, 108
- tooltip in, 122-123
- XUL is Cool Theme in, **131**, 131

time/timeDuration/Instant/Period, 38*t*, 38
titledbox component, 84, **84**, **85**, 87, 224
titles, 85, 224
token, 37*t*
toolbars/toolboxes, 9, 11, 15, 90-91, **91**, 94, 168, 224
tooltip, 122-123
transform text property, 71
trees, 9, 11, **12**, 17, 18, 23, 49, 56, **57**, 88, **88-89**, 143, 224, 270-271, 271-272
<triple> element, 145-156, 147*t*, **156**, 159
twisty, 11, 88, 107
type attribute, XBL, 184
type selectors, 54

U

underlines, 71
Unicode character set, 21-22
Uniform Resource Identifier (URI), 24, 27, 32, 33, 96, 135
Uniform Resource Locator (URL), 144, 144*t*
unique identifiers, 86, 90, 91, 176, 182, 185
Universal Character Set (UCS), 21-22
universal selectors, 58
unsigned data types, 37*t*
uriReference, 39*t*, 39
user interfaces, 1-2, 16-17
UTF character sets, 22
util package, jXUL, 227

V

value attribute, 91, 93
value of attribute, 24, 30, 40, 54, 83, 86
vbox, 224
version attribute, 21, 83
viewItem(), 276, 281
views, 92-93
visited pseudo class, 58, 59*t*

W

wait state, in animation, 115
Web sites of interest, jXUL, 210
WebFonts, 74
well-formedness of XML and HTML, 7, 27
widgets, 4, 9-10, 17, 168
- jXUL Open Source Project, 211, 218-224

wildcard operator (asterisk), 58

wildcard particles (wildcardType), 42
window element, 5, 9, 10, 15, 22-23, **22**, 83-84, 96, 218-219, **219**, **220**, 224, 269-270
WinEdit, 108
WinZip, 108, 126
word spacing property, 71
World Wide Web Consortium (W3C), 49, 50
wrapping elements, 22, 29

X

XFORM renderer, 229
XML Binding Language (XBL), 4, 7-8, **8**, 167-168, 174-207
- accessing bound elements and, 176
- addBinding method in, 178*t*
- anonymous content and, 176, 179, **180**, 183, 186-191, **186**
- <binding> and <bindings> elements in, 176, 182, 183, 207
- <body> element in, 183, 185, 194
- Cascaded Style Sheet (CSS) and, 176-177, 179, **180**
- CDATA and, 194
- <children> element in, 183, 187-188, **188**, **189**
- <content> element in, 176, 179, **180**, 183, 186, 192
- Customizable Browser Portal, 231
- Document Object Model (DOM) and, 177-182, 178*t*, 197
- elements in, 182
- event handlers in, 201-206, **203-205**, **206**
- explicit content and, 176, 186
- getAnonymousNodes method in, 178*t*, 197
- getter and setter functions in, 185
- <getter> element in, 183-184, 192, 194, 197, 198, 200
- Grading Application example of, 194-200, **195-201**, **202**
- <handler> and <handlers> elements in, 176, 184, 201-206
- <implementation> element in, 176, 184-185, 192
- inheritance of attributes in, with anonymous content, 189-191, **190**, **191**, **193**
- inheritance of binding in, 206-207
- insertion point in, 187-188, **188**, **189**
- JavaScript event handlers and, 176-184, 194, 199-200, **200**
- jXUL Open Source Project, 211
- <label> element in, 191
- loadBindingDocument method in, 178*t*
- <method> element in, 185, 194
- methods added to bound elements using, 192-200, **193-194**
- My Sidebar Customization in, 236
- Opinion Poll example using, 178-182, **178**, **179**, **180**, **181**
- <parameter> element in, 185, 194
- properties added to bound elements using, 192-200, **193-194**
- <property> element in, 185-186, 192
- removeBinding method in, 178*t*
- rules for, 187
- <script> element in, 183
- <setter> element in, 186, 192, 194, 197, 199
- syntax of, 176-186, **177**
- unique identifiers and, 176, 182, 185
- XPath and, 183

XML declaration, 5, 21-22, 25, 26, 36, 83
XMLNS, HTML attribute, 84
XMLSpy text editor, 82
XPath, 183
XPCOM Toolkit, 107
XPToolkit, 3-4, 18, 133
XSL Transformations (XSLT), 9, 49
XUL is Cool Theme, **131**, 131
XUL Runner, 211, 212-213, **213**, 224-227, **225**
XUL templates, 133-134, 142
- <action> element in, 145, **146**, 149, 156-158, **156**, **158**, 160, 236, 242
- binding in, 148-149, 158-160, **161-162**, **163**
- bookmarks in, 149-152, **151**, **152**
- <conditions> element in, 145, **146**, 184-149, 160
- container attribute in, 145
- contract identifiers in, 144, 144*t*
- in Customizable Browser Portal, 231
- datasource element in, 143-144
- datasources attribute in, 144, 144*t*
- dynamic content and, 143
- in E-commerce UI, 257
- local filenames in, 144, 144*t*
- member attribute in, 145
- merging content from multiple rule sets, 157-158, **158**
- multiple rules in (Book example), 152-158, **153-154**, **156**, **157**, **158**
- in My Sidebar Customization, 236-237
- pattern matching in, 146-147, **147**, 149-152
- RDF and, 143
- ref attribute in, 145
- <rule> element in, 145, **146**, 148
- singular rules in, 149
- syntax of, 143-149
- <template> element in, 145, 149
- test elements (<content>, <triple> and <member>) in, 145-147, 147*t*, 149-156, **156**, 159
- testing of, using Mozilla and Netscape, 162-163, **164**
- Uniform Resource Identifiers (URI) in, 135
- Uniform Resource Locator (URL) in, 144, 144*t*

XULElement, 86
xulexample.xul, 98, **99-104**, 209, 210
xulrunner package, jXUL, 227

Y-Z

year, 38*t*

zip files, 108, 126